Love's Story Told

Love's Story Told

A LIFE OF

Henry A. Murray

▼

FORREST G. ROBINSON

HARVARD UNIVERSITY PRESS

CAMBRIDGE, MASSACHUSETTS

LONDON, ENGLAND

1992

Design by Marianne Perlak

This book is printed on acid-free paper, and its binding materials
have been chosen for strength and durability.

Library of Congress Cataloging-in-Publication Data

Robinson, Forrest G. (Forrest Glen), 1940-
Love's story told: a life of Henry A. Murray /
Forrest G. Robinson.
p. cm.
Includes bibliographical references and index.
ISBN 0-674-53928-1 (alk. paper)
1. Murray, Henry Alexander. 1893- . 2. Morgan, Christiana.
3. Psychologists—United States—Biography. I. Title.
BF109.M86R63   1992   150'.92—dc20   92-8705
                                [B]   CIP

For Colleen

Preface

Henry A. Murray's place in the annals of American psychology is secure. The same may be said for his distinction among scholars of Melville. Yet his accomplishments in the public sphere, though estimable, may not at first seem to justify the elaborate reconstruction of his life ventured here. Murray's name is hardly a household word. To baffled inquirers I often respond that he was the cofounder of the Harvard Psychological Clinic; that he wrote *Explorations in Personality,* a classic text in that brand of personality psychology he defined as personology; that he had a major hand in the development of the widely used diagnostic tool, the Thematic Apperception Test (TAT); or that he figured centrally in the "discovery" of Herman Melville. This sometimes helps; but not always. "Why didn't you settle on someone *really* famous?" an eminent senior colleague once asked, rather grudgingly I thought. "It's a long story," I replied, taking shelter in the mild, evasive irony.

It is also a very personal story. When I first broached the topic of the biography with Murray in the spring of 1970, he allowed—with a gentle irony of his own—that there was little to tell. Nothing much to it, he said, except for a secret love affair of more than forty years. We never looked back. The challenge, as I understood it, was to work together with Murray in developing the materials for an integrated biography of the public and the private man—of the scientist, the littérateur, and the romantic. What was the interplay between the "parts" of this complex, fascinating human being? Happily enough, Murray was almost as interested in having the story told as I was. His zest and candor were great assets in our work together. We completed nearly a hundred interviews, more than half of them in the early 1970s and dozens of others during annual summer visits in the years that followed. As the life gradually fell open, it became clear that the secret love affair was the key to it all. It everywhere energized and informed the public career; it was the hidden center, the focus, the source of inspiration and direction. But its secrecy was cause for no little frustration to Murray. Love had revolutionized his life. By his own reckoning, such good fortune bore with it the obligation to spread the word to others in need of its saving light. For reasons that will become clear in what follows, Murray failed to meet that obligation. But in a biography of the kind that I proposed he glimpsed an acceptable compromise. His American *La Vita Nuova*, a still vital if diminished thing in his life, might at last be revealed. Thus, my arrival on his doorstep was a happy instance for us both of what Pasteur called "chance and the prepared mind."

It was also agreed early on that the biography would not appear in Murray's lifetime. Several of those I interviewed wanted it that way. They spoke openly only on the assurance that their commentary would not be shared with its subject. Murray had no quarrel with this arrangement. He wanted love's story told, but he could neither tell it himself nor comfortably witness its telling to others. "How such esoteric, unexampled and utterly private experiences can be fittingly and inoffensively represented by you in my life-time," he wrote in November 1972, "is still beyond my imagination." The agreement to delay publication was the obvious way past the dilemma; it opened the full life's experience to the telling. Murray made it clear to me—both by what he revealed in interviews and by the intimate, not always flattering, materials he left behind— that he wanted the "esoteric, unexampled" dimension to figure centrally in the biography. The narration of his life in its rich, fascinating human entirety was for him, as for me, the principal justification for our years of work together.

In two decades and more of research and writing, I have accumulated many debts of thanks. The deepest of these is to Murray's wife, Nina. Without benefit of her interest, patience, penetration, humor, and wisdom, this book would never have seen the light of day. Nina Murray knows more about her late husband than anyone alive. It is my extraordinary good fortune that she has been willing to share that knowledge with me. Murray's daughter, Josephine, has also been steadily and generously supportive. She is a rich mine of information and insight. Nina and Josephine have been especially helpful in offering their advice on the emerging chapters of the biography. In this they have been joined by several others. Brewster Smith, who draws on years of friendship with Murray, has responded promptly and copiously to my many requests for guidance. His support has been a terrific boost. Edwin Shneidman has been equally generous with his time and advice, and with myraid warm memories. Alan Elms, Bevil Hogg, and Robert White read the manuscript and commented in helpful ways on what they found there. I am also grateful to Daniel Aaron, Howard Gardner, Justin Kaplan, and Arthur Rosenthal for valuable counsel along the way.

My narrative has its foundation in an archive of personal interviews, about half of them with Murray himself, and nearly as many more with his relatives, friends, former students, and various associates. Of the latter, a number have died during the years since this project first got off the ground. I regret that they have not survived to read this book and to accept my thanks for their part in it. But to all who have given generously of their time and knowledge in interviews, I am deeply grateful. They are: Daniel Aaron, Conrad Aiken, Mrs. Gordon Allport, Alvan Barach, Frank Barron, Leopold Bellak, Carl Binger, John Bowlby, Paul Buck, Arthur Couch, Henry Dicks, Barbara Du Bois, Erik Erikson, Jessica Feingold, Louis Finkelstein, Maurice Firuski, Jerome Frank, Sanford Gifford, Herbert Goldings, Ina May Greer, Albert Guerard, Calvin Hall, Edward Handy, Harrison Hayford, Ravenna Helson, Robert Holt, Evelyn Hooker, Leon Howard, Elliott Jaques, Bert Kaplan, Alfred Kazin, Isabelle Kendig, Kenneth Keniston, Ted Kroeber, Lawrence Kubie, Harry Levin, Gardner Lindzey, Kenneth Lynn, Donald MacKinnon, David McClelland, Ann McDonald, Barry McLaughlin, Leo McNamara, Rollo May, Edwin P. Maynard, Harvey Meyerson, James G. Miller, J. O. Moreno, Councilman Morgan, Hallee Morgan, Ben Morris, Lewis Mumford, Rev. Michael Murray, Gene F. Nameche, Edwin B. Newman, Robert Newman, Osgood Nichols, Dan Ogilvie, Talcott Parsons, John Perry, Carroll

Pratt, Jack Pritchard, Rosemary ("Molly") Pritchard, I. A. Richards, Henry Riecken, David Riesman, Paul Roazen, Nevitt Sanford, Edwin Shneidman, Jeanne Shneidman, Neil Smelser, Brewster Smith, Larry St. Clair, Mrs. Larry St. Clair, Morris Stein, S. S. Stevens, John D. Sutherland, Lynn Swanger, Eugene Taylor, Florence R. Taylor, Virginia Thomas, Silvan Tomkins, Robert Trivers, Howard Vincent, Robert Penn Warren, Alan Watts, George Weller, Robert White, George Wilbur, Mrs. Frank Wigglesworth, Robert Wilson, and Frederick Wyatt. I am grateful as well to those who replied by mail to my inquiries: Dean Acheson, Alan Elms, Norris M. Getty, Eric Gordon, Harriet L. Gratwick, Robert K. Greenleaf, Joseph Henderson, Susan Howe, Devereux Josephs, Rod Kessler, Marianne Lester, Jay Leyda, James Lieberman, Peter Loewenberg, Grafton Minot, Zerka T. Moreno, John Parke, David Ricks, Saul Rosenzweig, Robert Scott, Robert Shenton, Jean Stafford, Rodney Triplet, Franklin Watkins, and Donald Yannella. For the use of their correspondence with Murray, I must thank Conrad Aiken, Alvan Barach, Edward Hardy, Elizabeth Handy, Robert Holt, Lewis Mumford, Josephine Murray, John Parke, Jack Pritchard, "Molly" Pritchard, Paul Roazen, Edwin Shneidman, and Howard Vincent.

Special thanks to David Thomas for introducing me to Henry Murray, and for guidance in the early going. I am grateful to Margaret Gordon for many years of faithful support and encouragement. Nancy Sullivan worked long hours at low pay over endless interviews; I am reminded on a daily basis of my great debt to her. I am grateful for favors along the way from Richard Onorato and Rodney Triplet. Daniel Wenger has been a wizard on the mysteries of the Macintosh. Dr. Harold Gordon offered expert advice in medical matters; his wife, Annette Gordon, made the index. Peter Bragdon, Dick Savage, and Dave Williams were very helpful during my visit to the Governor Dummer Academy. Anne Boutelle, a most able assistant, provided aid and comfort in the checking of the footnotes. Finally, Angela von der Lippe and Susan Wallace of the Harvard University Press have been unflaggingly patient and generous. Their encouragement has been invaluable to me.

Institutional support has been plentifully forthcoming over the past two decades. I had benefit at the very outset of research grants from Harvard University. During subsequent years I have had similar support from the University of California, Santa Cruz. A Guggenheim Fellowship in 1972–1973 gave me the time to get a firm foothold on the project. Much more recently, Darwin H. Stapleton, Director of the Rockefeller Archive Center, provided grant support for a research trip to North Tarrytown. I am grateful to American Studies, my Board at UC Santa Cruz—and especially to the Chair, Michael Cowan—for unwavering support over the years. The Reference and Interlibrary Loan staffs at the McHenry Library have been invaluable—patient, indefatigable, expert—in their assistance. I am indebted as well to the staff members of the Kresge College and Oakes College Steno Pools (at UCSC). I am grateful for special favors from Janet Morrison of the Lane Medical Library at Stanford, Ellen Slack of the Van Pelt Library at the University of Pennsylvania, and the Department of Special Collections at UCLA. Harley Holden, Curator of the Harvard University Archives, has been unfailingly accommodating. His staff—and most especially Curatorial Assistant Mike Raines—helped in many ways to lighten my labor.

Along with the Harvard University Archives, Nina Murray, Josephine Murray, and Alexander M. Davis have given me their permission to reproduce photographs from their collections. They have my gratitude.

It says something about my good fortune in life that I have a rather large family *and* that I work at home. Three of my children—Renate, Emma, and Marie—are not "into" books like this one yet. But they know quite a good deal about Henry Murray; they have been good sports about letting me write; and they keep my study colorfully decorated with their artwork. My oldest daughter, Grace, *is* "into" books like this one; indeed, she has been one of my most faithful readers. I very much value Grace's judgment, in books, as in all things. Colleen, my wife, keeps us all warm and full and on keel. This book, like so much else in our family life, rests squarely on the foundation of support and encouragement that she provides. It's simple, really. Colleen is the greatest, and this book is dedicated to her with love.

F. G. R.
Santa Cruz, California

Contents

Love's Story Told

▼

chapter one

Loomings

There was a stir of excitement on board the Cunard liner *Scythia* one early mid-August morning in 1924. She was just three days out from Boston when her captain, William Prothero, a stout Welshman, was brought down by a great pain in his belly. Fortunately, expert medical aid was at hand in the person of Sir John Bland-Sutton, President of the Royal College of Surgeons, who happened to be aboard and who saw almost at once that the Captain's acute appendicitis required immediate attention. Assisted by the ship's doctor, and by a young American M.D., Henry A. Murray, who administered the chloroform, Bland-Sutton went straight to his task. Heavy weather compounded the difficulty of cutting down through several inches of abdominal fat to the severely ruptured appendix. And though he kept his misgivings to himself, Murray was ill at ease working with chloroform, which had been replaced in American medical practice by gas and ether. Still, Captain Prothero pulled through. He had a rough time of it for the duration of the voyage, and for a few weeks in a Liverpool hospital. But by early November he was—as Bland-Sutton later wrote to Murray— "in excellent health, and grateful to all of us."

Once the Captain's needs had been met, the doctors retired to the lounge, where they settled into drinks and conversation. Murray explained that he was en route to Cambridge University for a year's research in biochemistry. For his part, Bland-Sutton was on the return leg of a whirlwind four-day visit to America. He had

1

come over to explore New Bedford, Massachusetts, the seaport from which Herman Melville had embarked on his first whaling voyage in 1841. Melville's *Moby-Dick,* he explained, had for many years been a kind of Bible with him. He kept a well-thumbed copy by his bedside. Bland-Sutton's brief pilgrimage had its more immediate occasion in a speech that he was scheduled to deliver to the Royal College of Surgeons at the opening of a major addition to their Surgical Museum. The new wing was designed to feature the work of Dr. John Hunter, the famous eighteenth-century anatomist, whose essay on the dissection of whales had been a definitive source for an admiring Melville. Bland-Sutton wanted to highlight the Hunter/Melville connection in his address, and he had traveled to New Bedford to learn more at first hand about the unheralded American novelist.

Some 32 years later, while preparing a speech of his own (for the members of the Harvard Social Relations Society), Henry A. Murray had occasion to recall that memorable day at sea. "I have read," he began, "that next to the feeling of genius in yourself, the most thrilling intellectual experience is the apperception of genius in another person, especially if it has not yet been seen and celebrated by any arbiter of merit." Melville experienced a thrill of this kind in his first serious encounter with the work of Nathaniel Hawthorne. He described his reaction—in his 1850 review of "Hawthorne and His Mosses"—as a "shock of recognition." Murray went on to explain that his own "first great shock of recognition" occurred on board the *Scythia,* during the several days just before Captain Prothero's attack of appendicitis. By the most striking coincidence, a "surgical friend" in New York had given him a copy of *Moby-Dick* as a kind of going-away present. Murray accepted the book—"a good sea yarn," his friend assured him, "by an unknown author"—and promised to "read it on the ocean where it should be read." Still, he was at first inclined to steer clear of the novel. A man should *live* adventures, not read about them. But once at sea, Murray had time to kill and nothing else of interest at hand. So he dove in, little knowing that much of his life's adventure lay on the pages before him.

The "rediscovery" of Herman Melville was complete in 1956,

when Murray prepared his remarks for the Harvard Social Relations Society. *Moby-Dick* was by then virtually unchallenged, save perhaps by *Huckleberry Finn,* as the greatest of the great American novels. In 1924, however, the word on Melville had just barely begun to spread. D. H. Lawrence, E. L. Grant Watson, H. M. Tomlinson, Van Wyck Brooks, and a few others had written appreciations; and the first life, Raymond M. Weaver's *Herman Melville: Mariner and Mystic,* had just recently appeared in New York. Ironically, Melville had his largest and most informed following in England, where the first complete edition of his works was published by Constable and Company in 1922–24. Meanwhile, it was into the World's Classics edition of *Moby-Dick,* published by Oxford University Press in 1920, that Murray took his maiden plunge. Indeed, it is no great exaggeration to say that the American rediscovery of Herman Melville took a major step forward on board the *Scythia* in 1924.

"Call me Ishmael," the familiar opening to *Moby-Dick,* "was the first shock," Murray later recalled. Other shocks followed in rapid order as he navigated the first third of the novel. The rich, powerful orchestration of the language ("Beethoven's *Eroica* in words"), the spacious maritime setting, the array of striking characters (Captain Ahab most notable among them), the mingling of dark emotions with unexampled, extravagant humor, and the over-brimming, fated inevitability of it all—these elements combined to draw the fascinated reader along. Murray was impressed with Melville's concreteness, his regard for natural objects and implements and tools— for things. But to "the fidelity of the scientist" the artist added a genius for delivering those things of their vital, human meanings. In this extraordinary fusion of "pure perception and relevant emotion" Murray first glimpsed—what he would later analyze and celebrate—Melville's rare myth-making powers. The novel dramatized in fully knowing ways the mysterious movements of mind that give rise to our shaping, all-informing constructions of reality. Long before Freud and his followers, Melville had penetrated to the hidden well-springs of human meaning, and he had done so, Murray came to believe, "with more genuine comprehension than any other writer." It was this potent, procreative union of science and poetry, detachment and passion, that riveted Murray's attention and pro-

3

pelled him to the threshold of his life's work. He likened the novel to great natural upheavals—earthquakes, tempests, volcanic eruptions. It was towering, massive, "a wild Everest of art, limit of governable imagination," as he put it in his celebrated Introduction to *Pierre*. *Moby-Dick* "whelmed" him and then swept him along in its path. "The book changed me," he would later admit. This was saying something, for Murray was not a man to be overpowered; helplessness and surrender had no place in his conception of himself. If he was swept away by Melville, then it can only have been because he was willing to take the ride.

Murray was not alone on the *Scythia*. He was traveling with his wife and daughter, both named Josephine. They would be joined in Cambridge by Murray's brother, Cecil, his family, and by the Morgans—Will, Christiana, and their son, Councilman—all of whom were taking the year in England to advance their educations. The friendship with the Morgans had its ostensible foundation in shared intellectual interests. But they were also drawn together by the strong pull of an undisclosed romantic attraction between Murray and Christiana Morgan. The future of their secret was uncertain, as new passion wrestled with old loyalties. Still, the decision to travel en masse to Cambridge was evidence of an unwillingness to be apart; and it was that partial surrender to desire, we may safely surmise, that prepared Murray for the fateful advent of Herman Melville. For in Ahab's titanic struggle with the white whale Murray recognized an immemorial human protest against the tyranny of paternal restraint. The novel came to him as an anguished appeal for freedom—of poetry from science, of heart from head, of passion from the shackles of religious convention. So interpreted, *Moby-Dick* pointed the way past medicine and hard scientific research to explorations into the mysteries of the human psyche. More crucially perhaps, it clarified what had been uncertain in desire, suggesting, even demanding, that he join Christiana Morgan in an exemplary modern rebellion against oppressive—in this case Puritanical—prohibitions. Embracing their fate, their American *La Vita Nuova*, they would show the way to others and thus earn canonization for their love.

Murray was fascinated with moments of great insight and discovery, of momentous change. In explaining them, he almost invariably invoked Pasteur's equation of "chance and the prepared mind." His failure to apply the formula to his encounter with Melville on the *Scythia,* where it appears to apply so well, is conspicuous. To have done so would have been to acknowledge that he was prepared in advance to follow where *Moby-Dick* seemed to lead. Moreover, it would have entailed the revelation of his relationship with Christiana Morgan. To the very end of his life Murray was reluctant to go public with that information. He was constrained, quite ironically, by a sense of propriety. But his insistence on secrecy was more deeply the symptom of an ambivalence, never resolved, perhaps never fully confronted, about Christiana Morgan, about rebellion, and about the great enterprise that Melville helped open to the two of them. The mind was prepared, but never completely. Thus, in retrospect *Moby-Dick* did not appear to Murray so much a liberating chance readily seized upon as an irresistible force that swept him away.

But if *Moby-Dick* took hold of Henry A. Murray, then Henry A. Murray just as surely took hold of *Moby-Dick,* not only by drawing it into alignment with personal desire but also more largely by laboring to bring it into the mainstream of American cultural life and by helping to shape the meaning that it has held for the millions of Americans who have read it since it was "rediscovered." His lifelong engagement with the novel well illustrates the dialectical interplay often observed between people and their institutions, individuals and social roles, actual human experience and dominant cultural fictions: We shape and modify the forms that shape and modify our lives. Murray knew this, of course. He regarded the construction of the self as a crowning human achievement. His leadership in the development of the Thematic Apperception Test, and his acclaimed acuity at "reading" the persons in the fictions it produced, bear this out. But so does his entire life. Henry A. Murray knew that he was his own greatest invention. He delighted at playing freely in the spacious field of his self, improvising, slipping puckishly in and out of roles. It was the direct corollary of his pleasure in the play of self that he regularly set it free in others. Almost invariably, people came away from encounters with Murray feeling exhilarated, pleasantly enlarged, gratified that their best selves had been liberated and on display.

Though he rarely let it show—that would have spoiled the game—Murray was intensely self-conscious. Little wonder that narcissism (he preferred "narcism") was a leading topic with him. It was one among many of the preoccupations that he shared with Melville. The *Scythia* was just getting under way when he read, in the first chapter of *Moby-Dick,* "that story of Narcissus, who because he could not grasp the tormenting, mild image he saw in the fountain, plunged into it and was drowned." Unlike Melville's protagonists, however, Murray was not prone to dally at the brink of personal annihilation. The free-floating self inspired him with *jouissance,* not the existential jitters. He rarely settled fully into his own fictions; rather, his self-absorption manifested itself in buoyant, brilliant self-command. He knew when he was being funny, or wise, or demanding, or cruel, and he was masterful at picking his spots. At rare intervals, as in his account of being overpowered by Melville, there is the hint of mild delusion in Murray's self-presentation. But even at such moments the biographer must proceed with respectful caution. After all, Murray must surely have glimpsed that "the shock of recognition" precipitated by *Moby-Dick* had its energizing source in his own poised readiness to be moved. The novel was the element of chance; his, the prepared mind.

chapter two

▼

Call Me Harry

His full name was Henry Alexander Murray, Jr., but that was rarely used. He represented himself professionally as Henry A. Murray. More generally, however, he steered away from formality. Over a long life he answered to numberless nicknames: Hen, Henro, HAM, Hamlet, H, and Murr come most readily to mind. I will call him Harry. That was what he asked of his friends. There was just a hint of noblesse oblige in the invitation. The name was obviously too small for him. His effortless, natural-seeming regality overflowed Harry, as Henry V overflows mere Hal. One felt a surge of pleasure, of special privilege, in being invited to address him informally. But the nonchalance aside, names, like all personal details, really mattered. Early along in our friendship I observed that except for the middle A his initials were identical to Melville's. He smiled, as if to applaud my penetration. Then, allowing a trace of archness to color his tone, he replied: "The A is for Adam, and he's in all of us." Clearly, Harry had been over this ground before.

Harry was born in New York City on May 13, 1893. Even by the standards of that opulent era, his family was extremely well off. They were comfortably superior in social position, and very rich. His mother, born Fannie Morris Babcock in 1858, was descended on both sides from old New England families. Her pedigree was on display in paired John Singleton Copley portraits of her prosperous New Haven forbears, Mr. and Mrs. Adam Babcock. Great-great grandfather Colonel Harry Babcock of Connecticut served on Washington's staff during the Revolutionary War. Her father, Samuel Denison Babcock, was an eminent financier. A founder and first president of the Guaranty Trust Company, and sometime president of the New York Chamber of Commerce, he was also an officer on numerous boards and a supporter of leading cultural institutions. Married for 55 years to Elizabeth Crary Franklin Babcock, whose forbears arrived from England in about 1680, he was blessed with seven children. His death in September 1902 was featured on the front page of the *New York Times*. A venerable patriarch, self-made, retiring ("He did not go into society very much"), respectable, he was remembered by his grandson, not very warmly, as the next thing to Jehovah. His fortune, Harry also noted, "was both ample and secure for succeeding generations."

In May of 1889 Fannie Babcock was married to Henry Alexander Murray, a well-bred Scot of very modest material resources. The fourth son of an army officer on Her Majesty's service near Melbourne, Australia, he was the descendant of John Murray, fourth Earl of Dunmore, the last Royal Governor of Virginia. After the untimely death of his father, young Henry, then about nine, went to England with his mother, who supplemented their meager resources by writing popular romances. Thanks to Murray family influence, the youngster was admitted to Christ's Hospital, the famous charity school once attended by Coleridge and Lamb. But his mother's death a few years later brought an end to Henry's education and prompted him to seek a fresh start in Canada. After a year in Toronto, he migrated south to New York, where he found employment as a clerk in a stock and bonds firm. After nearly a decade of slow but steady progress, his prospects turned sharply upward when he won the favor of Fannie Babcock and her family. There was love in the match, to be sure. "My father and his bride actually lived happily ever after," Harry once observed. But there was a calculated exchange of real and symbolic capital, too. Fannie was the fourth of six girls. As maidens went, she was getting on. For whatever reasons, an American male of the proper class and means was not available. But Henry Alexander Murray was. A talented, amiable young fellow, with Samuel Babcock's support he would do very well in banking. What he lacked in fortune he made up in background. "That counted, yes," Harry recalled, of his father's fine family tree.

At the time of Harry's birth, the New York Social Register indicated that the Murrays were members in good standing at fashionable clubs and lived in an equally fashionable neighborhood. Thanks to the wealth and influence of his father-in-law, Henry, Sr., rose to a respectable prosperity in banking. Securely installed in the social and financial elite, he was free of the ambition—or the need—to make an even bigger pile. He was a perennial vice-president. Wealth and warm security so dominated the lives of his wife and children that they seem scarcely to have recognized the extent of their good fortune. Comfortably patrician in outlook, they entered society only as they wished to, and knew nothing of the impulse to climb. They looked with dismay on the *nouveaux riches*, who in their vulgar ostentation gave money a bad name. Grasping plutocrats like Mr. Harriman, the father of Harry's classmate, who was ruthless in business and traveled in a private car on his own railroad, were little better. Politicians, and party politics generally, Henry, Sr., warned, were dominated by an inferior class, and hopelessly corrupt. Poverty was an unfortunate element in the progressive scheme of things. The Murrays saw it up close only in their servants, who were to all appearances content with their lot. Doubtless, life in New York was difficult for thousands of people, especially for immigrants. But all that seemed so foreign, and so far away.

In fact, of course, foreigners were increasingly visible in New York, and in the country generally, as eastern European immigrants arrived in crowded boatloads to accept the promise of America. For many, high hopes quickly gave way before the harsh realities of uncertain employment, low wages, the lack of basic protections against exploitation and abuse, widespread xenophobia, grinding urban squalor—all the horrors of rapidly expanding, unregulated industrial capitalism. The failure of the promise was a painful symptom of contradictions within the American scheme of things. In the land of opportunity, only a few prospered; in the land of equality, class divisions had grown into chasms; in the land of freedom, many were as trapped and degraded as slaves; in the land of peace, violence was epidemic and an appetite for conquest was on the rise. As it happened, such contradictions appeared in especially bold relief during the months just before and after Harry's birth. The financial panic of 1893, which set off a sharp increase in business failures and unemployment, served to confirm the worst fears of the burgeoning Populist movement. Hard times worked to sharpen class divisions. On one side, Chicago's White City, erected to celebrate four centuries of progress, heralded an opulent American future, to be won—according to historian Alan Trachtenberg— by the "corporate alliance of business, culture, and the state." Later on in the same year, Coxey's Army of the unemployed set off toward the national capital, hoping in vain to win sympathy and support for their cause. A few months later, in June of 1894, the bloody Pullman Strike gave evidence of labor's desperate need to be heard, and of government's refusal to listen. Things would get worse before they got better. McKinley, the Republican spokesman for business, won decisively in 1896, and Populism, along with the reform impulse generally, withered temporarily into silence.

Those New Yorkers who enjoyed the affluence and privilege of the Murrays were insulated against the storm that raged around them. They could see and hear, but the turmoil did little to disturb their repose. The specific terms of their detachment fell open to the eye of William Dean Howells, whose novel *A Traveller from Altruria* appeared serially in *Cosmopolitan* between November 1892 and October 1893. There is virtual consensus among Howells' leading characters—wealthy guests at a fashionable summer resort—that America is a country of distinctive, deeply divided social classes. "The severance of the man who works for his living with his hands from the man who does not work for his living with his hands," observes a prosperous banker, "is so complete, and apparently so final, that nobody even imagines anything else, not even in fiction." Mr. Homos, a visitor from the Christian socialist utopia Altruria, speculates that the problem may have its origin in the economic system. "Am I right in supposing," he inquires, quite rhetorically, "that the effect of your economy is to establish insuperable inequalities among you, and to forbid the hope of the brotherhood which your polity proclaims?" Glimpsing the awkward contradiction

10

emergent from the question, the narrator, Mr. Twelvemough, a fashionable novelist, resolves that it will be "best to evade it." Accordingly, he denies that "anybody is troubled by those distinctions. We are used to them," he insists, "and everybody acquiesces in them, which is a proof that they are a very good thing." A little further on, Twelvemough concedes that material greed is at the root of much evil in America. "'Mammon hath slain his tens of thousand,' I suggested lightly; 'we all like to recognize the facts, so long as we are not expected to do anything about them; then, we deny them.'"

It was by some such mechanism of denial, we must suppose, that privileged Americans preserved their moral composure in the face of glaring contradictions. The spell persisted unbroken for Harry until he was well along in his twenties; and it was not until the middle of his life that he emerged, quite proudly, into an enlarged social awareness. Even so, the charmed circle of his childhood was finally proof, in memory, against adult disenchantment. "My first years up to 22," he recalled in some late, rough jottings, "were spent in the world that has all but perished: a world of old New York: horse drawn & hansom cabs, victorias, buses on 5th Ave, horse-drawn cars to the Long Island ferry boat—a house-ful of servants, nurses, governesses, butlers, cooks, maids &c, gas light—no electricity—messenger boys—no telephones—coal in the grate—no central heating &c, &c. dress-suits, high-hats, white gloves—opera boxes &c dances. World of ladies & gentlemen—and common people—old families—vs upstarts, dirty politics, dirty business (vulgar Robber Barons), Tammany Hall (nouveau riche). Episcopal Church—Church boarding school—Sunday school in the afternoon—Charities organized." This is the world as it might have appeared in the popular novels of Mr. Twelvemough. It gives center stage to the pleasures of patrician adults. Such social conflict as appears is focused on the struggle for preeminence between the old money and the new. There are no immigrants here, no poverty, no disease; only servants, to help with the heat, the food, the children, the carriage, and the fine clothes. If there is suffering abroad among the "common people," it appears only obliquely, in the final reference to charity.

The city of Harry's childhood was a sprawling, bustling metropolis of great energy and sharp contrasts. By 1900 the population of greater New York exceeded three million. More than a third of the city's residents were foreign born. Many were illiterate; many spoke no English. A million and more lived in slums. Tall buildings had begun to dominate the skyline, and the Brooklyn Bridge was an acclaimed esthetic and technological triumph. But contemporary visitors were most struck by the brash, unbuttoned tone of New York. The hustle after quick money was unabashed and seemingly pervasive. Tammany Hall was equally bold and ruthless in its manipulation of political life. Clamorous with wagons and trolleys and elevated trains, checkered with slums and shanty towns, the city was rough, cluttered, and crudely cosmopolitan. "The more one studied it," observed Rudyard Kipling in 1892, "the more grotesquely bad it grew—bad in its paving, bad in its streets, bad in its street-police, and but for the kindness of the tides would be worse than bad in its sanitary arrangements."

At the center of this swarming, unkempt urban wilderness, the Murrays reposed, with others of their class, in a slender corridor of order and light running north and south along Fifth Avenue from 46th Street to 72nd Street. In the upper reaches of this enclave, hugging Central Park, the palaces of the super-rich rose in late-Victorian splendor. Further south, where the Murrays lived, the architecture was more modest and restrained. Harry's childhood homes—the first at 54 W 49th Street and the second, to which the family moved in 1904, at 38 W 51st Street—were demolished in the 1930s to make way for Rockefeller Center. Both were situated at the middle of the block between posh Fifth Avenue on the East and Sixth Avenue on the West. A 1894 photograph looking north at 48th Street along Fifth Avenue features rows of respectable, four-story brownstones with broad stairs sloping down to ample sidewalks and a clean, spacious cobblestone thoroughfare. Carriage traffic is light. Men in tall silk hats and ladies in long skirts, flaring sleeves, and elaborate bonnets promenade in the sunshine. The Fifth Avenue Collegiate Church, in handsome sandstone Gothic, graces the west side of the street. Further along, not visible in the photograph, are St. Patrick's Cathedral, the elegant Plaza Hotel, and the southern border of Central Park. It is the setting for a novel by Wharton or James, serene, civilized, and apparently oblivious to the squalor at its margins.

Harry was the second of three children. The first, Virginia, was born in 1890, and Cecil, Harry's younger brother, completed the family in 1897. Life at home was dominated by mother. By all accounts Fannie Babcock Murray was a responsible parent. She was proud of her children. Moreover, she was the efficient, thrifty overseer of a large household and several servants. She was a source of order and discipline. But Fannie was also a complicated, often difficult woman. Family members remember her with admiration rather than affection and invariably get around to reporting the wrinkles in her character. She was nervous, a little officious, inclined to meddle, given to sharp mood swings. She developed hypochondria soon after Virginia's birth and had a way of tyrannizing others with her high blood pressure. In later years she "saved string" and kept a lot of keys on a chain. In "The Case of Murr," Harry's carefully crafted autobiography, he introduces his mother as "the ambivalent parent: more often the focus of attention, affection, and concern than my father was, year in and year out, but also more resented now and then, mostly for correcting my abominable manners, for nagging about minutiae, or for enforcing duties or requesting services which interrupted my activities. Of the two, she was the more energetic, restless, enthusiastic, enterprising, and talkative—giving us daily reports of her personal preoccupations, her doings, encounters, worries, and frustrations—also the more changeable, moody, and susceptible to melancholy."

Fannie's ambivalence, it is clear, produced an answering sentiment in her son, who is by turns affectionate and resentful in reflecting on his mother's self-absorption. Basically, she didn't love him enough. Harry was "abruptly weaned at two months," took food only fitfully in the year or so that followed, failed hopelessly in the competition with his brother and sister for maternal affection, and thus came to "the grievous (and valid) realization that he could count on only a limited third-best portion of his mother's love." The bond of emotional nurturance having been severed, the youngster drew back into "venturesome autonomy," repressed his suffering and resentment, and displaced his self-pity on to—who else?—his mother, who thereafter ruled him with her poor health.

As chronicled in "The Case of Murr," Fannie's maternal shortcomings had profound consequences for her son. Most centrally, perhaps, they promoted the formation of "a marrow of misery and melancholy repressed by pride and practically extinguished in everyday life by a counteracting disposition of sanguine and expansive buoyancy." Harry's optimism—the "sanguine surplus," he liked to call it—overlaid a stratum of gloom that surfaced in a preference "for tragic themes in literature," especially in Melville and Shakespeare; in "an affinity for the darker, blinder strata of feeling . . . this being a representative of the feminine component" of his nature, readily "evoked by art" and vital to his "conversion" to psychology; and in "a hypersensitivity to the sufferings of other individuals, especially women." At the same time, "pride, denial and repression" merged in "the conviction that I could get along well enough with a minimum amount of aid, support, appreciation, recognition, or consolation from others; . . . in solitude and privacy I could be happily independent of all that." Later in life, Harry continues, as ideas (notably the concepts of inviolacy and nurturance) "began bubbling autonomously in my head, these became the foci of my nurturant disposition and there was not much energy left over for the miseries of others." In sum, Harry was at first drawn by "the marrow of misery" toward tragic themes, suffering women, and a career in psychology. In time, however, the emotionally needful and responsive youth gave way to the fiercely independent, intellectually detached adult. Head triumphed over heart. A confession of sorts thus emerges. I have been unresponsive to the emotional needs of others, Harry concedes; but my failure as a provider has been the reflex of my mother's failure to provide for me. I am sorry; but it is not my fault.

As if to underscore his own helplessness, Harry goes on to describe himself as a nine-year-old, "innocent as could be," returning from school "to find the dining room transformed into an operating room, with two white-gowned surgeons and an anaesthetist awaiting my arrival, and my mother confronting me with the option of a pain-eliminating general anaesthetic or an aquarium as prize for getting on without it. *Explanation:* Four years earlier, my mother, ever on the lookout for deviations from the norm, detected a slight crossing of my eyes (internal strabismus) which became steadily more accentuated." Harry opted for the fish, of course, but he developed a stutter in the bargain. Moreover, the operation produced a slight overcorrection which went undetected, even by the patient, for more than a decade. The physician who finally diagnosed the condition confirmed that the lack of stereoscopic vision had been the cause of numerous humiliating athletic failures, especially in baseball, and suggested that the sensorimotor defect was also tied in some way to the stuttering, which had persisted.

Harry had less to say about his father, though virtually all of it was positive. Henry, Sr., appears in "The Case of Murr" as "an unself-centered, even-tempered, unpretentious, undemanding, acquiescent, firm yet nonauthoritarian, jolly father who is scarcely capable of a veritable splurge of anger." Harry's tenderest childhood memories—afternoons at play in Central Park, the morning walk to nursery school, fishing and camping trips—invariably included his father. Henry, Sr., had been brought up in the old school of reserve and equable civility. A quiet, contented, peaceful man, he was by nature and training averse to conflict. Theodore Roosevelt's meddling with the trusts might provoke an occasional comment, but his conservatism most often expressed itself in a retreat from partisan political debate. He read a great deal, especially in nineteenth-century British fiction, though there was nothing of the intellectual about him. Books produced repose, not stimulation. He was equally British in his approach to sports. He encouraged his sons in their athletic interests but resisted the American emphasis on individual achievement and winning. Moderation in all things; play well and fairly; enjoy life; peace.

Harry was the first to admit that there was nothing heroic or "charismatic" about his father. But if he felt the need of a strong male model, or resented the lack of protection from his mother, he kept those feelings carefully to himself. Father and son were placidly comfortable together, especially in the early years. In some unstated way they must have conspired to give Fannie a wide berth. Rather than offer resistance, they kept their distance. She took no interest in sports and outdoor activities; they pursued them avidly. They shared an interest in books. Years later, when Harry "came upon Freud's conception of the father-son side of the oedipus complex, it did not strike home with any vibrant shock of recognition." In fact, he was delighted to have missed out on that nasty episode. Instead, he had grown into the sheltered space that his self-effacing parent had opened for him. In time, it is true, he outgrew his father. They had less and less to talk about as he advanced through school into maturity. "No bona fide intellectual ever crossed the threshold" of his childhood home, Harry recalled in "The Case of Murr." But this was not all bad. What he needed most from his father—emotional support, rules for living, simple self-esteem— he got. He found models as he needed them in life, and he had no lack of ambition. Already at five he felt a burning need to climb Mt. McKinley. A more aggressive, more demanding father, working in tandem with Fannie Babcock Murray, might have smothered that fire.

The real competition for his mother's affection came from Harry's older sister, Virginia. One family member describes her as a "terrier." An active, demanding child, and her mother's favorite, she made no concessions to newcomers. Harry felt sure that Virginia's complaints were the occasion for his early weaning. She tyrannized over him, he recalled, "until he was nine and had gathered up enough muscle to subdue her." In time the rivalry settled into an uneasy truce. They speculated after church on where babies come from and played doctor with such verisimilitude that father finally stepped in. Younger brother once served as an usher in his sister's play-wedding to their neighbor Averell Harriman. Still, Virginia had Harry's number. She criticized him for being too "analytical" and dubbed him "Hamlet." Later on in life they quarreled about politics. Their differences sharpened dramatically in 1922 when Virginia's husband, Robert Low Bacon, a very conservative Republican from Long Island, was elected to the Congress. After Bacon's death in 1938 Virginia carried on in Washington as a prominent political hostess. She did not figure on a regular basis in the events of Harry's life, though they continued to bicker, sometimes bitterly, and even in the midst of much laughter and sharing of old times, until she died in 1980. Harry never forgave his sister for her favored place in Fannie's eyes. Virginia recognized her advantage and seems to have enjoyed the power it conferred. Hamlet's composure, ordinarily in firm control, was always fragile in her company.

Things were much better between Harry and his younger brother, Cecil, who was born in 1897. Resistance to their mother's authority must have had a part to play in bringing them together. "She would run your life if you let her," recalls Cecil's son. The boys fought back. No one knows why exactly, but Fannie insisted on the name Cecil. Young Harry was mortified—Cecil sounded like "sissy." He proposed Nansen—after Fridtjof Nansen, the celebrated Norwegian explorer, who made a triumphant visit to New York in late 1897 and whose *Farthest North,* a vivid, copiously illustrated account of his exploits, was Harry's first and favorite childhood book. Fannie would have none of it. Cecil in turn never forgave his mother for the name. He plotted with his brother to change it to plain, manly "Mike," but Harry stuttered so badly that it came out "M-M-M——Ike." Even that was better, much better, than Cecil. Thanks to such small triumphs, the brothers got on "famously." Ike was the smaller of the two, a "cute kid" whose mechanical ingenuity contrasted with his older brother's more literary and intuitive disposition. But he followed Harry's lead in most things, at first in sports, later on—not always wisely, perhaps—in a variety of personal and professional interests.

Harry's affectionate ties to father and brother did not fully offset his mother's alienating influence. In rejecting her son, and in making him feel guilty for her constant headaches ("You'll be sorry when I die," she warned), she set the stage for Harry's later gravitation to Unamuno's "tragic sense of life." The presence in the Murray household of Fannie's two younger sisters, both, by Harry's account, "neuropsychiatric suffers . . . one the victim of seasonal psychotic depressions, and the other, a sweet hysterectomized hysteric," cannot have helped in this regard. Aunt Kitty, the psychotic, once fled from the house up Fifth Avenue toward St. Patrick's Cathedral, her nightgown fluttering about her body in the breeze. Harry took compassion on these poor souls, who triggered an "analytic interest" in human suffering that would later figure in his decision to become a psychologist.

But this is to focus too narrowly on the "marrow of misery and melancholy." Harry's childhood was notable, after all, not for its hardship but for its lavish privilege. Here indeed was a fair field for the play of optimism and native buoyancy. The Murrays were members of the elite, but they were not socially very active. Much to Harry's delight, he was often invited to join his parents in their box at the opera. He took equal pleasure in regular trips to Europe. Father liked to tour in Britain, while mother preferred France (she was an avid reader of Madame de Sévigné and insisted that the children study French). The elder son had patchy memories of a first visit to Edinburgh in 1896 and much clearer recollections of several other crossings during his childhood and youth. Nor did Harry seem to mind the weekly attendance at St. George's Church, the massive Episcopal pile across town in Stuyvesant Square. His parents were hardly devout, though they enjoyed the sermons and saw to it that their offspring were properly educated in the faith. In all such activities, and in their lives more generally, the Murrays operated as a close family unit. Virginia and Harry and Cecil saw a lot of their parents and were spared the heavy social demands often made on children of their class.

Such children were almost invariably sent to private schools. Harry's education commenced with a year (probably kindergarten) at Miss Henley's, followed by regular attendance until he was thirteen at the Craigie School, just three blocks from home on W 46th Street. There, along with about forty other boys, he applied himself to the disciplined development of mind and body (*mens agitat molem*—"intellect animates matter"—was the school motto). His grades in most subjects (English grammar and composition, mathematics, and history, his favorite) fell into the middle range, though he faltered somewhat in Latin and excelled in drawing, attendance, and conduct. He was also an editor on the school magazine, the *Craigie Current,* a monthly compendium of school gossip, sporting news, execrable (mostly ethnic) jokes, brief essays (on the evils of socialism, for example), and tips on the best books and plays. But

Harry's heart was in athletics. Elected captain of the football team in his last year at Craigie, he most enjoyed playing quarterback— "not too well," he recalled, though he "never stuttered when he gave the signals." A team photograph taken when he was about ten makes him appear a small but willing competitor whose attitude of boldness is rather comically belied—let it be acknowledged—by the skewed alignment of his eyes.

Harry enjoyed books, though he was not always willing to follow his father's lead into Scott and Dickens. Left to himself, he gravitated to narratives of adventure and heroism (Nansen was preeminent in this category), nature stories for boys (Ernest Seton Thompson was a favorite), fairytales (the collections by Andrew Lang were best remembered), and, rather oddly, the Horatio Alger novels. Harry seems to have been happiest, however, when he was out-of-doors. When they were not in Europe, the Murrays took a beach house for the summer at Far Rockaway on Long Island. A little after the turn of the century, thanks to a lucky streak on the market, they built Wave Crest, an enormous shingle-style residence on a rise near the ocean. "We were a little ashamed of the house," Harry once confessed. Still, until they sold it a few years later (it became a country club), Wave Crest was a happy summer retreat where Harry "built sand fortresses and claustra of barrel stays (his mother fantasied that he was cut out to be an architect) until his father taught him how to swim, fish, and sail, and later to play tennis, golf, and baseball with limited proficiency. More enticing than those games, however, were his animals—goat, dog, and hens—and the woods back of the house where he could climb trees, put up a teepee, and pretend he was an Indian."

In 1906, when the Murrays decided to send Harry away to a more high-powered preparatory school, their son was a healthy, active, good-natured boy of thirteen. He was slow to enter puberty, and a little on the small side, but would soon develop into a tall, well-formed young man. Contemporary photographs show us an alert, well-scrubbed, sweet-faced youngster whose earnest demeanor and slightly errant eyes combine to attract sympathetic good will. He was almost as innocent as he looked. True, his friend John Hodges, with whom he had spent parts of several summers on

Long Island, had given him a small taste of the high life. John's father drank, told stories about his wild youth, and boasted of having cheated his way through Harvard. His mother introduced Harry to the torrid novels of Elinor Glyn. Late at night, after the party guests had gone to bed, the boys stalked through the house, emptying all the glasses. Harry went along, to be sure; but he was properly scandalized by what went on at his friend's house. None of it rubbed off, and he was in actual fact the "clean, honorable and manly" fellow described in a letter of recommendation by his headmaster in May 1906. Young Murray is "popular alike with the masters and his school mates," the letter goes on. "I can truthfully say that I have never had a boy leave the school whose loss has been more deeply felt."

These words were directed to Endicott Peabody, the founder and headmaster of Groton, a small, elite preparatory school situated just outside Boston. Peabody came from an old, wealthy Salem family. His educational philosophy, which emphasized hard work and hard play, had been formed during years at school in England and at the Episcopal Theological School in Cambridge, Massachusetts. Many have compared him to Thomas Arnold of Rugby. Peabody's insistence on balance—a "muscular" Christian training of rigorous minds in vigorous bodies—reflected an ambition to build "character" in the sons of the patriciate, America's traditional leaders, who had lost the initiative to ruthless, unprincipled outsiders in the years since the Civil War. The program was akin, both in its anxieties and in its ideals, to Theodore Roosevelt's call for virile Anglo-Saxonism and "the strenuous life." "If we wish to do good work for our country we must be unselfish, disinterested, sincerely desirous of the well-being of the commonwealth, and capable of devoted adherence to a lofty ideal," the future president had argued in the mid-1890s; "but in addition we must be vigorous in mind and body, able to hold our own in rough conflict with our fellows, able to suffer punishment without flinching, and, at need, to repay it in kind with full interest." The full-blooded American warrior-prince marched with equal authority through Peabody's imagination when he opened Groton to its first class in 1884.

Harry was no doubt in awe of Peabody. All the boys were. The

Rector stood for manly Christian morality. In the chapel, in the classroom, on the playing fields, he was Groton's conscience. Affable in a formal sort of way, he approached the boys with affectionate, paternal condescension. His sense of humor surfaced on special occasions—most notably when he gave animated readings from Dickens before the whole school—but was otherwise pretty scarce. In the face of lapses from virtue, it vanished entirely. Peabody's sermons were not renowned, and Harry came to feel that their limitations were a window on the preacher himself. He had a tendency to wander from the point and seemed to lack the mental edge requisite to the coherent development of his own favorite views. He was better at brief spiritual pep talks delivered at chapel before classes in the morning. Here platitudes served adequately in place of freshly formed ideas. "Hypocrisy," he once assured Harry, "is the compliment that evil pays to goodness."

But it was not until Groton was behind him that Harry came to such mingled judgments of the school's spiritual leader. At the time of his graduation in 1911 he was still as pliantly susceptible to Peabody's influence as he had been in 1906, when his father, pleading his son's youth and inexperience, persuaded school officials to admit him to the second form and not the third. Grafton Minot, a classmate, remembered Harry as "straight and well-formed, carrying himself with style. His manner was open and agreeable, and I can remember no temper or ill-nature. He was not conceited, but had a certain reasonable dignity. The foregoing is almost negative, an attractive boy from the 'right sort of people' growing up in the 'right sort of way,' but there was much more to him than that." Having said this much, however, Minot neglects to mention what it was that set Harry apart. "Brains? Not much visible interest in scholarship, probably in the first quarter of the class in marks, which did not mean much in our case." Harry was a bright, privileged boy among others of his kind. He was a solid student with strengths in History and French, less evident aptitudes for English and Latin, whose grades never wandered too far from the middle of the class. The Rector's brief comments on Harry's report cards—"A very satisfactory boy," "Good, as usual," "Deserves credit for having taken so high a place in this form," "Came very near to disobedience the other day"—indicate steady progress, never brilliant, but with occasional lapses, toward graduation.

All the evidence indicates that Harry worked and played hard at Groton, and had a wonderful time doing it. He appears in his regular letters home to his father—which Henry, Sr., carefully dated and saved—as a positive, engaged, well-balanced, rather uncomplicated adolescent. Athletics were always first in his mind, and football, the premier sport at Groton, filled the foreground, especially in his first years at school. He rose no higher than reserve quarterback—his eyes no doubt betrayed him—but very sensibly took up other games, most notably golf, cross-country running, and crew. By his final, sixth form year he was a skilled oarsman, a regular member of the first eight, and a good prospect for collegiate rowing. His letters also give attention—though much less—to his school work, at which he labored faithfully, and with generally good results. He makes frequent mention of his many activities—debating, choir, stage managing class plays, teaching at a local Sunday school, serving as sports editor for the *Groton Weekly*—but never complains of boredom or fatigue. "I am terribly busy now," he wrote in early October 1910. "Football takes every afternoon. Then there is missionary [Episcopal church work] to Shirley. Pres. of the Museum Society, Grotonian, stage manager for two plays, rehearsals, Camp committee & Civics club, beside my regular studies which are very hard." But such constant, unreflecting motion was entirely to his taste. "The sixth form year is swell," he closed.

Harry's general health was excellent ("I feel perfectly bully" is a frequent boast), though he had his adenoids removed in the spring of 1908 and endured serious bouts with scarlet fever and mumps along the way. The rather slow pace of his physical development gave him no apparent concern. In March 1908, just before his fifteenth birthday, Harry was still able to compete in the 100-pound division of a boxing tournament. In September of the same year he reported home that he was no longer able to take soprano parts in the school choir. Less than two years later the school newspaper reported that at 5′11″ and 141 pounds he had moved to the bow seat on the varsity crew. He asked his father to send him a razor ("everyone that came along said 'You need a shave!'") in November

was not much help. Intellect was no handicap, provided it was tactfully concealed." As its final condition, the system exacted strict conformity to type. "You must do, wear, the 'right thing,' avoid the company of all ineligibles, and, above all, eschew originality."

Thanks to his stuttering and his wayward eyes, Harry fell short of the ideal that his class and background set before him. In all other respects, however, he seems to have been the perfect embodiment of what was, it can hardly be denied, a deplorably shallow standard of excellence. His academic record was distinguished only by the consistency of its mediocrity. He earned a few Bs in history but redressed the balance with Ds in chemistry and physics. For a short period at the beginning of his junior year he was on probation but promptly did what was necessary to get off. None of this bothered his parents, who were perfectly well pleased with a steady procession of Cs. Harry was equally ready to settle for the minimum required to get by. "Yesterday when a 1200 word theme was required for English," he explained to his father in March 1912, "I handed in one of 800 (an old Groton composition on which I had been given a C) and the Harvard professor said good & gave me a B. Pretty nice! as I have all my Groton compositions & I only have to rewrite them now."

Harry's well-concealed intelligence, in tandem with his Groton background, gave him a leg up on the college social ladder. His winning a spot on the freshman crew cannot have hurt, either. He kept rooms at Claverly Hall, far and away the most desirable of the Gold Coast dormitories. Thus, he was surrounded by prep school boys, many of them athletes, many of them from Groton. Years later Harry would reflect that he had no close friends at Harvard, that he was still inclined to be a loner. By his mature standard of judgment, which required of friends that they exchange ideas, his college relationships were rather shallow. But at the time he certainly thought of his acquaintances as friends, and all the evidence indicates that he had lots of them. Midway in his freshman year he wrote to his father that he and Sam Lothrop, his Groton friend, had reserved "a fine double room on the ground floor of Claverly next year." He was pleased that the location would land him in the midst of an especially agreeable prep school crowd: "Walter Trumbull

(1915 football team & probably crew) Philip Winsor (1915 hockey) Donald Cottrell (1915 football) Alfred Hoyt (son of Henry Hoyt) Be Bradlee (1915 football & probably crew) Francis Brooks (1915 track team) Lawrence Hemenway, Paul Courtney, and Harry De Ford (all Boston). I give you the names of these fellows because they are about my best friends I've made and you'll probably see some of them at the river this summer."

Virtually all of Harry's friends came from wealthy families and major prep schools. Their names turn up with striking regularity in all of the most socially desirable places. Trumbull and Lothrop rowed with him on the freshman crew. Every one of the boys mentioned in his letter to his father was elected to one of the two prestigious freshman clubs. Harry was the only member of his class invited to join both. He was also in the very elite first "ten" of D.K.E., along with Trumbull, Bradlee, and his old friend Hardwick. When he accepted the invitation of the A.D. Club, which he vastly preferred to the Porcellian, he was joined by Courtney, De Ford, Trumbull, Bradlee, Cottrell, and Hemenway. Griswold Webb and John Hodges were also members. The same contingent turned up at the coming-out parties for Boston's debutantes, the all-night dances, and the weekend gatherings in country houses that were *de rigueur* for the members of Harry's set. Not that he minded. At 18 he was already a veteran of high society, at ease in the most fashionable company, comfortable in all varieties of formal dress, and happy to be in constant motion between engagements. In early November 1912, having complained to his father about his poor marks and the pressure of unfinished school work, he announced: "Tonight I go to the Slater's fancy dress. Elsie Burr at whose house I'm dining is making my costume. I'm spending the night at Hemenway's. You see the dance is at Readville. Tomorrow the Princeton game & in the evening I'm going to the theatre with the Thachers and Nunsy. Sunday I'm spending at North Andover with the Trumbulls."

Harry commenced a diary toward the end of his sophomore year, in April 1913. The volume is the surest evidence that he was intellectually quite without sophistication on the eve of his twentieth birthday. The cover bears the warning (reminiscent perhaps of *Trea-*

sure Island), "Cursed be he who reads this book without permission from the author." What follows is tame enough, even by contemporary standards. He begins by reviewing his freshman year, a long season, he recalls, of "loafing, rioting and rowing." He acknowledges that his grades were only so-so; and "as for rioting I made a fool of myself several times, [and] made some close friends but managed to keep pure despite the fact that many of my best friends fell by the wayside." Harry's purity was in jeopardy almost from the day of his arrival in Cambridge. He joined his friends in the obligatory tour of the brothels on Shawmut Avenue, where several of the boys—Harry perhaps one of them—sampled the fare. Harry's account of his collegiate sexual adventures are notably ambiguous. His diary protests his virginity, but it may have been protesting too much. In later life he readily acknowledged visiting the red-light district and even took some pride in recalling the names of the most famous madames. He allowed that black prostitutes may have figured in the fun. But he also remembered that his earlier dread of venereal disease had hardly abated and that it grew worse when one of his closest friends turned up with gonorrhea. Part of him, even in his diary, was pleased to have gone along with the boys; another part would have preferred to stay home. Sex for Harry was thus charged with the fascination of the illicit. Sexual pleasure was best taken off limits. Its delights were bound up with its danger and immorality. One did not discuss it with parents or with proper, marriageable girls. There was sympathy for the fellow with VD, but the friendship was never the same.

The would-be libertine in Harry never quite got free. The figure of the genially dissipated young carouser and rake was prominent in his social world. The men of A.D. took a certain pride in their excesses. Harry played along from time to time; he drank his fill and roared with the boys down to Shawmut Avenue. But the man of character would not finally give in. High principle and purity were certainly involved; fear of contamination, and the refusal to relinquish control, also had parts to play. Harry was more the product of the late Victorian ethos than he liked to admit. His heroes— John Brown, Abraham Lincoln, Nansen, Grenfell—were men of determination and clear moral purpose. He felt the strong pull of

TR's summons to clean, virile Anglo-Saxon manhood. In later years he would insist that dogmatic Christianity had little influence on his youthful idealism. Unitarianism, he told Endicott Peabody, was an "ethical society rather than a religion." Still, Harry's daybook of uplifting quotations, very tidily executed in 1914, is suffused with Christianity. Biblical quotations—"I am the Way and the Truth and the Life"; "I will arise and go to my Father"—set the opening tone. Thereafter, muscular idealism from Kipling and Service is interspersed with uplift from Shakespeare, Tennyson, Browning, and Longfellow, and sage advice from the likes of Newman, Emerson, Lincoln, and Phillips Brooks. LeBaron Briggs, the enormously popular and influential Dean of the Faculty of Arts and Sciences, mentor to generations of Harvard undergraduates, and Harry's favorite advisor, is also represented. "Do not let your ideals get shopworn," he counselled, in books such as *School, College, and Character* (1901); "What students do (or don't) when they are in love is a pretty good test of their character."

Harry the Rake and Harry the Pure seem to have reached a kind of truce in Harry the earnest, busy man about campus. Lawrence Kubie, who was a year behind him at Harvard, recalls that Harry was a "prominent figure" in the college. In addition to his athletic and social activities—which came to include the Hasty Pudding and the Signet Society—he was involved in a variety of service and student organizations, among them the St. Paul's Society, the Natural History Society, the Student Council, the Annual Junior Dance Committee, the Harvard Memorial Society, the Student Register, and the Executive Committee of the Harvard Varsity Club. When, during his junior year, he was elected to lead the Phillips Brooks House Association, a local paper announced, rather baldly, "Capt. Harry A. Murray of the varsity crew, the son of a New York multimillionaire, is chairman of the superintendents, whose task it is to look after boys' club work." No doubt because of his hectic schedule, Harry disciplined himself to a strict "efficiency system" in the spring of his sophomore year. Rising at 6:40 AM and allocating time for study, reading, writing in his diary, meals, exercise, "dressing & odds & ends," and club activities, he harnessed himself to a tight, closely watched regimen. Subsequent pages in his diary make room for detailed lists of friends, programs for physical development, exercise records, and columns of golf scores. All is carefully planned and tidy. "Efficiency," he concluded, "is the keynote in life." He later augmented his system with daily percentage ratings of success in key areas. In much of his earnest rage for order Harry was following Jules Payot, the French sage whose *Education of the Will* (1909) appears regularly in his daily reflections. "One must toil in these early years to improve oneself," he admonishes his diary. "Christ never went out to help his brethren until he was older." Supplementing Payot with Dean Briggs and Endicott Peabody, his guides for the year ahead, he assured himself that "Society means little to me. Blood, family etc. do not come in to my thought at all."

Again, one suspects that Harry protested too much. Society and family meant everything to him, though they counseled—as Peabody and Briggs and even Roosevelt counseled—that it was the obligation of privilege to serve. Harry's youthful earnestness echoes the Progressive spirit of his class in the years just before the Great War, when Anglo-Saxon Protestant males of means reasserted what they took to be their rightful authority in the public sphere. The country had fallen on evil times. Unregulated big business, hordes of immigrants, and ruthless urban politicians had combined to contaminate the national life. America felt unclean to right-minded Progressives. The title of Lincoln Steffens' *Shame of the Cities* (1904) catches the mood. There was no dearth of smugness and paternal condescension in this movement for reform. But there was good will, too, and a readiness to take a part and to make sacrifices in the service of others. Family and class could hardly be dismissed from consideration; nor was it anticipated that their social importance would diminish with the solution to America's problems. It was a cleaning up that the elders had in mind, not a leveling down.

The summer of 1913 was a fairly typical college vacation for Harry. Toward the end of June, with the rowing season just completed, he joined his family at Mid-River Farm in the Thousand Islands. It was his habit to rise early, help with the milking on the dairy, and then to pass the days entertaining the numerous Harvard friends who came up for a visit. After a month given over to boating, fishing, tennis, golf, reading, and general loafing, he took the train south to Cape Cod, where his unit of the National Guard, Battery A, an artillery outfit, gathered for a week of training. Moved by patriotic zeal, by the prospect of good fellowship, and in order to gain a commission in the event of war, Harry had joined up in 1912. In late July and early August, he served as a counselor in a camp for poor boys from Boston. Then he boarded the luxurious Twentieth-Century Limited for the long journey via Chicago to Portland, Oregon, where he spent five weeks with friends and guides on horseback hunting deer and bear, fishing, mountain climbing, and taking in the color and excitement of life outdoors in the far west. "I feel like a rip-snorter & am in the pink of condition," he wrote to his father. There was just time to return home with his trophy (a small buck) before classes resumed in September.

Harry's diaries for his junior and senior years do little to complicate the profile emergent from earlier college records. The young man just entering his twenties is earnestly attentive to his moral condition and to his vocation in human service. He continues to keep lists and tabulated records; he is a mine of resolutions in matters of thrift, self-improvement, family relations, moderation, and health. Measured units of his carefully monitored time are assigned to school work, but his mind is elsewhere, with the crew, in varieties of social activity, and in affairs of the heart. Harry was by now a handsome, muscular athlete—he appeared in the *Boston Globe* sports section at 6′ 1″ and 168 pounds in May 1912—and a familiar figure in and around Harvard Yard. Yet there was still something decidedly boyish about him—in his fair, friendly face, his ready optimism, the reserve that went with stammering, and the untried freshness of his spirit. The warning on the cover of his journal for 1914—"This book is quite private and anyone who reads its contents is hereby damned"—is less floridly archaic than its predecessor but suggests a still imperfect submergence of the pirate in the man about campus.

Harry was protective of his diaries, no doubt, because they contained the intimate record of his romantic relationship with Josephine Rantoul. Rowing and romance—the varsity crew, which he captained as a senior, and Jo, as she was called, to whom he was engaged in June 1915—were the twin centers of his life during his

34

speech, and then sat, a forgiving audience of one, through several trial runs in Sanders Theater. He was also there, an assuring older face in the audience, when the young captain of the crew delivered his speech, without a single hitch, to 200 of his peers.

Harry had learned a valuable lesson for the future—that stammering was not a factor when he knew in advance what he wanted to say. But it was quite another matter to control the words of others. On several occasions during his senior year the press made the going rough for him. Early on in the season, for example, a Boston paper declared it "unfortunate that Captain Murray is not a leader in rowing as he is in spirit. He makes a wise and heady captain but lined up with the other 16 men competing for the first eight places he does not seem at present to outstrip all the available talent." The article went on to acknowledge that "Murray develops well in a season" and predicted that he would "come to the front rapidly." Still, the writer had rankled a wound first opened by Jim Wray's remarks the preceding spring. Harry was captain, all right; but was he athlete enough to take a place alongside the men he was supposed to lead? The coach wasn't sure; perhaps Harry wasn't either.

One thing is certain—Harry was very uneasy with Jim Wray. He found him nervous, fretful, and too quick to find fault. Wray's habit of talking with reporters after races, and of taking the occasion to isolate individuals for criticism, was especially infuriating. The crew diary casts Wray as an unpredictable grouch who often inadvertently undermines a fragile *esprit de corps*. In April, just before the Navy race, Harry observed "a feeling of uncertainty in the crew which is instigated by Jim. He gets all excited just before a race and curses us out, & it doesn't serve any purpose except to disconcert us." Personal doubts were compounded by major disagreements over strategy. Wray was in favor of frequent shifts in personnel back and forth between the first and second boats. The point was to find the elusive perfect combination and to bring out the best in the men. Harry took the opposite view. Constant shifts were destructive of morale; the best results were to be had by staying with the same crew over the long haul. Quite in keeping with his temperament, Wray was also an advocate of fast starts. He wanted to run away from the competition. For his part, Harry liked to go out smooth and steady. The best money, and the highest drama, he felt, were in heroic come-from-behind finishes.

The power to enforce decisions was divided somewhat indefinitely between the coach and the captain. Wray had years of experience; he was regularly out in front of the competition; he was paid to give guidance. On the other side, Harry was closer to the members of the crew, not only in age but also in background. His closest friends in the program were young men of the upper class who approached rowing with a gentleman's eye to camaraderie and good sportsmanship. Winning was important, but insisting upon it, and losing badly, were vulgar. Wray was by contrast an employee of modest means paid to produce winners. Victory was his business. Indeed, he stood for professionalism in what seemed to many a properly amateur pursuit. This difference in attitude worked subtly to drive a wedge between the coach and many of his oarsmen. Harry was of course very much on the side of those whose feelings about Wray were colored by "old school" condescension. Thus his formal authority as captain was substantially augmented by close class affiliations with major actors in the rowing program.

Ties of this description came into play at secret meetings of the crew, convened and presided over by the captain. The first such gathering took place at the beginning of the fall season, when Harry summoned the members of the varsity boats to his rooms. "It was a private talk," the crew diary records, "& it was stated that everything that was said was just between ourselves." Harry took the occasion to spell out his views on Coach Wray's faults—specifically, his "poor sportsmanship" (illustrated in the "articles in the paper after the Yale race") and his indecisiveness (presumably in making crew assignments). Harry went on to urge "that it was up to everyone on the squad to minimize these faults as much as possible." To that end, he proposed "that no-one should 1. complain to Wray about anything; but that all complaints should be registered with me, and 2. that no-one should give their opinions about other men on the crew or express any ideas whatsoever, except that things were going O.K. This should keep Wray humored, and prove a valuable asset in having him as a coach."

46

Harry had no trouble drawing the majority to his side. The coach was not widely admired by the members of the crew, which made it all the easier for them to imagine that lining up against him would ultimately serve Wray's best interests and the best interests of the program. The effect of their agreement was to isolate the coach in ignorance and to turn all important decisions over to the captain. In return, Harry promised that Wray's irascible outbursts would be contained and that the boat assignments would be as firm and final as possible. He was as good as his word. Wray's moods were carefully monitored, and on numerous occasions potential flare-ups were successfully averted. Harry noted in the crew diary— not without irony, perhaps—that letting the coach win at croquet "is one of the big factors in handling him." And with help from Robert Herrick, the exemplary amateur coach of the victorious Henley squad and chairman of the Harvard Rowing Committee, he made Wray "swear not to say anything to the newspapers" after the Cornell race. Meanwhile, the composition of the first and second boats remained stable. This departure from precedent was entirely the captain's doing. It is Harvard's greatest "asset," the crew diary proudly reports, "that we've been able to develop without any changes."

Harry's strategy of containment and continuity seemed to pay off in the early going. Effectively strapped by the crew's silent resistance, Wray was forced to capitulate to the captain's policies. His authority was further undermined by an inquiry, undertaken by Dean Briggs in March 1915, into allegations that he verbally abused his oarsmen and imposed "commercial" values on the sport. Meanwhile, morale on the boats was high. Wray was a distraction to the crew before the Navy race, but the middies fell easily to a confident Harvard varsity. Harry found faults with the performance but viewed them as valuable lessons for the much more challenging race with Cornell. It was now his "absolute conviction" that Wray's "tendency to raise the stroke like hell" was a grave tactical mistake. "Emphasize the finish," he reiterated. On May 22 that strategy had its reward in a great victory on Lake Cayuga. No Harvard crew had ever before defeated Cornell at home. "Come on & shove" had been the "big signal" for the final push. It worked perfectly. "We rowed in the same order as we have all season," Harry noted in the crew diary.

Two days after the Cornell victory the crew gathered to celebrate at the Tennis and Racquet Club in Boston. Harry's ally Robert Herrick, who arranged and paid for the spread, left the coach off the list of invited guests. "Coach Wray of Harvard Crew is Snubbed" read the headline of a local newspaper account that Harry dutifully included in the crew diary. Taking a lead from "those who are supposed to know," the article traces the trouble to a source in the Yale race of 1914, in which "the crew disregarded Wray's instructions to row hard all the way and followed graduate advice. Wray scolded the crew afterwards and Herrick was perturbed." Noting that the coach "has been forbidden to talk to the newspapers," the article speculates that his job may be in jeopardy. "Friends of Herrick" concurred but added that "the dinner was merely a club affair to which no paid professional would be invited anyway."

Clearly enough, Harry was working with Herrick against the coach; just as clearly, class antagonisms had their part to play in the rejection of the "paid professional" by those more at home at "a club affair." Wray was outraged and carried his complaint to the captain. "I let him get everything off his chest," Harry recorded in the crew diary, "so that when we got to New London he would be O.K." In the greater privacy of his personal journal, however, he was less restrained. "Wray is one of the most interesting persons in the world," he wrote. "1. He is a moral coward & will never tell you directly what he thinks to your face. 2. He is a great family man. This is about his weakest spot. Treat him as your social equal & it tickles him to death." Charges of deviousness come rather oddly from one who had earlier imposed secrecy on the crew. Moreover, Wary had been quite direct in airing his grievances and had been muzzled for his trouble. In fact, whatever his offenses may have been, caste prejudice worked to deny the beleaguered coach a full, fair hearing. Harry's dairy makes this painfully clear.

In the weeks preceding the Yale race, Harry labored over an essay on "Rowing at Harvard" which his mother's good friend Frank Crowninshield, the witty editor of *Vanity Fair,* had commissioned for his magazine. The article, brief but gracefully brought off, describes the pleasurable "sensation of slipping over the water swiftly and easily after a powerful stroke of the oar." Somewhat predictably, Harry gives the main emphasis to the necessity for developing a sense of unity among the members of the crew. It is best, he insists, "to select your men as early as possible and let them row together for at least three weeks before each race." This readiness to highlight his own controversial policy reflects a self-confidence that surfaced more than once as the great event drew near. "Right and good sportsmanship seem to be on our side in this race & therefore we should win," he observed in the crew diary on June 24, just a day before the race.

But something in the formula was awry. The Elis went out fast and never looked back. "There is no story to tell except that of a procession," Harry wrote. "They gained a few inches every stroke & crossed the line in record time—7 lengths to the good." It was a massacre. Containment and continuity had failed utterly. Harry took brief refuge in the thought that the professionalism requisite to victory was ruining the game. Paid coaches—such as Yale's Nickalls, for example—"are poor sports in many ways & have not the proper gentlemanly instincts to maintain the sport on the high standard which it should enjoy. I admire the English system of amateur coaching," he went on, but despaired of its future in America. Even so, he concluded, "Wray would lose 4 times out of every 5 to Nickalls."

"Here endeth the lesson of 1915," he wrote on the penultimate page of the crew diary. And there, it seems clear, he wished to leave it. "I put all I had into the race and into longing for my girl after that," reads his personal journal. "It was a day of sensations all right—but oh I'm happy inside because I know that for once in my life (with Jo's help) I've done my best. Took the midnight train to Boston. I arrived at the Copley-Plaza at 7 A.M., was paged at 8:15, arrived in room 488 at 8:20, was engaged by 8:23." Thus he moved from defeat to victory without so much as pausing to catch his breath. "I hereby end this diary as Jo and I start on a new era together in perfect love."

But the lesson of 1915 was not so readily absorbed. The pain of the defeat, and a nagging sense of discomfort with his own role in

49

it, never went away. Toward the end of his life Harry endured a season of nightmares in which his greatest personal failings thrust themselves into view. The Yale race was always high on this nocturnal agenda. His ambivalence on the subject was striking. It seemed such a small matter, after all, and he dismissed it as such, only to come back to it again and again. Fifty thousand spectators, including his family, Jo, and many friends, had been there in New London to witness the ignominious defeat. But the shame was not simply in the losing. Harry's code of sportsmanship equipped him to handle defeat with grace, so long as he gave his best effort. If you played the game in the right spirit, his *Vanity Fair* piece had concluded, "victory or defeat in any particular race is but a trifle." The real trouble, insofar as he could locate it precisely, lay in his behavior as captain. "Those were the years when I was an autocrat," he admitted more than once. There appeared to be ample justice in his opposition to Wray's public attacks on individual oarsmen. But what of his refusal to compromise in the matter of moving men back and forth between positions? Was that justified? Harry wasn't sure. "No," he replied on one occasion, "I didn't know whether I'd made a mistake or not, but I didn't feel I had." A few moments later he shifted ground. "I think I just had a fixed idea, and like all fixed ideas, they're apt to defeat you in an emergency." Such uncertainty had been there almost from the beginning. Less than a year after the race, when he was living in New York, the sound of the boats on the Hudson seemed especially melancholy to Harry. They put him in mind of the wail of horns and sirens that went up immediately after the disastrous defeat in New London.

The press coverage of the Yale race—copiously represented in Harry's scrapbook for 1915—offers a window on the deeper sources of his uneasiness. A *New York Herald* story highlights "Talk of Friction in Harvard Camp" and reports, on reliable authority, that Wray could not place his "best oarsman" on the varsity boat because of opposition from "the persons who controlled the rowing policy in Cambridge." Another article, entitled "Favoritism at Harvard Beats Crews," asserts that "Captain H. A. Murray is the storm centre," and identifies Eugene Soucy, Harry's competitor for a seat in the 1914 Yale race and a graduate of Boston Latin, as one of three oarsmen unfairly kept off the varsity boat. The article details Harry's maneuverings to exclude Soucy and then asks, "Did Murray also have the future in view in disposing of Soucy, who is far from being a member of the exclusive set at Harvard? With his rowing two years in the Harvard shell he would have been the logical man for the captaincy next year. This would have deprived D. P. Morgan, who is a close friend of Murray's, of that honor."

Other articles—one of them announcing Coach Wray's dismissal by an eight to one vote of the Harvard Athletic Committee—echo the suggestion that Harry unjustly favored his friends on the crew. Given the evidence of the diaries, there can be no denying the plausibility of the accusations. Nor is it likely that Harry failed to recognize the truth of what was being leveled against him. But it was quite another thing to admit in so many words that class prejudice had figured in his treatment of James Wray; or to allow that injured pride had played a major part in his campaign to silence the coach; or, finally, to acknowledge that making permanent rowing assignments relieved him of the nagging fear that he, the captain of the crew, might end up on the second boat. Harry knew all this, or at least glimpsed it; and he came as close as he could to expressing his regret in the admission that he had been an "autocrat" with a foolishly "fixed idea" in his head. Soon enough he would thrust prep schools and clubs and cotillions, and the people that went with them, from his life. Indeed, the vigor with which he rejected that world expressed something near contempt for the part of himself still at large in it.

▼

chapter four

Misgivings and Preparatives

In "The Case of Murr," Harry looks back on his years in medical school as a period of decisive personal change. "Murr had been brought up on the conservative Republican Episcopalian side of the traditions of a relatively stable society, with a moral code, cluster of tastes, and privileged status that were taken for granted by his parents and unobtrusively exemplified. Molded by these values, which had been reinforced by the Rev. Endicott Peabody of Groton, Murr arrived at medical school not suspecting that in due course his analytical mind would identify their ethnocentric determinants, and that before he graduated he would refute a basic Marxian theorem by saying good-bye to his implanted prejudices in favor of Christianity, the Republican Party, and the class of people with whom he had been reared." By this account, aptly entitled "Egression from the Husk of His Youth," Harry's years in medical school produced a complete revolution in his life. Murr went to New York "with the express purpose of detaching himself from his playboy and athletic friends in the Harvard–Boston area; but the separation that was intended to be temporary turned out to be a permanent divorce of interests and viewpoints with no remaining valid bridges of communication."

Even in its telling omission of Jo—who was inseparable in fact, and in Harry's mind, from what was left behind in Boston—this view of the period seems just. His life turned almost completely around in New York. Medical education initially appealed to his rage for order and classification. Over time he came alive to the subtleties of the diagnostic process, to the interior lives of his patients, and to the challenge of medical research. But his extraordinary personal transformation was just as closely keyed to changes in his physical environment. New York brought Harry face to face with a much wider range of human experience and thought and expression than he had encountered in Cambridge. Freed almost by surprise from his role as Harvard clubman and athlete, he embraced this wide, various world with unexampled gusto. Explorer at last, a new Nansen in Gotham, he discovered science, books and ideas, people, and a fascinating new self.

Harry first heard the call to medicine during his freshman year at Harvard when a professor in a human physiology course suggested he'd be good at it. He went on rounds with the father of his friend Paul Courtney, a genial Boston neurologist and Francophile who encouraged him to read widely in medical history. Harry began to build a personal collection of books in the field and spent a full day in Paris during the summer of 1914 looking for a suitable picture of his hero, Louis Pasteur. His mediocre academic record was no obstacle to admission to Harvard Medical School, but the Columbia College of Physicians and Surgeons was much closer to home. "I like the New York spirit of research, the Rockefeller Institute, the hospitals—the big city with its enormous opportunities & I think it's far superior to Boston as a place to conduct your life work," he wrote to his diary late in his senior year. "Therefore it's P. & S., Presbyterian Hospital & New York City for me—no question about it."

Harry spent much of the summer of 1915 with Jo and her family at the Rantoul summer home outside of Boston. It was an easy commute to the city, where he took Harvard summer school courses in elementary histology and bacteriology, lab methods and dissection. In September, leaving fiancée and rowing and playboy friends behind, he moved to New York. From his parents' house on W 51st Street, where he lived for the next year, it was not a very long walk to the College of Physicians and Surgeons, on W 59th Street between 9th and 10th Avenues. The campus bordered on two very rough areas, Hell's Kitchen and San Juan Hill, both notorious for their gangsters and red-light districts. In time, Harry would venture out into this neighboring underworld. At first, though, he gave himself entirely to the new routine, and to missing Jo. His diary for 1915, which he resumed briefly in September, alternates between elation ("New friend—my partner in Organic Chemistry—I'm absolutely delighted!") and depression ("I find I am in bum shape mentally. . . . I forget. And I stammer worse than usual. Perhaps it's the effect of leaving Jo. God only knows how terribly I miss her—my own girl"). Troubles with concentration persisted, though by the second week Harry found himself "getting more interested in Medical School all the time." Up at 6:30, to bed at 11:30, he put himself on a schedule demanding 13 hours of study each day. Before long, he was happily absorbed in his work.

Harry was, in his own words, "crazy about medical school." It came very easily to him, and he was at the top of his class right from the start. He was well liked and social enough, though he had fewer friends than at Harvard and lost no sleep over his failure to win the election for class president. Edwin Maynard, a friend and classmate, remembered him as a bright, friendly fellow with a good sense of humor. His closest friend was Alvan Barach, another stammerer and a prodigious intellectual enthusiast who did more than any other person to draw him out of "the husk of his youth." Harry ranked Barach foremost among those "redeemers" who won him away from the values of his sheltered and privileged upbringing. It mattered greatly that Barach was Jewish. Harry had never had a Jewish friend. Anti-Semitism was prominently a feature of his background; Jews must have seemed exotic to him, and a little dangerous. But Barach was brilliant, unabashed, very funny, and in love with talk. He introduced Harry to Goethe, Dostoevsky, and Wilde. They engaged in marathon conversations, sometimes filling whole weekends, on art, love, politics, and the meaning of life. The talk was so animated that they had to set rules of procedure governing interruptions and control of the floor. Early on they were both elected to the Omega Society, a fraternity of leading students that met regularly to hear from distinguished guests. Barach primed his new friend for a conversion to Democratic political values, a shift completed in Harry's vigorous support for Wilson's 14 Points and the proposed League of Nations. As much by example as precept, Barach also helped to free Harry of the prejudice that came with his privileged background. For the first time, he glimpsed the absurdity of the upper-class pretension and snobbery that he had been brought up with. "I'd been given a bias that was right down in the marrow," he recognized. "I was very ashamed of it." Because he was intelligent, voraciously curious, irreverent, Jewish, and a great bringer of light, Barach, who went on to a brilliant career in medicine, became a valued, durable friend.

But Harry's vastly enlarged horizons did not change everything. He was still a rich man from an established family with habits and tastes that marked him for life. He became critical of his parents for their unreflecting caste prejudice, but he did not abandon them or cease to be entangled emotionally in their lives. He came to think less of Groton and Harvard clubs and the friends linked with them, but he did not attempt to banish them from sight and mind. As time passed, and as experience accumulated, Harry became conscious of himself moving back and forth between worlds. His old self did not change completely or go away. He continued to enjoy fine houses and possessions; he lived in the best neighborhoods and employed servants. But even away from home there was something unmistakably superior in his social bearing. Clothing had a part to play; so did his accent and his range of personal reference in conversation. Most of all, perhaps, it had to do with the way other people seemed to grow brighter and funnier and more interesting in the warm sun of his regard. One expanded in Harry's ample presence; one lifted gratefully toward his eminence. The patrician in him was never concealed, but it appeared in the midst of much else—intelligence, learning, discipline, generosity, creativity—that was more conventionally estimable. So situated, it made him seem a prince among American men.

The personal transformation that commenced at Columbia in 1915 continued for many years, even for decades. Harry's unfolding was singular both for its duration, and for the extraordinary depths it revealed. But while he expanded, Jo remained the same. She was very comfortably a patrician, in part, Harry believed, because of proud Saltonstall family traditions of service and principled dissent. Jo was so at ease with people of all classes and backgrounds, and so ready to give, that she lost sight of her own advantages. Most crucially, of course, it was not the part of young women of her high station to go to college, or to enter at all seriously into the world of ideas. Jo moved gracefully and unself-consciously within the taken-for-granted. It never occurred to her to be someone else.

Had Harry and Jo waited three or four years instead of one to marry, they would never have made it to the altar. But there was no reason to hold back, it seemed. Certainly there was no shortage of what Harry liked to refer to as "cash." Both families were pleased, even delighted, at the match. The engagement was celebrated in mid-July at what one Boston newspaper described as "an informal 'at home'" at the Rantoul estate in Beverly Farms, "the aristocratic West Beach neighborhood" on the North Shore. "Messenger boys were kept busy all day . . . bringing beautiful and exquisite baskets, boxes and bouquets of flowers, while letters of congratulation just poured in for Mr. Murray and his fiancée." Jo appeared in "a dainty and girlish frock of white silk muslin." She is described as "a clever sportswoman" who "drives her own car" and "inherits the blonde type of beauty and fine coloring for which her mother was distinguished." Her "costly pieces of jewelry," it is recorded, were gifts from her wealthy husband-to-be. The New York papers were equally attentive to the event, though more restrained. "The date of the wedding has not been set," observed the *Times*.

"It is a good thing for the world when two such people decide to throw in their lot together," wrote Endicott Peabody, praising Jo for having "shown the perspicacity of the clan." His daughter, Rose, offered a word of caution to Harry: "I should think the idea of relating yourself to the Lees, Saltonstalls, Peabodys and in fact most of Boston would have frightened you a little, but I guess it is worth it in spite of that!" "Harry Murray is a corker," observed Barrett Wendell, Jr. "It's up to me now," Ike declared. "You've got to get Jo to pick one out for me, one that is good, but that isn't expecting much." Harry's father sent less complex sentiments: "There is nothing finer in the world than the love and companionship of a good woman—they stimulate you in your career, and help you in maintaining and developing high standards and ideals." Meanwhile, the families exchanged warm letters. Lucy Rantoul, Jo's mother, wrote regularly to Harry after he left for medical school. "Your girl's eyes are big," she reported. "I heard some little sobs last night. . . . I suppose we can get along somehow. But it will be hard. Just this I ask you to remember, dear, that love comes first in a woman's life—while it is only a side issue in a man's. Remember that when things are difficult, which I hope and pray may be seldom."

They were married at noon on May 30, 1916, at St. John's Episcopal Church in Beverly Farms. Endicott Peabody performed the ceremony, while both families, a legion of bridesmaids and ushers, and many of Boston's best looked on. The papers were predictably effusive, featuring pictures of Jo, detailed descriptions of the reception at the Rantoul's, and long lists of distinguished guests. Though all agreed it was "a brilliant society wedding," Harry and Jo wasted no time in making their getaway. They left that afternoon for a few days of fishing and hiking in the Thousand Islands, before moving west via Chicago (where they looked in on the Republican National Convention) for the Grand Canyon and Los Angeles. Jo's fascination with show business took them to the lot of the Flying A Moving Picture Company in Santa Barbara. They saw a film in production and then took a hydroplane ride out over the channel. "It was certainly the most fascinating journey I ever took," Jo told a local reporter. Making stops in San Francisco ("the next best city to New York") and Yosemite, they traveled north through Oregon, where they fished the MacKenzie River, to Seattle and Vancouver. Harry made note of the troubles along the Mexican border ("It looks as if I might have to return immediately cutting short my honeymoon") and of Harvard's victory at New London. Turning eastward, they enjoyed climbing and fishing in the Canadian Rockies and then stopped only briefly in Minneapolis and Chicago en route to New York.

They arrived on July 11 and settled into their new home, a very comfortable apartment at 129 E 69th Street, in Manhattan's most fashionable residential district. Harry spent most of the summer in Boston doing independent research at Harvard Medical School. He had not yet accepted the fact that a conventional career in medicine had no place in his future. In part because of his incapacity for stereoscopic vision, surgery, his initial preference, would not finally suit him. More crucially, he was from the very outset of his medical education drawn towards research. Though his summers at Harvard—studying anatomy and other introductory subjects in 1915, embryology a year later—yielded little of practical significance, they gave evidence that surgery would not be enough to hold his interest over the long term. But even as his career plans changed, Harry was consistently energetic in his approach to medical school. Whatever the specific goal, he was anxious to get on with things.

His sense of urgency was intensified by an ambition to take a part in the war in Europe. Harry was hardly unusual in viewing the struggle as a summons to heroic endeavor. In his senior year at Harvard he corresponded with friends who had gone over to work in the American ambulance service. As a next step, he wrote to Theodore Roosevelt, seeking advice. The old hero of San Juan Hill urged him to prepare for strenuous action as a medic or ambulance driver. He encountered Roosevelt again, this time by chance, outside of Carnegie Hall in early 1917. A small crowd had gathered, and TR took the opportunity to inveigh against Woodrow Wilson. "Our president thinks that he can fight a war with a fountain pen," he sneered; "I believe in fighting with a sword." Within a few weeks the toll taken by German submarines forced the reluctant Wilson to make the world safe for democracy. Harry wrote more letters, trying to find his own way into the war. Finally, he was drafted in August and ordered to report for duty in September, though in the upshot he was obliged as a medical student to complete his training before moving into action. This was discouraging.

Harry responded by going without summer breaks for the duration of medical school. But of course graduating in January of 1919 was no help. By then the war was over; the opportunity had passed. While good friends fought and died for glory, he was obliged to go to school. Worst of all, his little brother had made a hero of himself in the skies over Europe. The story of Ike's war service falls open like a romantic adventure story written for teenage boys. As a nineteen-year-old Harvard sophomore, Ike tried to enlist in the naval flying service but was refused because of his age. Undaunted, he sought private training, qualified himself as a flier, and this time earned his enlistment as a Lieutenant, junior grade. Sent overseas as a member of the Dunkirk bombing squadron, he twice crossed the Alps in Caproni bombers and took part in several missions behind the lines, including raids on the German submarine base at Zeebrugge toward the very end of the war. For his conspicuous valor he was decorated with the Naval Cross.

Ike's letters home must have filled Harry with a mixture of pride and helpless, aching envy. "I don't want you to tell anyone about this plan," he confided, "especially ma. I think in the near future there will be an opportunity for us to do night bombing over the lines, which as I have written you is the prize job of all others— from my point of view anyway." Such fearlessness in the face of danger had its reward in a most gratifying scrape with disaster. "I nearly got mine the other night," he wrote. "We counted 79 bullet holes in our machine. Of course, this seems a lot to me; but the pilot (I was the observer in back—learning the country) was very casual about it. This only happens rarely, & is nothing to worry about." In July 1918 he served as a rear gunner in an exhilarating attack on an aerodrome behind enemy lines. "The raid itself lasted slightly over 3 hrs," he reported to his brother, "& these were probably the best 3 of my life."

Harry held up well enough in the face of such glamorous exploits. This was so, no doubt, because medical school had a firm hold on his interest. He continued to succeed brilliantly in his work. His notebooks are alive with questions and observations, titles to consult, research topics to pursue, books and articles to write. He had become friendly with Hans Zinsser, a professor of bacteriology and immunology at Physicians and Surgeons, an avid equestrian, and a poet of some note. Thanks to Barach's friendly guidance, Harry was giving more of his time to literature. But the leading figure in his education was Dr. George Draper, a professor of medicine who gave a course in physical diagnosis at the end of the second year. It was in this course that Harry developed what his friend Edwin Maynard remembered as a fascination and special adeptness with difficult diagnostic problems. In later life Harry often elaborated on Draper's genius for drawing inferences from apparently insignificant clues. While the medical students gave their attention to the heartbeat of a woman with tachycardia, the professor noticed that she had a habit of jerking her head to the right. Had she been in an accident recently? he asked. She said no. Had she come close to having one? Yes, the woman replied, nervously. A train had nearly hit her car at a crossing. Had the train come up on the right? Yes, she said, it had come up quite suddenly and she barely got across. Once the connection between this frightening episode and the patient's condition was made manifest, she recovered fully.

Harry made a special place for Draper in "The Case of Murr." "At medical school and later," he recalled, "there were many occasions to be astonished, stimulated, and instructed by [his] pinpoint observations and brilliant intuitive diagnoses of patients with what was later to be called psychosomatic illness. For some years he was Murr's most uniquely influential teacher, both by exhibiting these talents and by expounding his very original conceptions respecting varieties of human constitution, many of which would eventually be more systematically set forth by W. H. Sheldon." Draper instructed his students to ignore textbooks. Preconceptions and pat answers were obstacles, not aids, to correct diagnosis, he insisted. Write your own book, he challenged them, and do it on the basis of original observations. He divided his classes into pairs and asked the students to begin by examining each other. He urged them to use all of their senses in gathering information and to trust their intuitions. Draper's resistance to convention, his insistence on direct observation, and his emphasis on the free play of imagination in developing insights were the elements that most impressed Harry and stayed with him. Diagnosis on this model was a kind of adventure, a wide-open challenge to explore afresh the signs and unlooked-for clues that patients might betray to a searching, sympathetic observer.

Draper's mingling of scientific objectivity with imagination and individual intuition appealed to Harry because it called upon a rare combination of resources that he himself possessed in an unusual degree. Draper's influence overflowed into Harry's essay, "Groton and Adaptation," which was featured in the graduate number of the school magazine in May 1919. He tinkered with the piece for a year or more and then sent what he had produced to Dean Acheson for comment and criticism. Acheson's response was both helpful and very encouraging. He made numerous adjustments to the structure of the essay but offered his unequivocal assent to its basic message. Emboldened by the support, Harry sent the manuscript to Ellery Sedgwick, editor of the *Atlantic Monthly,* who nodded his approval but suggested that the *Grotonian* might be the best place to publish it.

"Groton and Adaptation" offers itself as a modest attempt to stimulate "reflection and discussion" on the school's educational philsophy. Illustrating his points with examples from science, Harry opens with an assault on the intellectual rigidity encouraged by the Groton system. "The value of habit is very much overemphasized," he observes, "and it is allowed to enter into fields where not stereotyped conduct but rather original and independent thought is needed. . . . Progress in the world depends not upon the maintenance of habits but rather upon adaptation." Clearly enough, Harry was speaking from personal experience and from the exhilarating sense of freedom and discovery that medical school in general, and George Draper in particular, had fostered in him. He goes on to acknowledge his mentor, underscoring the "fundamental truth" that "all knowledge in the world is derived through the senses." Granting that education should make room for "the most enlightened opinions of others," he nonetheless emphasizes close observation and the free play of the imagination. Teaching dogmatically and by rote cripples creativity. "Boys should not be taught *what* to think, but *how* to think." It follows as a corollary, he insists, that attendance at morning chapel should be made optional. He closes by praising Groton graduates for their exemplary service in the war. The school "will always have the respect of people who prize physical stamina and moral fibre," but it is now time to "establish in the realm of thought the high standard which she has maintained on the field of action."

Strong of body, feeble of mind, the average Grotonian emergent from the essay is as much self-portrait as composite photograph. Harry, it seems quite clear, was at once settling an old score and celebrating his arrival at a new phase. Even so, his recommendations for reform will strike most readers as pretty mild stuff. Not so the editor in charge of the volume, who thought it best to slip the essay in at a moment when Peabody was away. Harry was right, apparently, about rigidity at the top. The Rector's response, when it came, was perfectly civil. He granted the importance of teaching "boys to think," and observed that the school had changed since Harry's time. Debating was on the rise; mathematics and science were given greater emphasis than in the past; not all boys were required to take Greek. As to the care of the spirit, Peabody was not personally inclined to bend and saw no great demand for change. "At present the boys go to chapel as naturally as they go to dinner or to recitation," he observed. Nor could he satisfy Harry's demand for greater student independence. "We do not believe in self-government, but in co-operation," he wrote, rather stiffly. "So far as I know, the experiments in self-government have not been successful. Co-operation is our method, and we find what seems to me a remarkable response from our boys." So much for Emerson, and Dewey, and Murray.

George Draper's approach to medicine played to Harry's natural strengths and thereby reinforced his growing self-confidence. "Groton and Adaptation" is more or less direct testimony on this score. But Draper had touched something deeper still. He demanded above all else that students pay attention to their patients as people; correct diagnosis depended upon it. Harry was immediately taken by this feature of his mentor's method. He had been appalled at the insensitivity of the professors who took groups of students with them on "grand rounds" through the hospital and who seemed to regard the patients as mere things, to be poked and probed and discussed without regard for their feelings. Harry found himself more drawn to the suffering of the patients—most especially the female patients—than to the medical instruction they occasioned. Watching their expressions, he said, "was just like watching my mother's face. I learned a lot from watching my mother's face. I suffered in those rounds." When possible, Harry would circle back after rounds, to try to repair the damage done by the doctors. A few of his peers faulted him for getting too close to the patients. But the spectacle of female suffering stirred the old, unanswered craving for maternal love, rekindled the ambition to relieve the pain that blocked that love, and awakened the fear that mother's distress, echoed now in all women's distress, was somehow his fault. How could he turn away?

In Harry's highly self-conscious narrative of his life, his mother appears, for good and ill, as a prime mover. We are not bound to accept his constructions in such matters; indeed, the artfulness of Harry's self-portraiture may at times seem to invite skepticism. But the evidence tends strongly to confirm that Fannie was very much with him in his life, just as he says she was, and most especially in shaping his melancholy predilection for tragic themes and suffering women. His sister Virginia was doubtless shrewder than she knew in dubbing him Hamlet, for Fannie would play Gertrude to more than one Ophelia in her son's life. During his first week of medical school, after complaining to his diary of his longing for Jo, Harry made note that his mother "was all in from what she thought were swollen ankles & bad kidneys. A great deal of imagination mixed in with it—unfortunately. I wish I could help her. Maybe I can." He was obviously ready for George Draper's brand of diagnosis, though it is clear as well that he did not discount his mother's suffering simply because it was imagined. He wanted and needed to help. When Fannie complained—as she was wont to—of high blood pressure, he took her to a famous doctor at Physicians and Surgeons. The special treatment was no help, for the patient had too much invested in her poor health; she would live to be an old woman, dying the whole way.

The deeper authority of Fannie's suffering was forcefully brought home to her son in the face of one Alice Henry, a totally ravaged young prostitute who lay dying in a women's ward on Blackwell's Island. Harry was in a group of students on rounds with a professor who drew along side the patient's bed and announced that she was afflicted with syphilis. Harry wrote two accounts of his association with Alice—a formal medical history, and a more personal narrative, perhaps designed for magazine publication, that he left unfinished. In the latter he describes his first view of "a young woman with what seemed to me a peculiarly appealing face, but at the same time deadly pale, care-worn, cachexic & sad." The doctor in charge prepared the students to palpate the patient's liver. "Rudely pulling the bedclothes down and the night shirt up, the man exposed a thin white abdomen—the patient showed the submission of one who had born [sic] much at the hands of mortal men. Each student in turn . . . passed by the bed and clumsily poked about her abdomen in an attempt to feel the liver—and at each touch the poor woman winced with pain for it was exquisitely tender." The doctor went on to advise against wasting time on poor incurables such as Alice and then moved along to another section of the ward. But Harry stayed behind. "A peculiar attraction for the pathetic little figure in bed held me," he wrote. He made a more thorough physical examination, asked a few questions, concluded that "it was a hopeless case," and hurried away. But Alice was not finished with him. "That night I tossed restlessly in bed as the picture of that pathetic face reappeared time and time again before my mind's eye." Early the next morning he was back at Blackwell's Island, puzzled perhaps at his own behavior but fascinated, answering from his own depths the mysterious pull of the dying woman.

The more personal, perhaps even somewhat fictionalized version of Alice Henry's story goes on to give details of her life as a lonely, vulnerable immigrant woman in New York. It is a depressing tale of betrayal and violence, rape and virtual captivity in brothels, of pimps, gangsters, encounters with the law, heroin addiction, attempted suicide, and rapid physical deterioration. The facts are not in all respects consistent with the much longer medical history that Harry composed, using materials gathered from interviews and correspondence with people who had information about his subject. He learned, in the course of a good deal of research, that Alice was something of a figure in the New York underworld. She had once testified before a grand jury against a notorious criminal who operated brothels in the city, and she had been around long enough to know many of the actors in the sordid drama of the urban underworld. In following the broken trail of her life backward through Ellis Island to Drogheda, County of Meath, Ireland, he revealed an uncommon interest, even an obsession, with the fate of this simple, doomed girl.

There was a history to Harry's fascination with the city's other half. During his Harvard years he made inquiries with the New York police commissioner about visiting Ellis Island and the Tombs. During the same period he opened a correspondence with Wilson Gandy, a convicted sex-offender who saw Harry's name in the sports columns and wrote from the penitentiary. But the fascination with Alice went far beyond amateur sociology and good works. Harry took Edwin Maynard along on a visit to one of the houses where Alice worked; he asked Maynard to look after her when he was out of town; he paid her funeral expenses and corresponded with her family when she finally succumbed on July 17, 1918. He gave considerable time and energy to the reconstruction of her life. His attempted personal narrative is evidence of an impulse to make sense of his strange attraction to Alice and of a failure to achieve satisfaction. He was not yet prepared to see that it was his mother's face behind Alice's, brimming with pain and reproach, drawing him in. Harry's frustrated childhood demand for intimacy resurfaced in the fascination with the beautiful, utterly beaten woman. Desire, clearly, was dangerous. It was dangerous in infancy and childhood, for it made him vulnerable and it intensified the sting of his mother's rejection. Desire was no less potent in 1918, and no less threatening. But the sexual component had become fully manifest, and the penalty for its indulgence, now bearing the impress of adolescent phobias, was disease, disfigurement, and death.

This is not to diminish the large measure of compassion in Harry's response to Alice Henry. True to the analysis outlined in "The Case of Murr," the self-pity arising out of rejection is here displaced on to its chronically ailing source, his mother—or, in this instance, her stand-in, Alice. The identical pattern appears in Harry's brief summary of a "really astonishing (and uninterpreted) dream" that surfaced years later in analysis. "I was comforting my mother in my arms as if she were a baby," he recalls, "while she was vomiting over my left shoulder." It is no great strain, in context, to see past Harry's maternal role in the dream to his gently nurturing treatment of poor Alice. The extremity of his mother's suffering in the dream invites similar interpretation. It is a good question whether Harry would have gone along with such a reading. He acknowledges that the dream leaves room for "a great deal more analysis," but makes no gestures toward an answer. Quite evidently, he recognized the importance of the dream—else why include it?—and most likely he had a feeling for its general drift. Just as clearly, however, he wanted no part of the oedipal script in his life's story. Freud, he says, "had no concepts at all" for a father like his own. Most crucially, he had taken the painful measure of his mother's rejection "quite a while before the traditional oedipus hunting season." The implicit thrust of this semijocular commentary is to minimize the sexual component in his early development. Given this much, it is little wonder that he did not expand on what he may have glimpsed in his "really astonishing" dream. As "The Case of Murr" makes clear, he was willing to hint at the wrinkles in his sexuality but not to parade them openly. Perhaps he knew no more than he actually reveals; more likely, he feared that others might ridicule or condemn the sexual implications obliquely emergent from his dream, and more directly manifest in his attraction to suffering, degraded, dangerous Alice Henry.

Harry's encounter at Blackwell's Island substantially augmented his increasing awareness and sympathy for other human beings. In the hospitals, and in the tough neighborhoods around Physicians and Surgeons, he came into close physical contact with a world that had rarely so much as crossed his mind in earlier years. In venturing out, he ventured in as well. As the world grew, and grew more complex, more challenging to his sheltered illusions, he grew along with it. He was taken immediately and completely by Alice Henry's wasted face because it mirrored back to him his own pain and thereby gave much fuller play to his sympathy and compassion. Medicine was less a mere profession to him now and was increasingly an outlet for his growing need to relieve pain and promote healing.

Maybe it was Alice's face—a book that fell open before his discerning eye—that prompted Harry to take up physiognomy, the pseudo-scientific endeavor to measure character in facial features. It was not long after her death, at any rate, during his final half-year at medical school, that he got hold of a popular manual on the subject. Finding that he had a real knack for reading faces, he de-

same period of life, and the same process, this time less encumbered in theory, are the subject of a letter written in mid-1945 to his friend Lewis Mumford. Reflecting on Mumford's recent experience of "renewal," Harry recalls caring for the dying Alice "during the influenza epidemic of 1918–19. I became *her* during her illness, a death rattle developed in my throat, I was in the valley of death for a night, & then suddenly the next day I was possessed by an immense exaltation. It was as if I had experienced all the possible pains, discomforts, anxieties & neglects that patients—that is, the sick—have had to suffer since the beginning of time, and, knowing all this inwardly, I could now be like a giant rock in a weary land, a tireless source of strength & consolation to every patient that came to me in the future. The great thema is that of Death & Resurrection—the death of a beloved being, or a profound melancholy, or extreme pain as a necessary overpowering first phase which may last months or even years, & then the reaction—creative power & exuberance coming out of grief. Pregnancy—the inward turning & withdrawal, the labor & the pain—& then the birth, a new life, hive of potentialities." The self, like the Phoenix, arises from the ashes of what has gone before, from death and loss and grief into a brave new world of its own engendering. Life is renewed, one's calling is clear, the spirit brims over with energy and optimism. "There is no key to the renewal as such," he goes on, taking a notably organismic line. "It just happens as a gift of Nature, evidence of the abundant fertility of the universe, the quenchless spirit of man."

Harry's renewal had multiple sources and occasions; the "immense exaltation" that came to him in the wake of Alice's death was but one of numerous similar experiences spread over a period of several years. The process moved into its final, most exhilarating phase in 1923, at the time that he first read C. G. Jung's newly translated *Psychololgical Types.* The book was a bright point of intersection for numerous convergent strands in his life and thought, not the least of them the matter of vocation. "Up to 1923," he recalls in "The Case of Murr," he "had been immune to the enticements of all encountered versions of the science of psychology: a single lecture at Harvard by Professor Münsterberg, the course in psychiatry at the Columbia College of Physicians and Surgeons, and a single hour at the hospital with Freud's *Interpretation of Dreams* had been enough to cancel whatever potential gust for that sort of thing was in the offing. But then suddenly Murr was in a blaze, a blaze which would go on for three years and eventually pressure him to embrace psychiatry and psychology, and so to take the last step in his slow and devoted recapitulation of the order in which the disciplines pertinent to modern medicine were founded: anatomy (Vesalius), physiology (Harvey), biochemistry (Claude Bernard), and psychiatry (Kraepelin)." All of which illustrates "that the publication of Jung's book at just that moment in the course of Murr's mental and emotional metamorphoses is an example of what Pasteur called chance and the prepared mind." Harry's pathway to the final goal, to psychology, though clear enough in retrospect, was not experienced as a series of deliberate steps. His mind was "prepared" for change, but the process took direction, variously, from impersonal historical sequences, chance, or the "pressure" generated by unseen interior fires. This is to highlight once again Harry's inclination to regard his life's course as something not so much consciously chosen as happened upon and haltingly pursued.

Harry thought he knew where he was going at the Rockefeller Institute. He conducted his research under the direction of Alfred Cohn, an innovator in the field of electrocardiography and a specialist in diseases of the cardiovascular system. Cohn was an influential teacher (Harry's friend Carl Binger was one among his many well-known students) who combined strong interests in clinical research and public health. Harry's research, on the development of chicken embryos, was loosely tied to Cohn's work on the aging process in tissue as it related to heart disease. The two got on very well. In an unpublished memorial sketch written at the time of Cohn's death in 1957, Harry paid tribute to his "unexampled friend and teacher." Cohn, he emphasized, was a tactful and supportive guide who took an interest in his students' work but who also gave them ample room to develop their own ideas. Harry enjoyed his freedom. With the aid of an assistant, and employing techniques developed by Alexis Carrel, a Nobel laureate who had been at the Rockefeller Institute since 1906, he performed experiments on fragments of the hearts of chicken embryos. Afloat in shallow dishes, the tiny particles of tissue continued to beat and to reproduce cells at an astonishing rate. Harry was excited, even temporarily transported, by what he beheld in the microscope. The embryos were a breathtaking allegory of life itself, in all its orderly and creative abundance.

The research with Cohn was sufficiently promising that Harry decided to advance it a step or two further by taking a year's work in England, at the Cambridge University laboratory of F. Gowland Hopkins. He had it in mind to broaden his scientific horizons generally, and, more narrowly, to measure the changing concentrations of glutathione—a substance that Hopkins had recently isolated—in chicken embryos. He gained admission as a research student and Ph.D. candidate at Cambridge for the fall of 1924, with the provision that he would return to the Rockefeller Institute to complete his degree, under Cohn's supervision, the following year. With his way prepared by extremely flattering letters of recommendation ("on the whole the finest young man whom I know," wrote Henderson), Harry was warmly received by Hopkins, had the pleasure of working in the same lab with such distinguished young scientist-intellectuals as Joseph Needham and J. B. S. Haldane, and made excellent progress in his research. He had no trouble completing the work for the Ph.D. at the Rockefeller in 1926, though the final step, a rather perfunctory oral examination (with Henderson presiding) was not taken until the following year.

Harry's Ph.D. thesis was published in a series of twelve papers that appeared under the general title "Physiological ontogeny" in professional journals between 1925 and 1927. Harry was solely responsible for eight of the papers, Cohn for two; they collaborated on two others. Some of the papers, it is clear, were completed before Harry left for England; others were written while he was at the Biological Laboratories at Cambridge; and the last three were finished after his return to New York. In the final paper, a theoretical overview written by Harry, with additions, mostly of a clinical nature, by Cohn, the purpose of the investigations is declared to be the discovery of "relationships between the structure and the behavior of an organism as functions of age." This general goal is amply served in specific studies of weight and growth rates, chemical changes, metabolism, and other variables as observed in incubating chicken embryos. In reporting on such experiments, Harry determines, among many other things, that the percentage growth rate of organisms "decreases progressively with age"; that cells and their environment (the *milieu intérieur*) interact reciprocally; that common assumptions about the parallel development of functions need to be refined; and, more tentatively, that "the elaboration of organic substances and biological evolution" may indeed be "considered as mutually dependent."

Fascinated though he was with the day-to-day development of the embryos, it is clear that Harry was most engaged—more, certainly, than Cohn—by the larger implications of what he was doing. In this he was influenced by Henderson, whose interest in the complex interaction of multiple components within whole, self-regulating systems is everywhere evident in the papers generally and in the concluding overview most particularly. In the conclusion Harry insists that "a comprehensive view of the developmental process" cannot be achieved without "the simultaneous analysis of numerous functions over the same developmental cycle." He is a mechanist of the holistic Hendersonian variety, emphasizing that parts must be studied in their relationship to whole systems. Teleological vitalism is dismissed as the projection of a fond human wish. His entire enterprise, he concludes, "leads naturally to the belief in the importance of a comprehensive investigation of the same organism simultaneously undertaken from a number of distinct standpoints over the entire ontogenetic period or at least over a certain specified portion of the life span. A study so planned seems especially significant when the present day trend of biological interest towards an examination of the togetherness or totality of the organism is appreciated." When this last passage was read to him in 1970, nearly 45 years after its composition, Harry smiled and observed, "It's as if I outline my whole life plan there."

To Henderson's influence we may add that of Alfred North Whitehead. *Science and the Modern World,* first offered as the Lowell Lectures at Harvard and published in 1925, appears in the bibliography of the final essay of "Physiological ontogeny." Of course it is not always possible to distinguish Whitehead's influence from Henderson's. Henderson read *Science and the Modern World* with enthusiasm and referred to it in confirmation of his own views on key theoretical issues. Many others were similarly impressed. Whitehead gave eloquent philosophical expression to a widespread movement away from mechanism, and toward organicism, in the scientific thinking of his time. Harry's attraction to *Science and the Modern World* is thus evidence of his engagement in this broader intellectual ferment. With Henderson, he took support for the general thrust of his research from Whitehead's theory of "organic mechanism," which featured the idea that "the plan of the *whole* influences the very characters of the various subordinate organisms which enter into it." But there is evidence, in details, and in overall tone, that Harry was even more closely caught up in the philosopher's sway. His thought takes root, as Whitehead's does, in a celebration of burgeoning natural abundance. A key word for both is "creativity." "Peering through a microscope, through a little fabricated window in the egg's shell," Harry recalled, "spellbound as any libidinous voyeur, I witnessed the procession of momentous transformations that mark the hours when the embryo is no bigger than an angel perching on a pin point." Harry's angel is a playful spirit, to be sure, but the reference faithfully conveys the mood of awe and reverence that swept over him as he gazed into the microscope.

The sexualization of his response is equally playful and equally freighted with significance. His breathless tone conveys an exuberance, and an inclination to equate natural creativity with the divine, that are reminiscent of Whitehead. Both men viewed evolution as the unfolding of progressively more complex organisms. Such development, they agreed, was the essence of the natural and required for its explanation no recourse to "ultimate" realities. They shared decided emphases on process, on the necessity for multiple perspectives, and on the play of hidden agendas in the formation of scientific theory. Harry was deeply impressed, as Whitehead was, with the Romantic repudiation of arid scientific abstraction. Both valorized sense experience; both embraced change and contradiction as thresholds on progress; and both stressed that all true creativity is a cooperative enterprise. Harry would in time come to share the philosopher's sense of the human need for a viable—supple, resilient, progressive—mythology.

In the broader social and political frame of reference, Whitehead's emphasis on process was the analogue to an enhanced respect for the inherent worth and purpose of human activity. The retreat from mechanism had its parallel in a rejection of Social Darwinism and the tendency, most pronounced in the decades just before and after the turn of the century, to regard human beings as so many units in the grinding mechanism of evolution. It is notable in this regard that Henderson's physiology and sociology were linked by his sense of the interplay between many elements in a dynamic—rather than static—equilibrium. Keynesian economics had a similar appeal. Something of the same broad-based humanism, with its attention to human creativity within complex, evolving systems, is clearly discernible in Harry's development during this period. It is there, of course, in his attraction to Whitehead and in their shared suspicion of narrow academic specialization. Whitehead was preeminent among those scientists in Harry's ken—Zinsser, Pearl, and Henderson were others—who ranged comfortably outside the boundaries of their major disciplines. *Science and the Modern World* succeeded in part because of Whitehead's mastery as a prose stylist and because of his easy fluency in literature and *belles lettres.* Harry's respect for such humanistic virtuosity is manifest in a letter of 1924 to John Jay Chapman, in which he defends true scientists—by contrast with mere technicians and inventors—as "accomplished musicians, lovers of fine literature, poetry and the Classics."

In defining and defending the true scientist—the man of discipline and reason who ventures confidently, and with clear human purpose, into the domain of high culture—Harry was of course making a very personal claim. The schedule at the Rockefeller Institute was relaxed by comparison with the long days and nights demanded of him as a surgical intern. Harry used his free time to cultivate interests in literature, philosophy, and the arts which had developed in the years since medical school and that now moved to the foreground of his consciousness. Carl Binger recalled that Harry gave every spare moment to reading, music, and the theatre. He avoided society, stayed up late with his books, and kept company with people who shared his expanding interests. "The most potent external stimulants besides Bordeaux wines," Harry wrote in 1925, for his tenth annual Harvard class report, "have come from Ecclesiastes, Shakespeare, Goethe, Wagner, Nietzsche, Shaw, Anatole France, Henry Adams, Emerson, and William James." Continuing, as no ordinary scientist could have, he declares that "the single greatest influence . . . has come from our American Herman Melville, who with a vulture at his heart, penetrated deeper into the spiritual core of man than any writer with whom I am acquainted." Harry prefaces this vivid rehearsal of mere "objective facts" with the warning that "it takes an artist to tell any human story." There is more here, apparently, than meets the eye. "My principal interests," he sums up, again offering himself as a broadly cultivated man of many parts, "centre around psychology, biological and medical science and literature."

Harry had always been a theatregoer, but his pleasure in the stage increased markedly in the early 1920s. Jo shared his enthusiasm, and she especially enjoyed hobnobbing with theatre people after the show. She invited Clare Eames, Alfred Lunt, Katharine Cornell, and other prominent actors and actresses to the 79th Street apartment for drinks and conversation. Harry was absorbed in the theatrical interpretation of deep psychological themes. If a play seemed particularly profound, he would return for a second and third viewing until he had fathomed its mysteries. He buttonholed playwrights with questions about their artistic intentions and sometimes went to rehearsals to grill the players about the meanings of their parts. Sidney Howard, who later exploited oedipal themes in *The Silver Cord* (1926), was so impressed with Harry's psychological penetration that he asked him to serve as a "scientific consultant" on one of his plays. Nothing came of the proposal, though Harry tried his hand at a one-act play about witchcraft in Salem. "It was," he recalled rather vaguely, "about this girl who was a sort of a witch." The manuscript has not survived.

Carl Binger introduced Harry to Edward ("Ned") Sheldon, the Harvard-educated playwright who became a celebrity overnight with the success of *Salvation Nell* in 1908. For the next decade Sheldon was the acknowledged master of stage melodrama and a brilliant man about town. But in 1917 his career was cut short when he was struck down by a virulent, crippling arthritis that gradually reduced him to total invalidism. Binger befriended Sheldon in the early 1920s and remained an intimate until the playwright's death in 1947. When he brought Harry to Sheldon's bedside in 1924, the two quickly developed a friendship. Sheldon was famous for the selfless generosity that somehow grew with his affliction. Harry was impressed both with his friend's intelligence and fund of theatrical lore and with his noble character. "The concrete fact of your transcendence over bodily affliction fills me with awe and humility," Harry wrote. Over time, however, Sheldon's refusal to voice his suffering, and to acknowledge the bitterness of his fate, began to pall on Harry, and he drew away.

Paul Robeson entered Harry's life in 1920, on a stretcher. The tall, broad young football star was wheeled into Presbyterian Hospital with a severely torn muscle in his thigh. Harry assisted in the surgery on the injury and was then assigned to look after the patient during his recovery. He was very much taken by the friendly, obviously talented Robeson and decided to introduce him to Eslanda Goode, a beautiful, well-educated technician in the pathology lab. The two promptly fell in love and were soon married. Harry and Jo befriended the newlyweds and took a close interest in Paul's brilliant stage career. They got the best tickets to all of his performances— Harry was most impressed with *The Emperor Jones, All God's Chillun Got Wings,* and the stunning London production of *Othello* in 1926—and held receptions at their home to celebrate his triumphs. Their friendship endured for many years.

There was a briefer but more intense encounter with Eugene O'Neill, whose verbal mastery and complex psychological preoccupations caught Harry's attention in the period just after the war. It appears that they were introduced in 1924 by Carl Binger's friend Robert Edmond Jones, O'Neill's collaborator and a noted set designer. Harry made no secret about his admiration for O'Neill's plays; he was profoundly stimulated by their plausible dramatic rendering of the psychoanalytic ideas he had begun to pursue in his reading. Jones, known familiarly as "Bobby," invited Harry to rehearsals. In due course O'Neill turned up at the 79th Street apartment for a memorable evening of drink and talk. Harry went on in Jungian terms that the playwright found both apt and flattering. His guest responded with stories about his childhood in New London, his father's drinking, and his own tumultous life. O'Neill so enjoyed himself that he made gestures about getting together again. Harry quietly declined. He was comfortable in his friendship with Bobby Jones, and later urged him to undertake an analysis with Jung. But in the company of America's greatest playwright he felt like an awkward, inarticulate dabbler. When O'Neill sought his medical advice in 1927, Harry referred him to Alvan Barach.

Fortunately, Harry was not always so constrained by his inexperience. He dabbled quite happily in sculpture and produced a bust of Jo that was, he recalled, "very representative—anatomically perfect, but artistically horrible." He was sufficiently self-assured to discuss with Essie Robeson the possibility of his writing a play for her husband. Nor did he hesitate to tell his friend Archibald MacLeish that he thought he was "too healthy," too immune from misery, "to be a poet." Harry would never overcome a certain insecurity about his prose style and about his qualifications as a literary critic. But in general he had confidence in his powers of self-expression and considerable independence of esthetic judgment. He knew what he liked. In opera he favored Wagner and Puccini. He arose in the early morning and walked through the darkness to the box office at the Met, where he waited in line to get the best possible seats. He was not satisfied until he had heard one production of *Tosca* six times. The *prima donna* came to recognize his eager face in the audience, and she gave him her picture when he appeared at the stage door. Harry was just as vigorous in developing his interest in classical music. He purchased a phonograph and subjected his friends to long sessions over his favorite composers. It was the same with books. He bought, and read, Shakespeare, the English Romantic poets, Tolstoy, Chekhov, and Dostoevsky, along with the major American writers. He took a walking tour through Thomas Hardy country with his father in 1924. Two years earlier, Heywood Broun, the literary pundit and later Harry's patient, asked him to join the Coffee House, a literary club presided over by an old Murray family friend, Frank Crowninshield. There, when he could get away from the Rockefeller for lunch, Harry encountered such leading literary lights as Sherwood Anderson, Edmund Wilson, and F. Scott Fitzgerald.

Harry was the first to acknowledge that his headlong plunge into the arts seemed to lack direction. "Nothing was pulling it together," he once observed. "It was an explosion from within . . . it was diffuse, going in all directions." He adopts a similar perspective in "The Case of Murr," describing his experience as a "profound affectional upheaval that swept [him] into the unruly domain of psychology." Life, rather characteristically, is out of his control. By way of explanation for Murr's discomposure, Harry observes "that up to that time an assemblage of emotional potentialities had been denied adequate participation in his work," and that his "evolving genetical program" had triggered the release of "something wholly novel and astonishing, never dreamt of in his philosophy, with a dimension of depth and elevation which landed him in a vast brew outside the husk of his contemporary world." The arts were instrumental, Harry points out, "in effecting and reinforcing this transition," but the ultimate wellspring of change was finally mysterious. Interior energies that were his, but not his to control, propelled the latter-day Hamlet to a point of vantage on reality different from, and presumably superior to, that enjoyed by the majority of his contemporaries.

The center of attention in all this was, finally, Harry himself. This much is clear. He was enthralled by creativity itself, by the abundant, unfolding variety of life, first as it emerged from within and then as it was manifest in chicken embryos, Beethoven symphonies, and all between. He saw that the inside and outside were related; indeed, the more he took the pulse of things, the more he recognized that the sermons in stones—and embryos and symphonies—are composed principally by those who witness them. The world, he saw, was a human construction. But he saw further that his world was more fully alive, more exciting, more full of promise than the reality inhabited by ordinary people. Something within himself, it followed, brought him into company with that select few who, like O'Neill, took a stand "outside the husk of his contemporary world." Harry's prodigious unfolding made him acutely aware of himself as different, as a privileged explorer whose search for truth led invariably from the outside to the human inside, and ultimately to the *fons et origo,* the deep, mysterious recesses of the self.

This inward trajectory had its analogue at the Rockefeller in Harry's increased attention to the assumptions and concealed personal motives informing ostensibly objective scientific inquiry. If his fascination with chicken embryos was in some degree the expression of his own uncharted interior, then presumably a similar kind of claim could be made for others in the field. "I began to wonder, after several years of research in biochemisty and physiology," he declared, "why some of the men with whom I was associated at the Rockefeller Institute clung so tenaciously to diametrically opposing views about the simplest phenomena." More specifically, Harry confessed that he "was repeatedly confounded by a radical theoretical (if not metaphysical) opposition between the Institute's then-most-famous members, Jacques Loeb, who stood for an extreme variety of mechanism, and Alexis Carrel, the defender of some type of vitalism. How, Murr asked himself, can one account for such irreconcilable interpretations of identical phenomena?" His question arose from the center of his own scientific work; this was the issue to which his research had invariably led him. And yet to pose the question in this way was to transfer the focus of inquiry from the merits of individual theories to the personal qualities of those who held them. To what extent, Harry wanted to know, do students of nature discover themselves in their objects of study? His hypothesis—that they do so to a considerable extent—was radical in its time and certainly put him "outside the husk" of contemporary views on scientific objectivity. His way from here, he recognized years later, lead "down the pecking order of the sciences" to lowly psychology.

Questions of professional status were of little concern to Harry in the mid-1920s. He was on fire with an idea. His mind was once again perfectly prepared, and chance this time put Carl Jung in his way. Their encounter, Harry makes clear, was a decisive turning point in his development. "The notion that science is the creative product of an engagement between the scientist's psyche and the events to which he is attentive prepared Murr for an enthusiastic embracement of Jung's *Psychological Types* on the very day of its timely publication in New York (1923). . . . This book by Jung came to him as a gratuitous answer to an unspoken prayer. Among other things, it planted in his soil two permanent centers of preoccupation: the question of varieties of human beings and in what terms they can be most significantly represented and discriminated, and the question of what variables of personality are chiefly involved in the production of dissonant theoretical systems. These questions were at the root of Murr's first spurt of veritable intellectual interest in the direction of psychology." The language of procreation in this passage is carefully chosen. It echoes Melville's account of Hawthorne's potent entry into his creative life. "I feel," wrote Melville in the summer of 1850, "that this Hawthorne has dropped germinous seeds into my soul. He expands and deepens down, the more I contemplate him; and further, and further, shoots his strong New-England roots into the hot soil of my Southern soul." Can there be any doubt that Harry's debt to Jung was a deep one?

Psychological Types distinguishes between people who are dominantly introverted or dominantly extraverted by nature. Introverts are shy, inward, and solitary but usually independent and imaginative, while extraverts are outgoing, gregarious, and optimistic but often rather conventional and insincere. Introverts and extraverts are more narrowly distinguished by their most developed "function"—sensation, thinking, feeling, intuition, or some combination of the four. Thus, for example, the scheme yields the extraverted thinking type. The thought of such a person is positive and productive. He or she is naturally drawn outward to "new facts or to general conceptions of disparate experimental material." By contrast, the thought patterns of the introverted thinking type begin and end in the subjective realm. "Facts are of secondary importance; what, apparently, is of absolutely paramount importance is the development and presentation of the subjective idea. . . . Its goal is to see how external facts fit into, and fulfil, the framework of the idea." Numerous additional traits attach to the various types. Introverts and extraverts tend to misunderstand and dislike one another; women are inclined to the feeling function, men to the thinking function; introverted intuitive types are often visionaries and poets; and so on. It should be added that an ideally balanced person would combine introversion and extroversion; in practice, however, and in varying degrees, people tend to repress one side of their nature. Just so, according to Jung, we possess all the functions but tend to favor some over others. The proper integration of the total personality, involving the recovery from the unconscious of those dimensions of the self that have been repressed, results in what Jung calls "individuation." Its achievement, issuing from an often painful embrace with personal contradiction, culminates in a religious experience of unity with all things. Individuation is accompanied by the emergence from the unconscious of vivid, even perilously overpowering images. These are the archetypes of the self, arising from the collective unconscious, whose appearance signals the discovery of God within.

Psychological Types was intensely exciting to Harry because it seemed to have been written in response to his most pressing personal concerns. He received Jung's book, as Melville received Hawthorne's, as a long, intimate letter from a remote brother in the spirit. *Psychological Types* was the surest, most gratifying evidence that the drift of his own thought brought him into company with the intellectual leaders of his time. During his internship at Presbyterian Hospital Harry had settled into the view that Christianity is a product of the human imagination. No sooner had he arrived at that liberating perspective than he was overtaken by the ambition to explore the origins of what attracted him to religion—its yield of order, and value, and beauty—in the history of the human psyche. His questions about religious belief were obviously cognate with his puzzlement at the divergent creeds of his colleagues at the Rockefeller Institute. Scientific theories, like religions beliefs, Jung would help him to see, arise from the interiors of their possessors. *Psychological Types* contrasts Darwin and Kant as examples of the extraverted and introverted thinking types. "The former speaks with facts; the latter appeals to the subjective factor. Darwin ranges over the wide fields of objective facts, while Kant restricts himself to a critique of knowledge in general. But suppose a Cuvier be contrasted with a Nietzsche: the antithesis becomes ever sharper."

95

Religions, Jung observes, are similarly shaped by human variety as it expresses itself collectively, in distinctively Eastern (introverted, subjective) and Western (extraverted, objective) types, over long periods of time.

Harry's mind was also prepared for Jung's advent by stirring developments in his personal affairs. The cooling of his sexual attachment to Jo, reinforced no doubt by his rapid intellectual flowering and by a gathering antagonism to his own social class, made him vulnerable to what he would have considered an inconceiveable lapse just a few years earlier. Times had certainly changed since the war. So had Harry's crowd. Sex was more open, more acceptable, more interesting, and more available than ever before. And perhaps he found, when he looked carefully, that his gentleman's code of strict marital fidelity had a small print provision on discrete, seventh-year liaisons. Some such array of elements combined to prepare Harry for Alma Rosenthal, his bright, cultivated, very attractive young Viennese lab assistant at the Rockefeller Institute. Ubiquitous chance was palpably at play again. Or so it must have seemed. Alma was well educated, a devotee of the arts with a special passion for opera, and a friend since school days of Anna Freud. She was possessed of a gay, worldly-seeming sophistication and an exotic allure that went, for Harry, with her being Jewish. She made no secret of her attraction to him and seemed to assume that he would respond in kind. He did, of course, and without much of a struggle.

Alma was unprecedented in Harry's experience. She was frank and uninhibited in her desires. Love-making with her was natural, copious, unrestrained, and as close to fun as it could be for a man of Harry's background and makeup. There was nothing solemn about Alma; she was playful, undemanding, even frivolous. In all of this, as in her cultivation and rather casual familiarity with ideas, she was Jo's antithesis. Jo was New England and family and convention and hunting trips to Newfoundland; she was handsome and hearty, but more helpmate and "pal" than lover. Alma was unattached and entirely novel; she was urbane, plaint, pretty, and sensuous. She liked nothing more than escapes to Fire Island for long walks in the sand. Withal, she was light where Jo was not so much

96

heavy as sturdy. Still, Harry was deeply attached to his wife, and—in spite of himself at times—to much of what she stood for. Alma's love was too light—easily taken, ephemeral, and, finally, too sunny—for a man of Harry's somewhat gothic predilections. She liberated him sexually but could not sustain the full weight of what she had set free. The fire between them soon died down, though they remained warm friends for many years.

Alma helped to prepare Harry for Jung by opening up a largely repressed side of his nature. One of the *femmes inspiratrices* that he encountered "here and there along the way," she was, as he once put it, "a sort of symbol" for the feast of the senses and the imagination that he indulged in during the Rockefeller years. It must have soothed his puritan conscience to reflect that in embracing Alma he grew more fully into his true self. She was—happy thought!—a source and sign of his improving mental health. But Alma could not take him the whole way. She was, he later recognized, just a "little blaze" lighting the way to the much more substantial "woman" who, with "several other fructifying influences," made him "feel and think at once, instead of separately." Thanks to Alma, buried Jungian functions rose to the surface; but it took another woman to integrate Harry's scattered selves.

Christiana Morgan was born in Boston in 1897. Harry describes her background and personal qualities best. She was "the second of three variously cultivated daughters of intellectual parents. Father, Dr. William Councilman, was the eminent and widely-beloved, un-professorial professor of pathology at the Harvard Medical School. Christiana seems to have felt that she and her revered, humorously wise, handsome father were bound together by a secret reciprocal understanding engendered by a shared adoration of Nature as they experienced it together at the family summer place proximate to the York River, Maine. For Christiana in later years the Eden of child-hood was a composite memory image of father and self, the former with spade in hand—maybe planting shrubs or seedlings—as he conveyed to his intently watching daughter precious botanical lore interlaced with fantasy. As she grew older her role in the mystic scenario became more active in two respects: she learnt to work alongside her father, doing as he did, and she learnt to ask the questions that kindled his eagerness to transmit whatever intellectual news he had in mind. One potent result of all this was a durable father complex with a readiness to exalt a series of passionate thinkers, starting with Chaim Weizmann and ending with Alfred North Whitehead (who delighted in honoring her, for instance by insisting that she be seated at his right on his 80th birthday celebration at Harvard). Of this distinguished series Carl Jung was certainly the most influential. . . . She had an intuitive understanding of the aims, methods and principles of the life sciences; but she was neither, in any strict sense, scientifically educated nor, to any degree at all, mathematically minded. . . . Her formal education, limited to private schools, ended with one (senior) year at boarding school. No college. Instead there was World War I, nurse's training in a New York hospital, and marriage to a convivial man of good-will, Harvard graduate and war veteran, whose sense of humor was likened to her father's."

Christiana's mother, Isabella Coolidge, was a well-born Boston blue-stocking. She enrolled her pretty, very independent middle child in all the right schools but generally failed to offset the influence of her husband's more relaxed style and winning "common touch." Christiana was, her sister recalled, a sensitive, inward girl who disliked the proper social "run of things" and kept to herself, or to a small group of select friends for whom she wrote romantic stories and poems. In one brief tale a girl magically restores her lost brothers to life. There is an epistolary fragment between Dulcinea Montague and Geraldine Mason, a poem to Isa—"another sister fair/Who has not golden curly hair/She ties it up against the door/And makes a giant pompadour"—and much else that is fanciful and bright, though hardly distinguished. She was, evidently, a great reader of melodramatic girls' book. During a stretch of several years in her mid-teens Christiana was bedridden with rheumatic heart disease. Her time, much of it passed in solitude, was occupied with shelves of romantic fiction and a long, memorable detour through Dante's *Inferno*. She emerged from adolescence a beautiful, intensely romantic young dreamer, persuaded in some half-knowing and therefore vaguely melancholy way that reality could never satisfy her inward hunger for strong passions. The fire inside gave a special, almost sibylline glow to her quiet outward demeanor.

Those that knew her well agreed that Christiana had "a thing" for her father. That she could never possess him helps to explain both her lifelong attraction to powerful older men and a secret, prophetic sense that desire was the parent to disenchantment and tragedy. She was frequently depressed. At times—most especially when overtaken by unprovoked spells of weeping—she feared that she had been born depressed. William O. Morgan was a cheering influence. A graduate of St. Paul's School and Harvard—where he was casually acquainted with Harry—Will, as his friends knew him, was a bright, affable native of Chicago whose comfortable private income spared him the necessity of settling into a vocation. He tried one thing and another and then fell in love with Christiana just in time to go off to the war. She worked as a nurse while he was away and gave some thought to a career in medicine but set all that aside to get married when the war was over. In good part because he bore little resemblance to the romantic figures at large in Christiana's imagination, Will was a safe choice. He was a generous provider, got on well with the Councilmans, and in his mild, forbearing way served as a stay against Christiana's inner turmoil. They lived for a year or so in Cambridge while Will tried his hand at the Harvard Law School but then moved on to New York, where their only child, Councilman, was born in 1921.

Christiana was much too distracted and unstable to succeed at motherhood. She withdrew from her infant son, who was cared for by a nanny, into a postpartum depression so severe that she was obliged to consult a neurologist. A few sessions with the doctor were in themselves little help, though they had the beneficial effect of stirring Christiana's interest in European depth psychology. It was a relief, she found, to read and speculate about her condition. She studied Freud with interest but was more personally taken by Jung's *Psychology of the Unconscious,* which brought her home to herself in an especially compelling way. Thanks to Jung, and more generally to her discovery of the unconscious, Christiana was now in earnest what she had always been in fact, a rapt spectator to her own inner drama.

Christiana "was beautiful, and she knew it," recalled her good friend, Ina May Greer. "All she had to do was sit and people would come—men." Harry was no exception. He first met Christiana in

January 1923, when she was 26 years old, at a performance of Wagner's *Parsifal*. Harry's memory of the occasion was remarkably clear. He recognized Will Morgan during an intermission and took him up on an invitation to meet his wife. They found Christiana—thin, tense, nervous, wearing a blue dress—engaged in animated discussion of "a certain visionary artist" with Frank Wigglesworth. "She turned," Harry recalled, "a little irritated to be interrupted—shook hands (or nodded) & then immediately resumed conversation—cold shouldering me." Will did his best, "in his usual healing fashion," to smooth things over.

Subsequent encounters were more encouraging, though Christiana's moods were sharply changeable and Harry was inclined to be cautious. But there was something in her look that began to take hold of him. She was elegantly lean, with sharp features and intensely searching eyes. Her clothes and jewelry and makeup inclined to the exotic, lending something of the far away, of the gypsy, to her appearance. She had a warm, slightly jaundiced complexion that put Harry remotely in mind of Alice Henry. And when the mood took her, she could be bold and flirtatious with men. Harry remarked to Jo that he thought their new friend was a little "neurotic." He didn't add, but Jo could not have failed to perceive, that it was the smoldering intensity and rebellion in Christiana that had begun to fascinate her husband. She was in the flesh what he had once urged Jo, quite against her nature, to become.

They soon met again, at a "rather boisterous" dinner party given by the Morgans in the spring of 1923. Christiana smoked heavily and sat in silence until the drinks had begun to do their work. Then, quite abruptly, she turned to Harry and inquired what he thought of Jung as compared with Freud. He allowed that he had no basis for an opinion but listened carefully as she contrasted the two thinkers, evincing a decided personal preference for Jung as she proceeded. His stance on religion and morality, she said, had helped to open her eyes. Prompted by the lead, Harry purchased a copy of *Psychological Types* that June. Christiana shared the book with him and the excitement it gave; she listened intently as he described Jung's stunning anticipation of his own reflections on scientific objectivity and his exemplary summons to a career in psychology.

Harry went on promptly to *Psychology of the Unconscious*. Christiana said she knew it had something for him, and she was right.

Shared enthusiasm for Jung gave focus to their participation in an evening course on nineteenth-century thought offered by the philosopher Morris Cohen at the New School for Social Research. The course featured background readings in Romanticism—Rousseau, Fichte, Schelling, and Coleridge—along with more substantial doses of Kant, Hegel, Schopenhauer, and Nietzsche. Jo did not participate, but Harry was vigorously involved, along with the Morgans and an assortment of friends, including Carl Binger, Robert Edmond Jones, Alvan Barach, and the prominent journalist Walter Lippmann, who made occasional appearances. There was, Christiana noted, "tremendous excitement over it all." Everything seemed to connect. The group gathered after the lectures at Binger's apartment for continued discussion. Christiana, who was especially active, gave a paper—presumably inspired by Jung—on Hellenic religions. Harry worked for a while on German that he might better appreciate Nietzsche. The play of ideas centered on the predicament of modern, alienated humankind in a waning Christian civilization. Matthew Arnold's "Dover Beach" was no doubt very much with them, as were T. S. Eliot's striking new variations on the thematics of decline.

But it was to Jung's spacious perspective that Harry found himself returning. At his urging, others in the group looked into *Psychological Types*. They measured one another against Jung's classifications, vying playfully for membership in the "Extravert and Introvert Club." Rather more seriously, and in line with his vocational deliberations, Harry circulated a transparently Jungian questionnaire designed, as he put it, to reveal "certain aspects of the thinking faculty." The questions, covering varieties of logic, attitudes toward problem solving, patterns of thought, and assorted intellectual preferences and predilections, were sent to several dozen friends and associates. In a genially self-effacing cover letter, Harry admits to having "one or two theories regarding types of thinking which correspond with certain psychological syndromes—to verify which I thus encroach upon your limited time." Thirty-eight responses have survived, along with a fragment of Harry's quantitative analysis of the total sample. He divides the group into more or less straightforward Jungian classes (intuitive thinkers, extraverted feelers, and so on) and characterizes individuals in terms of the relative strength of their leading functions. Thus Will Morgan is an Intuitive/Thinker/Feeler, Edwin Arlington Robinson is an Intuitive/Thinker/Senser/Feeler, and Carl Binger—departing slightly from the Jungian scheme—is a Feeling/Instinctive/Intuitive/Thinker. Harry rates himself a Thinker/Intuitive/Feeler, while Christiana comes out at the opposite end of the spectrum, an Intuitive/Feeler/Thinker/Senser.

The questionnaire was a preliminary expression of Harry's impulse, amply reinforced by Jung's timely example, to align specific personality types with differing worldviews. It was an installment on his project to correlate thought with temperament and thereby to challenge prominent, notably scientific, orthodoxies. It was also a stage in his descent from biochemistry to psychology. This epistemological foray, taking rise from his work at the Rockefeller Institute and dramatically accelerated by his discovery of *Psychological Types,* had its moral and spiritual counterpart, springing from his experience with Christiana Morgan, in his reading of Jung's *Psychology of the Unconscious.* In the eighteen months after their first meeting Harry and Christiana saw one another regularly, at dinner parties, lectures, and discussions. It was as yet an affair of the mind; they were interanimated, as Donne might have said, by the embrace of their ideas and longings. But Donne also knew that bodies follow the spirit. Both Harry and Christiana remembered vividly the night she sat on his lap as they raced across Manhattan on the way to Binger's apartment. They met by chance one early morning on Lexington Avenue and walked together between tall buildings in the moonlight, discussing Unamuno's *Tragic Sense of Life.* Jo could not fail to see what was happening; nor could Will. Binger felt sure that his friend had gone out of control. Harry might have agreed. He recognized with sadness the strain on Jo, and on their marriage. Will's suffering was additional cause for regret. And it was clear to him that Ike, his follower in so many other ways, was also fascinated with Christiana. He saw the potential for greater confusion and suffering and scandal gathering on all sides; yet he would not, or could not, turn back.

Jung's *Psychology of the Unconscious* was important to Harry and Christiana because it seemed to offer an explanation, and a justification, for their situation. The book offered itself as a reason for choosing the road that desire had already taken. Their powerful attraction for each other, Jung helped them to see, had its mysterious origins in the unconscious recesses of their fullest selves. They were, as a pair, profoundly well matched. But their personal drama took its extraordinary force from the broad collective human experience that flowed through it. Modern men and women, Jung explains, veer away from full adult reality into the imagined satisfactions of the past, most especially to the comfort and protection of an idealized parental "imago." This is a variation on the Freudian oedipus/electra theme, with the important difference that the misdirected libido, though sexual in its remote origins, is understood more broadly as the sum of the individual's vital and creative force. The introvert's psychic investment in the opposite-sex parent is thus a crippling handicap, one that Christiana must have perceived in her inflated regard for her father and that Harry recognized both in his tie to his mother and in the infantile dependence of his sexual feelings for Jo. Jung explains that it is the high calling of the hero (or heroine) to break free of the libidinal bond with the devouring parent and to rise toward the expression of his or her full creative potential. Viewed in this light, their attraction for each other may have appeared to Harry and Christiana as a release from such regressive patterns and therefore a blessing, a way to sanity and health.

It must have appealed to Harry that Jung stresses man's biological relationship to all life, defining libido as the source of energy and direction for the entire organism. In her lucid introduction to the edition of *Psychology of the Unconscious* that Harry and Christiana read, Beatrice M. Hinkle declares that "it is in his privilege as a self-creator that [man's] highest purpose is found." Thanks in part to Jung's work, she goes on, man "need no longer be unconscious of the motives underlying his actions or hide himself behind a

changed exterior, in other words, be merely a series of reactions to
stimuli as the mechanists have it, but he may to a certain extent
become a self-creating and self-determining being. Indeed, there
seems to be an impulse towards adaptation quite as Bergson sees it,
and it would seem to be a task of the highest order to use intelligence to assist one's self to work with this impulse."

Against this broad, creative evolutionary background, Jung
views religion as the the principal historical obstacle to the liberation of human creativity. For nearly two millennia, he argues,
Christians, recoiling in horror from the sight of their "sinfulness,"
have been blind to the fullness of human nature. He does not deny
that Christianity elevated man above mere brutishness; individuation, the unfolding of the God within, is one among many religious
residues in Jung's thought. Yet the freeing of the libido reveals that
man is, after all, an ego-centered creature, bound up in his demands
for pleasure and self-perpetuation. It would be folly, Jung insists,
to deny this truth by returning to the "sentimental and ethically
worthless pose" of conventional Christian values. He decries the
"unhappy combination of religion and morality" that distracts and
hinders us in our vital present concerns, insisting that it "must be
overcome." In its place, we must recognize and accept selfishness
and sexuality as integral to our biological makeup, trusting that
unhampered self-expression is the way of happiness and creative
adaptation.

Here, then, was a clarion call to freedom that Harry and Christiana were primed to hear. Cast off your neurotic ties and suffocating
Christian morality, Jung seemed to demand, and expand to the
margins of your richly complex natures. *Psychology of the Unconscious*
offered a plausible moral and psychological mandate for the surrender to desire. It made a virtue of passionate necessity. And it did so
in a broadly compelling way. Jung's turn toward biology and his
emphasis on process, movement, and internal self-regulation were
doubtless impressive to Harry. (Christiana, apparently taking a cue
from Jung, gave him a copy of Bergson's *Creative Evolution* for
Christmas in 1924.) There was another link to his scientific work
in the notion, boldly advanced in *Psychology of the Unconscious,* that
dreams and imaginative productions recapitulate the psychological

104

evolution of the species. "Ontogenesis," Jung declares, quoting liberally from Nietzsche, "corresponds in psychology to phylogenesis." Harry made this idea his own, writing to John Jay Chapman, most probably in early 1924, that "subjective impulses & aspirations are inherent predispositions (which constitute what might be called the collective unconscious of man) & represent racial memories to the extent that they have become fixed in their particular form by experience & become phylogenetic traits. This is my hunch, intuition." The biological version of the same idea figures prominently in Harry's concluding overview of the essays on physiological ontogeny.

It was more of chance and the prepared mind. For not only did Jung speak directly and positively to Harry's most pressing personal concerns but in the same voice he pointed the way from biochemistry to psychology. His emphasis on creativity, anchored in the erotically charged libido and radiating in all varieties of human expression, overlapped in striking ways with the content and mood of Harry's scientific ruminations. It was also compelling in Jung that he professed to describe and analyze not some merely local and current phenomenon but the interior life of Western man as it had developed over several millennia. To find your place in *Psychology of the Unconscious* was to become an actor in the vast sweep of human evolution; and compliance with its program for change was the reflex, Jung suggested, of heroism. There is, to be sure, something grandiose in all of this, though a certain inflation was probably necessary if Harry and Christiana were to continue on the course that Jung had helped to open for them.

Their way would be precarious for a number of reasons. Were they making a choice? or had the grand tide of history simply swept them along? *Psychology of the Unconscious* seems to make room for both perpectives—Beatrice Hinkle has it that man "may to a certain extent" be self determining. "Chance and the prepared mind" is a more clearly self-conscious formula for deferring closure on this issue. But was a real contradiction coiled up inside the apparently principled compromise, waiting for an occasion to lay them low? There was a kindred ambiguity in Jung's approach to Christianity. In discarding what he viewed as the sentimental altruism of his

Protestant upbringing, Jung loosened the restraints on his intense
narcissism and what Peter Homans calls the "grandiose self." Jung
contrived to partially recontain what he had set free, but at the
price, Homans goes on to argue, of having it both ways with Christianity. The same contradiction threatened Harry and Christiana.
Would they find it necessary to retrieve on one side the very values—fidelity, modesty, self-sacrifice—that they had jettisoned on
the other? Would the higher union they might achieve finally justify the human costs of its pursuit? Would the aggregate of their
combined—and readily acknowledged—narcissism be a transcendence of contradiction, as in a metaphysical poem; or would their
efforts collapse in moral futility?

The posing of such questions may seem premature; after all,
Harry and Christiana had not yet gone to bed. But they both recognized as 1923 gave way to 1924, and as Harry laid his plans for
a year's study at Cambridge, that something powerful had them in
its grip. That Christiana managed to persuade Will to follow the
Murrays to England is testimony on that score. Harry knew perfectly well what was happening. He recognized that there was more
than vocational uncertainty at the root of the depression that bore
down on him in the year or so before he left for Cambridge. There
was the weight of sadness for what Jo had been forced to endure.
She had bent patiently to his drift, hoping that the storm would
pass. But Harry was most deeply troubled by an inability to gauge
the probity of his involvement with Christiana. It so ran against the
grain of what he had been trained to expect of himself.

Yet on all sides there were signs—Jung's books not the least of
them—beckoning them forward. Christiana saw immediately why
Harry was so spellbound by *Tosca*. The tragic heroine, with whom
she identified, had a special, magnetic purchase on Harry's repressed
libido. "Jo's complete lack of sympathy or understanding" for this
side of her husband's nature, Christiana complained, was the source
of great pain to him. In O'Neill's *Hairy Ape* they witnessed a parable
of the modern dilemma which it was their calling to transcend.
Christiana modeled a rough, agonized, death-like figure in clay,
hoping thereby to communicate her "pain and longing" to Harry.
A lonely figure in Dmitri Merezhkovski's *The Romance of Leonardo da*

Vinci was yet another embodiment of her own soul's need, and confirmed that Harry was a godsend.

The results of the Jungian questionnaire spoke a different language but carried the identical message. Opposites attract; absolute opposites attract absolutely. Harry's responses to his own questions indicate a preference for orderly thought, uniformity, and clear expression; for her part, Christiana likes drifting, diversity, and cares little for clarity. She is consicous of abundant emotion and intuition in her thinking; he is not. There are a number of shared traits, of course. Both admit to having weak memories, prefer profound or imaginative thinkers, and gravitate to Willam James and Henry Adams (Harry dislikes Franklin "because he's practical," Voltaire "because he is a scoffer," Roosevelt "because he is too much action," and Henry James "because he is emasculate"). But in the large view it is the great differences between them that stand out. She is intuitive, emotional, tolerant of disorder, and visually oriented, while he is logical, controlled, organized, and verbal. They are both creative, though she is the artist, he the scientist. They were to each other, in other words, as sun to moon, day to night, yin to yang, incomplete things made whole by union. The pull between them was strong, the questionnaire made clear, because the complementary fit was so perfect. It was thus a kind of narcissism *à deux;* Christiana was Harry's buried self, his unconscious, and he was hers.

"She regarded him as a part of herself out there," observed Ina May Greer, and "he regarded her as a part of himself out there. And they were both conscious of this." Plato's *Symposium* of course came to mind; they were the ancient, sundered halves of love at last come together again. In the Jungian terms that they would soon make their own, Christiana was Harry's anima, and he was her animus. Viewed in this way, their relationship was indeed a metaphysical poem.

> This ecstasy doth unperplex,
> We said, and tell us what we love;
> We see by this it was not sex;
> We see we saw not what did move;

> But as all several souls contain
>   Mixture of things, they know not what,
> Love these mixed souls doth mix again,
>   And makes both one, each this and that.
>
> (Donne, "The Ecstasy")

There was, in such a view of love, no necessary urgency in the matter of bodies. They would find their own proper time, perhaps in Europe. But Harry and Christiana knew pretty well where they stood in the summer of 1924, when they sailed, on separate ships, for England. "Alma Rosenthal telling me that she was in love with [Harry] and he with her," noted Christiana of the period just before their departure. "My telling her to go ahead and do something about it."

▼

chapter six

He Crosses the Rubicon

Harry didn't finish *Moby-Dick* on board the *Scythia*. There was the recovery of Captain Prothero to attend to; and he was enjoying the company of his new friend, Sir John Bland-Sutton. Besides, he had fallen upon a novel of great girth, and he was reading deliberately, with relish. But Melville was very much with him once they arrived in Cambridge. "I have recently read Moby Dick," he wrote to John Jay Chapman, "and believe it to be the greatest stroke in American Literature—particularly the last 1/2 & especially the soliloquies." Harry promptly purchased the new Constable edition of Melville's complete works and, beginning with *Typee,* made his way through the entire published oeuvre. As he read and learned more, he began to look for opportunities to test his untrained critical eye against the judgment of literary professionals. On a trip to London he met Henry M. Tomlinson, the novelist and travel writer, who "had a habit," he recalled sixty years later, "of berating Americans for seeking the Great American Novel when it had actually been written in 1851." E. L. Grant Watson, a *Pierre* enthusiast, was another useful contact. Harry also took what he could from Raymond M. Weaver's *Herman Melville, Mariner and Mystic,* the only full-scale study of the novelist yet to appear. It was "an exciting book," he found, brilliant in its intuitions but limited by its shortage of factual evidence and the failure to arrive at "balanced judgments of Melville's personality or . . . literary stature."

By the end of his year in England Harry had become, as he once put it, "pretty thoroughly involved with the currents of Melville's mind." The more he learned about the novelist, the more he wanted to know. He had taken the measure of the available commentary and found it sparse and notably mixed in value. Gradually, but pretty firmly by the time of his return to America in the late summer of 1925, he arrived at the decision to write his own book, a critical biography of some sort, on the author of *Moby-Dick*. "I had never taken a course in English literature or English composition," he admitted, adding, much too modestly, that he "had no native talent" for the undertaking. But he was made bold by the sense, born at his first encounter with *Moby-Dick* and confirmed by the subsequent year's reading, that he had a unique, very personal purchase on the sense and spirit of the great writer's work. Melville was virtually unknown, Harry felt sure, because his message was too dark and too deep for ordinary readers. Hawthorne had been similarly misunderstood, he knew, until Melville penetrated to the core of his genius. "It is that blackness in Hawthorne," Melville wrote in 1850, "that so fixes and fascinates me." Hawthorne was like Shakespeare, he declared, a master of "deep far-away things," given to "quick probings at the very axis of reality," and possessed of insights "so terrifically true, that it were all but madness for any good man, in his own proper character, to utter, or even hint of them." Hawthorne and Shakespeare conceal their subversive wisdom because, "in this world of lies," the vast majority of people cannot or will not face reality. Thus, "Truth is forced to fly like a scared white doe in the woodlands; and only by cunning glimpses will she reveal herself, as in Shakespeare and other masters of the great Art of Telling the Truth,—even though it be covertly, and by snatches."

By Melville's reckoning, then, the inspired author of *Hamlet* was misunderstood because he wanted to be; Shakespeare hid the truth from a world that would have scorned him for revealing it. Just so Hawthorne, who "takes great delight in hoodwinking the world . . . being willing to reserve the thorough and acute appreciation of what he is, to that party most qualified to judge—that is, to himself." To himself, rather, and to Herman Melville, who—if his analysis was correct—revealed about Hawthorne what the novelist had taken great pains to conceal. But there was no cause for alarm. Hawthorne "is immeasurably deeper than the plummet of the mere critic. For it is not the brain that can test such a man; it is only the heart."

Melville's understanding of Hawthorne sprang from an intimation of profound personal affinity. He felt that it was somehow his destiny to mingle on intimate spiritual terms with his fellow novelist. Harry was no doubt astonished when he first read Melville's description of Hawthorne, for it eerily anticipated his own sense that in the author of *Moby-Dick* he had found a true soulmate, a brother in the spirit sent before him on purpose in order to show the way. "The shock of recognition," Harry declared, following Melville's description of his first, rapt encounter with Hawthorne, began to register as he feasted on the language of *Moby-Dick.* Viola Meynell, in her brief Introduction to the World's Classics edition that he read on board the *Scythia,* described it best, he thought. Melville is "one of the greatest of all imaginative writers," she claims, because, among other things, he is the master of "scientifically accurate" prose. "There has never been such imaginative description of fact," she insists. Here, surely, was the novelist to please a young laboratory scientist with a passionate flair for the arts. "The infinite detail of the whale," she goes on, "its measurements, its blubber, its oil, its lashless eyes, its riddled brow—these are the reality with which the wild spirit of thought is interlocked." Melville situates the reader in the visible, palpable world but then expands "to the comprehensible limits of marvellous imagination." The results are "absolutely unsurpassed." And while Melville's "fame may still be restricted," she concludes, "it is intense, for to know him is to be partly made of him for ever."

It was only the first of many coincidences that Meynell surveys *Moby-Dick* from precisely the point of view that Harry would himself adopt. It was as though she had seen him coming. But then so, it seemed, had the blubbery Captain Prothero, and Sir John Bland-Sutton, the distinguished surgeon and sometime big-game hunter on the homeward leg of his Melville pilgrimage to New Bedford. The entire cast turned up in Harry's dreams on the night after the surgery—"a mixture," he recalled, "of whales and elephants, butchery and surgery, Ahab, Starbuck, Bland-Sutton, and the outcast Ishmael." All of these elements—the time, place, and cast of leading characters—conspired to reinforce the aura of inevitability that attached to Harry's first encounter with *Moby-Dick*. He was meant somehow to read this book. But how, precisely, did it speak to his condition?

Harry came to regard *Moby-Dick* as "a drama written out of grief, out of a secret inward bleeding too desperate for tears; and yet it was pervaded by the comic spirit, countless humorous touches and reflections which engendered the most enjoyable abdominal chucklings." To the extent that they dipped irreversibly toward the tragic, the novel and the novelist's career served well enough as an object lesson. Accept your losses in life, but do not let them bear you down. Trust your instincts, and don't look back, for fear that you, like Ahab, and like Melville, will drown in the sea of your obsessions. The novel was thus a summons to advance boldly. Harry would finish what he had started at the Rockefeller Institute and Cambridge University, but he would also begin to take the first steps toward a career in psychology. His view, never modified, that Melville was "the greatest depth psychologist America ever produced," shaped itself during and just after the voyage to England. The novel not only sealed him in his decision to take up psychology, but it helped to define the specific direction that his new interest would take. The unconscious, libido, myth, symbol, archetype— these and other concepts took on dramatic form in Ahab's furious rebellion and in the whale's impersonal wrath. Taken in tandem with *Moby-Dick,* Freud and Jung looked more compelling than ever.

So much for work; but what of Christiana? While Harry viewed Melville's masterpiece as "everything that one could ask of literature," he acknowledged in the same breath that it was "everything this side of love, everything except love, the summum bonum." In fact, however, there was no separating work and love, for depth psychology and Christiana Morgan were intertwined in Harry's thinking. To move toward one was, by the ingenious logic of his self-persuading, to move toward the other. Hers was the reflected face in the pool, the tantalizing image of his buried self. But she was also the gateway to the unconscious; she gave him access to the submerged human terrain that he was setting himself to explore. Thus between them they were a whole world, the united subject and object of passionate inquiry. Christiana was his love and work; he hers.

Years later, Harry would conclude that in *Moby-Dick* "Ahab-Melville's aggression was directed against the object that once harmed Eros with apparent malice and was still thwarting it with presentiments of further retaliations." The responsibility for this crime against love lay with that harsh strain of American Calvinism "which conceived of a deity in whose eyes Eros was depravity." Harry had been formed in the shadow of this oppressive tradition and would come to view his relationship with Christiana as symbolic of his liberation from its influence. This position, in its full critical elaboration, was a thing of the future. In 1924 it was perhaps enough that *Moby-Dick* summoned him in unequivocal terms to deep psychological diving. Melville's other works, he soon discovered, covered all the other important bases.

Typee (1846) was a protest against the straitened sexual mores of mid-century America and a proleptic rejection, as Harry saw it, of the prison-house of "an incompatible marriage." *Omoo* (1847) was another chronicle of the novelist's numerous youthful "egressions" from civilized restraints. Harry ranked *Mardi* (1849) with *Moby-Dick* (1851) and *Pierre* (1852) as novels that Melville "wanted to write," that were "dictated by his daemon." The book was important to him for reasons that were probably pretty clear even on a first reading. It records the philosophical quest of Taji, an idealistic young man whose passion for the truth is bound up with his pursuit of Yillah, an exotic island princess who has been "etherealized" by her childhood exposure to "wild conceits" and who therefore regards herself as "a being of the land of dreams." Harry viewed Taji as the personification of Melville's frustrated Eros and of his search, outside of conventional marriage, "for the ideal person to complete his life." In elaborating Taji's journey, the novelist wound deeper and deeper into himself and thereby discovered his vocation as a "pioneer" explorer of the unconscious. It is notable that Taji, feeling as "fixed as fate," persists in his quest against the advice of his friends. He must go on.

113

Redburn (1849) and *White-Jacket* (1850) were of interest as additional chapters in Melville's autobiographical exploration of his inner development. They were followed by *Moby-Dick* in 1851, and a year later by *Pierre,* the novel which more than any other confirmed Harry in his initial shock of recognition. The protagonist, young Pierre Glendinning, is handsome, athletic, sheltered, idealistic, and born into great wealth and position. Here, in short, was Harry himself. Pierre's mother, proud, independent, dominating, and the object of her son's adoration, fits neatly enough into the profile of Fannie Babcock Murray. His fiancée, Lucy Tartan, is blonde, virginal, aristocratic—a kind of prototype for Jo. It was undoubtedly with his wife in mind that Harry later—in the Introduction to his 1949 Hendricks House edition of *Pierre*—described Lucy as "a finely human creature, sensible, acquiescent, modest, whose great worth resides in her capacity for faithful unselfish devotion to those she loves." Such irresistible parallels between art and life were stunning, to be sure; but they must have paled for Harry when he first came across Isabel, the darkly sensuous woman of mystery who erupts onto the scene to persuade Pierre that she is his abandoned illegitimate sister. Prompted by high ideals, but moved as well by unconscious sexual impulses, Pierre rushes to Isabel's side, leaving his bright prospects in a shambles. Masquerading as a married couple, they move to New York City, where Pierre makes bold to "gospelize the world anew" in a book setting forth the moral implications of his experience with Isabel. Ironically, however, Pierre's mission to revolutionize humanity leads to his own confusion. "For the more and the more that he wrote, and the deeper and the deeper that he dived, Pierre saw the everlasting elusiveness of Truth; the universal lurking insincerity of even the greatest and purest written thoughts."

Isabel is the mystery that attracts and then consumes Pierre. Sister or not, she is that buried side of himself to which young Narcissus is reunited at the price of his life. Isabel, Harry would argue in his Introduction to *Pierre,* is a Jungian anima. As such, she expresses Pierre's repressed feminine dimension, which has been shaped both by experience and by the unconscious archetype of woman, and projected outward on the important females in his life.

Very often it is something mournful and deeply (if vaguely) mean-
ingful in the anima's look that draws attention. Melville gives Isabel
"one of those faces, which now and then appear to man, and without one word of speech, still reveal glimpses of some fearful gospel.
In natural guise, but lit by supernatural light; palpable to the
senses, but inscrutable to the soul; in their perfectest impression on
us, ever hovering between Tartarean misery and Paradisaic beauty;
such faces, compounded so of hell and heaven, overthrow in us all
foregone persuasions, and make us wondering children in this world
again." This is the strangely seductive face of fallen, hopeless Alice
Henry; and of course it is Christiana's face, dark, mysterious, re-
plete for Harry with potential for good and ill. These women's faces
drew him, as Isabel's drew Pierre, toward what was partially or fully
repressed in himself. Harry observes that Isabel, the unshaped orphan, has "the tired, unloved and unloving woman's desire to let
go and sink back into oblivion rather than make a forward effort
into life." He might as well have been describing Christiana, who
was baffled and depressed in 1924, incapable of caring for her child,
"drowning"—as he says of Isabel—"in her unconscious." In fact,
he had Christiana in mind as he wrote about Isabel, just as he was
thinking of himself when he described her fascination for Pierre.
"She embodies the repressed and the as-yet-unformulated components of the man's personality: the child in him who felt unloved,
the passivity and the death wishes which were forsworn, the grief
and the self-pity which have been bottled up, the feminine dispositions which have been denied, and, in addition, scores of nameless
intuitions and impulses, the open expression of which has been
barred by culture. Isabel," he concludes,"is the personification of
Pierre's unconscious."

Here, thinly disguised, Harry gives us himself, rejected by his
mother, emotionally and sexually repressed, but inwardly a rebel
against society and his own conventional upbringing, waiting to be
born. The way of his deliverance and growth is through the resurrection of Christiana, a prospect which opens up to him the promise
of love and sacrifice, issuing in the emergence of a new, fully indi-
viduated self. But the same road may lead to a disastrous, irrever-
sible descent into the unconscious. Either way, there is no apparent

choice in the matter; the anima must be obeyed. "Pierre was not arguing Fixed Fate and Free Will," Melville writes. Rather, "Fixed Fate and Free Will were arguing him, and Fixed Fate got the better in the debate." Harry comments, thinking of Christiana: "Pierre's love for Isabel is irrational: it overcame him suddenly, compulsively, and unaccountably, and threatens to disrupt every plan he has made for his future. It will be a horror to his mother. What has poor Isabel to offer him? For her sake he may be forced to suffer much, as well as to renounce many satisfactions to which he is accustomed. And yet, somehow, her claim is incontestable."

To have found Christiana mirrored so exactly in Isabel, and to have found his own response so perfectly represented in Pierre's, must have been a stunning revelation. For now more than ever the fateful incidents on board the *Scythia* seemed to limn out a definite pattern. To be sure, much that is striking in *Pierre* might pass for coincidence. Many young men love their mothers and fall in love with handsome, blonde, sensible, rich girls. But the coupling of Pierre and Isabel was another matter altogether. Their entangled souls were in some nearly literal sense the parents to Harry's encounter with Christiana. Or so it felt. Little wonder that Harry concurred—where few others did—in E. L. Grant Watson's opinion that "the center of Melville is *Pierre;* if one would understand him, one must understand this book before all others." But what precisely did *Pierre* signify? What course of action did it seem to enforce?

As Harry read it—both in 1924 and again twenty-five years later—the novel makes a basically positive case for Isabel's influence on Pierre. She carries him, as Christiana carried Harry, "beyond the reach of ordinary thought" to a virtual "declaration in favor of the unconscious as a directing influence in his life." Harry acknowledges that the anima is invariably "an ambiguous, or ambivalent, object, compounded of heaven and hell. . . . Isabel is an irresistible, irrational power that separates [Pierre] from all his present happiness, produces an intolerable conflict, and transfigures him into an enemy of all the good that he has known." But this painful descent, he insists, is the necessary first step toward liberation. Following Henry James, Sr., and Charles Peirce, Harry elaborates on "the doc-

116

trine of creative, or evolutionary, love," which "prescribes at each critical point of spiritual or mental growth, the embracement by the thesis of its antithesis, and the creation of a new synthesis. Usually the antithesis which is called evil is the potential source of a greater good than has been realized theretofore. This is the case for Isabel."

Thanks to Isabel's influence, Harry argues, "we find Pierre standing at the threshold of a saving evolutionary way through relationship." This may be so, though Pierre's way is vexed from the outset by the menace of incest. The assumption that Isabel is his half-sister provokes a certain perversity of repressed desire, and leads Pierre into "a long series of fantastic errors of judgment and treacheries of the heart." In the upshot, he squanders his precious opportunity but retains "the distinction of having once gazed on the promised land, even though, like Moses, he never inhabited it." Strongly inclined as he was to trace his own fate in Pierre's, it was essential that Harry salvage an affirmation from the general disaster of his alter ego's history. He concedes that Pierre makes a mess of his life, but insists at the same time that the anima experience held the potential for great good. Read this way in 1924, *Pierre* was a beckoning forward toward the promised land; it was a call to make good on the opportunity that Pierre and Isabel let slip away. Reading the novel in this way twenty-five years later was obliquely to testify that the journey had been successful.

As forecasts go, in fact, *Pierre* was a mixed blessing. Isabel is never represented as an unequivocal good. From the beginning she is an ominous figure, "vaguely historic and prophetic; backward, hinting of some irrevocable sin; forward, pointing to some inevitable ill." There is just a hint of humbug in the shadow of mystery that surrounds her; likewise, there is evidence of self-deception and self-indulgence in Pierre's surrender to his half-sister's dark allure. Harry recognized all this, just as he recognized that *Pierre* was a falling off from *Moby-Dick*. For all of his great interest in Melville's life, he could never get comfortably past 1852, the year in which *Pierre* was published. In betraying signs of the mental instability that would finally silence its author, the book also cast doubt on the enterprise that it had helped to inspire in Harry and Christiana.

Even as he was coming to regard himself as Melville's biographer, Harry began to have dreams in which he asked the great novelist to discuss his long period of decline. "Scarce might I have the heart to write it," Melville replied. It was too painful for words.

That Harry ignored the warning in *Pierre* is hardly surprising; after all, the novel conformed readily enough to his preferred reading. This is not to suggest that his interpretation was a heedless distortion; it is simply to indicate that another, less sanguine perspective was available to him. In a sense he made a virtue of necessity. There was no ignoring the novel; and there was no turning back. So he moved forward boldly, taking *Pierre* as one sign among many that he was on the right track. On occasion he would refer to Christiana as Isabel. And as the Morgans were taking their leave one cold afternoon during the winter of 1924, Harry looked at Christiana and blurted out, "You fertilize me." The words had emerged without conscious summons, though he recognized immediately that they were Pierre's, addressed with great feeling to Isabel toward the end of Melville's novel. Jo and Will were startled, naturally, but said nothing. Harry's allusion escaped them completely. But who could fail to see what he meant?

The year in England was outwardly rather placid and uneventful—or so it appeared to Ann McDonald, Josephine's governess, who kept a close eye on things. Soon after their arrival in Cambridge, the Murrays rented Leckhampton House, a large Georgian mansion set on sixteen acres, formerly owned by Frederic W. H. Myers (1843–1901), a noted spiritualist, sometime president of the Society for Psychical Research, and friend of A. Conan Doyle. The house had at one time welcomed all the famous mediums and was rumored to be haunted. It had an oak study set up for seances and a clock that began to tick just as Harry opened the room in which it had stood idle for many years. It was also within easy reach of Trinity College, where Harry had his lab, and of the Morgans, and of Ike and Veronica Murray, who had settled nearby. There was occasional company—Alvan Barach, L. J. Henderson, and the youthful scholar of literature, Theodore Spencer, passed through—but Harry was principally occupied with his work. He explained to the English literary critic and poet I. A. Richards—with whom he became friendly at Cambridge—that he was undecided about whether to be a physician and scientist, a psychologist, or a literary critic and biographer of Herman Melville. As an interim solution, he worked at all three. During the day he was engaged in research at Trinity; during the evenings, often until well past midnight, he immersed himself in his other interests. In fact, Harry came to England knowing that he would probably find his way into psychology once his research on chicken embryos was completed. Melville was a late addition to his plans but seemed to fit in as a kind of literary adjunct to his psychological pursuits. "I put Jung and Freud and Melville all in one pot," he once remarked; "there was so much similarity, so much overlap."

Things were placid because Harry was forever at work. There was a minimum of socializing with the English—they were so reserved and aloof—but frequent meals and outings with brother Ike and the Morgans. Harry made time for rowing on the Trinity crew, revealing only belatedly that he had once been captain at fair Harvard. Jo thoroughly enjoyed regular trips to London, where she shopped, visited with friends, and went to the theater. To Harry's chagrin, she arranged to be presented at Court in the spring of 1925. Ike and Will were also studying physiology at Cambridge. Ann McDonald observed that Harry's younger brother was tense and rather ragged in his outward appearance. His marriage was failing, in part because Veronica "was all brains," but no doubt at least as much because of his deepening attraction to Christiana. By contrast, Harry appeared healthy (in spite of a chronic smoker's cough), composed, and apparently fully satisfied with his life. To a large extent, this was an accurate picture. He was in many ways happy with Jo. Involvement with Christiana jeopardized that happiness, but it did little to influence his basically positive feelings about his wife. His attraction to Christiana was evident enough— he was "very, very fond on her," observed Ann McDonald—but where Ike's romantic agitation was there for all to behold, Harry's was not. He kept his deeper feelings pretty much to himself. Inwardly exhilarated with all dimensions of love and work, he was outwardly energetic—he had everyone talking about *Moby-Dick*— but never out of control.

The parallel strands of Harry's life converged dramatically during the Easter season in 1925, when he traveled on his own to Zurich for a meeting with Carl Jung. He had first written to Jung during the summer of 1923, just after reading *Psychological Types,* requesting an interview. Jung agreed to the proposal and thereby helped to fuel the Murrays' plans for a year abroad. Harry was excited, it will be recalled, by the way Jung's book illuminated the relations between personality types and individual preferences in matters of ostensibly "objective" theory. Though his appreciation of Jung had deepened over time, he made his way to Switzerland in mid-March with that original topic foremost in his mind.

As he approached Zurich, however, it became clear that other matters were astir in his unconscious. At a hotel in picturesque Fribourg he had what he later described as "a mini-anima experience." A tall, dark, very striking woman walked past in the dining room and took a table by herself. Later, after he had finished his meal, Harry saw her again, seated in the lobby, reading. There was something about her face that he couldn't resist. On impulse, he approached her. "I've never seen you before," he began, "but I know I've known you for years and years; I've dreamt about you." As it happened, the woman was a sophisticated English aristocrat, Lady Winifred Gore, who was herself on a mission to a Swiss psychiatrist and who took the abrupt intrusion comfortably in stride. She listened while Harry explained himself and responded with her own very interesting story.

Little more came of it. A friendship grew up between the two; they exchanged letters and occasional visits over the years. But Harry arrived in Zurich with the anima experience freshly in mind—to find, as chance would have it, that his host was full to brimming on the same score. They met first at Jung's house in Küsnacht, a pleasant suburb south of the city on the Lake of Zurich. Harry spoke briefly in praise of *Psychological Types* but saw immediately that Jung was little engaged. So he turned instead to an account of his adventure in Fribourg and, by way of explanation, to a preliminary discussion of his relationship with Christiana. Harry warmed quickly to his subject and found, quite to his surprise, that while *Psychological Types* had been the conscious occasion for his visit, love was the deeper agenda. More surprising still, he had barely opened his personal narrative when Jung jumped in with a story of his own. This was not the solemn, restrained psychoanalytic manner. There would be no long silences in Zurich. Harry's opening contribution was also his longest; thereafter Jung did most of the talking.

And as Jung talked, Harry must have felt once again, as he had so often with Melville, that there were no accidents in his life. Zurich had come into his way, it seemed, as *Moby-Dick* had, that he might better recognize what the future held. Of course it occurred to him, as Jung went on about the anima, that he was hearing what he had, in some mysterious fashion, come to hear. But of such secret designs he had little conscious awareness. He had not planned that the shift in Jung's interests, from types to the anima, would shape itself so perfectly to his own deep drift. Nor could he have anticipated that Jung's personal experience with the unconscious would so vitally anticipate his own.

Harry spoke in detail about Christiana and about what he had discovered in Melville. He was forthright about immanent crises in the domestic, vocational, and moral dimensions of his life. Jung responded by describing his own period of crisis a decade earlier, at the time of his break with Freud. He acknowledged an initial dread of the descent into the unconscious and expanded in memorable ways on his archetypal dreams and visions. He gave special emphasis to individuation, the process by which autonomous unconscious contents are assimilated to consciousness and thus stripped of their power. Harry was impressed with Jung's flair for earthy, concrete language and his instinct for the apt metaphor. It was obvious from the beginning that Jung's system had its foundation in his long personal encounter with the unconscious. This was gratifying confirmation of Harry's hunch about subjectivity and science. Moreover, the ready application of Jung's ideas to Harry's situation was freighted with the implication, lost on neither of them, that their lives and personalities were in key respects the same. They met in sessions of at least an hour each on a daily basis for more than three weeks. On weekends they sailed together up and down the lake in Jung's boat, pausing on shore for meals, and talking, talking, talking. When they were done, Jung had joined Melville on the template of Harry's destiny.

Some of what Jung had to say about the unconscious would appear years later in his autobiography. But much else was intensely personal and would have no place in his published writing. This was especially the case with his commentary on the women in his life. He was unusually candid on this subject with Harry, it seems clear, because the parallels between their experiences, as they emerged in discussion, were so numerous and close. Both of them were influenced during their formative years by strong mothers. As to their wives, Emma Jung, though more of an intellectual than Jo, was just as squarely anchored in reality; she was handsome, sensible, faithful, and forbearing, an able homemaker and helpmate. Thanks in good part to her stabilizing influence, Jung survived his long, perilous "confrontation with the unconscious." "It was most essential for me to have a normal life in the real world as a counterpoise to that strange inner world," he acknowledges in *Memories, Dreams, Reflections.* "My family and my profession remained the base to which I could always return, assuring me that I was an actually existing, ordinary person." He contrasted himself with Nietzsche, who "lost the ground under his feet because he possessed nothing more than the inner world of his thoughts. . . . He was uprooted and hovered above the earth, and therefore he succumbed to exaggeration and irreality. For me, such irreality was the quintessence of horror, for I aimed, after all, at *this* world and *this* life." Harry's approach to the unconscious would be equally cautious; he had no wish to share Nietzsche's fate, or Melville's, for that matter. He would venture to the edge of the abyss, but never without a lifeline back to wife, family, home, and work.

Most crucially of all, both men were brought to a reckoning with their interior lives by remarkable young women. When Harry began to describe Christiana, her look, her manner, her mind, and her mysterious hold on him, Jung quickly took fire. He hastened to describe an identical encounter in his own life, a decade earlier, with Antonia Wolff, a young woman of twenty-three who had come to him as a patient but who soon became his fearless guide to the underworld. Toni, as she was called, has been described by one who knew her as the consummate vehicle for projections of the anima. "She was not beautiful in the strictly classical sense, but she could look far more than beautiful, more like a goddess than a mortal woman. She had an extraordinary genius for accompanying men— and sometimes women too, in a different way—whose destiny it was to enter the unconscious." Her role, it appears, was to awaken and in a sense to embody Jung's unconscious that he might recognize and control its contents and thereby achieve wholeness, or individuation. Harry felt sure that he recognized this extraordinary woman, alongside Jung himself, in the discussion of the anima and animus that appeared in the 1928 edition of *Two Essays in Analytical Psychology.* The personal could penetrate no further than this into the realm of theory!

Toni Wolff was to Jung, then, as Christiana might well become to Harry. More astonishing still, the Old Man—as Jung was called—and his young coworker and lover had entered a permanent relationship with the consent, and even the approval, of Emma Jung. Harry was overwhelmed, of course, not merely with what to an American sensibility appeared outrageous in their triadic relationship, but also with what it suggested—however shockingly at first—might be possible in his own life. On their return to Küsnacht from a long sail down the lake to Jung's newly constructed tower in Bollingen, Harry and Jung were greeted by Emma and Toni, who had prepared tea. Here they were, then: the Old Man, his dark mistress, and his fine wife, serenely taking tea together. The arrangement was a carefully guarded secret in proper, unbending Zurich. But that made Jung's openness the more remarkable. Harry had the impression that his host had gone out of his way to dramatize the harmony of the situation. But he needed little persuading. They had made a go of it, he could see. Toni and Emma had a good deal in common. They were both dark and shy and quiet.

It was central to the great impact of his stay in Zurich that Harry felt far "removed from the ordinary run of things. . . . When you go to Zurich you cut connections with your everyday life. . . . Everything that happens is extraordinary; you're ready to receive it in an extraordinary way." At the apex of such heightened awareness was the unconscious itself, which "got operating right away," Harry recalled, primarily in his dreams. For a few days he recorded his nocturnal adventures in a notebook but then destroyed what he had written. He found, as others have, that words were inadequate to the experience. Many dreams seemed to betray the perversity of the unconscious, its delight in frustrating conscious wishes and expectations. Others seemed insane, incomprehensible; a few were freighted with what he took to be telepathic communications. His first dream, which occurred on the night after his initial meeting with Jung, was by Harry's reckoning a very important one. It finds him on a street corner in Zurich, waiting for a tram. When the tram arrives he sees that the conductor has black hair, a black beard, and black clothing. "I looked at him and recognized him as Freud," Harry recalled. "Then I put my hand up to get onto the car, and I looked up and the whole car was just filled with these people, all exactly alike. I saw this was the devil and his legions. Then I woke up."

The conductor was actually Jung, Harry felt sure; but he appeared in the dream as Freud because of his association with sex— more specifically, because of his electrifying revelations about his relationship with Toni Wolff. Boarding the tram—continuing the analysis—was thus to undertake a journey that might well terminate in adultery. True, Harry had already indulged himself, without much ado, in at least one extramarital fling. But with Christiana it was different; the deeds of love were in this case heavily consequential. Harry's uneasiness was sharpened by an analogy that Jung had drawn between adulterous relationships and the German invasion of Belgium in World War I. The Germans acknowledged that overrunning their neighbor was a violation of treaty agreements, but they invaded it anyway, without excuses, "because they had to." It was the same, Jung said, in his relationship with Toni. He allowed that the infidelity was a moral wrong but insisted that its coming to pass had been inevitable. To view the matter this way was far better, he said, than pretending that the transgression was justified, or making excuses for it after the fact.

It was of course the application of Jung's analogy to his own affairs that gave Harry pause. Taken in that context, the Old Man's

reasoning seemed nothing short of devilish; it was an invitation to
trample moral scruple under foot in the headlong surrender to desire. Just as clearly, however, when it came to the translation of "I
want to" into "I had to," Harry had himself to fear far more than
Jung. He knew this; and yet, understandably enough perhaps, he
was inclined to pose the issue as though his analyst bore the burden
of moral responsibility. "Shall I trust myself to Jung?" he asked.
But he did not force the question; and thereby, in temporarily setting it aside, he answered it. A week or so passed before he mentioned the dream to Jung. By that time the momentum of the
analysis had gathered behind Jung's example with Toni, which now
had all the force of Necessity. The irony of the situation was not
entirely lost on Harry. For a brief while he looked askance at the
Old Man's moral dereliction; "but that," he said, "was quickly repressed, and when I went away, I had nothing but a good impression of him."

Jung was a decidedly ambiguous mentor. On one side, he gave
very positive emphasis to the ways in which his own life might be
construed as a model. He responded to Christiana with Toni and
allowed that he and Harry were both introverted thinking intuitive
types. On the other, Jung gave stern warnings. He could take no
responsibility for what his patients did. "You take your life into
your hands" when you come to Zurich, he said. He steered Harry
away from a career in psychology, and he was not encouraging about
Christiana. Stay where you are, he seemed to suggest; you have a
good life. But Harry took such gestures as tests of his resolve. It
was Jung's "regular method," he decided, "to put difficulties in the
way to see how enthusiastic you were." The more Jung "talked
against" things, the more Harry favored them.

It is virtually impossible to exaggerate the importance of the long
visit to Zurich. Jung was "the first full-blooded, spherical—and
Goethean, I should say—intelligence I had ever met," Harry wrote
in 1940. Under Jung's guidance he *experienced* the unconscious,
something not to be drawn out of books." Harry had by this time
gone back to *The Interpretation of Dreams,* but such dealings in "ordinary sexual symbolism" seemed tame and reductive to him now
that he had encountered the anima. "Within a month," thanks to

Jung's guidance through the realm of the archetypes, Harry found that "a score of bi-horned problems were resolved." He specifies but one of these—"I went off," he says, "decided on depth psychology"—leaving the rest to the reader's imagination. But in opting for depth psychology he decided on Christiana as well; and that decision in turn brought a world of changes—for Jo, for Will, for Ike, and for their families—in its tow.

Harry's misgivings about Jung were swept aside by the waves of illumination pouring from the unconscious. In the excess of light, Harry admitted, he was temporarily blind. But probably not completely, and certainly not for long. At one level, the fit to things was irresistible; Jung's life, like Melville's in *Pierre,* seemed virtually interchangeable at key points with his own ("I'd been through the whole thing" once before, he later observed). At another level, it was obvious that Jung cared little—much too little—for facts. He made no effort to familiarize himself with basic details of Harry's life; his fancy took flight at the slightest provocation. He was, Harry felt, "a borderline psychotic" with "a terrific imagination" and a "terrific way of making up reasons" for his constructions of the world. In dedicating himself to the "service of the psyche," Jung also legitimated his intense self-absorption. His tower at Bollingen, which made a special impression on Harry, was a monument to the unconscious, "a kind of representation in stone," Jung wrote years later, "of my innermost thoughts and of the knowledge I had acquired." He regarded the building as "a maternal womb," a place to be "reborn." "There is nothing in the Tower that has not grown into its own form over the decades, nothing with which I am not linked. Here everything has its history, and mine; here is space for the spaceless kingdom of the world's and the psyche's hinterland."

"I admired and respected him more than any man I've met," Harry once declared of Jung. And for good reason. Jung *was* "spherical"—fully rounded, complete, at home outside of science, at once the model and the premier student of the whole human being. He had also achieved in his personal life what had once been inconceivable to Harry. Thus the Old Man, the sage guide to the underworld, was exemplary in work and love. Still, Harry was bothered by Jung's inflated preoccupation with the products of his own "larger

126

self." This was manifest in an inclination to view the anima as a figure of blind eros, useful to the male logos as the projected embodiment of its unconscious, but inferior, and possibly expendable. Jung regarded Toni Wolff as a hetaira, a woman "not meant to bear physical children" but to "give rebirth to a man in a spiritual sense." Harry shared some of this obvious prejudice. With most people of his time, he associated women with feeling and intuition and regarded them as rather uncritical in their thinking. Men, by contrast, were more objective and logical in their approach to the world. He once remarked that Christiana found little to criticize in Jung because "she was a woman." It followed that Harry was the bearer of reason and science in their relationship, while Christiana proceeded feelingly and with sudden flashes of insight.

Harry was sharply aware of such continuities between Jung's views and his own; indeed, they were integral to the attraction between the two men. But there were differences as well, and these were important to Harry because they set him apart from Jung at those points where their association made him most uneasy. Harry thought of his relationship with Christiana as a potential union of very distinct people in an equal partnership. It was important that they were about the same age. There was no temptation to fall—as Jung and Toni had fallen—into the roles of wise old man and spirit of eternal youth. Christiana was not Harry's child, or student, or satellite; she was his anima, and he was her animus. From two would come one in which both would share. Theirs would be a mutual rebirth. This is what they aimed for. In time, Harry and Christiana would come to think of themselves as a dyad, a unit of two interdependent entities. This well described how they felt about each other; it also served as a check against the kind of inflation that Harry witnessed in Jung and that threatened all deep divers into the unconscious. Lewis Mumford would speak for them in observing that Toni found no place in Jung's autobiography. The omission is unfortunate, Mumford comments, "in the case of a man whose personal experiment in open erotic relationships influenced the marriage of more than one patient who came to him for advice." The omission was also symptomatic of the kind of self-absorption that Harry wished to avoid.

Harry left Switzerland feeling like "a reborn man." He went by train through the mountains and down to Florence, where he caught up with Jo and the Morgans, who had been in Rome for Easter. All agreed that he looked different, renewed, as though he was just back from paradise. Appearances were of course revealing, for Harry was experiencing a rather mild inflation of his own. He felt that his earlier perspective on life had been narrowed by the pressure of trivial quotidian concerns. But now that Jung had opened his eyes, the world seemed large with possibility. At the source and center of this expanded vision was Christiana. It was clear now that she was essential to his fulfillment, he to hers. Their drawing together might take time, but it was, he felt sure, inevitable. It was equally clear that divorce was out of the question. The family, society, career—all would suffer as the result of a break. Jung's solution was the best one. If Jo and Will could see their way to it, an arrangement acceptable to all might be worked out. Harry would begin to move in that direction as soon as the time was right.

He did his best to explain to Christiana what had happened to him in Zurich. She understood. At the famous Dominican monastery in the village of Fiesole, just outside of Florence, they had a few minutes together in the courtyard. It was evident to both of them that "something was going to happen." They felt possessive of one another, and jealous of each other's mate. Soon they would begin to lay plans for Christiana's visit to Jung. By late April they had returned to Cambridge, with a stop in Paris en route. Harry began to round off his research and went into training for Henley. Jung wrote, thanking him for his "nice letter." He cautioned against saying "too many good things, as I have to be careful not to be swayed away by Megalomania. It is so important to keep close to the earth, as the Spirit is always soaring up to Heaven like a flame as much destructive as enlightening. I appreciate your genuine reactions and I sympathize with your enthusiasm, because I am so deeply convinced, that those ideas that came to me are really quite wonderful things. I can easily say that (without blushing), because I know, how resistant and how foolishly obstinate I was, when they first visited me and what a trouble it was, until I could read their symbolic language, so much superior to my dull conscious mind.

Your visit has been a joy and a refreshment to me as there are so few
people capable of understanding the clarity of the 'profunda coeli.'"

Jung goes on to recommend an analyst for Christiana. The man
he has in mind is an "artistic and intuitive" fellow, quite without
"philosophical or scientific clarity" but perfectly suitable for "a
young woman." Harry apparently declined the suggestion, urging
Jung himself to work with Christiana. "Mrs. Morgan can come Oct.
5th," came the terse reply. "Then I am at home." In the same note
Jung responds bluntly to Melville. "I have read Mardi and cursed
it. It is too long. He was eaten up by his sexualized Coll. Unconscious." The novelist's eccentricities notwithstanding, however,
Harry was "welcome always" in Zurich. Emma Jung had written
earlier, with thanks for *Mardi* and for Henry Adams' *Mont-Saint-
Michel and Chartres* (Harry's oblique comment, perhaps, on Jung's
tower). She promised to send a picture of her husband. Meanwhile,
L. J. Henderson visited while giving lectures at Cambridge. He had
read around in *Psychological Types* and liked it about as well as the
Old Man liked *Mardi.* He conceded that Jung might be "very good
with people" but complained that he wasn't "too clear about his
concepts." Henderson soured on Zurich, we may suppose, in about
the same degree that Harry warmed to it.

After the Henley races at Oxford in mid-June, the Murrays returned to Cambridge, settled their affairs, and set off in August for
a month of touring in France. Ike and Veronica had left earlier with
Will and Christiana. They were to rendezvous in Carcassonne,
where Harry would join them, while Jo stayed for a few days with
friends in Paris. She would catch up later, to take over the back seat
of the Morgans' car with Harry, while Ike and Veronica continued
from Carcassonne on their own. The children, meanwhile, were
settled with their nannies and governesses in Houlgate, a coastal
village in Normandy, not far from Le Havre.

Carcassonne, with its remarkable double-walled medieval forti-
fication, was as good a place as any for a scene. It was clear to Harry
from the moment he arrived that something was brewing. Christiana's behavior had been erratic and impulsive. She had recently
complained of the heat and took relief by walking fully dressed into
a shallow river, where she lay with her head on a rock, just above

129

the water. Ike's feelings for her had become painfully obvious to everyone. Veronica took Harry aside and explained, on Will's say-so, that Christiana was in love with him, not his younger brother. Christiana said as much herself. "I'd make an effort with you," she told Harry, dismissing Ike as a "nice easy child." That evening, as they sat drinking in a cafe, an old French woman asked them if they were married. "No," Harry replied, "she is my sister," thinking of the relationship between Isabel and Pierre, which, by chance, they were just then discussing. Later on, after dinner and more drinks, Will went into town and organized a band. While he roared through the streets with his friends, Ike, who was drunker still, began to climb down the steep outer wall of the fortress. Veronica must have told him the truth about Christiana. He was desperate and half-suicidal—and one slip away from the end of his misery. Harry went over the side after him, in good part to help, but also, he acknowledged later, to show that he was "up to it." Ike resisted at first but finally agreed to head back up the wall. "It was quite risky," Harry recalled, "just fingers and toes" the whole way.

From Carcassonne, Harry and the Morgans traveled west for a week or so through the French Pyrenees. Jo had rejoined them now, and they drove slowly through the rugged countryside, making stops along the way at Tarascon, Lourdes, and Pau. Harry and Christiana talked incessantly about Melville and *Moby-Dick*. At St-Jean-Pied-de-Port, a pleasant tourist and fishing center, a festival was in progress. It was a version in miniature of the annual gathering at Pamplona, just south across the Spanish border, which would achieve a kind of immortality a year later when Hemingway made it the setting for *The Sun Also Rises*. There was dancing in the streets of St-Jean-Pied-de-Port; and when Jo and Will drifted into town, following the fun, Harry climbed up to the balcony of Christiana's room. There in the warm southern night, with the music and the lights lifting softly from the streets below, they made love for the first time. That embrace marked the real beginning, they agreed, of their new life together.

Harry and Christiana came to bodies at last because the time and place were perfect and because they could wait no longer. Their grand embrace in St-Jean-Pied-de-Port was momentous, to be sure;

but it was also, as such things go, rather belated. Occasion and desire had not been wanting, after all. The delay was more Harry's doing than Christiana's. He would never be completely sure that they were right; it never occurred to her that they might be wrong. It mattered to them both that they had gone forward without Jung's imprimatur. His example was vitally important, of course; but the fire was all their own. No doubt the pressure to act increased as the trip through France drew to a close. After a final week at Houlgate, Harry and Jo and Josephine were scheduled to take ship at Le Havre for the voyage home to America. The Morgans, meanwhile, would return to Cambridge, where Will would complete his work in physiology and Christiana would prepare herself for Zurich. Had they missed St-Jean-Pied-de-Port, their parting that September might have been a final one. Who cared for Jung's approval if they were thousands of miles apart? At such a distance, love would surely cool.

But they did not miss their chance, and love grew very warm indeed. From St-Jean-Pied-de-Port they traveled to St-Jean-de-Luz, a coastal fishing town, where Harry and Christiana spent the night on a cliff overlooking the ocean. They talked until dawn about "the devious-cruising Rachel," the forlorn whale ship that takes the orphan Ishmael on board at the end of *Moby-Dick*. Next to Biarritz, where Christiana walked on the beach with Will and told all. He was deeply hurt, of course, but hardly taken by surprise. Will was too gentle to make a scene and too much in love with his wife to oppose her. Christiana's records indicate that passion grew even bolder as the end drew near. "*Bordeaux.* A.M.," she noted; "*Tours.* A.M.," and "*Blois.* Adjoining rooms. P.M. Chaise Longue." So it went, on through Chinon, Chambord, and Chartres, and west finally to Houlgate, where they rejoined their children.

The last few days were very tense for everyone. Jo and Will were no doubt as relieved as their mates were distraught at the prospect of separation. They all knew this, but no one dared say it. The night before their farewell, the lovers met one last time on the beach. "*Houlgate.* Bathing naked at night. Touching [Harry]," Christiana recorded. It was daring, almost flagrant, for they were in easy view of the houses set back from the water. It may be that they felt the need to declare unequivocally who they were and what they meant to each other.

The next morning the Murrays embarked from Le Havre. Harry would not see Christiana again for a year. "I remember leaving," he reported, nearly a half century later; there were "tears pouring down into the water, and Jo next to me holding my arm, despite the fact that they were all against her in a sense. They were not for her. The tears." Christiana was no happier. "Terrible depression after his departure," she wrote.

▼

chapter seven

Mardi Behind,
an Ocean Before

The return to New York restored a measure of order to the Murrays' lives. They reoccupied the apartment on 79th Street, which had been let out to another family while they were away. Josephine continued in the care of her governess, who recalled that socializing was held to a minimum in order that Harry might meet his busy work schedule. Opera and theatre were the leading diversions, though time was also set aside for visits with Fannie and Henry, Sr., and for occasional dinner parties. Harry was regularly at the Rockefeller Institute, where he completed the research and writing for his Ph.D. He was also immersed in the study of psychiatry and psychoanalysis, with heavy reading in Freud, Jung, Adler, and Rank. He made a call on Frances Wickes, said to be the most able and enthusiastic of the New York Jungians. On several weekends he joined his old mentor George Draper on tours of the clinics at the Manhattan State Hospital for the Insane. Finally, he found time—quite a good deal of it, in fact—to begin hunting and gathering for a biography of Herman Melville.

Harry had not been home more than a few days before he contacted Raymond Weaver, whose *Herman Melville, Mariner and Mystic,* published in 1921, was certainly the most substantial study of the novelist to be found. Weaver was very helpful. He lead Harry to Eleanor Metcalf, Melville's granddaughter, who was unfailingly generous with memories, letters, and assorted possessions of her esteemed kinsman. Weaver also mentioned the Morewood sisters, granddaughters of Melville's brother, Allan, who took a dim view of their literary relative—he had been an erratic, half-insane, sometimes violent husband and father—and had so far refused to cooperate. Forewarned, Harry approached the Morewoods gingerly, and with an arsenal of charm. He wanted what they had. So he plied them with ingratiating letters, took his mother along on visits to their home in New Rochelle (Fannie conspired, with a show of refined condescension, to please), performed chores, gave them an airedale pup, paid for letters and memorabilia, and even acquiesced when they observed that he was "the spitting image" of their deranged brother. Over time, and not without regular doses of coaxing, the Morewoods shared all that they knew and possessed of mad, moody Melville.

The more Harry learned of Melville, the deeper his personal identification with the novelist grew. He was especially attentive to what the Morewoods revealed—belatedly, almost evasively—about their forbear's fractious discontent with marriage. But the richest return on Harry's labor was the discovery that the Morewoods held the deed to Arrowhead, the fine old farm in Pittsfield, Massachusetts, where Melville wrote *Moby-Dick*. More wonderful still, they allowed that the place was on the market. "I am absolutely overcome to think that Melville's house is intact and for sale," wrote Christiana in late October 1925. "This mustn't slip by. . . . I have the most wonderful picture of that fireplace, the bookshelves, and the porch." She was struck by the suggestion of auspicious design in Harry's discovery—"It is almost unbelievable," she wrote, "to have found it as we wanted to find it—alone, apart." Harry was even more sharply alive to the implication of the thing. On his first visit to Pittsfield—just a week or so after returning to New York—he found himself shaking all over. "I don't know what it was," he recalled. "It was just as if I was going to meet the man himself. . . . I had a religious feeling; this was a sanctified place, a sacred place." He let it be known that he was interested in buying the farm. It might be suitable for use as a rural psychiatric clinic, he speculated; or he could turn it over to the state as an historical monument. Time and circumstance would eventually frustrate Harry's ambition to make Arrowhead his own. But in late November, when Agnes

Morewood sent him the key to the house, he took spiritual possession of the place. He stood beside the enormous fireplace immortalized in "I and My Chimney." He entered Melville's study, with its grand view of Mt. Greylock. He sat at the writing table on which *Moby-Dick* had been written. He slept in Melville's bed. To the extent that such a thing is possible, he laid hands on the novelist's life.

Inspired by Arrowhead, Harry moved quickly to learn everything there was to know about Melville. He followed the novelist's trail through New York and New England and all the way out West to Galena, Illinois, where young Herman had visited his uncle Thomas Melville in 1840. He pored over the papers made available to him by Eleanor Metcalf and the Morewoods. He made efforts to locate and purchase Melville's books and possessions. There was the riveting news, second-hand but reliable, that *Pierre* was in fact closely autobiographical. Here was additional fuel for Harry's hunch that Melville's youthful idealism had been permanently shattered by the discovery that his father had sired an illegitimate daughter. The trail grew warmer when Harry located the so-called "chair portrait" of Allan Melville, a picture that turns up in *Pierre* as telling evidence of paternal frailty. He was also able to make contact with Julian Hawthorne, the novelist's son. "I know of no secret passages in [Melville's] career," Hawthorne wrote, apparently in response to questions about young Herman's traumatic discovery of his half-sister, and about the role of that knowledge in his precarious mental health. "I think his mind became unbalanced at or before the composition of Pierre, and continued to be more disordered for the rest of his life. I think he was seldom cheerful, and toward the last became constantly depressed." Hawthorne goes on to underline Melville's "extravagance and morbidity" and concludes that "he was a wanderer, in mind and body, but too much of a poet to be an atheist, and not enough of a poet to write poetry."

Harry moved with equal speed in his planning and early drafting of Melville's story. In mid-September 1925 he sent Christiana an outline which featured major thematic considerations—among them, "Melville as forerunner of modern psychology." At year's end she advised him to set aside his concerns about style—"It will be good I know, because you are in it completely"—and to send something of what he had written. A month or so later she applauded his "idea of writing about Melville from several angles." Van Wyck Brooks, the noted chronicler of American literary and cultural development, was less sanguine about the design of the biography. Brooks learned about Harry and his rage for Melville from Ned Sheldon. In March 1926 he wrote asking to see a chapter of the work in progress. "Your scheme for a double biography, so to speak, one subjective, with another objective biography interpolated," he observed later in the same year, "strikes me as mighty interesting, though certainly difficult." Brooks advised Harry not to overdo the subjective commentary; "you are in danger of getting rather confused here," he cautioned.

The research for the biography was virtually complete by the end of 1928. Harry had worked with such thoroughness and passionate speed that two decades would pass before others in the field began to catch up with him. This was so in some part because he failed to publish what he knew. It is clear that he got down to drafting early chapters soon after his return to New York in 1925. But it is also evident that Harry was uncertain in matters of style and was wrestling with what Brooks called the "subjective"—presumably the personal and the intuitive—dimension to the work. That he regarded Melville's story as an extension of his own made its telling all the more difficult—made it, finally, impossible. "Everything Melville writes is about himself," Harry observed, later in his life. "We might call his condition a narcissistic psychosis, which is what makes all his writing so intensely psychological. He looks into himself, reports what he sees, and depicts it through characters and events. He surpasses Freud, who looked there only briefly, whereas Melville spent literally decades wandering in the deep."

Wandering indeed!—going half mad with bafflement at what he found, and passing finally beyond words into silence. Perhaps Harry glimpsed early on that diving into Melville was, after all, a narcissistic plunge, at one remove, into himself. His pursuit of Melville enabled and at the same time largely concealed that personal agenda. The story behind the narrative of Melville's life, moving and shaping it, was a "subjective" tale of self-discovery, of a marriage of true minds at once fabulous and verging on the grandiose. It was the shroud of self-absorption, Harry saw, that finally silenced Melville. Did he recognize that it was narcissism above all things which he shared with the lapsed Titan of American letters? Clearly, he did; just as he saw, perhaps less clearly, that his close identification with Melville, precisely in those terms, would be the principal obstacle to the completion of the biography.

"I am my own soul's emperor," proclaims Taji at the end of *Mardi,* "and my first act is abdication! Hail! realm of shades!" Harry seized upon this kindred deep diver into the "endless sea" of the unconscious as the essential Herman Melville. Having discovered this unknown genius, he was determined to protect him from exposure until the story, as he saw it, could be perfected. The true Melville would be his to unveil. Thus he took careful precautions with the evidence. The Morewoods promised to grant him first priority on all their records. Eleanor Metcalf was equally cooperative, assuring him in May 1926 that she would be "very *discrete*" with her holdings and comment. Two years later, when Lewis Mumford asked her for assistance with his nearly completed biography of Melville, she put him off. "Do you want to help Mr. Mumford out?" she asked. "I shall say nothing about your activities unless I hear from you." A week later she wrote again, urging Harry to "have no fear—Mr. Mumford will not duplicate you." Still, she would say nothing to the newcomer about Harry's special angle on things.

Mumford was in 1928 already well known for his work on utopias, architecture, and American culture generally; he was also approaching the first great flowering in his long, celebrated career. In taking arms against a grasping, mechanized modernity, and in looking to artists—Emerson, Whitman, Melville—for answers, he was a man after Harry's heart. In the first of the hundreds of letters they would exchange in their long friendship, Mumford asks for permission to look at Melville materials in the New York Public Library to which Harry had secured first priority. It is his wish, he writes, to allay any fears of their "books overlapping or competing with each other." He has learned from Raymond Weaver that Harry has "a great deal of first hand data about Melville's life" which he will not share. But this is no problem, Mumford protests; his own work on Melville is primarily "literary criticism" based on published writings, and with rather sketchy attention to the life, especially in the vexed period during and after the composition of *Pierre.* Thus he can get along quite well without the Melville papers in the New York Public Library; though he asks to see them nonetheless, as "objective data" against which to test his own "independent conclusions, drawn from a study of Melville's literary work."

Harry replied that he had "*no* priority whatsoever" with the papers in New York and wished Mumford well with them. He goes on to describe his own project as a full length biography with attention both to the facts of Melville's life and to the analysis of its "principal trends, major conflicts, impasses & regressions." He is also interested in what he calls "the esoteric Melville—subjectively, poetically & metaphysically apprehended." He was, in short, taking all of Melville into his sights—even that kindred deep diver who took him by storm on board the *Scythia.* Harry denies that his approach will be systematically psychoanalytic; it is the novelist's "attempt to break the Gates of Paradise" and his "teasing the world for grace" that hold him. He makes no attempt to minimize the overlap between his work and Mumford's; indeed, he exaggerates it. "If there is anything left for me to write," he ends, "I might finish within 18 months." The two met for lunch at the Harvard Club in New York that September, found that they had much more than Melville in common, and were soon fast friends. Before the year was out, they joined Hans Zinsser and others in coming to the aid of Van Wyck Brooks, who had suffered a devastating mental breakdown. As to Mumford's questions about Melville, Harry could not promise to answer every one. "We all have our pet little vanities," he wrote, "of which we are not entirely purged."

Harry was generous with Mumford because he respected him and because they were personally compatible. He admired Mumford's encyclopedic learning, his literary acumen, and his steady sobriety of judgment. For his part, Mumford was drawn to Harry's energy and imagination and to his strong intuitive hold, buttressed by science, on the human psyche. He likened his new friend to his old mentor, Patrick Geddes, who at thirty-five was "eager, active, intense, plastic, not yet limited by his thought-cage." But Harry's readiness to cooperate was also, rather ironically, the measure of his disagreement with Mumford on key fundamentals. He went to the heart of matter in one of the two reviews that he wrote when *Herman Melville* appeared in 1929. At the end of several paragraphs of praise he rounds to the admission that "there are moments when Mumford's attitude seems too rational—I might say too consciously elaborated." Mumford fares well enough with the straightforward early novels; but his literalism and objectivity are inadequate to the deep diving in *Mardi, Moby-Dick,* and *Pierre,* where Melville "discovered the Unconscious and commenced to explore it. . . . This casting adrift was better, it seemed to him, than subjugating himself to a straight course in a humdrum world." At the end of *Mardi,* in setting a course for the "realm of shades," Melville declared his intention to surrender to the unconscious and thereby to accept the "annihilation of the Ego." To properly measure Melville's achievement, Harry goes on, we as readers must also "let go the common ways and allow ourselves to be carried down in the undertow" of the novelist's greatest works. "This is hazardous," he admits, "for at this point we are on the borderline of disintegration. But such a sojourn in darkness and chaos," he suggests, thinking of his own approach, "might lead to an awareness of Melville's dilemma which would differ somewhat from the intellectual formulations presented by Mumford." In conclusion, Harry observes that "Mumford is not mysterious or ambiguous. He is supremely conscious, and his book is so lucid that the reader is never lost, but remains a willing and appreciative listener to the end."

The two friends sometimes jested that theirs was happier version of the Hawthorne/Melville relationship. Harry was the bold, romantic, impetuous diver, while Mumford was cool, detached, analytical—a landsman. From Harry's side, the jest implied—what his review implied—that Mumford had never experienced the unconscious and that the lack handicapped him as a reader of Melville. More privately, Harry believed that Mumford's reluctance to venture out into the deep had its price in a certain innocence and superficiality. But of course that lack rendered him safe; it was precisely what Mumford could not reach in Melville that Harry wanted to preserve from exposure. He suggests as much in his review, hinting that he will be the one to return, like Ishmael in *Moby-Dick,* a singular survivor bearing a singular tale.

Raymond Weaver saw it the same way. He had no sooner finished *Herman Melville* than he wrote to Harry condemning it as "bowelless" and anemic. "But in one way," he reflected, "Mumford's book gives me unqualified rejoicing: it heightens your own opportunity and advantage. . . . You have the real stuff to offer—and until your book appears, all other books must be romanticizing pretty much in the void. . . . You, now, are the only person alive that can throw any real new light on Melville." Mumford sent a much milder version of the same response after reading Harry's reviews. "Your praise is generous and your rod is gentle," he wrote. "I didn't get to the bottom of Melville's unconscious, and I am inclined to think that the reason is that I have never opened the trap door to my own." Thus he acquiesced in Harry's critique, bowing gracefully to the prospect of a better, bolder biography. This, they had agreed, was to be the way between them. "Our friendship shall redeem the emptiness of Hawthorne's and Melville's," Mumford had written, adding in a later letter that he embraced Harry as one with whom he could share all "attitudes and interests—with no disguises." "It is inevitable," Harry replied. "We shall make up for all the promising friendships in the world that came to nought."

Melville was one of three major concerns in Harry's adult life. The other two were the study of dynamic psychology and union with Christiana Morgan. These strands, tightly interwoven as they were in his experience, formed an anchor line sunk in the vast ocean of the unconscious. All three took him where he most wanted to go; and all three brought him back to himself. The second of these concerns, which had prompted him to undertake a rigorous independent course of study, began to show real promise early in 1926 when Harry learned that a new Psychological Clinic had been proposed at Harvard. Morton Prince, a pioneer in American psychopathology, best known for his work with hypnosis and multiple personality, had approached President Lowell with the idea, and with the money—more than $140,000—to back it up. Prince conceived of the Clinic as a teaching and research center in Abnormal

Psychology. He came to Lowell with his proposal for several reasons: because he knew he would get a favorable hearing from his old friend and classmate; because he was convinced that research in psychopathology would flourish in a university setting, at a comfortable remove from the distracting practical demands made upon students at medical schools, the traditional locus of study in the field; and because he wanted to be remembered for his contributions to science. "La Salpêtrière is a monument to Dr. Charcot," Prince declared just before he died; "I want no other monument than the Psychological Clinic."

He had his way, largely because Harvard was quick to take hold of a bargain. President Lowell accepted Prince's offer, appointing him—at a token salary—to head the new Clinic, beginning in September 1926. L. J. Henderson was just as quick to recognize the perfect fit between Harry's interests and the full-time assistantship built into Prince's budget. He arranged meetings between the two, he lobbied Lowell, and he used his influence with the members of the Department of Philosophy and Psychology—which would have jurisdiction over the Clinic—on his old protégé's behalf. Thanks to these and other "high-hushed finaglings," the chances looked good. Henderson coached Harry through delicate passages with Prince— who quite properly counted the candidate's lack of formal training and clinical experience against him—and provided regular, generally optimistic forecasts. "I have the impression that you will be offered the job unless Prince objects," he wrote early in March. "Efforts will be made to please him."

Within a few weeks Henderson had helped to set up a dinner meeting with the faculty members in Philosophy and Psychology. Harry was summoned by telegram to join a large group—including Whitehead, William Ernest Hocking, James Woods, Ralph Perry, William McDougall, Henderson, and two or three others—at the Harvard Club in Boston. The evening went very well. The hosts took turns sitting next to the candidate. Whitehead reminisced pleasantly about the old days at Trinity College, Cambridge. Ralph Perry was pleased to learn that Harry had once taken one of his courses and apparently made little of his former student's failure to remember anything about the experience. Grades, happily, did not

141

come up. Perry mentioned in passing that his summer plans included a visit to Salamanca. "To visit Unamuno?" Harry asked. "Who?" Perry replied, giving the candidate an opportunity to shine. McDougall was more self-conscious in creating an opening for Harry. He had just come from a session with Margery, the famous Boston medium, who claimed to be able to exude animate material—she called it "ectoplasm"—from her body. McDougall had pocketed a sample, which he passed to Harry, asking him what he made of it. "Rabbit's lung" came the response, an informed guess that accorded precisely with the good-natured McDougall's view. The others were at once amused and impressed.

Harry received a one-year appointment as Research Fellow in Abnormal and Dynamic Psychology, at a salary of $1,800, toward the end of April. It was, he rightly observed some years later, "another glorious instance of chance and the prepared mind." He was the first to admit that he was unqualified for the job; though he had done a good deal of reading, he was quite without the requisite clinical background. Prince made the same point, though he readily acknowledged that there were no properly qualified applicants. In such a vacuum, Harry looked very promising. He was an M.D., a seasoned research scientist, and his commitment to the field was manifest. Henderson's support was of course vital, especially when Prince, glimpsing the broad streak of independence in Harry's nature, began to back away from the appointment. But the Department finally approved, and Prince made the best of the situation. "I am delighted to learn that you have been appointed," he wrote. He went even further in a letter to Harry's sister, Virginia, whom he knew socially. "I may say to you, if not to him," Prince confided, "that if he finds this field of research as interesting as he anticipates that I shall look forward to having him succeed me in the chair as head of the department."

Jo was happy to rejoin her family in Boston. Mrs. Rantoul found a house on fashionable Brimmer Street, which held the Murrays for two years, until Fannie bought them a larger and even finer place, around the corner on Mt. Vernon Street. It was an ideal location, bordering on the Charles, convenient to downtown Boston, within easy reach of good schools for Josephine, and close enough to Har-

142

vard that Harry could walk when he chose to. Life was outwardly uneventful. The Murrays gave one night each week to leisure—entertaining, or the theater. Harry occasionally socialized with old friends—Charles Codman, Jefferson Coolidge, Ives Gammel, Hans Zinsser, and others—while Jo gave her free time to numerous charitable organizations. Otherwise, Harry worked full time at his new vocation. The Mt. Vernon Street house spoke rather boldly of his concerns. A picture of Melville's mother, Maria—a gift from Fannie—dominated the entry. Just beyond were the large living and dining rooms. The second floor held a sitting room decorated with pictures and expensive bibelots sent by "Nanon" (as Fannie was known to the family). Down the hall was Harry's spacious study, filled with books, whaling pictures and curios, and painted to resemble the ocean (the floor was cobalt blue flecked with white, the walls were a washed blue). There were two floors of bedrooms above.

During the warmest of the summer months they left Boston for the country. Late June and July found them on their farm in Topsfield, which Harry purchased in 1927. Here they were just a few miles from the Rantoul summer estate in nearby Beverly Farms and within easy commuting distance of Cambridge. When at home on the farm, Harry worked in another symbolic study, this one painted in shades of red, orange, and yellow to suggest the inside of a volcano—or the "infernal regions," as Harry remarked years later. "It's a pre-creative thing. It may take you over into insanity. But it's the eruption of the id; eruption of the unconscious." In August they moved further north, to Mid-River Farm, the Murray outpost in the Thousand Islands. Here more than ever Harry faced what Josephine's governess, Ann McDonald, referred to as his lifelong "struggle to get people to leave him alone." Jo was especially hard on readers, Harry often complained. She would interrupt constantly, though always with the best of intentions. A few years more at Mid-River Farm, and Harry built himself a small, sturdy retreat, at a decent remove from the main house, where he could retire for study. "No Hawkers," he called it.

It was probably just as well for Harry that the Clinic got off to a slow start. They were quartered in two small rooms on the third floor of Emerson Hall, an arrangement that proved very trying to the patience of the philosophers and psychologists. Space was tight; and they were uneasy with clinical practice, especially as it involved hypnosis, which Whitehead—among others—considered unsafe. Prince's course on abnormal psychology featured demonstrations in which his subjects—almost always veteran hysterics with whom he had worked for years—dipped promptly into trances and then performed impressively under his control. Harry admired Prince for his skill and learned something of hypnosis from him; but he was frustrated in his efforts to duplicate the master's sensational effects and troubled that the shadow of P. T. Barnum fell a little too palpably over the entire operation. He complied only minimally with Prince's suggestion that he attend psychopathic clinics at local hospitals. He much preferred reading at home or developing experiments—on variations in the galvanic skin response occasioned by the loss of normal consciousness—with Donald MacKinnon, his first graduate student. Fortunately, it was easy enough to keep a distance from Prince, who usually took his departure once classes were over.

Harry was promoted from Research Assistant to Instructor in Abnormal and Dynamic Psychology for a second year, beginning in September 1927. Things improved dramatically at the Clinic, in good part because they moved to an old house, owned by Harvard, at 19 Beaver Street (since demolished to make way for Dunster House). The building was dilapidated and unfurnished but happily remote from Emerson Hall. Funds for furniture and equipment were in short supply (a chronic problem), but Harry did not hesitate to make up the difference out of his own pocket (a perennial solution). He continued to teach with Prince in Abnormal Psychology, now the permanent replacement for a course formerly given by McDougall, who had resigned. In addition, Harry offered his own seminar on the Psychology of Human Personality, which attracted a sizable audience of students, both graduate and undergraduate, with an interest in the ideas of Freud. His stammering was especially pronounced in the new course, but it did little to dampen student enthusiasm. Indeed, it seemed to make him "more charming," recalled Donald MacKinnon. Harry began to see a few patients on a casual, nonpaying basis. He found almost immediately that Freud's ideas were much better suited than Jung's to the treatment of ordinary neurotics. One of his first cases, a protracted affair involving a boy with a severe compulsion neurosis, drew him into the center of a heated medical controversy. Prince complained to his friends at the Tavern Club that he had had little success in trying to get to know his junior colleague. Still, failing health obliged him to turn more and more of his teaching over to Harry and to bow before the necessity of retirement. Despite his misgivings— including a thoroughgoing hostility to Freud—Prince satisfied himself, and then persuaded President Lowell, that Harry was the best candidate available to replace him as Director of the Clinic. "I am somewhat discouraged and at times feel that my old hour glass had about run out," he wrote to his successor during the summer of 1928. He died the following year.

Harry could not have foreseen in 1925 that the Clinic would fall into his hands three years later. Nor, in the light of his interests and ambitions, could he have imagined a more promising development. Prince's brief tenure had given him time to catch up intellectually and to establish himself in the university environment. With his appointment to a three-year renewable assistant professorship in 1928, he was ready to take over. When the Clinic was moved again, this time to much more permanent quarters in a clapboard two-story house at 64 Plympton Street, he lost little time in making the place his own. He filled the house with family furniture, much of it antique, which he brought out of storage. There was a library upstairs devoted entirely to literature; another downstairs given to psychology. Harry had his office just off the landing on the second floor. Expensive paintings and *objets,* dominantly maritime and Melvillian in theme, were everywhere on display. The main meeting room was spacious and featured a large table used for staff meetings and for the luncheons that soon became a fixture in the legend of the Clinic. Harry invited leading scholars and public figures— poets, novelists, scientists of all kinds, political types, entertainers, many of them his close friends—to join the staff at fine midday meals, carefully prepared on the premises. The talk was wide-ranging, open, and stimulating. Harry presided with great tact and even greater pleasure in the civilized adventure in ideas that he had fostered. Many came away feeling that the life of the mind could be no better than this.

It took a little longer to settle on the specific mission of the Clinic. Harry was interested from the beginning in studying unconscious psychic processes; this general objective was never in doubt. Such is the implicit thrust of his "What to Read in Psychology?" a brief survey for the modern newcomer to the field, published in 1927. The article opens with the observation that modern man, bereft of "religious fables" and without faith, is "unable to rationalize his conduct on a dramatic and cosmic scale." Life on such terms is "a mean and paltry thing." The article concludes that books on psychology may sharpen the mind but provide scant spiritual nourishment. For that, we "must be initiated into deeper mysteries." In between, Harry gestures in the direction of a remedy, though without specific references to his own recent deep diving. "What is strictly new about modern psychology concerns itself with the unconscious," he observes, "and it is of this that I write." Freud is the great innovator, a modern revolutionary who fired "a shot that *really was* heard around the world." Harry features Freud's work, along with selections from Jung, McDougall, Prince, Janet, and from the literary and philosophical writings of C. K. Ogden and I. A. Richards. As Rodney Triplet points out, contemporary biological and behavioral theories, not to mention current work in experimental psychology, are largely excluded. This is so because they do not address themselves to Harry's real concern, the modern malaise. Theorists in abnormal psychology find a place in his curriculum because they lead us back to the unconscious, the wellspring of human spirituality. Great literature, he suggests, is an even richer source of such nourishment.

Like so much that Harry wrote, "What to Read in Psychology?" is a veiled report on his own experience. It is perfectly clear from our privileged vantage that the "deeper mysteries" he alludes to have personal referents in Christiana, Melville, and Jung. His espousal of "the hypothesis that derives all ideal and divine love, as well as the creative instinct in art, from the principle of Eros" is similarly grounded. In fact, though it is brief and oblique and woe-

146

fully overwritten, "What to Read in Psychology?" is Harry's first public declaration of what we may think of as his program—the study of the human condition, with close attention to its variety and complexity over time, with an emphasis on its interior and spiritual dimensions, and with an eye to its amelioration. It was the vocation of a scientist and physician who had abandoned the faiths of his childhood, plunged boldly through love and literature into the unconscious self, and returned with what he took to be an answer to the troubles of his time. Driven by curiosity, ambition, desire, and no little narcissism—by what he called "the sanguine surplus"—Harry embraced the biggest picture of all.

The Clinic, a main branch of this enterprise, was a site for the systematic study of human nature. Here Harry would attempt to combine the insights of Freud, Jung, Melville, and Christiana Morgan with the brand of imaginative scientific inquiry that he admired in Henderson and Whitehead. To the degree that it was possible, he wanted to make the unconscious available for objective scrutiny. At the same time, following Aristotle, he recognized the necessity for accurately gauging the degree of precision appropriate to one's chosen field of study. There was much below the threshold of consciousness, he knew, that eluded the web of science. The pursuit of this vital but elusive human dimension would find its proper place in the biography of Melville and in Harry's continuing relationship with Christiana. To some extent at least, these activities were present to the life of the Clinic. It was part of the magic of the place that it welcomed—indeed, advocated—the mingling of art and science, the creative interplay of objectivity and intuition. Still, there was much in his personal life that Harry was unwilling to share. Here, to be sure, was a contradiction. What profit, after all, in secrets, especially in a setting dedicated to their unmasking? Yet Harry had his limits. His private explorations of the unconscious would interpenetrate with the work at the Clinic, but never completely.

It is tribute to the success of Harry's undertaking that so much of what he stood for has now merged with the taken-for-granted in his discipline. It was not obvious in 1928 that the Clinic, with Harry at its helm, had a future in American psychology. To the contrary, there was good reason to suppose that the rootless, under-funded, and still groping little institution might falter badly. Harry wanted the Clinic to become a bridge, as he later put it, between "the old academic psychology and the new dynamic psychology." It was foremost among many related problems that the old guard were not inclined to smile on his operation. The American academy in the 1920s made no room for abnormal psychology and psychother-apy, which were condescended to as "applied" fields and relegated to the medical schools. Personality research was rarely undertaken on a systematic basis. The American Psychological Association had about a thousand members in 1928 (as compared with about 100,000 in 1990), most of them experimental in orientation. This is to say that they consciously emulated the methods and objectives of physical science. Cornell's Edward Titchener, reductionist par ex-cellence and advocate of psychology as pure science, and John B. Watson, father of behaviorism, were dominant figures. Gestalt psy-chology had not yet taken root in this country. Freud and his follow-ers were not unknown, but they had virtually no influence with leading academicians, who viewed them with suspicion. Mc-Dougall—who left Harvard for Duke University in 1927—was an exception, but his professional influence was in steep decline. The major journals—the *Psychological Review* and the *American Journal of Psychology*—were almost exclusively devoted to narrowly defined ex-perimental research, with copious attention to sensory perception and experimental apparatus. Papers on behaviorism were also on the rise, while psychodynamic psychology was little heard from.

American academic psychology, in short, was either hostile or indifferent to the kind of work that Harry wanted to pursue. The climate at Harvard was representative in this respect of the broader professional environment. The chairman in psychology, Edwin G. Boring, a devoted student—as he put it—of "the brilliant, erudite, magnetic, charming Titchener," was a scientific purist and a noted historian in the field of experimental psychology. His suspicion of Freud was confirmed by an unsuccessful analysis with Hanns Sachs in 1934–1935. Boring was understandably resentful of the fact that Prince and Lowell had settled on the Clinic without so much as notifying him. It is not unlikely that his feelings spilled over on to

Harry, whose class affiliations and personal style were additional sources of irritation to a man raised among poor, rather astringent Quakers. Boring was critical of Henderson; and his opposition to Harry's candidacy as Prince's successor grew more vigorous when he learned that his Ph.D. was in biochemistry and not, as he had originally assumed, in psychology. Boring's preference in colleagues ran to Karl S. Lashley, a radically empirical neuropsychologist and former student of Watson, whom he was trying to recruit, as Mc-Dougall's replacement, from Chicago. Lashley declined, at least for the time being, and in this Harry was very fortunate; for in Lashley's place, at the insistence of the philosophers, came Gordon Allport, a future eminence in personality theory and an effective supporter of the Clinic.

Harry's barely restrained contempt for the opposition cannot have made things any easier. He came into academic psychology on the wings of an encounter with charismatic, all-embracing Carl Jung. Somewhat naively, he supposed that he would meet people of a similarly broad gauge at the university. Instead, he was "absolutely amazed" to find that most of his new peers were narrowly specialized, rigidly empirical, and devoid of any burning interest in human beings. By comparison with the medical people Harry had known, they seemed drab and decidedly second-rate. They shared none of his fascination with "the darker, blinder recesses of the psyche." To the contrary, Harry soon learned that delving into the unconscious was "anathema to the majority of academic psychologists who were militantly engaged in a competitive endeavor to mould psychology in the image of physics. . . . To be among the leaders in this race it was necessary to legislate against the 'blinder strata,' to keep away from those events which intellectuals at large assumed to be the subject matter of psychology, to disregard individual and typological differences, and to approximate universality and certainty by measuring the lawful relationships of narrowly restricted forms of animal behavior, of physiological processes in general, and of the simplest sensory and sensorimotor processes of human beings in particular. In short, methodological excellence was dictating (more than it did in any other science) the phenomena to be investigated." As for Watson's "proposal to limit the science of psychology to concepts that pointed only to perceptibles," it struck Harry, "the former biochemist—all of whose critical concepts had referred to imperceptibles—as a naive, juvenile perversity." Psychophysics, as practiced by Boring's protegé, S. S. Stevens, he dismissed as "eye, ear, nose and throat psychology." It was guilty, as experimental psychology in general was guilty, of what he called "scientism"—of sending "a mountain of [scientific] ritual" after "a mouse of fact more dead than alive."

Harry was only slightly less disillusioned with Prince. He admired his predecessor's ingenuity in devising experiments and paid him homage, in a memorial written for the *Harvard Alumni Bulletin,* as the only American to make a "thoroughly original and authentic contribution" to the early exploration of unconscious psychical processes. He was also careful to contrast Prince with those academicians "so pedantically circumscribed" in their thinking "as to exclude from their horizons a consideration of the unconscious psyche." But in the midst of much praise Harry makes note of Prince's "exhibitionist vein," his "brusque, erratic, and volatile temperament," and the utter lack in his makeup of the "artistic sensibility" and "fine cultural discrimination" required of a fully rounded intellectual. This latter shortcoming, in combination with misplaced scientific rigor, rendered Prince insensitive to "the more mysterious, subtle, and poetical facts of subjective experience" and thus hostile to the genius of Freud and Jung. As the result, during his later years he "fell out of the mainstream of contemporary psychopathological thought." As if to lend ironic emphasis to his critique, Harry frames Prince's career in a description of the unconscious that features leading Freudian and Jungian ideas. Their bold innovations, he suggests, will in time "transform our most axiomatic propositions of value, and hence our ethics and our religious sentiments." While Prince missed the chance to participate in this revolution, his successor, it is implied, will not.

Privately, Harry found Prince coarse and insensitive. He bridled at the suggestion that the Clinic should model its future on the founder's ideas. No doubt he shared Jung's view that Prince was prudishly deficient in self-knowledge, and Freud's, that his account of dissociation was insufficiently dynamic. He was inclined to agree with those students who found the old man's teaching disorganized and repetitious. It was clear to Robert White, one of the first graduate students at the Clinic, that Harry was impatient with his senior colleague and restless to get on with his own agenda. This included an increased interest in normal psychological functioning (and thus a movement toward Allport's domain) and a concomitant decrease in attention to psychopathology. Harry continued for a time to work with hypnosis, but in the growing conviction that Prince's claims for the technique were inflated. His first research paper in psychology—"Hypnotizability as a Personality Trait"— and his last to touch substantially on hypnosis, is based on research undertaken with Herbert Barry and Donald MacKinnon in 1928 and 1929. Their results indicate that suggested correlations between hypnotizability and other elements of personality—dissociation, submissiveness, extraversion, intelligence, and so on—have little scientific support. This was apparently discouraging, though Harry was little surprised, and hardly set back, by the outcome. In fact, the paper seems to have been of value as the occasion for putting Morton Prince and hypnosis behind him.

It was probably not long after Harry's takeover as Director that 64 Plympton was first described as having "wisteria on the outside, hysteria on the inside." Certainly it was lively. Harry's lectures, which he delivered in the large, converted basement, drew capacity crowds. Graduate students, bored with the experimental program at Emerson Hall, turned out in increasing numbers. They were attracted both by Harry's independent variations on Freud and Jung and by the comfortable, intellectually stimulating environment at the Clinic. Donald MacKinnon, Isabelle Kendig, Robert White, Saul Rosenzweig, and H. A. Wolff were among those who worked closely with the new Director. Their research increased in volume and began to find a common focus. True, hysteria of sorts had its place on the inside. Harry and Rosenzweig sometimes locked horns; controversy flared up over the use of hypnosis; and funds were forever in short supply. Moreover, it was now clear that Boring could not be relied upon to support the Clinic.

But none of this weighed very heavily on Harry's spirit. He was harassed and overworked and delighted with it all. "Things have come in so fast during the last two years," he complained to Barach in 1929; "however, I do not hurry, have no publisher's dates, promises to myself or anyone else. I am so happy and serene that I am ashamed to acknowledge it." His high spirits are equally on display in a piece he prepared for the *Harvard Crimson* early in the same year. David Riesman, then an aspiring undergraduate reporter, came to the Clinic looking for a story. The result was a full page article headed "Professor Murray Describes Department of Abnormal Psychology." Harry's tone is intermittently solemn and irreverent, playful, even mischievous, but throughout confident. Harvard is a "coolbed of conservatism," he jests; "our professors are by nature prudent, our students docile." He speculates ironically on why "a university first fashioned by high churchmen should admit this troublesome child within its august portals." More seriously, he insists that Harvard needs the Clinic, just as "psychopathology needs the university." Espousing Whitehead's philosophy of organism—which "dissolves the old dichotomy of mind and matter"— he celebrates the variety and zestful iconoclasm of his field. "Let a man once smack his lips on abnormal psychology and it will lead him to the end of his days on a hunt through the cultural activities of man to find an answer to his questions." Harry's comically voracious figure of speech catches something of the headlong excitement that he brought to his work at the Clinic. It is all here, he exulted; "there is no end to it."

"Your life is yourself," Jung wrote to Harry, just a day before the *Crimson* piece appeared. "Nothing matters but the completion of the self." This was seductive but perilous advice. How easy it would be, Harry saw, to become infatuated with an inflated conception of the self. He traced his own narcissism to "an uprush from the unconscious of feelings and emotions that had been held down" since childhood. With Melville, Christiana had been instrumental in the awakening of his buried self. She was of course similarly stirred by Harry and shared his sense of elation and of peril. Theirs was "a strange relationship," she acknowledged in her notebook for June 1, 1925, "and one which for the first time in my life I fear. I am taken beyond my powers. I am made strong. I am given my own life, which by myself I am hardly conscious of. I see and understand my own spirit. . . . It is strange this effect of looking into a mirror and find[ing] that the image comes back intensified, clear cut, resplendent. I had thought this only possible as a response to art. I am greatly and terribly moved to find it in a human relationship. Its dangers are manifest. Narcissus gazing into the pool."

Christiana was less fearful of self-absorption than of self-engulfment, of a descent without return into the labyrinth of the unconscious. She was also apprehensive about Harry. He was so involved in ideas, so detached, so quick to rise to the mind. "There is no genial basking in the friendly presence on his part," she complained. Her notebook for May 1925 records a dialogue between them in which she accuses Harry of holding himself apart, of engaging with other people only that he may study them. "You give greatly of your intellect," she observes, "but you give no warmth." He concedes the point but adds in his own defense, "I take now to give later. I want to give with a great gesture." The exchange is finally indecisive, involving her unanswered appeal for intimacy and his unfilled promise to deliver it. Christiana feared that she might be nothing more than a mirror for Harry's restless mind, a datum in his cool calculus of human motive. She wanted the "great gesture" to be theirs, an outpouring of heart and head, passion and science, in celebration of their union. But would he go along? Could he rise above mere science into art?

The relationship between Harry and Christiana—the dyad—is fully recorded in notes, journals, letters, dialogues of the kind just quoted, and in draft chapters of unpublished books. Virtually all of this writing is Christiana's; she was to be the archivist and chronicler of the affair. But the records are seldom literal ones. The lovers had more than a literal transcript in mind. In many cases the same events appear in more than one place and give evidence of revision—omission, elaboration, dramatization—always perforce involving interpretation. The dialogue just quoted, for example, appears to have been reconstructed from memory at some remove from the actual event. It is conspicuously a construction. Much of what Christiana left of herself and Harry is just as unguardedly semifictional.

The point to be drawn here is not a simple one. Christiana

wanted to preserve her experience because she felt, as Harry did, that the dyad might become a new age *La Vita Nuova.* She was Beatrice, source of inspiration, while Harry was Dante, the coordinating intelligence of their exemplary union. The literary motive was with them almost from the beginning. But for Christiana there was increasingly a note of desperation in the effort to record and enhance. There is everywhere the suggestion that experience could never rise to the romance in her imagination and that in her revisions she was drawing a limited, transient reality back into alignment with her dreams. But her dreams, it is vital to add, were not uniformly or even dominantly taken up with romantic fulfillment. "Good night, dear one," she wrote from Zurich in September 1925. "Keep all your shining armor. Let no one take it from you but me." If there is a trace of ambiguity here, it is slight by comparison with her appeal, earlier in the same letter, for assurances that "with us there is no destroying—only creativeness. For once we have cheated the law of paradoxes. Haven't we in this triumphed over the opposites? Tell me that there is no destruction, no ugliness, only creativeness, and beauty, and a new strength." But of course the mood of triumph surfaces amidst shadows of defeat and betrayal. Such fears arise on one side out of doubts, clearly expressed, about Harry's readiness for the prescribed romantic role; but they arise as well from Christiana's characteristic inclination to expect the worst and to cast herself in tragic parts. Suffering, mysterious and unrelieved, is the key to the anima's authority with men. Animas are not for saving. Against this backdrop, it is willy-nilly Harry's part to fail as the romantic hero and in doing so to precipitate the tragic denouement that Christiana had more deeply in mind for herself. They both glimpsed this dimension to their relationship, even as they both most often denied it. Still, the dialogue of May 1925 ends with a passage from Melville's *Mardi,* in which Taji confronts the possibility of failure in his perilous search for "the world of mind." He seems to speak for Christiana in accepting the prospect of defeat, but only when it is construed in romantic terms, as a tragedy of Promethean defiance. "If after all these fearful fainting trances, the verdict be, the golden heaven was not gained;—yet, in bold quest thereof, better to sink in boundless deeps, than float on vulgar shoals; and give me, ye Gods, an utter wreck, if wreck I do."

Christiana went to Zurich in September of 1925 with a long handwritten list of questions for Jung. These she kept, later typing them on five single-spaced pages as part of the history of the dyad. She opens by casting herself as Ahab, furiously independent, at odds with society, a romantic rebel living only to strike out at an elusive reality. At the same time that she follows Ahab in demanding a unified vision, she finds the spectacle of irreconcilable opposites "thrilling and moving." She is witness to opposing forces of creation and destruction in herself; the latter, she admits, spring to life when she is with Harry. At such times she feels unhappy but very powerful. "Why," she goes on, "am I predestined to the tragic sense of life? Why is everything dark rather than light? . . . Why in Art do I hate everything that seems overflowing and exuberant? and can only enjoy something in which I can see the elemental struggle of the soul, the agony about something?" The relevance of Ishmael's observation on Ahab—"There is a wisdom that is woe; but there is a woe that is madness"—was not lost on her.

Christiana locates her problem in a personal conflict between thought and feeling. "My thought can and does inhibit my feeling—even sexual feeling. When I am in the country all thought goes and I regain my sex feeling. I cannot seem to make them work together." She regards her pronounced thinking function as masculine. It makes people afraid of her; it inhibits her maternal impulses; and it makes her much prefer the company of men. At the same time that she enjoys masculine habits of thought, however, Christiana admits that her own mind is "definitely illogical and feminine." She goes on to describe herself as an introvert, allowing that she is often made fearful by the sense that she is poised at the edge of a great gulf. She admits to a craving for stimulants. "Is this an effort to increase psychic activity, to overcome inhibitions, or both?" She associates her creativity with the unconscious but sees no way to avoid "the neurotic strain" that attends its cultivation. As an alternative activity, she has been advised to work as Harry's associate in the study of psychology. What, she asks implicitly, does Jung make of all this?

During meetings spread over about two weeks in late September and early October, he told Christiana pretty much what she had come to hear. This is hardly surprising. Her questions, amounting to a tentative Jungian self-analysis illustrated out of Melville, were really answers seeking Jung's confirmation. This he readily provided. Christiana wrote excitedly to Harry that Jung's ideas opened "the possibility of a truly great advance, an advance equal in magnitude to that of Christianity." The unconscious, for centuries held in check by religion and explored at great peril by Melville and Nietzsche, can now "be used in the service of a heightened consciousness without insanity or the engulfing of the personality as a result." The old dogmas have failed, she insists; so has "the solution of the age—Science. In the end we have come back to ourselves. The only thing we believe in is ourself." Jung has made great strides on his own, she continues in a closely following letter, but "the full philosophy remains to be worked out. Let's do it, Harry! To go on with what Jung has begun would be the biggest thing that could be done at the present time. Is there a bigger whale or a whiter whale than the chains of the outworn attitudes which fetter and hinder the spirit?"

Christiana was just as excited by what she took to be the drift of Jung's response to Melville's *Mardi*. The book is evidence, he said, that the novelist squandered his libido on an idealized conception of woman. This was the psychological reflex of his refusal "to recognize his sexuality, to accept his anima in life, in the flesh . . . as Jung put it, 'to be up to his shoulders in the mud.'" While Melville pursued his barren ideal into the sea of the unconscious, his soul languished because it was not fed by real life. *Moby-Dick* and *Pierre* dramatize his terrible decline and serve as a cautionary tale to those in similar straits. The task, Christiana goes on, is to forge a synthesis of body and soul, to mingle feeling with thought, to countenance multiplicity, to invest sexuality with the spirit. "I understand now even more than before," she concludes, "why you and I have talked to each other through Melville. Can we now be the gateway into life for each other, dear one?"

It seems unlikely that Jung took Melville this far. Dyads were not his line. While he made no objection on principle to the love affair between his clients, he cautioned that the present instability of Harry's life would probably work against them. Still, Christiana made the most of even the slenderest encouragement. She reached out to Harry as the answer to an old longing for beauty, passion, and a place in history. "There are big things in the air," she wrote. "I need you." It mattered little that Jung found her too much the thinking type, too abstract and rational, too masculine. "You have killed your love," he said, presumably referring to her shortcomings as wife and mother. He added that her intellect was an obstacle to creativity—"I haven't learned to let myself be taken possession of,"— Christiana explained to Harry. But she was half-wedded to her alleged defect, especially as there was no shortage of powerful feeling in her life. Harry, she knew, was the true intellectual in the relationship. His complaints about the incoherence of her letters were, quite ironically, a source of reassurance on this score. The point, after all, was to achieve a balance of head and heart. "It seems to me impossible that any thinking individual of the present could fail to know in his own life the fact of the intellect being too far advanced," she declared. "The body can scarcely support the present weight of the head." Between them, if Christiana had her way, they would set the balance straight, in the dyad, in a psychology of whole human beings, and in their example to the world.

If the visit to Zurich gave rise to serious concerns, they had to do with the emergence of a radical turn in Christiana's thought and with the fear that Harry might not be able to follow her lead. It is fair to say that she was the more adventurous of the two, if we add that an admixture of desperation on her side was a good part of the difference between them. "For some people," she wrote, "the only clarity in life is in themselves." But in their quest for the truth, such people cannot get past the "dark chaos of unintelligible life" they discover within. It was a variation on a lesson out of *Pierre*— "appallingly vacant as vast is the soul of a man!"—that Christiana witnessed in herself. Still, there was a sensible drift to her purchase on chaos. Harry's scruples, an unreadiness to appear selfish or to give pain, were potential obstacles to the fruition of the dyad. At a distance of several thousand miles, he had begun to waver, most especially out of concern for Jo and Will. But he was also determined to protect his new career, both from distraction and from the varieties of scandal—divorce and kindred personal embarrassments—that had cost others at Harvard and elsewhere their jobs.

It was the effect of Christiana's broadly antinomian declarations to sweep aside all such illusory constraints and to embrace unharnessed impulse, even if it led to almost certain disaster. "Isn't this the very kernel of the tragic sense of life," she asked, "the chaos and fecundity and in short the meaninglessness of life, providing the only meaning." But would Harry see it this way? Would he be able to discount his misgivings as supine illusion? Or, alternatively, would the weight of Christiana's conviction bear him along, misgivings and all? Perhaps, deep down, Christiana was gambling that Harry would capitulate to desire only on condition that she took the initiative, and the burden of moral responsibility with it. Was it the anima's part, after all, to ease the white knight's way to forbidden pleasures?

Whatever the case exactly, much that passed between them in the months that followed had implicitly to do with measuring and distributing the moral responsibility for having one another. Christiana returned to England where Will was to complete his graduate work. She wrote during the winter that they had decided to go back to Zurich the following June for six months of analysis with Jung. In April she announced that the Old Man was willing to see them all just before going on holiday in mid-summer. Robert Edmond Jones would be along. Wouldn't Harry and Jo come, too? He replied that they would, and that Alfred Cohn and his wife would join them, both for meetings with Jung in Zurich and to spend a month or so afterward touring Germany.

Christiana's early sessions with Jung, during June and July, centered on her dreams. These strongly confirmed Jung's impression that she was burying her feminine spirituality under an unnatural weight of masculine rationality. This, he said, alluding to Plato's *Symposium*, would alienate men. "What fascinates a man is Diotima—the mystery. This she forfeits when she becomes Socrates." Jung had no difficulty persuading Christiana that she had it within her power as Harry's anima to awaken his spirit. He compared her to "a pioneer woman. Your function," he assured her, "is to create a man. Some women create children—but it is greater to create a man. If you create Murray you will have done something very fine for the world." This explained to Christiana's satisfaction why she

158

had so little feeling for her child and why she felt fully alive only in male company. Most importantly, of course, it represented the cultivation of the dyad as a vocation, a call to serve Harry, and through him the world.

Christiana was also very frank in discussing the all-important sexual side of her relationship with Harry. "I feel him to be clutching and tearing at me for something," she complained, "as though he wanted to tear the secret of his own love out of me—and at times with him I feel absolutely exhausted and drained dry. Although he gives me much of mind & spirit he gives me nothing of warmth and of earthiness. Even last summer I felt that I was a divine goddess to him and he kissed my feet—I fertilized his mind, he felt creative as he had never felt it before—but he fled from my lips. I somehow felt this and told him that I couldn't be a spirit—an inspiration—that he must love my body as well as my soul. And that same night out on the beach he came to me quite naked and I touched him all over with my hands—but even then there was a sort of white and sublime purity." Jung replied that men were less spiritual in their sexuality than women. Harry recoiled from the sexual as from a descent into the pit, and diverted his erotic energy into intellectual activities. His "building great structures of ideas is autoerotic," Jung explained; "they are terribly highly sexualized." Christiana's task as anima was to bring Harry to recognize that "no religion has so violated eros as Christianity," and that "sexuality is the sina qua non of spirituality." In the complete sexual relationship that he urged her to pursue, "the man becomes more the woman and the woman more the man—so that in complete fulfillment you are neither man nor woman." Christiana made reference to the price of such ecstasy for Jo and Will. "Harry is much more tied by pity than I am," she admitted. "He can't bear to hurt—and he always says of me that he wishes he had that quality more. I am afraid that he will blame on me any hurt that we might inflict on his wife." Jung's response to her concerns, if he made one, has not survived.

Harry's hesitation to take fire sexually had thus been a matter of concern to Christiana for some time. It was important in itself, of course, but it was also the leading obstacle to the relationship that she wanted above all things in life. In a letter to Harry earlier that year she goes on at length, and in rather intimate detail, about her new friend, Billy Richards, an American traveling in Europe. He is fascinating to her because of his unsuccessful effort "to throw off his Puritan background in regard to sex." Such artificial restraint, she complains, "kills the creative life." The implied comment on Harry's hesitation, and the prod to his jealousy, surely registered.

It may be that Christiana was preparing Harry for the most crucial question of all, about the future of the dyad. She brought it up in a letter of June 17, written in the midst of her early analysis with Jung, and probably shared with him. "You have spoken to me and I have spoken to you," she begins, "from the innermost places where storms and profoundest quiet lie together in dark embrace. From that terrible and beautiful world can we now come and speak to others?" It was time, in short, to reveal their intentions as lovers, as a dyad, to Jo and Will. "If you don't want to do this, dear Harry," Christiana continues, "then let this letter go." But the only way to "know whether our love is great enough to be fulfilled is to test it against the love we have for Will and Jo. And we will have to take their pain and somehow or other carry it with them." To break with Will is inconceivable, "because him, too, I love. And it must be the same with you and Jo." But can it be made to work? "Perhaps the pain of the others will be too much for us. . . . You must not feel that you carry me, nor I you. . . . At such moments one is quite alone."

Christiana closes by making it clear that she plans to discuss the matter with Will right away, without waiting for Harry's response. This was a bold, preemptive move—a display of initiative, commitment, and of confidence that Harry would follow suit. "If you wish," she reiterates, "let all that I have said in this letter go by. After all we are human, and we may undertake something that will be too great for either of us to manage. We might live thereby, or we might destroy ourselves and others, for we would have to walk where there are few footsteps to show us any way." "If you want," she adds in a postscript, "show this letter to Jo." Christiana's intentions, and her willingness to bear the moral weight of having taken the first long step, could not have been clearer.

It was a proposal that Harry could not refuse. When he and Jo arrived in Zurich, they took a room in the Morgan's hotel. There was ample occasion for lovemaking, and for making grand plans. The dyad was now a sure thing. Christiana was warm and festive, if rather annoyingly chummy with Billy Richards, who had come over from England ostensibly to consult Jung. Will met with Toni Wolff, who explained how it was with lovers like Harry and Christiana. He was terribly shaken but acquiesced and did his best to remain on friendly terms with his rival. Jo had a meeting of her own with Jung. Harry brought her to the tower in Bollingen, where Jung suggested that she join him on a walk along the lake. They sat and talked for a while, no more than twenty minutes or so. Jung insisted that Harry was no more a model of purity than other men. We are all part animal, he said. Marriage had once been Harry's ideal, but that phase had now passed. His love for Jo was enduring, but Christiana was also important to him, not least in relation to his work. The animal in men had been a burden to women for centuries, he assured her. It was an old story.

Jo came away with the impression that Jung was a dirty old man. She was of course upset, and she protested that the meeting had been a waste of time. But Jung's characterization of the affair—as base, but typically so—seems to have helped Jo to accept it. She agreed, as Will had, that divorce was out of the question. They would make the most of a bad situation. Jo was wonderful, Harry remembered, bearing up with dignity and good humor under the strain. During their driving tour with the Morgans and the Cohns she occupied herself with the pleasures of sightseeing and with the opera in Munich. But her composure finally cracked at a rathskeller in Nuremberg. Christiana was engaged with Alfred Cohn in a characteristically lively discussion of Jung. As time passed, and as the drink flowed, the speakers grew more playful, even flirtatious. Jo and Cohn's wife, who had observed the entire show in silence, finally rose in unison and walked out. The tour was never quite the same after that, and it was a relief for everyone when they finally broke up, the Morgans returning to Zurich, the rest to the States.

Satisfied now that Harry was fully committed to the dyad, Christiana was more determined than ever to explore the unconscious. For here, she felt sure, the precise direction and meaning of the

161

relationship were to be found. In early July, prompted by Jung to relinquish the intellect and to be passively receptive to the upsurge of her feelings, she had a vision of a beautiful peacock perched on a man's back, with its beak in his neck. Jung interpreted the vision as a "feeling judgment" of Harry. This was good, he said; but even better, the vision was evidence that Christiana had begun to grow. More such visions followed, as Jung helped her to master the technique he called "active imagination," which he had perfected years earlier during his own "confrontation with the unconscious." Christiana was instructed to concentrate attention on individual images as they emerged from her unconscious and to probe them for the messages they bore from below. She drew some of the images—an eye, an owl, three circles, a man drinking wine out of a double goblet—for Jung's inspection. He was pleased with her impulse to create but found the results too vague. Try to involve yourself more fully in the images, he suggested, and "paint them as beautifully as you know how." In time the visions "will be your church," he assured her, "your cathedral—the silent places of your spirit where you will find renewal."

Jung spoke from personal experience. "The years when I was pursuing my inner images were the most important in my life," he later declared; "in them everything essential was decided. . . . It was the *prima materia* for a lifetime's work." Christiana's visions came to play a similar role in the evolution of the dyad. They would be the foundation and the light, the sacred text. The Old Man was delighted with her progress. On evenings out drinking beer with his students, he would point to Christiana proudly and declare, "Here is my Olympus!" Others had visions but none that so closely approximated the symbolic clarity and richness of his own from years gone by. "You are always a living reality to me," he wrote, long after her departure from Zurich, "whereas other former patients fade away into oblivion, becoming unreal shadows in Hades." When she showed him her complete collection of illustrated visions in October, he pronounced them "very fine," enough "material for the next two or three hundred years." He reciprocated by showing her his own images before she left in November. There would be continued difficulties with Harry, he predicted, but the struggle would be well worth it. He urged Christiana to continue to summon her unconscious to the surface. In this she would become more feminine, less intellectual. "You are like Brunhilde," he said. "You have never been broken in. There ought to come to you a Siegfried who would break through your ring of fire—who would make you into a woman."

The Morgans made Cambridge, Massachusetts, their new home. Harry and Christiana had agreed that she would join him in his work, no matter where it took them; and Will had decided—taking a by now familiar route—to abandon physiology for anthropology, which he would study at Harvard. Harry was furious when Christiana turned up at her coming-home reception with Billy Richards in tow. The storm passed quickly enough, but a point of sorts seems to have been made. Will found a comfortable apartment on Memorial Drive and soon developed a friendship with the new neighbors, Alfred North Whitehead and his wife. Christiana lost no time taking her place as a volunteer at the Clinic, where she kept a safe distance from the ailing, rather baffled Morton Prince. After a good deal of looking around, she and Will found a lovely piece of property on the Parker River, just north of Boston, where they would build a small, rustic summer house. Harry meanwhile leased and furnished an apartment in Fairfax Hall, on Massachusetts Avenue just across from Harvard Yard. A well-kept secret, the rooms were to be Harry's rendezvous with Christiana for many years. As it happened, the apartment had been home a few years earlier to Kenneth Raisbeck, a friend to Thomas Wolfe, who describes the place in *Of Time and the River*.

Christiana's dreams, which began early in her analysis with Jung, continue to appear in her notebooks until well into 1928. Much more closely personal than the visions, they are troubled in predictable ways, extending and confirming patterns of ambivalence about marriage, motherhood, and the dyad. They were of scant concern to Jung—especially after the advent of the beautiful peacock—and of comparably diminished interest to Christiana. Her visions, which she found much more compelling, also continued for about eighteen months after her return home. Many of these she handprinted, illustrated, and sent along to Zurich for the Old Man's review. Harry grew concerned that her involvement with the unconscious had become too intense. Beatrice Hinkle, who took her as a patient in January 1927, agreed, advising that she suspend the visions for a while. Still, Christiana persisted and thereby earned Jung's warm approval. "Let me thank you most sincerely for your pictures and the text," he wrote in December 1927. "I think your technique has marvellously improved." He compares one of her pictures favorably with the work of St. Hildegard of Bingen, a German mystic of the twelfth century. "Your material is *most valuable* to me," he goes on. "I often think of working through it, because it seems to me as if it were a most beautiful example of the original initiation process." At about the same time, however, the visions began to round to a close, and within a few months the last of the images had made its appearance.

Beginning with the peacock in the summer of 1926, the visions had emerged steadily for nearly two years. Harry accurately estimated that there were finally more than one hundred in all. They are preserved in various forms, ranging from preliminary notebook and journal jottings with crude, preliminary sketches to carefully hand-printed prose accounts accompanied by elaborate watercolor illustrations. The content of the visions is equally various. The first fifty or so are generally brief and sharply focused on a single, arresting image—an animal, a human figure, an abstract symbol. Thereafter they unfold as continuous but episodic narratives, with movements back and forth through natural and constructed settings and featuring encounters with animal and human figures from assorted mythologies. The illustrations are generally rather spare and abstract, combining a few elements in flat, highly formalized spatial arrangements and painted with manifestly symbolic intent. They are almost hallucinatory in their sharp clarity but oddly decorative at the same time. The nightmarish potential of the images—many are violent and bloody—is moderated, if not altogether neutralized, by the pervasive evidence of design.

The overall thematic unity of the enterprise, most especially in its earlier stages, is not easily discerned. From the midst of a great profusion—of bulls, pigs, stallions, goats, rams, snakes of all colors and sizes, winged birds, golden cows, scarabs, a sphinx, satyrs, a classical youth with flute, giants, dragons, earth mothers, an Indian, wise old men, women transfixed and transfigured, spears, swords, the sun and the moon, Christ, great negroes, Indians, anonymous men and women alone and in crowds, blood and fire and water in abundance, icons, badges, crosses, spears—certain trends emerge. The journey, the transforming revelation, death and rebirth, physical and psychological metamorphosis, transcendence—these are the general topics that Christiana's very active imagination brought her back to. The earliest of the visions, which surfaced in Zurich and in the United States during the weeks just after her return, would later serve as the subject matter for Jung's Vision Seminars, which he offered on a regular basis in Zurich between 1930 and 1934 and which were published in 1976. They center on individual images of initiation and transformation, veering briefly toward apocalypse after the return home, and then settling into the first of the much longer visions, which move forward from one scene or symbolic tableau to another. About this earliest material Christiana left little comment.

The final visions—the several dozen that do not come up for analysis in Jung's seminars—are entirely of the linked, continuous variety. Unlike the earliest of Christiana's images, these have some of the qualities of an allegory by Spenser or Bunyan. We are witness to a series of fantastic episodes, most often involving challenges to the spiritual development of the female protagonist and issuing in her gradual growth toward enlightenment and wholeness. There is a wise old man who makes regular appearances, and a younger male figure who is at one point actually identified as Harry. The speaker moves toward her final goal, a large blue mountain, with the aid and protection of a magical star—the symbol, clearly, for her true self, which emerges in triumph as the mountain, and the final visions, draw near. There is development as well in the speaker's gradual growth in confidence and authority; toward the end she is more than ever the agent of the action, with power to influence the forces in her environment.

Christiana's progress toward individuation is irresistibly the theme of the later visions, manifesting itself both in the content and in her increasingly conscious control of what she produced. In clearly discernible ways, she began to take over her own story. In the eightieth of the visions she meets a man who is perishing in a land of ice. "My sin was the sin of refusal," he confesses, sounding very like Harry in a repentant mood. "I kept my body from the fires of life. I desired clarity. Now am I here where all is clear, transparent, bloodless." At one point the speaker encounters a woman who calls out to her from a dark pool. "Bel-bel-bel," she murmurs, in the manner of the mysterious, maternal guitar that speaks to Isabel—"poor Bell," as she refers to herself—in *Pierre*. The Ten Commandments are discovered and promptly declared obsolete; the modern industrial world is condemned as the last obstacle to human wholeness. Dreams and interpretive notes were also entered into the last of the vision notebooks. In June 1927 Christiana declared herself "strong—held together. I read my old trances. I am moved by them, fascinated, awed." She notes that Harry is now involved in the process, but then falls prey to anxiety as a new vision rises before her. "Oh this is terrible. Perhaps my feet are no longer on the ground. Perhaps I have lost myself and am being swept [away] & will never get back again. . . . I am afraid. I will stop this. I refuse to feel this sensation any more." But another vision promptly follows. Three days later, exhausted and still afraid, she summons the courage to be strong for a while longer, to see the visions through. "I must dare to be great, not to step things down—to make things small. I must dare to live to express this much life."

Despite the very positive drift of the visions, then, Christiana found the process arduous and even painful. Her states of mind are characteristically extreme, moving suddenly and rather frequently between positive poles of calm or elation and negative phases of fear and depression. The successful completion of the visions did little to modify the dominant pattern. Indeed, the pain and fatigue, it is increasingly evident, are integral for Christiana to her role as anima, as the deep diver for the dyad. Even as she asserts, with Harry's enthusiastic agreement, that "the new spirit will be wrought out by the man & the woman together," she concedes that the process leaves her feeling annihilated. She readily admits to a penchant for confusion and excess. "The destructiveness in me," she argues, "was the urge toward the unconscious, the tearing down that new life

166

might spring up." Again shouldering the moral burden for the dyad, Christiana admits that her "ruthless and daemonic" behavior has "destroyed others." But this, she adds, has been the price of their "integrity" as a couple. "Without that quality in me and your springing up to meet it, this that we have now would have been forever impossible." Nor will the painful process end. Growth for the two of them can only result from increased tension and even more tearing down. "I must dare it further and further," she declares. "I will be torn. That is inevitable."

Christiana seized upon suffering as her *raison d'etre*. She felt incomplete without pain and viewed tragedy as the only real sense to life's "meaninglessness." This is not to deny that the visions inspired intervals of optimism. In September 1927 Christiana registered a pleasurable "letting go. A sort of flowering—a new ability to release my energy in whatever I am doing. And this must have come from the progress of our relationship. The soul and the spirit are now in reality between us." Without her, she now felt sure, Harry would be "lost." But enhanced confidence had its paradoxical corollary in heightened vulnerability. For she was now more than ever lost without him, too. "The naked soul of me is for no one but you," she wrote; "without you I have none." The following January brought her to a recognition of Harry's central role as the logos for the dyad. "I want the greater clarity, the greater order, which you have. It is like a physical need for you. I hunger and thirst for you because knowing my own limitations I am unfulfilled here as in all things without you." She makes the poignant discovery, in her new power, that it is strange to feel beautiful.

The human price to be paid for the dyad surfaced only slightly less dramatically in the lives of those closest to it. Not long after the return from Europe, Will's health began to fail. At first the doctors suspected tuberculosis—the disease, according to one reliable observer, that had killed his father. Later they called it asthma. Jo had meanwhile been overtaken by bouts of uncontrollable weeping. Young Josephine could not help overhearing the sobs; nor could she understand why her father, at work in his study, made no effort to help. Harry knew that talk would only make matters worse. He had met his private commitment to give Jo more time;

167

but there was no denying the painful truth that real intimacy between them was a thing of the past. More than ever before he was struck with the vast differences between his wife and his lover. Jo didn't know she had an unconscious, while Christiana—her sister once remarked—"didn't know she had anything else." Harry was also aware that his wife suffered because their daughter always lined up on his side against fashionable Boston society. Jo wept because at times she felt very lonely in her own home.

The problems internal to the relationship—Harry's "sublime purity" and guilt, his deep commitments to the Clinic and to Melville, and Christiana's maneuvering around them—were just as formidable and just as chronic. Yet the dyad flourished, in part because so much was riding on it, in part because so much had been sacrificed in its name, and mainly because Harry and Christiana were so much in love. "We have gathered a new strength," Christiana recorded at the end of 1927, by the "complete physical expression of our love." Enhanced sexual satisfaction was a manifestation of Harry's much deeper penetration into the spiritual dimension of their common experience. Earlier in the year Christiana had written "The Creation of the Star," a brief account of the culminating phase of her visions. It was an attempt to help Harry better understand what they had both agreed was the foundation for their mission as a couple. Alternating trends toward order and disorder had finally stabilized, resulting in "a feeling of elation, a feeling that I could never be destroyed or lost or disrupted. I felt that now at last that I was secure in some deep principle of my own being." Christiana imagined that she had arrived at what Jung called individuation, a reconciliation of conscious and unconscious issuing in the emergence of the true self. A feeling of wholeness and of union with all creation was the result. She felt "healed of original sin." The star, a prominent motif in the visions, was the archetypal symbol of perfection used by her unconscious to mark the arrival at this high psychological plateau. "Man must have always sought for this," she exulted.

Harry responded with what Christiana referred to in her records as his "First Great Recognition" of her spiritual authority. Composed in September 1927, it is Harry's full, formal acknowledge-

ment that the visions—or what he sometimes calls "the trances"—
"represent, express, [and] *order* our love. Thus they are central. We
cannot go ahead without them. They are our language." But the
truth of the visions is not merely personal. Christiana is possessed
of a "cosmic" perspective; she is witness to "the universal truth" for
her epoch. Thus, it is their larger task to express the visions to the
world. "Our purpose," Harry declares, "is the creation of a trance
epic." It will be divided into three parts. A "realistic" narrative of
Christiana's life; an account of the visions, "more or less poetically
transcribed"; and an "objective cold analytical" treatment of the
whole story, drawing widely on psychology, history, and myth. "I
do not know of anything as big as this ever being attempted," Harry
concedes; "but I feel fully capable of doing it *with you*."

Harry did not arrive at this position without help. In fact, his
pronouncements are the compromise that he and Christiana settled
on in the wake of the crisis precipitated by her approach to individuation. "The Creation of the Star" confirmed for Christiana the absolute primacy of the visions in the definition of the dyad. But how,
it followed to ask, did her breakthrough influence the ordering of
Harry's priorities? Too much of his time and energy, she decided,
was going to the Clinic and to Melville; not enough to her truth as
it unfolded in their relationship. And so she delivered an ultimatum. "Lover, you must choose between me and Melville." You must
choose, she meant more broadly, between those things that primarily concern *you* and those that *we* share together. This demand forced
the issue and brought Harry to his "First Great Recognition." The
dyad, he agreed, would be primary; the visions would be their
guide; and the creation of the "trance epic" their highest goal. To
that end, Harry conceded, the Melville biography would be no
more than "a training ground."

▼

chapter eight

No Return through Me

"You are the center of my world and the compass of all my hopes," Harry assured Christiana at the end of his First Great Recognition. "Your center is spiritual, and your truths soul-truths, so you must determine the climate for our life, and be the leading principle of our life. I live gloriously when I mass upon your vision. Keep me at the center. Drive me always toward The Book." She was his true love; her visions were the inspiration for their union; and the story of the dyad, once revealed, would transform the world. "The whole spiritual course of man will pivot on you," Harry concluded. This, they decided, was the way it was meant to be. They had been called as a couple to take a leading role in the history of the human spirit. It appeared to Lewis Mumford that they imagined themselves the founders of a new religion. Christiana now referred to herself as "Wona," immemorially the woman, the feeling guide to the future. Harry was "Mansol," her complement, yang to her yin, the active, worldly weaver of their message. Apart, they were mere automatons; together in the dyad, their separateness dissolved, they possessed "synergy," the strength of opposites transformed and united. "When the two become one," reads the epigraph to Christiana's visions, "And the outside as the inside/And the male with the female/Neither male nor female/Then shall ye see God."

Ina May Greer, a veteran Jungian who was close to Christiana for many years, classified her friend as a classic inspiratrice. By contrast to the mother type, who is oriented to the domestic and the social, the inspiratrice is oblivious to the outer world and turns inward to the individual and the subjective, in herself and in men. Because she is immersed in the productions of the unconscious, she may possess the magnetism that self-absorption sometimes produces. At her best, she mediates the mysterious and the intangible and may serve as the source of profound inspiration. But in her alienation from social reality, the inspiratrice is prey to an inflated regard for her interior experience and for her authority as visionary and prophet. Christiana reckoned with her life in terms such as these; and as a budding Jungian analyst she surely recognized the perils of complete identification with an archetype. She had had her fill of the pain and panic that went with a steady diet of visions. In their aftermath, she may have sensed that the fruition of her role as inspiratrice had its price in a deepening dependency on Harry. By her own urgent admission, she could not be completely herself without him. She was "the introverted Anima woman" of her diary. "Alone she has no fruits. She perishes without a creative lover who will bring ideas & people to her & enfold her." The dyad bound them together as lovers, but with some of the desperation—especially on Christiana's side—that survivors at sea must feel, holding on against the loneliness of the deep.

If Christiana's role was formed by an artist with a taste for the tragic, Harry's was the product of a decidedly picaresque sensibility. True, he confessed to a certain penchant for darkness—it was there in his attraction to Melville and to Christiana. But Harry's was surely the much brighter hemisphere of the dyad. He came in time to deplore the excess of woe in the author of *Pierre.* "A creative person can never be disillusioned," he wrote to his friend Alvan Barach. "I never use the word 'anxiety,'" he once declared; "I'm not aware of anxiety." Harry was not insensitive to the grief—much of it tied to his love affair—that overtook him in the mid-1930s. Trouble came with the territory, he knew; but that was no reason to welcome or cultivate it, save perhaps as a piquant supplement to life's many pleasures. Christiana's notes for June 1933 record her "coming to Mansol after Pa's funeral. Remote in the closeness to death and grief. His taking my body. My joy." For both of them sex was the rapturous sequel to pain. But while desire was mutual, the anguish that gave it rise was Christiana's. It was her part—as it had been Fannie's—to suffer, Harry's to heal. And so the cycle began to gather momentum; increasingly their pleasure had her suffering as its necessary precondition. Indeed, the pattern was already emergent in the last of the visions, where affirmation gave way, in Christiana's eye, to the ceaseless renewal of pain. "Oh my love this is so dangerous," she exclaimed. "I am utterly terrified."

Christiana's fear was rooted in the recognition that Harry's professional work drew him outside of her orbit. "You have lectures to write," she observed. "Your energy must be withdrawn from me to do this—withdrawn from your unconscious. Our rhythms together must slow down—there must be more delay in what happens between us—more tension." She lived in dread that she might "become unreal" to him, that the intensity of their "unconscious life together" would fade, only to be revived for him with "some other woman." They were obliged to be rather stiffly polite with one another at the Clinic. This was painful for Christiana; they seemed to be playing at what she most feared. For Harry, on the other hand, the obligatory formality opened a space between them, room to engage with other people and to indulge his intellectual interests free of the constraints of intimacy. He had several lives; she had but one. He worked; she waited. He called; she dropped everything to be with him. During the summer months Harry divided his time between his wife and his mistress. His days were full, even overfull. So were Jo's; she had adjusted reluctantly to sharing and had no want of things to do. Not so Christiana. When Harry was with her alone, she flourished; but when he was gone, her self and her life were at loose ends, and it was all emptiness and waiting.

Within a year or so of his taking over at the Clinic, Harry began to find the focus that would carry him through the first major phase of his career as a psychologist. Culminating in 1938 with the publication of *Explorations in Personality,* this decade of development brought Harry to prominence as a theorist of human personality and established the Clinic as a model institution in the field. By all accounts, this was his peak professional period, a long season of creative research and writing in company with a team of bright, committed, companionable co-workers, several of whom would go on to become the leaders of their generation in American personality psychology. Harry—wellspring of new ideas, charismatic leader, and conjurer of the Clinic's magical ambience—was the grand progenitor and key to it all. He thought it up; he made it go. His program was at once simple and, in the American academic world at least, revolutionary. "My aim," he declared, "was to understand man and human nature in all its phases." Fascinated by his own interior life, by Christiana's, and by Melville's—and through it all by the unconscious—he wanted to explore the human psyche anew for his times. Central to his interests was the formation and evolution of values. In a letter of 1930 to Lewis Mumford he heaps scorn on the reactionary neo-humanism of Irving Babbitt and Paul Elmer More, calling it "an emasculate rationalization of banal & arid prejudices." Such sentiments take their edge from Harry's implicit defensiveness about the dyad, which would not fare well at the hands of conventional moralists and required for its justification some willingness to honor the promptings of the unconscious. He defines for Mumford what he calls "humanistic psychology," the study "of human values as subjectively experienced—the conflicts that anteceded these emergent attitudes & the techniques of consciousness in respect to them—preparation, assimilation, etc." Harry's plans for the Clinic thus spoke volumes about his private life. The scientist and the man in love had virtually identical agendas. For both it was imperative to reassess and refashion American values with the exigencies of the unconscious foremost in mind. Deep diving into the psyche of modern man was the *sine qua non* of any authentic new humanism.

Harry's program for change registered prominently in his teaching. There were large turnouts for the standard introductory course, Abnormal and Dynamic Psychology, which he offered regularly during the 1930s and which featured heavy reading in Freud, Jung, and Adler. Students approved. The *Crimson Confidential Guide* gave generally high marks to his teaching and to Allport's, while condemning the others in the department as narrowly specialized psycho-physicists "still following the subject matter of the 19th century." The Clinic was a hub of intellectual activity, especially for the growing number of graduate students and volunteers who gathered there to conduct research under Harry's guidance. Donald MacKinnon, Saul Rosenzweig, Robert White, Nevitt Sanford, Isabelle Kendig, Jerome Frank, and Kenneth Diven were among the most prominent of the early group. Erik Erikson (then Homburger), recently analyzed by Anna Freud, arrived from Vienna in 1933. Merrill Moore, the psychiatrist and poet, joined them at about the same time. Money in limited amounts was also available to support a clinical fellow in psychotherapy and research (Dr. William Barrett held this post during the early 1930s) and to fund research fellowships for students who had completed their graduate work (these were filled by Carl Smith, Richard Sears, Walter Langer, David Wheeler, and others).

Group identity and loyalty were very strong. There were all the usual tensions and dramatic subplots, but the main action—working at close quarters on aspects of the same large research project— was for virtually all involved the most memorable intellectual experience of their careers. The Clinic flourished because Harry brought new ideas into an environment that sorely needed them. He excited the imaginations of able, energetic students who came to think of themselves as explorers in uncharted but obviously important territory. Evidence of disapproval from Emerson Hall and elsewhere in the university produced an exhilarating maverick camaraderie. The Depression also had its part to play. Young intellectuals were in a mood to break fresh ground. This of course drew them to Harry. He was perhaps a decade or so older than most of them but still youthful. He was independent in all the important ways. Broadly trained, he could move from molecules to Melville to motivation with effortless authority. He had earned the right, it seemed, to challenge the established academic boundaries. His money and personal style also set him apart. He supported the Clinic, and many of its students, during regular periods of need. Much more than his striving, middle-class colleagues, he worked at his own pace and at tasks of his own choosing. He took more vacations and leaves than others; he dressed well, traveled constantly, entertained lavishly; the rumors about his personal life took some support from appearances and conferred an aura of romance. His was a princely manner of living. Other faculty may have taken

174

offense, but there was little complaint from students. Harry put his money where it helped them most, and there was nothing ostentatious in his bearing of privilege. He was friendly, enthusiastic, supportive of their enterprises, tolerant of their differences and idiosyncrasies, and willing to let his hair down at regular, hard-drinking Clinic parties. Forever coming and going, willing at intervals to work closely with his many students, a hive of ideas, genial host to a glittering procession of lunchtime guests, he was always several steps ahead of those around him. He read more, and more widely; he thought more, and with a greater yield. He seemed to live for the creative interchange of ideas. At Emerson Hall colloquia he was forthright with his views and able to defend himself—and, it went without saying, the Clinic—pretty much single-handedly. Nevitt Sanford recalls that the Plympton Street crowd "felt proud that he was able to give as good as he got" on such occasions. Harry was a good prince if there ever was one.

"The Clinic staff," Harry reported in 1934, "have collaborated in an investigation of the total personality. Each member has worked with a particular experimental technique, by means of which he created for the subjects a type of stimulus-situation or environmental pressure designed to bring into prominence a particular aspect of personality. The persons who served as subjects were tested in turn by each experimenter. By means of the data collected in this way, it was possible to study and compare the reactions of single individuals to many varied situations. An attempt could then be made to construct an intelligible abstract portrait of each individual." The research was premised on the assumption that personality is "a complex of numerous mutually dependent processes" or variables whose "relations must be known and appraised if one is to give an adequate description—analysis and synthesis—of even a single human reaction. One must understand the whole to understand the part." The leading features of the program—attention to the whole personality, to individual differences rather than "average" results, and to multiple variables—were directly derivative from Harry's medical and scientific training. The same may be said for the unique model of assessment beginning to emerge in the collaborative or team approach to personality assessment. These were the research strategies that would in time earn for Harry the reputation as a major innovator in his new field. A more emphatic endorsement of the interdisciplinary approach is not easily imagined.

"Although we have barely taken the first step in the direction of our goal," Harry goes on to acknowledge, "it is our impression that the general procedure which we are pursuing should tend eventually to a significant advance." The number of subjects will soon reach its final total of fifty. He includes a selection of the studies involved—of aspiration, latent aggression, mirth, varieties of perseveration, hypnotizability, and so on—among which the Thematic Apperception Test makes an appearance. Far and away the most famous of the techniques developed at the Clinic, the TAT invites the subject to tell stories based on pictures of dramatic events. In a co-authored essay on the test published in 1935, Harry and Christiana describe the TAT as a kind of brief, inexpensive alternative to psychoanalysis, especially for young people. It is, they write, "an effective means of disclosing a subject's regnant preoccupations and some of the unconscious trends which underlie them." Among the procedures employed at the Clinic, it has yielded "the best understanding of the deeper layers of personality." They advance persuasive evidence for this claim in detailed analyses—both notably Freudian in emphasis and terminology—of the test results for two of their subjects.

Here, then, is good evidence both of Harry's now fully developed interest in "normal" psychological phenomena and of his continuing effort to forge keys to the unconscious. Years later he observed that "every man knows something about himself which he's willing to tell; he knows something about himself that he's not willing to tell; and there's something about himself that he doesn't know and can't tell." It was the latter of these that most interested him, and that the TAT was designed to summon to the surface. Papers based on other experimental procedures betray a similar emphasis. In a study designed to demonstrate that "the emotional state of a subject may affect his judgments of other personalities," a positive correlation between fear and estimates of malice in others was obtained. To have discovered otherwise would have been a great surprise, of

Harry's father, Henry A. Murray, Sr.,
circa 1915

Fannie Babcock Murray,
circa 1892

▼

Harry at about age three,
circa 1896

Top: Harry in 1905. Bottom: At Craigie School
(seated second from left), 1902.

Gaston Lachaise's rendering of
Christiana Morgan, 1934

Top: Christiana at the Axis Mundi, 1940, and seated
on the lawn near the Tower. Bottom: Christiana at sixty.

"Then I knew that I had become a tree . . ." (an illustration
of one of Christiana's visions).

Portrait of Christiana
by Mary Aiken, 1939

Top: Josephine Rantoul Murray, 1946
Bottom, left: Josephine L. Murray, 1945
Bottom, right: Henry A. Murray, 1946

Harry and Nina, 1969

Nina and Harry, 1971

The Tower

course. But Harry's more urgent business appears in the assertion that his results are best explained by recourse to the hypothesis of unconscious processes, and in his underscoring consistent patterns of difference between individual subjects. Two papers on humor published in 1934 develop equally self-evident hypotheses; indeed, the first paper features the admission that its results merely "demonstrate what is already a matter of common knowledge." Once again, however, the discussion comes round to the discovery of unconscious processes—as previously identified by Freud—in the dynamics of the humorous response.

Harry's pursuit of the unconscious led him to the Boston Psychoanalytic Society, which he helped to found in the years after 1928, when Dr. Isadore Coriat invited him to meet with a handful of others to discuss psychoanalysis. When the group grew too large for Coriat's private home, it was decided, at Harry's invitation, that they gather at the Clinic, which became their meeting place for the next few years. Franz Alexander, a leading Freudian from Berlin, arrived in Boston in September 1931 and commenced training analyses with a number of the Society's members, Harry among them. Alexander moved on to a position at the new Chicago Psychoanalytic Institute in 1932 but recommended Hanns Sachs, one of Freud's inner circle, as his replacement. Despite his international fame as "the analysts' analyst," the distinguished newcomer was not warmly greeted by many in the Society, who were opposed on principle to "lay" analysts—those, like Sachs, who lacked an M.D. Harry did not share this view; nor was he in a mood to endure the outbreak of contentiousness that it provoked among his associates. From the beginning he had been impatient with what he regarded as the "fanatical adherence" to Freudian orthodoxy among some members of the organization, and the power-mongering of others. The Sachs dispute, he felt, was yet another distraction from the educational mission of the Society. It marked the beginning of the end of his active involvement.

It is not entirely surprising that Harry's analysis with Franz Alexander failed to get off the ground. They met for a total of about nine months, in Boston during Alexander's tenure with the Boston Psychoanalytic Society and for a few final weeks in Chicago just before and after the New Year 1933. Harry was a cautious admirer of Freud. He judged his "contribution to man's conceptualized knowledge of himself" as "the greatest since the works of Aristotle" but added immediately that Freud's view of human nature was woefully "one-sided." Harry's chief complaint was the common one that the Freudian "libido has digested all the needs contributing to self-preservation, self-regard, and self-advancement, together with a host of others, and rebaptized them in the name of Sex; and that sex itself is never given either its profound evolutionary status or its interpersonally creative status." Harry's views on this score had been decisively influenced by Jung, who rejected pansexualism and the oedipal doctrine and defined libido in very broad terms as "psychic energy." All of this conformed with Harry's experience and predilections, as did Jung's view—conveyed to Harry with special emphasis during his first visit to Zurich—that the liberation and cultivation of human sexuality are vital both to happiness and to creative adaptation in the modern world. Freud's pessimism on this score, as manifest in *Civilization and Its Discontents,* impressed Harry as the symptom of "a black despair." Nor were his objections to Freud merely theoretical. After all, he had staked his personal life, both in its positive dimension with Christiana and in its painful costs for Jo, Will, and Josephine, on the sanguine prospects of the Jungian scheme.

Thus, Harry's resistance to Freudian analysis was deep and virtually unshakable. It was never overt. He was personally drawn to Alexander and in principle committed to their work together. But his accounts of the experience are characterized by an insouciance edged with condescension. "I accepted his entire frame of reference just as all of us accept the conventions of stage scenery when we go to the theater," he recalled. Alexander "was rather bored (yawned continually), and I was less aggressive than in ordinary life. I liked him from the start—he had a sense of humor (an indispensable requirement) and could tell good stories—and I had to search hard to find excuses (borborygmi and other tricks of his) to stir the aggression that I thought should, according to the rules, erupt. I was too busy, otherwise-attached, and happy to be transferable." Stammering was "the symptom chosen for attack." Important but hardly central, it was a telling choice and got them nowhere. Harry discussed Christiana but felt that his analyst's preference for flashy, extroverted women disqualified him as a judge of the dyad. Something of this view emerged in Harry's habit of referring to Alexander as "foxy grandpa." There were other complaints: transference was not possible with a man so unlike Henry, Sr. (and Harry was a "non-Freudian child," anyway); Alexander was distracted; Alexander was bored; Alexander had nothing to say. In Chicago, as they approached the last of their sessions together, Harry asked for a summing up. Alexander could provide none; he had no notes and no special insights to offer. Harry objected, though not strenuously; he had not planned on being impressed. They parted on genial terms.

Precisely because it did not open significantly on his personal life, Harry's subsequent "control" analyses under the guidance of Hanns Sachs were much more productive. Christiana had recently completed her own brief training analysis with Sachs. Neither of them wished it longer. Her resistance was as deep as her loyalty to Jung was strong, and she made little attempt to conceal her prejudice. "She really gave it to him," Harry recalled. But so long as his own interior life was not involved, Harry had little but praise for the Freudians and their approach. "Time and time again," he observes, Sachs "could predict my patients' trends several days or even weeks before they were exhibited. A theory that can do this is valuable."

Harry encountered another valuable theory in the work of Vilfredo Pareto, the Italian economist and sociologist whose works were featured in a seminar organized by L. J. Henderson in 1932. The group, the so-called Harvard Pareto Circle, met regularly for about two years and included George Homans, Charles Curtis, Joseph Schumpeter, Talcott Parsons, Bernard DeVoto, Crane Brinton, Harry, and a few others among its regular members. Pareto's intellectual appeal—which ran parallel in some respects to Whitehead's—had its foundation in systems theory. Henderson was given to drawing analogies between Pareto's construction of the "social system"—in his *Trattato di Sociologia Generale* (1916)—and physico-chemical systems as understood by scientists of the time. Both schemes of thought foreground the notion of equilibrium or homeostasis (versions of the earlier *milieu intérieur* of Claude Bernard), and both abandon cause and effect explanations for analysis—as Henderson wrote—"involving the simultaneous variations of mutually dependent variables." The social order, in other words, is at once extremely complex and profoundly resistant to change. The people who inhabit that order, meanwhile, are in Pareto's view hopelessly incapable of rational thought or behavior. It follows that they are well served by strong political leaders who take the preservation of the status quo as their highest priority.

The conservative political thrust of the *Trattato*—H. Stuart Hughes has characterized Pareto as "the great rationalizer of authoritarian conservatism in our time"—was hardly lost on the members of the seminar. Henderson's misgivings about human nature, democracy, and liberals found confirmation in the man he celebrated as the modern successor to Machiavelli. And Homans, a Boston patrician, made no secret of the fact that Pareto served him well as a line of personal defense against the Marxists. Harry was more optimistic about human beings than Henderson, and less pleased with his social status than Homans; still, we must suppose that he was engaged at some level by the politics of the *Trattato*. It is worth adding, however, that Harry supported the New Deal, while Homans—in his book on Pareto—heaps scorn on those who worship "Action in the shape of Roosevelt." By his own account, Harry was most taken by "Pareto's representation of society as a system." Further "encouraged by Whitehead's speculations," this developing fascination with systems analysis fostered "the perilous practice of discovering analogies among events at different levels."

Nor was Harry as thoroughly converted to Pareto as other members of the seminar. The *Trattato* appealed to Henderson, Homans, and many of the others because of its pretense to scientific rigor. "Pareto applies to sociology the method to which the physical sciences owe their growth," Homans was pleased to report. Harry was of course familiar with the methodology of the natural sciences; more than the others in the seminar, he had made it his business to apply that method to the study of human nature. Experience at the Clinic had reinforced his belief that the marriage between scientific rigor and the study of the human psyche could never be complete.

The misguided attempt to force that union had trivialized American psychology by blinding its practitioners to the richest insights available in the field. Much to Henderson's displeasure, Harry began to offer his views in the meetings of the seminar. On one side, Harry faulted Pareto for a lack of intuition into social phenomena; on the other, he praised Freud and Jung for their valuable, if scientifically unverifiable, contributions. Henderson was unaccustomed to such resistance, and his irritation was at times obvious to everyone. "Well now, look, don't get angry, Professor," Harry would say, only half in sympathy. "I'm not angry," the notoriously irascible Henderson shouted in reply.

It was not Pareto alone that came between them. Henderson had never fully accepted Harry's defection from physiology; and Ike's subsequent decision to follow his older brother into psychology compounded the grievance. Meanwhile, as he gathered momentum in his new field, Harry achieved a measure of intellectual independence from his old mentor. He saw a connection between Henderson's worship of power (in men like Mussolini) and his autocratic style as a scholar and teacher. "I really got pretty fed up with his authoritarianism," Harry admitted years later. Matters grew worse before they got better. Privately, Henderson condemned his former protegé as disloyal; meanwhile, the student grew more persuaded than ever of the teacher's rigidity and arrogance. The approach of war later brought them back together. Henderson repudiated Mussolini when he joined forces with the hated Nazis. And Harry relented, especially as illness overtook his old friend. He was regularly at Henderson's bedside during the months before he died, in 1942.

Harry reflects on the break with Henderson in a letter to Lewis Mumford written in April of 1933. For all of its shortcomings, he confides, the analysis with Alexander shed useful light on his relationships with the strong men in his life. It revealed "that I was a sort of Patricide (the old familiar) who had been surreptitiously seeking the Perfect Father but critically & skeptically & maliciously; that I had been drawn to one Master after another, proved them wanting, discredited them & then passed on to the next victim; & now I had got to a position where I could do no work because I was playing each of them off against the other—the chief figures being L. J. Henderson (Science & Pareto) Jung and Melville (poetical and religious and literary) Freud (psychoanalysis). Any one of these attitudes was attacked by the other two & more or less annulled." In another mood Harry might have recognized that his virtually unexampled intellectual latitude was a great asset. That he could sit down together with Henderson and Jung and Melville and Freud is striking; that the gathering sometimes cost him a little ambivalence is not. Patricide, surely, is too strong. Harry was hardly exceptional in his craving for independence; on the other side, he was more generous than most people of his stature in honoring his intellectual debts. Harry was no more a father-slayer than other children, and he knew it. "This ambivalence from the start is of course as old as the hills," he goes on to Mumford, "but somehow I seemed to see it differently. It illuminated the fact that just when H[erman] M[elville] was writing Hawthorne affectionate letters, he was writing the Duyckincks that there was something wrong with N. H. He needed rare beef."

The fraying edges of his friendship with Henderson were not the worst of Harry's difficulties in 1933. Even as the Clinic flourished, as the talented staff pulled more closely together around their leader and his ideas, and as 64 Plympton Street emerged as a place to reckon with in the field, signs of trouble began to surface. Money was scarce. Harvard fiscal policy placed the burden of support on the individual academic unit—"Every tub," as the saying went, "stands on its own bottom." Income from the Clinic's endowment had dwindled as the Depression ground along. Harry sacrificed the lion's share of his salary to help meet expenses; in addition, he made regular contributions out of his own pocket. Still, the budget was a virtual allegory of want. "The Psychological Clinic is in a precarious economic condition," he wrote in a 1933 appeal to Harvard Medical School. "There is no money for a secretary ($1,500 a year), nor for apparatus and supplies ($700 a year), nor for psychological books and journals ($400 a year), nor for the salary of a trained Research Fellow to superintend the large research project which has been undertaken ($2,500 a year)." This effort failed, as all inside negotiations for increased funding failed. In 1934, as the situation grew worse, Harry began in earnest to seek outside support.

Edwin Boring, for more than a decade the *de facto* chair of Harry's branch of the Department of Philosophy and Psychology, was another problem that wouldn't go away. In *Psychologist at Large,* one of his autobiographies, Boring imagines himself an agent of "the deliberate forces of History" that brought about the founding of the Clinic. In fact, the actual founding took place without his knowledge, and his impact on the subsequent history of the Clinic was largely negative. This is not to suggest that Boring was without his grievances—the founding among them—but merely to highlight his failure to mention them. His oversight may have had a partial source in what he describes (in a second autobiographical essay) as the "outstanding characteristic" of his personality, an "eternal conflict" between the "need for *power and success*" and the "need for *approval and affection.*" Boring traced his problem to "a lack of security and love in childhood." Whatever its source, his ruling ambivalence found a compelling object in the director of the Clinic.

There is evidence that Boring wanted to rise in Harry's esteem; just so, there is evidence that Harry was a vexing obstacle to the full flowering of Boring's ambition. It had for many years been his goal to make Harvard a national leader in a rigorously scientific brand of experimental psychology. The Clinic was an insult to his ideals in this regard; worse still, it was a success. Boring was at once jealous and in awe of Harry's charisma and of his privileged style of life. In a letter of 1929 he sneers in a glancing way at his junior colleague's membership in "our local aristocracy" but brags nonetheless of Harry's loyalty to Harvard ("I don't suppose that a ten thousand dollar salary would interest him in the least"). Tensions flared over administrative details and over the evaluation of graduate students. Most often, however, Boring worked behind the scenes to frustrate Harry's ambitions. He tried—and failed (thanks to Whitehead's intervention)—to make an issue of Harry's relationship with Christiana. Moreover, he was entirely two-faced in responding to Harry's plans for the tercentenary celebration in 1936. It was symptomatic of his ambivalence that he gave his support and encouragement in minor matters along the way but grew more fixed in his opposition to the Clinic as the struggle over its survival drew toward closure.

That struggle began in earnest in the fall of 1933, when James B. Conant, a distinguished chemist, took over from A. Lawrence Lowell as president of Harvard. Where his predecessor had given his best energies to the development of the undergraduate program, the new president was primarily concerned with excellence in research and graduate training. Henderson shared Conant's viewpoint on this score and therefore brought all of his very considerable influence to bear on his election. This meant that Harry had a friend near the throne. He would need such well-placed friends now more than ever, for Conant insisted on regular publication as the leading index of merit. Publications were as yet few and far between at the Clinic; Harry and his staff were laboring in uncharted territory and just beginning to find their way. To make matters worse, Conant was a "hard" scientist with a strong personal aversion to psychoanalysis and an initial impulse, Harry believed, to banish the Clinic to the Medical School. As one of his first acts as President, Conant appointed a committee to review psychology at Harvard and to make recommendations for its improvement. According to Boring, who was one of those selected to serve, the committee was "chosen to favor biotropic psychology, not the philosophical kind" practiced at the Clinic. Conant also asked the committee to "find 'the best psychologist in the world' to elect to a chair at Harvard." They finally settled on Karl S. Lashley ("whom I had been backing all along," Boring crowed), who joined the faculty in 1935. By the time of Lashley's arrival, Boring had also set in motion the formal separation of Philosophy and Psychology. The chairman had never been stronger, the Clinic never more vulnerable.

Harry had no illusions about Boring. He knew what his gestures of support were worth and how things would settle out when push finally came to shove. He knew, too, that Conant was a very uncertain quantity when it came to psychology. The new president called him in toward the beginning of 1934. They had had a passing acquaintance during undergraduate days, and Conant knew something of the Clinic and its director from Henderson. He listened carefully to his visitor's comments on the present and future of the field. Then he turned to Harry's recent article in the *Boston Herald*, which set forth a vigorous defense of Howard B. Gill, the progressive administrative head of the Norfolk Prison. Conant described the piece—disapprovingly—as "radical." He went on to acknowledge that Henderson had helped to make him president. He was no less straightforward in expressing his doubts about Harry's brand of psychology and about its uncertain future at Harvard.

Harry had been routinely reappointed as an Assistant Professor without tenure in 1931. That three-year position was due for review in 1934; only this time, in part because of Conant's new policy on research and in part because of the Clinic's failing finances, success was not assured. Boring was ready with a favorable prognosis and some advice. "I do not expect that the University is likely to fire you at the end of your present term for lack of productivity," he wrote in January 1933. "I think it is going to see that you had a very difficult undertaking to put through and that you have done what is about humanly reasonable; but I think it is also going to continue to put pressure upon you for personal productivity in addition to the work of your students." He closes the subject in the hope that Harry's book on personality will be "out long before the problem has to be considered again" in 1937. The Clinic staff responded to the challenge with a flurry of scholarly papers, three of them by Harry, six more by Saul Rosenzweig. At the same time, Harry let it be known in various quarters that a book—at one point tentatively entitled *Studies in Total Personality*—would be ready for publication during the next year or two. His reappointment went forward without further difficulty.

Harry moved just as vigorously on the fiscal front. "If you knew of a psychological laboratory-clinic where the most original and promising research work in this country was being done, and where the best opportunity for pre-medical and pre-psychiatric training in the elements of normal and abnormal psychology prevailed, and if you also discovered that this laboratory-clinic was the most impoverished organization of its kind in this country, would you be inclined to assist it?" Harry addressed his question—composed early in February 1934—to Dr. Alan Gregg, the Director of the Medical Sciences Division of the Rockefeller Foundation. His tone suggests a certain optimism about his chances with Gregg. They had been at the Rockefeller Institute during the same period in the mid-

1920s; perhaps Harry knew that as a young man Gregg had actually met Freud, Ferenczi, and Jung at the time of their visit to America in 1909. "I saw Freud . . . in the flesh," he later recalled. In any case, the passage of time had hardly diminished Gregg's enthusiasm for psychoanalysis. He welcomed opportunities to use his influence, and the financial resources of the Rockefeller Foundation, to support its development. Once again, Harry had landed in the right place at the right time.

At Harry's invitation, Gregg came to Cambridge in late April for a complete tour of the Clinic. His notes indicate that he was impressed with what he found and certainly alert to the urgency of the financial need. Just days before his visit he received a letter of warm support from Dr. Stanley Cobb, a neuropathologist at Harvard and mutual friend, who praised Harry both for his research program and for his effort to create a place for psychoanalysis in the university. Two weeks later, Alfred Cohn wrote in a similar vein. Gregg was anxious to extend support but held back, waiting for Conant's committee to submit its report. Harry pressed for a decision. "Why shouldn't financial help be given to those experimenters who have the most promising researches in mind?" he asked, pointedly, in September. He urged Gregg to make another visit to the Clinic and sent him the draft of an article on "Psychology and the University," an attempt, Harry explained, "to outline what I think should be the course of psychological growth in the future." Harry wrote again in October, to thank Gregg for returning to 64 Plympton. "I hope you were not too much shocked by the bluntness of my article," he went on. "If you think it should be toned down, I hope you will say so. I can not promise that I will follow your advice because I feel that a bit of indignation at the shameless provincialism of the separate classes of psychology is appropriate at the present time, and I can better afford to make myself the goat than many others who feel as I do but whose very existence depends on academic favor."

Here was a commendable readiness to accept the responsibilities of privilege by stepping first and boldly into the breach. Harry enjoyed playing the Knight of Truth; but he was also very effective in the role, as "Psychology and the University" makes clear. He was ambitious for the piece, and sent it first to Ellery Sedgwick at the *Atlantic Monthly,* who thought it too specialized for a general magazine. It was finally published in 1935 by the *Archives of Neurology and Psychiatry.* The essay is a compact, sometimes funny, often blunt review of the field by one who finds little to admire in what he beholds. "If psychology is defined as the science which describes people and explains why they perceive, feel, think and act as they do," Harry reflects, then "properly speaking, no science of the kind exists." The vast majority of psychologists are "encrusted specialists," narrowly trained adherents of one or another school, from whose "web of activity consideration of man as a human being has somehow escaped." As the direct result, "academic psychology has contributed practically nothing to the knowledge of human nature"; its practitioners are the "vestal virgins of unusable truth prolonging without profit the culmination of a spent impulse." Harry is little gentler with the psychoanalysts. He pays his respects to the advances of Freud and others in discovering and describing the unconscious. But because the leaders in the field have been "untrained in the fundamental sciences," their theories often "resemble myths or metaphysical doctrines rather than authentic scientific formulations." Freud is himself "a strange genius who has made some of the shrewdest guesses that have even been recorded"; the Freudians, meanwhile—with "their simple-minded technical patter, their polymorphous perversities of logic . . . their hostility to research, their touchiness, their inability to get on with themselves or with others—in short, their pervading neuroticism"—are often flatly insufferable. In the upshot, "no critically minded person practiced in scientific research or in disciplined speculation can accept psychoanalysis on the basis of the writings of Freud or any of his followers."

The field, then, is in complete disarray. "Academic psychologists are looking critically at the wrong things. Psychoanalysts are looking with reeling brains at the right things." The universities are crippled by the perverse refusal on virtually all sides to admit psychoanalysis to the curriculum, and by the lack of a "common scheme." Harry proposes as a corrective the development of a broad-based interdisciplinary program that makes room for a variety of approaches. He adds that "the establishment of a unifying theory would be the noblest aim" such a program could set for itself. Clearly enough, Harry believed that the Clinic was the closest thing around to what he had in mind and that he was the man—physician, scientist, psychoanalyst, biographer, *littérateur,* preeminently the humanist—to handle the theory. "Perhaps it is not too fanciful to suggest," he goes on—with the question of value as always in mind—"that this emotionally sick world is in urgent need of a workable theory of personality."

Gregg liked "Psychology and the University" just fine. "Don't tone down your article," he wrote, "I like pickles that taste of brine." Boring didn't. No sooner had he read the manuscript than he rushed down to the Clinic, shaking all over. He was horrified, and with good cause. After all, the essay made a laughing stock of his life's work. A psychologist from Baltimore had been ostracized completely for having written such an attack, he said. It was no time to risk a similar setback. Inwardly, Harry must have been pleased. The point of his essay had found its proper target. Certainly he was not intimidated. Gregg had seen the point, too, and decided in mid-October, without waiting any longer on Conant's committee, to give the Clinic the support it needed. A grant-in-aid of $2450 for one year was issued at the end of October 1934. "I am glad," Gregg wrote, "that it has been made and will be in such good hands." It would be enough to keep the Clinic afloat until Conant had made up his mind. Time enough then to deal with Boring and Lashley.

Boring and Lashley! Taken in tandem, the names have a decidedly allegorical ring to them. Boring suggests a villain who works below the surface, attacking relentlessly from underground; Lashley is of course the sadistic punisher, the cruel master of the scourge. All of which brings us back to the Knight of Truth. Harry no doubt indulged himself from time to time in perspectives as fanciful as these. His imagination ran quite readily to spectacles of combat between good and evil. He recognized this strain of romanticism in his own makeup, just as he readily admitted that he enjoyed the combat. "My relations with the university were just right as far as I was concerned," he later reflected. It was bracing to have "a certain amount of enmity around." He took pleasure in bearding the establishment, even at his moment of greatest vulnerability to attack. He was sure of his cause, and of his own fitness to advance it. And of course he was right on both scores. The heyday of psychoanalysis and depth psychology in America was drawing nigh, and he would be recognized as one of its proudest pioneers—especially in the university—when that time came.

"There is reason to believe," Harry declares in the first sentence of "Psychology and the University," "that in coming years the university which contributes most to the advancement of learning and the cultivation of the human spirit will be the one which develops and sustains the greatest school of psychology." He wanted Harvard—the Harvard of 64 Plympton Street—to be that school. He took his appeal directly to the old grads in "The Harvard Psychological Clinic," an essay published by the *Harvard Alumni Bulletin* in 1935. Having outlined his research program, he announces that its results are "now being prepared for publication in a book to be entitled *Explorations in Personality.*" He underscores his interest in "events exhibiting the influence of unconscious psychic processes" and, at the same time, highlights a concern for "what the educated layman supposes to be the proper subject matter of psychology— facts and theories leading to various *interpretations* of why in *everyday life* different *types* of *men, women,* and *children* feel, act, think, and perceive as they do." He insists that the Clinic is the ideal site for such inquiry and concludes, following the philosopher John Macmurray, that "the development of a scientific psychology is perhaps the most urgent need of our time." Harry pauses toward the end of his discussion to express his gratitude that Harvard now has "a first-rate animal laboratory under the direction of Professor Lashley." There is little alternative to an ironic reading of this apparently generous gesture. Harry was broadly latitudinarian in intellectual matters, but he was hardly naive. Lashley—whom the temperate Robert White once described as "a hateful person . . . he really was the bad guy"—had just arrived from the midwest, where he had recently evened his score with psychoanalysis by laying waste to Franz Alexander's enterprises at the University of Chicago. The Knight of Truth would have his hands full for a while yet.

It is entirely to Conant's credit, and to Whitehead's, that nothing was made of Boring's revelations about Harry and Christiana. Not surprisingly, the lovers kept this side of their lives carefully to themselves. While they seem always to have underestimated the number of insiders to the dyad, it is significant that they tried to keep track and that they wished to keep the roster of *cognoscenti* small. Still, Harry was at times inclined to be a little coy with his secret. Toward the end of "Psychology and the University" he looks ahead to the widespread "creation of enduring and emergent synergies—erotic and communal"; and in "The Harvard Psychological Clinic" he pays tribute to a special breed of "women—gnostic women—who have the gift to quicken minds in their fertilities, a power which some creative men in their indebtedness have had sufficient stature to acknowledge." Such brief glimpses of the dyad were tributes of a sort to Christiana, whose contributions were too often obscured by the need for secrecy. But it may be that Harry enjoyed this mild flaunting of his rebellion; it was as close as they had come so far to educating the world in their radical new way of love.

Harry's work on Melville, which had progressed with such speed and promise in the years just after his return from England, slowed to a virtual halt as Christiana and the Clinic drew increasingly on his time. He wrote to Mumford in 1931 that he had completed a chapter on the Hawthorne/Melville relationship. More typically, however, he was silent on the subject, or brought it up only to comment on his failure to keep pace. "I, myself, was ensnared within the Ambiguities of Pierre six years ago when I first discovered Melville," he confessed in an earlier letter to Mumford; "& that perhaps was the element of personal identification which caused the Vesuvian explosion in me. It was the *same,* to such a mysterious degree—even to the mother, the color of the hair, the dreams, the stating of the problem &c. that I attributed much of my Insane Delight with Melville to a Narcissistic feeling of feeling rather than to a detached & yet interpenetrating oneness. For I was almost Insane then, & guessed Pierre before reading it, i.e. after Moby Dick & Mardi—for Pierre is merely a restatement in more concrete terms of the same soul turmoil. So that I dismissed my immediate & spontaneous larva, until I had solved the problem within & without. Melville's heroic attempt—though vain—made it possible. The only decent thing I have done in my life was to follow all the riddles that this situation presents & for myself at least solve them to the ecstatic limit & give them some assimilative form. Now that I have passed on to other knots it seems harder to return to Melville. Somehow one can gather oneself to the white heat & pitch in behalf of an attitude for which one is reaching, better than for one which has become a part of the tissue of personality. Nevertheless I have begun to think of Melville again & I may return to him this summer, but I have a hunch I may never be able to write it." This letter is instructive on a number of fronts. It is a reminder of the ardor with which Harry first embraced Melville. It draws attention as well to his gathering impression that Melville had finally come up short, in fiction by his failure to properly resolve the problem— erotic, metaphysical, moral—of *Pierre,* and in life by surrendering his creativity to woe and madness. There is the suggestion here that Harry has "solved" Melville, that he has himself passed successfully through the fires of *Mardi, Moby-Dick,* and *Pierre* and has now moved forward, as the author of those books could not, to the next, more settled phase. This was one mood among many, to be sure; but it was evidence of a drawing back from Melville's explosive example and hinted at a certain weariness with the constant tumult of the dyad.

Christiana was not happy at the Clinic. She disliked plodding "scientific psychology"; she rejected Freudian terminology because it had few "concepts which could express her"; worst of all, she felt cut off from Harry. "At the Clinic this morning you were so busy," she complained, "your energy so withdrawn from me & all that was left in its place was politeness. We had no sense of each other's reality." Christiana wanted more of Harry than he was willing to give. She blamed him, and she blamed the "complete split" between their public and private lives. It may have helped that Harry's new friend Conrad Aiken picked her out immediately as "the Sibyl" of the Clinic. Her face and clothing, and most especially her "oblique glance," gave it away, he said. But Harry saw that it would take more than compliments to bring Christiana around. He urged her, without much success at first, to take a more positive attitude

191

toward the work at the Clinic. More and more, however, she found a creative outlet at the property on the Parker River. She planned and cultivated an elaborate garden, with trees and shrubs assigned names and ritual significance. She carved shutters, decorated walls and doors with symbolic paintings, and supervised the digging of a well and the construction of a dock. It was here, alone, or alone with Harry, that she was happiest. When the Whiteheads visited the property for the first time in June of 1929, they observed—as Christiana was careful to record in her diary—that she was a "truly creative person."

Still, her restlessness and discontent gathered to the breaking point. She grew increasingly aggressive "against current psychological formulations." The Clinic was suffocating. Perhaps she resented the fact that all the subjects were male. Her frustration boiled over one afternoon at Fairfax Hall when she threw down the "tablets"—the collection of books by Melville, Jung, Whitehead, Nietzsche, and others—that had inspired the dyad. "I cannot follow you," she told Harry; "you confuse me." It was time, she decided, to have "another man in her life." Ralph Eaton, a bright but very unstable young philosopher, Whitehead's protegé, was certainly willing to take the part. Christiana seems to have encouraged him. They drank together at her apartment. Later he came out to the Parker River, confessed his love, and then, when his suit fell short, tried to get himself run over on a nearby turnpike. Alcohol had a place in Eaton's difficulties; so did an uncertain sexual identity. He was more trouble than Christiana had bargained for, and she drew back. But the episode was another element in the crisis that finally broke toward year's end.

December 2, 1929, appears in Christiana's records as "The Day of Fiery Particles," on which she adopted a "new mana"—an improved attitude—at the Clinic. December 3 was "The Tempest Day," when she vowed to try "to control the forces"—the impulses arising out of the unconscious—that had recently taken over her life. For his part, Harry—he appears as "Mansol" in the records—had a "revelation" directing him, as Wona's "chief Disciple," to help her to "express the creativity of her trances in actual living at the Clinic." Between them they would try to "see a new form." "The

Day of Confirmations," when Wona accepted the authority conferred by her mate's most recent "recognition," followed on December 5. There is evidence that the lovers drew a few drops of each other's blood into a small cup and then drank to the unity of two in one. Finally, they engaged jointly in a "Severance of Past Loyalties"—a vow to put the dyad first, at all times and against all competing moral and emotional claims.

The elaborate naming and ritualizing and recording were to become more and more characteristic of Christiana. She viewed herself as the inspiration for the dyad, the agent through which its forms emerged, and its holy scribe. Her passion for ceremony and recordkeeping was at once the measure of her spiritual involvement with Harry and of her fear that the high romantic life she longed and grasped for was falling away. It was symptomatic of the frailty of her ecstatic dream that it required constant refabrication. She saw this; she glimpsed her own hand in the fantastic scheme but turned away, preferring a rapturous half-truth to the bathos of the everyday. Little wonder that in shoring up her crumbling Xanadu she sometimes mistook the parched rush of anxiety for the real romantic thing. Both were intense, and for Christiana quivering intensity itself, almost regardless of its source, was increasingly the goal.

Harry played along side her in the drama of the dyad. He believed, as she did, that they were bearers of a precious message. He was Mansol just as surely as she was Wona. But, again, Harry had several parts to play, while Christiana had but one. He moved between settings, genuinely invested in each, yet alive to the fiction of himself in each as well. It was his essential challenge in life to balance ironic detachment with a sustaining credulity, to preserve a tolerance for his mobile, multiple selves. Christiana could ill afford irony; it would have triggered a descent into the ordinary. She *had* to believe. Harry saw this; yet even as he penetrated her fiction, he helped to preserve it. In this he was moved by an answering faith in the creative authority of the unconscious, by love, and—because he saw her suffer—by compassion. As she grew more precariously fervid, he encouraged her to express herself in art, ceremony, and in the keeping of ever more elaborate records—the sacred dyadic texts, as it were. Thus she called the crisis of December 1929 "The

New World." Their restored unity was set down and parsed out in various journals and diaries. Just before Christmas, apparently to commemorate their ritual of blood, Christiana composed two brief poems of mortal sacrifice. The first, entitled "Crucifixion," is dated 19 December 1929.

> Then the weariness of death came over me.
> The strength of my love was as a terror to me.
> In the agony of death I struck at my love.
> In the defiance of death I commanded my love.
> Then was I crucified by fear of my love.
> Then did I die in the arms of my love.
> And my love knelt beside me, and touched his lips to the cup.

The second, "The Hand of Life," appeared four days later.

> I die into the suffering of my life.
> I die into the long wandering of my life.
> I die into an immemorial grief.
> I die into a world where no longer can I seek rest.
> Sustain me now, oh hands of my love.
> Sustain me now, oh hand of life.
> Pour forth your blood, that I may live again.

Was ever consciousness more in thrall to the idea of death! Despite the fact that they are paired—in "The Crucifixion" the speaker provides the sacrificial blood, in "The Hand of Life" she receives it—Christiana is in both poems the victim. She dies to give and she dies that she may receive. Dying is in fact so pervasive that it may be read as the figure for life itself, as experience taken in all of its linked moments—of love, hate, fear, grief—to an extreme mortal pitch. The immanent threat of its loss is finally the source of life's value. The poems do not so much express love as appeal for it (on grounds of the speaker's desperate need) or demand it (love me, or I *will* die). We can hardly envy Christiana the feelings that gave rise to the poems, nor can we envy Harry the feelings that the poems must have given rise to in him. The dyad was no picnic.

The rocky road leading to Christiana's "New World" illustrates in bold relief the pattern that the dyad would follow in subsequent

> Love is not love
> Which alters when it alteration finds.
> (Shakespeare)

But of course love altered quite a lot, even as it proclaimed its permanence; and the severance of old ties was evidently no obstacle to the creation of new ones. Such contradictions are themselves emergent from the texts Christiana selected to express the dyad in 1930. It was as though the tormented lovers fed on the irony of their condition; they felt they were going nowhere, it seems, unless they were going in both directions at the same time. The volume of quotations opens with several that proclaim the dyad an instrument of fate; Wona and Mansol, it is clearly implied, were made for each other. Harry makes the same point—obliquely but unmistakably—in his 1931 review of a new edition of *Pierre*. In their love for each other, he argues, the hero and his half-sister "are seized by the unambiguous hand of destiny." His remarks were published in April, just weeks after Christiana, recoiling in anger and jealousy and hurt, collapsed in what she describes as a "nervous breakdown." Will did what he could to comfort her; so did her friend Frances Wickes, who laid the blame on Jung's influence. The dyad was misbegotten, she said. Christiana could not agree. "In spite of my terrible grief I rose up and said she was wrong—that in spite of everything the trances were the Way. Not Jung—but Mansol was the failure." At intervals she derived some slender consolation from the memory of "what Jung had said—'He may not be good enough.'" More often, to judge from her records, it was "Anguish and anguish—stretched on the rack of wracks. Was there ever such pain?" Fate was having it both ways, too, it appears.

Eleanor Jones was in desperate condition when she arrived at the Clinic in the late summer of 1930. Dissatisfied with a marriage that she would not leave and badly burned in a recent love affair, she was confused, humiliated, guilty, and veering toward suicide. Harry took her on as a volunteer. For a while she worked on TAT pictures; later she was asked to gather impressions of subjects in unstructured "conversations." From the start, taking her cue from Conrad Aiken, she looked to Harry for guidance. He was struck by the deep division in her personality. Respectable, engaging, even motherly on the outside, she was inwardly prey to a welter of confused impulses, sudden cruelty not the least of them. The suppressed demon in Eleanor surfaced in her art, short stories and poems furtively composed and then squirreled away—so Aiken believed—in a bottom drawer somewhere. "It was obvious," Robert White recalled, that Harry "was stunned by her genius." She could do what he feared he could not—find language adequate to the expression of deep, complex, powerful human feeling. Harry admired and coveted—he loved—creativity of that sort above all else, Ina May Greer once observed, even above Christiana. And it was creativity of precisely that sort that his partner in the dyad lacked. Christiana could design and draw and paint and carve, but she had little talent as a writer. Harry opened his Melville manuscript to Eleanor. "She could write three times as well as what I had there," he readily conceded. She was one of a very small handful of people to have seen the manuscript during his lifetime.

Aiken was pleased and grateful that Harry had made room for Eleanor at the Clinic. "I'm so glad you gave Eleanor a covert—isn't she swell?" he wrote from England in November 1930. "What a glorious counterpoint, you two in that there place," he followed up a few weeks later. "Antichrist and the pythoness—the agonized Titan and the creative spider—thunderbolt and hoarfrost—oh well, what tripe, but you know what I mean." No doubt Harry was amused at Aiken's literary high jinks. But the affair had a much more serious side. Eleanor Jones pushed Christiana out of the picture; not for good, as it turned out, though it seemed final enough for a while. For more than a year Christiana stayed away from the Clinic; seeing Harry left her confused and exhausted. When it was all over he persuaded himself that she had never lost confidence in their future, that she had never lapsed into jealousy. A happy surmise. In fact, he knew better. In writing to Jung with news of the break, Harry did nothing to minimize Christiana's suffering. He was equally solemn in describing for Lewis Mumford what he took to be the end of six years of "intense high-frenzied love." "C. revealed to me the underworld—the maddened hollowed-out woe of

the whole world since Adam—Melville's world, Dante's Inferno—
the world of witchery, hate, Krakens & claws. The ugliest in both
of us was burned up by an utter unrelenting compassionate hospitable
love that welcomed All. E. on the other hand is a poet & a
genius who leads me back to the sun." Harry goes on to acknowledge
Christiana's pain and his own search for ways "how not to leave
her broken." He pauses as well to praise Jo—"the ever-loyal-disapproving,
of course—but yet maintaining with me all the original
ground structure of life"—but then catches sight of himself in
doing so. "I feel like a devourer," he confesses.

Harry was wrong about several things. Most obviously, he was
not the hardened, cross-breaking renegade from traditional values
that he sometimes imagined. Though he concealed it well, guilt
was a constant in his life. The "Severance of Past Affections" was
with him more a wish than a sober claim. He also misjudged
Eleanor Jones. True, she was a fine writer. But her writing, though
generally pretty obscure, reveals nothing if not that her imagination
was a chamber of nightmares. When Harry decided that Eleanor
was his sunshine, he was not reading her prose, or her personality,
with much penetration. Perhaps he was blinded by her technical
brilliance to the gravity of what she had to say. "No Margin," a
story "By E. C. J." published by the *Atlantic Monthly* in 1924, is all
shadows and gloom. The narrator, who writes from prison, describes
"an existence with no margin at all. . . . No reality, no
connection, no continuity of meaning." The story is a kind of allegory
of the creative process, a desperate grappling with "terrors and
depressions which—raising up defenses of comprehension and
beauty against themselves—translate themselves at last in art."
Creativity so construed is a flight into transparent fictions of order,
a temporary stay—as Frost would later have it—against confusion.
The identical message emerges from "The Basket," another well
wrought meditation on loneliness and the necessary illusions of art.
"Isn't she a seraph?" Aiken enthused, apparently without irony. He
was casting around for ways of getting more of Eleanor's work into
print. Harry tried to use his influence with H. L. Mencken at the
American Mercury, and with Ellery Sedgwick at the *Atlantic,* but to

no avail. Sedgwick replied that he was at a loss for words to describe "the ultimate horror" of what he had read. "Not that it isn't effective, but it is so hauntingly terrible."

Finally, Harry was wrong to suppose that he could sever the ties that bound him to Christiana. Slowly, as much by her initiative as by his, and only after her second nervous collapse in February of 1932, they repaired the ruins of the dyad. Christiana returned to the Clinic that spring. Granted, the old way looked better and better to Harry as Eleanor's dark side surfaced to view. The depression manifest in her stories had wide-spreading roots on the nether side of a rather prim exterior. Eleanor's preoccupation with pain was geared, Harry found, to an exquisite sensitivity to the slightest of social abrasions. Her interior life lacked the archetypal girth so characteristic of Christiana's. Because she was edgy, and because she made scenes over seeming trifles, her presence sent waves of tension through the Clinic. Finally, in a transparent projection of her own desires, Eleanor accused Christiana of secretly wishing that Will were dead. It wasn't true; but either way, the thrust was a cruel one. Harry felt that the time had come to ask Eleanor to leave the Clinic. She held on for a year but finally departed, not without a final scene, in July of 1933.

"I believe you've saved her life," Conrad Aiken observed to Harry of Eleanor Jones during her first year at 64 Plympton. Quite possibly so. He gave her work, counsel, and love in hard times. No wonder she objected when he took it all away. Harry was gentle but firm. Eleanor was increasingly a liability at the clinic; their romantic involvement had run its course. The time had come for her to go. Harry had fallen in love with Eleanor's creativity. It was as though he felt that through her he might find words gravely potent enough to solve Melville. Something of the same half-conscious aspiration found its way into his friendship with Aiken, whose nimble genius with language Harry at once admired and coveted. He supported Aiken generously, with affection and encouragement, and with quite a lot of money, during a lifelong friendship, through it all hoping for a small purchase on the poet's elusive authority. Had creative genius been negotiable, Harry would have given a fortune to increase his already very substantial holdings.

Lewis Mumford complained that Harry had poor taste in literature. "He didn't like Hemingway or Faulkner at all" but was swept away with the lesser genius of Thomas Wolfe and John Cowper Powys. Mumford quite rightly observed that his friend was most interested in a writer's "general theme for life" and often "overlooked the fact that the books were overwritten and overdramatized." Harry gravitated rather uncritically to fiction that confirmed his own view of reality—by most standards an overwrought and overdramatic view, it must be conceded. It is also true that he had none of the professional critic's interest in concealing the "subjective" side of his pleasure in art. He liked Melville because he found himself in Melville. He liked O'Neill and Wolfe for the same reason. He was in this, as he was—by his own admission—in so much else, a narcissist. He wrote endlessly to his friends about Powys' *Wolf Solent* (1929), an interminable meditative romance tracing the development of the title character through intricate, closely scrutinized internal changes. It is preeminently the novel of the self, complete with earth and spirit figures competing for the hero's soul, mother fixations, incest, and long intervals of introspection, all carried forward in a tide of myths, symbols, visions, and assaults on Christian morality reminiscent of Jung. It was uncanny the way the book mirrored Harry back to himself. He went out of his way to meet Powys in New York and made a point of sending him a copy of *Pierre*.

Mumford could not conceal his dislike for *Wolf Solent;* he found it puffed up with false wickedness. "The whole category of evil is non-existent to me," Harry replied. As to the fakery, he argued— no more persuasively—that it "was intended by Powys, and unconsciously intended (so as to produce the necessary dramatic tension for himself) by Wolf Solent." He held on to the novel, as to a part of himself, against all criticism. There were other books that achieved a kind of canonical status within the dyad. H. Rider Haggard's *She* (1887), a favorite with Jung, and William Henry Hudson's *Green Mansions* (1904) were admitted mediocrities valued for their treatment of the anima figure. Christiana was deeply stirred by Franz Werfel's *Goat Song* (1921). It gave dramatic confirmation to her belief that great good might issue from great evil, "a cleansing of the spirit from the blood and lust of sacrifice." She was also powerfully drawn to Susan Glaspel's *The Verge* (1921). Finally, George Weller's *Not to Eat, Not for Love* (1933) stands out among many other titles that would appear on a complete list of special favorites. Written just after Weller's graduation from Harvard, and with Harry's active support, the novel is an episodic, often satirical panorama of university life. Harry delighted in its irreverent critique of pervasive complacency and in the pulse of feeling carried by its language. He urged it on Aiken, who found it superficial, and on Mumford, who declined to review it. Unperturbed, Harry reviewed it twice, proclaiming it the best university novel ever written.

Harry admired *Not to Eat, Not for Love* because he felt it expressed better than he could the truth about something that mattered very much to him. His attraction to Eleanor Jones, and in a more moderate degree to many other writers, was similarly inspired. In overvaluing the admitted skills of such artists, he undervalued his own. He was a better writer than he knew—though fiction was not his strong suit and though his lack of self-confidence often caused him to overwrite. Keeping company with Eleanor Jones temporarily eased the panic that the Melville biography and the trance epic of the dyad stirred up in him. Of the first he had completed only a few early chapters; of the second not a word. And neither was going anywhere fast. Still, though work at the Clinic now filled his time, the other projects, the biography most especially perhaps, held a higher place in his estimation. "I was always more interested in writing Melville than I was in writing psychology," he observed in later life. But could he find words for what he knew and felt? That remained to be seen.

For now at least it was clear that talent like Eleanor's did not rub off. In returning to Christiana, Harry reclaimed the first and only living source of inspiration available to him. Time would tell if she could awaken in him the energy and eloquence to write what they both knew about Melville and love. Meanwhile, reconciliation after the long crisis of "the Witch" was properly extravagant. In late July 1933 Harry and Christiana met for a few days together in New

York. It was a glorious recoupling of physical and mental energies highlighted by an overflowing of tender forgiveness that Christiana memorialized as "The Compassion of Love." They agreed to think of the dyad as having three phases—visions, synergy (the living unity of two in one), and the proposition (the representation of their love in words). They also rediscovered their bodies. Christiana's notes record regular and increasingly intense sexual activity reaching a climax—quite evidently hers—on the day of "The Body's Rapture," September 4, again in New York. Harry wrote to Christiana that it had been "the most magical experience" of his life. For her part, Christiana felt "safe—completely enfolded," and ready to share all her weaknesses. "I want you again," she wrote. "I want to wander in & out of Fairfax very often before our winter begins." She was indeed Brunhilde, waiting, as Harry observed, for a "hero who would accept her pace. When [the] spiritual pace was accepted, then [the] physical pace was set." The hero was so pleased with himself, and with love's gentler, more leisurely rhythms, that he bought a new bed. They agreed on what they called "The Signs," a playful symbolic vocabulary of clothing, nail polish, and accessories. A red bracelet said "I want your body"; the gold necklace meant "I love you very much but do not need you"; white translated "I am tired, quiet, depressed. I want your arms"; and so it went. That winter Christiana experienced what she called "an extreme erotic consciousness." She kept records of meeting Harry for lunch at Fairfax Hall, "and making love afterwards, almost every day. Then going to Clinic meetings aflame with Mansol's body." This chapter in the history of the dyad was aptly entitled "The Wisdom of the Body."

Their season of bliss was as complete as the season of woe that preceded it. Once again, the pattern of the dyad ran to extremes. It was in the midst of this period of reconciliation that Christiana decided to insist that Jung bring the seminars on her visions, which had entered their fourth year, to a halt. Will had it from friends in Zurich that the identity of the American lady in the Old Man's lectures had somehow leaked out. Fear of gossip drifting back to Boston, and resentment perhaps of apparent carelessness, thus prompted the sudden move. But more was no doubt at stake. From the beginning Harry and Christiana had been put off by Jung's failure to deal at all closely with their personal histories. While both came away impressed with Jung's charismatic authority, and with the value of much that he had to say, they were disturbed that his attention seemed fixed almost exclusively on the ways in which their lives confirmed his "universal" theories. In Christiana's case particularly, he asked very few questions before launching into an analysis of her personality type. This worked well enough, in good part because she had long since found her place within the Jungian scheme of things. But it was nonetheless annoying and irresponsible in the Old Man that he failed so completely to see beyond the boundaries of his preconceptions.

The strange impersonality of Jung's approach comes through quite sharply in a letter of 1931 written in response to Harry's report of the breakdown of the dyad. "I am sorry for Christiana," he begins, "that she didn't succeed in whatever her quest was, or perhaps she succeeded and did not know it—which, alas, is a defeat just as well. I can't be sorry for you, because you learn and experience, and you got rid of a bother—a thing that became a nuisance. You have not learned the one thing through Christiana, beyond which there is no further experience, and therefore you have to try the opposite." To Jung's view, Christiana had been incorrigibly wrong-headed in her own designs and, worse, an obstacle to Harry's achievement of individuation, the only goal really worth pursuing. There is nothing here of love, nothing of loyalty, nothing of loss. Just good riddance to "a bother," to "a thing that became a nuisance."

Jung's evident lack of regard for Christiana's "quest" struck a familiar note. He had regularly chastised her during the analysis for relying too heavily on her obvious intelligence. It was a woman's nature, he insisted, to feel, not to think. Jung's theory made little room for thoughtful women, Harry often complained. "The moment they start thinking, they begin to get argumentative and contradict him." Jung's prejudice on this score is a conspicuous feature of *The Vision Seminars*, which open to a portrait of Christiana as "a typical intellectual" with "an extraordinarily one-sided development of [her] thinking function." It was even more annoying to Christiana that Jung showed so little interest in what concerned her most, the development of the dyad. When she discussed her relationship with Harry, or when she produced visions that involved male companion figures, he was without interest or comprehension. Individuation was the only goal he seriously considered. "These lectures," he declares at the beginning of *The Vision Seminars,* "are about the development . . . of the transcendent function out of dreams." While it is true that Jung had no opportunity to comment on the final cluster of visions in which the dyad is most centrally featured, there is little evidence—either in the accounts of his analytical sessions with Christiana or in his published remarks on the earlier visions—that he would have seen or sympathized with their drift. "It wasn't in his being" to have done so, Harry believed.

In his "Postscript" to *The Vision Seminars*—composed, he is careful to note, in response to the editor's invitation to "pen a few words about Mrs. Morgan"—Harry emphasizes that Jung's lectures were "devoted to the study not of a particular case, but of a set of *universal,* self-transforming processes." He shows that the Old Man's initial esteem for Christiana—verging at points toward "libidinous affection"—cooled markedly when, after her return to America, the visions no longer conformed (as Jung put it) "to the rules." In a passage excised by the editors from the published "Postscript," Harry observes that the offending visions occurred after Christiana's departure from Zurich and suggests that their "unlawfulness could conceivably be due to the absence of the law-giver." He is perfectly unequivocal in declaring that Christiana's understanding of the visions "was nowhere near the focus of her doctor's commentary" in the published seminars. Jung was interested in individuation; but what, Harry asks, could have moved Christiana to endure the suffering that the visions so clearly demanded? What was in it for her? "Wouldn't you . . . guess," he replies, "that love was the key to it all?"

In objecting to Jung's conformity "to the gender-expectations of his day" and to his treatment of Christiana's visions as the merest "gloss for his own conceptual scheme," Claire Douglas, a Jungian analyst, reiterates Harry's emergent critique. She goes on to place

Christiana in company with the other "special women"—Lou Andreas-Salomé, Anaïs Nin, Ruth Mack Brunswick, Beata (Tola) Rank, Toni Wolff, and Sabina Spielrein—whose lives intertwined with those of the leading male figures in modern depth psychology. These were women "of quick intuitive thinking, deep interested excitement in ideas, and vibrant charm" who possessed the "capacity to energize and inspire the men in their lives." They were all in analysis with leaders of the movement, and "each became for awhile her genius's inspirer, confidant, and friend." Most crucially for Douglas, each of the women was "more or less devalued when the great man turned to other interests." Harry often observed that Christiana had a place in this group, though he would have balked at the notion that she was as close to Jung personally as Douglas suggests or that she was "devalued" in any significant way by the Old Man's shifts of focus. Jung was "vexed," Harry says, at having to terminate the vision seminars, but it was Christiana, after all, who brought them to a halt. Douglas goes on to characterize the visions as "a newly recovered archetype of women's psychological development." This is doubtless a useful corrective to Jung's schematic reading, though it overlooks entirely the dyadic emphasis in the later visions. "With Christiana and myself," Harry insisted, "that was the crux." The dyad, as it emerged from the visions to define their relationship, was among other things a conscious response to the exploitative pattern that Douglas notes and objects to. "We were concerned with a new or different kind of value," Harry observed, "which came from a relationship that was mutual, that was double, as it were, that went back and forth."

Of course they often fell short; but they never lost sight of their creative, passionate, mutually reinforcing, life-affirmative ideal. The dyad was a new idea; there was nothing quite like it in the written records of romance or in the life around them. It would not come easily, they knew that. But they both craved a challenge. They recognized that their task was not to arrive at some fixed point but rather to keep moving and adapting and experimenting. But if process was the key, then there would be painful changes and bitter sacrifices along with way. Nietzsche's yoking of creativity and destruction was axiomatic with them. Nor were they blind to the obstacles that they set in their own way. They were narcissists, strongly inclined to veer off in opposite directions—Christiana downward into herself, Harry outward into the world and work. They saw the necessity for resisting the tragic allure of the anima scenario. Devotion to the dyad, it was clear, might serve to rationalize or imperceptibly to conceal varieties of selfishness and cruelty. This was as clear to them as the guilt that they both endured. It was all part of the larger alternating rhythm of dyadic life—systole and diastole, thesis and antithesis, crisis and reconciliation. It was a hard ideal.

True to form, the triumphant reunion of 1933 bore with it the early signs of future difficulty. Christiana's jottings for August 31, 1933, refer to the emergence of a dilemma, "Man's narcism vs. woman's narcism" and record an anonymous response: "Don't talk. I'm not listening. You can dismiss that problem. It hasn't come up." It had, though, and it would again. In December of the same year Mansol wrote from New York in gratitude for Wona's initiative in their sexual life. But he goes on to thank her for returning the lead to him, thereby acknowledging his "insistent, limitless need for control." Much graver challenges came from outside the dyad, as several of those closest to it came to the ends of their lives. Both of Christiana's parents died in 1933; Harry's father followed in 1934. These were real losses, but not unexpected ones. It was much more shocking when Ralph Eaton committed suicide in April 1932. It fell to Harry, who had taken a hand in Eaton's care, to lead a corps of workers from the Clinic in the search for his body. Billy Richards, another of Christiana's quondam admirers, was also a suicide. He destroyed himself while in the course of psychotherapy and thereby fueled his brother-in-law James Conant's suspicion of Harry's work at the Clinic.

The dark shadows of these deaths were ominous with implication. Were they the signs of some fatal flaw in the dyad? Will's sudden death in May 1934 and Ike's more protracted surrender to Hodgkin's disease a year later seemed irresistibly the response to that question. The toll of Will's personal anguish was evident to many in the chronic respiratory problems that finally brought him down. Harry did his part in consoling Christiana, though he held his own feelings carefully in check, as if fearful that the weight of remorse, once loosed, might crush him. But there was no side-stepping the grief that came with Ike's passing. His death at thirty-seven was a great waste. It was also a dark commentary writ large on his older brother's extraordinary path through life. Ike had followed Harry through medicine and physiology into psychiatry. He was yet another of Christiana's doomed admirers. Along the way he had had his own anima and his own encounter with Melville. He left his first wife for good on the morning after a long night of ruminating over *Pierre*. He remarried, prospered briefly in his career, but grew increasingly dependent on drink in the years just before his death.

Harry admitted in old age that Ike's death was a painful blow to him. He grieved. But there is little if any record of his more specific feelings about the loss. The guilt was surely extreme, especially as it had by then gathered such momentum. We may suppose, too, that he and Christiana were aghast at the ruins that had heaped up around them. The human cost of their bold experiment in love had risen terribly. Had they gone too far? Did all the dying have their self-indulgence as its common cause? Such questions crossed their minds, and the minds of many in their midst. One thing was certain. They were more alone than ever now in a world gone gray.

▼

chapter nine

The Pequod Meets
the Rachel

Toward the end of *Moby-Dick,* Ahab rebuffs the captain of the *Rachel,* who comes to him with a moving appeal for assistance in the search for his son, lost at sea. For many readers the episode confirms that Ahab has sacrificed all fellow-feeling to his vendetta with the whale. Thus convicted of heartless inhumanity, the old monomaniac is hurtled forward to his ghastly reward. Christiana took a different view of the matter. During the long night of love-making with Harry at St-Jean-de-Luz in the summer of 1925, she praised Ahab for refusing to buckle under the moral condemnation and guilt that fell to him for his defiance of convention. Ahab was great, she said, because he rejected the false purity of Christian values and because he stood naked and alone, an integral, authentic man, locked in mortal combat with the punishing Jehovah of a white whale. It was their task as bearers of her vision, she argued, to follow Ahab in his heroic defiance. The truth of the dyad would demand of them a readiness to bear the guilt that came with plowing past the plangent Rachels in their way.

Christiana mourned intensely but briefly after Will's death. Harry consoled her faithfully but restrained his own feelings, insisting that Will's demise "didn't change anything down in the heart of things." Ike's loss was surely a heavier one for him, though again he gave little outward sign of grief. He was mindful, no doubt, of the Rachel episode, and possibly braced by it. Christiana may have recurred to one of the several apposite tags from Nietzsche in her collection of dyadic aphorisms. "Yea," he had written, "much bitter dying must there be in your life, ye creators!" But "all creators," Nietzsche added, "are hard." Was it hardness in the mourners that they warmed with passion on the drive home from Ike's funeral? or that they left a few days later for a vacation in Mexico? Was it the expression of callousness in Harry that he wrote to Christiana in late August, celebrating the summer as one of great advances in the dyad? Perhaps, though the hardness was in good part recoil from the sting of grief and remorse. "Good bye, good bye," says Ahab to the captain of the *Rachel*. "God bless ye, man, and may I forgive myself, but I must go." He was not cold in pulling away, anymore than in counseling hardness Nietzsche denied that dying was bitter. Harry and Christiana drew stoically together after Ike's death as an alternative to collapsing under the weight of grief and guilt. In fact, their love had grown more dear as its human costs rose. This is to say that it was more precious; but also that it was harder than ever to conceive of letting go. Now as never before the dyad had become their fate. No retreat indeed!

"My work has been a long series of abortive failures for six years," Harry complained to Lewis Mumford in early 1935. "This is partly because with me Love & Life has come first." As the year wore on, however, the crisis at the university demanded more and more of his time. There were delicate passages with Boring, Lashley, and Conant to be negotiated; it was essential to maintain close, friendly relations with Alan Gregg and the Rockefeller Foundation; and most crucially, the survival of the Clinic depended on the timely completion of *Explorations in Personality*. It was a busy, anxious, often rather frantic period. Yet Harry faced the challenge with increasing gusto. "It was just hard enough to make it exciting," he recalled. "I would go out of the Clinic with an appointment at Conant's . . . as if I had a bayonet in my hand." He enjoyed leadership; he had confidence in the quality and commitment of his staff; he knew he was right. Success was hardly assured, but Harry was untroubled by doubts about the honor of his cause. On such terms, virtually any outcome was acceptable. By contrast, the dyad had fallen deeper into the shadows of moral uncertainty. So, too, in some subtle, answering drift of feeling, had Harry's bearing toward it. More than ever before the full title of Melville's novel *Pierre or, The Ambiguities* seemed to apply. It was not that Harry drew back from the dyad; rather, it was that the swing between poles of certainty and uncertainty grow more pronounced, as if gathering passion had its secret source in gathering doubt. Christiana surely sensed the shift, both in Harry's enlarged energy for the Clinic and in the extremes of their life together. It was the old pattern in bolder relief.

Lashley's arrival in the fall of 1935 set the final stages of the crisis in motion. He exceeded all expectations in the rigidity of his insistence on a narrowly scientific (Harry called it "scientistic") definition of psychology and in the doggedness of his hostility toward psychoanalysis. At a Clinic luncheon Lashley revealed that as a boy he was as baffled by people as he was skillful with mechano-sets. Psychology finally fell open to him, he said, when he recognized that human beings and machines had a great deal in common. "He was looking for a mechano-set wherever he went," Harry scoffed. The antagonists clashed once or twice at meetings but for the most part maintained a cautious civility. Still, Lashley's periodic outbursts on the subject of the Clinic left no doubt that he was an immovable obstacle in its way. Stanley Cobb, a member of the ad hoc committee that finally voted on Harry's promotion in December 1936, had no doubts on this score. Nor did Alan Gregg, or Allport, or Boring, or Conant, for that matter. Indeed, Lashley's opposition was so furiously fixed as to seem irrational. By one account, Conant grew concerned over the new senior professor's mental stability. Could such passionate disapproval have a properly objective foundation?

Boring's opposition was less rigid and inflammatory but for that probably more damaging. Lashley undermined himself by being passionately singular, while Boring's constitutional ambivalence concealed a deeper hostility and at the same time passed for judiciousness. It may be that he believed in his own freedom from prejudice in the matter. In September 1935 he shared with Allport his assumption that Harry would be one of the four "stable" members of the department. More than a year later he apprised Lashley of his opposition to having Harvard psychology "wholly physiologized."

213

By that time, however, his vote against Harry had been cast, and his remarks were relevant only to Allport, whose advancement he favored. Harry was properly quite sure that he would have to do without his chairman's support. As the final reckoning drew near, he reared up in anger at Boring's spiteful maneuvering. "It doesn't take a psychologist to see that during the last week you have eagerly grasped at every scrap of evidence . . . which might be used as a case *against* the Clinic & have overlooked many points *for* the Clinic. In your words I find everything treacherously twisted." If a reply was written, it has not survived.

Boring's ambivalence was nowhere more conspicuously on display than in his abortive analysis with Hanns Sachs. That he sought such assistance in the first place was remarkable, given his suspicion of "non-scientific" psychology. A writing block, depressed dissatisfaction with his personality, and a brief flirtation brought him to such extreme straits that he went to Sachs "as a last resource," taking care in public to save "face by the rationalization that the psychoanalysis of an experimental psychologist might result in some important insight into the relation between the two fields." His need for help thus only barely outweighed his doubt that he would find it on Sachs' couch. Still, from September 1934 until June of the next year he gave lavishly of his time and money to the search for answers. After 168 sessions, Sachs announced that the process had run its course and left for Europe. When challenged a few years later to respond to his former patient's critique of the analysis, Sachs defended himself plausibly enough. He had in no way departed from professional convention. Boring "had no neurotic symptom," and his defects of character, though real enough, seemed little amenable to modification. Sachs agreed that a good friend might have served Boring nearly as well as psychoanalysis but observed, quite pointedly, "that it was not accidental that such a friend did not exist." In effect, then, the analyst listened patiently—in part because no one else would—until it became clear that Boring's problems were neither very deep nor very likely to go away. "A patient who wants to be cured of a neurosis," Sachs noted pregnantly, "becomes aware that he cannot set himself free without giving up an important gratification." Apparently persuaded that Boring was not prepared to make the requisite sacrifice, Sachs offered little in the way of sum-mary or advice and simply urged that he wait patiently for insight. A month and more passed, but the dawn never came, so poor Bor-ing, broke, baffled, still deeply dissatisfied with himself, and feel-ing betrayed, wrote to Harry—another "last resource"—for help.

Once again, Boring's behavior revealed deep divisions of feeling. On one side, he urged Harry to believe that he had capitulated completely to the psychoanalytic point of view. "I went into analysis with the utmost faith," he insists, and "I held to the expectation that there would be at least a major miracle." On the other side, Boring abandoned his posture of surrender for a more assertive po-sition, suggesting that his acquiescence in the psychoanalytic per-spective was conditional and fraught with consequence for the Clinic. "There are many angles to this matter," he allowed, omi-nously—"e.g., how does this affect my attitude toward analysis in the University and what can I do to be sure that I am fair?" Tell me what I need to hear, or else! he seems to threaten, his best self giving fair warning of a worst self coiling for a strike.

This perfectly ambivalent letter held few surprises for Harry. Bor-ing had "become so dependent on Sachs," he later observed, that "he couldn't live a day without making a confession of some kind." Harry's reply was itself ambiguous, though its main elements—of genuine concern mingled with ironic condescension—were con-sciously controlled. Part of him reached out to his suffering antag-onist—"What a hell of a state!" he opens; "I am dreadfully sorry." Yet almost in the same breath he chastises Boring for trying to force the creative process. "You can push yourself & write a lot of papers just so long," he warns, "but then Nature—great mother Nature who will be a hive of ideas for us if we respect her & wait upon her, like a lover—rebels." By implicit contrast with the more "natural" pace of creativity at 64 Plympton, Boring's willfulness betrays "a consuming ambition, a form of power motive." Thus identifying the submerged aggressive impulses that threaten the chairman's health—and, it is hinted, the welfare of the Clinic—Harry urges Boring to slow down. "Whoever made up the old saw about a 'watched pot don't boil' was talking about that great pregnant pot—the Unconscious." But this was of course to offer as cure the very entity that had first given rise to dispute. Harry no doubt controlled the irony, and Boring almost certainly felt its edge.

This serio-comic episode had its denouement in late August when Boring joined a party of staffers from the Clinic—including Erik Erikson, Donald MacKinnon, and Nevitt Sanford—for a week of "resuscitation" at Mid-River Farm, Harry's retreat in the Thousand Islands. But relief was in short supply for the chairman. After supper on the day of his arrival the guests gathered to play a circle game that tested their knowledge of famous historical figures. The game was hardly designed to bring out the best in a man of Boring's highly specialized interests. He failed miserably on question after question which Harry's teenage nephew, who followed him in order, dispatched with evident ease. Poor Boring. In place of promised peace of mind he was treated to a humiliating confirmation of his inadequacy. Things went rapidly from bad to worse. He got terribly sunburned, and itched; he got hay fever, and sneezed; he went to his host for comfort, and got scant sympathy ("I was a little rough on him," Harry confessed). Finally, Boring got mad. I made up my mind "to damn psychoanalysis," he later reported to Allport; "and I did DAMN it to [Harry], MacKinnon, Sanford and Homburger [Erikson] assembled, all one evening, in the middle of the St. Lawrence." It was an embarrassing scene for everyone, in part because Boring's anger was so fully, even comically, on display, and in part because he was so isolated in his point of view. Still, there could be no doubt now how things really stood between the chairman and the director of the Clinic.

Harry's relationship with Conant was no less complicated. It was obviously necessary to do everything possible to win the President's good will. This included inviting him down to 64 Plympton for lunch and a tour of the Clinic. Nevitt Sanford, who was present on that occasion, recalled being "considerably let down with our heroic Harry, who was far too deferential toward this pipsqueak of a chemist." In fact, Harry shared Sanford's critical view of Conant. "I wasn't at all fond of this man," he later admitted. "He was all ready to be an enemy of the Psychological Clinic and Freud and psychoanalysis and me and everything else." Still, Harry did his best to maintain a level civility, though at times the hint of irony in his remarks, and an impulse to tease, made the President uneasy. Conant sought the advice of many, including Lashley and Boring, the latter of whom recommended that Harry be reviewed for yet another three-year appointment. But Conant, faithfully observing his own new "up-or-out" policy, insisted on a final decision between promotion to a tenured Associate Professorship or termination. Given the difficulty and importance of the case, he asked Alan Gregg to extend for a third year the Rockefeller support granted to the Clinic in September 1934 and again in September 1935 This would make time both for the completion of *Explorations in Personality* and for the deliberations of an ad hoc committee appointed to assist him in settling the matter by the end of January 1937. Gregg responded with a grant-in-aid of $5,000, issued on the understanding that no further support would be considered until a firm judgment on Harry's future, and on the future of the Clinic, had been reached.

Explorations had developed rather slowly, both because Harry was opening new territory and because he was prone to defer writing until the pressure to publish finally forced pen to paper. The actual research on the project had begun early in the decade and became more focused as the idea of studying whole personalities crystallized in Harry's mind. When word spread in the fall of 1935 that Lashley had advised Conant to close the Clinic, Harry advised his staff that the time to write was urgently upon them. They responded during the next year or so with a steady stream of articles, most of them geared to the *Explorations* research and many destined to turn up as sections of the completed volume. Harry published several such papers, two of which—"Basic Concepts for a Psychology of Personality" and "Facts Which Support the Concept of Need or Drive"—figure prominently in the pivotal *Explorations* chapter on theory. He had complained to Lewis Mumford in 1935 of his tendency as a writer to "build, tear down, build, tear down . . . and, then, in a kind of desperation write anything that happens to be in my head." He traced his difficulty to the lack of any "preliminary classification or set of fundamental concepts to go ahead on—there are too many empty spaces which need to be filled in before any adequate map is possible." The pair of theoretical essays were designed to help fill that vacuum. Two others—"Techniques for a Systematic Investigation of Fantasy" and "An Experiment in Judging Personalities" (with Richard E. Wolf)—would also find places in later chapters of the book.

Because he had more lives than most people, Harry was always very busy; but never more so than during the final years of crisis at 64 Plympton. The public man was visibly active as director of the Clinic, where, just after Christmas in 1936, he was host to a gathering of prominent American and European psychologists at a conference honoring Kurt Lewin. During the same period Harry organized a series of six seminars on aspects of psychoanalysis led by Hanns Sachs. Designed to build bridges between warring factions in the department, the meetings were variously subverted by Lashley and Boring. The chairman was no more helpful when it came to the elaborate Harvard Tercentenary celebrations earlier that year. Harry contributed in substantial ways, by helping to nominate the distinguished psychologists—Janet, Jung, and Piaget—to be honored with degrees and by welcoming them to a gala luncheon at the Clinic. Boring wrote to Harry that the luncheon "would be a splendid thing" but then immediately confided to Lashley that he felt "a little cool to the whole business." Fortunately, Jung and Conant got along famously. Meanwhile, Harry's expanding professional interests found an outlet in the self-styled "Levellers," a group that included Bernard DeVoto, Clyde and Florence Kluckhohn, and Talcott Parsons, among others, and that met regularly for wide-ranging discussions of social theory and American values. The same broad concerns surfaced in preliminary proposals, first to Boring in 1934 and then to the Rockefeller Foundation two years later, for an interdisciplinary Institute of Human Relations at Harvard. There was also time for a few patients, most notably the novelist Eva Goldbeck, a good friend of Lewis and Sophia Mumford, who impressed Harry with her plucky independence during the year or so before her death—of anorexia—in 1936. Finally, he completed two additional papers in psychology. The first, a brief study of dreams bearing on the kidnapping of the Lindbergh baby, finds little evidence to support the popular belief "that distant events and dreams are causally related." The second, a cogent discussion of the psychogenic origins of selected physiological processes, was first delivered at a Harvard Medical School colloquium in 1936. Drawing on the work of Claude Bernard, George Draper, and Franz Alexander, and copiously illustrated with examples from Harry's own practice, the paper is evidence of a continuing commitment to the treatment of the whole patient. "Seek in the body what the tongue cannot utter," Harry advised, "for what the mind conceals—even from itself—the body will display."

Still, until it was finally published in 1938, the developing manuscript of *Explorations in Personality* was at the center of Harry's often divided attention. The precise form of the project was slow taking shape in his mind. At first he seems to have conceived of it as two volumes. Nor was he at all reliable in estimating its likely date of completion. He assured Mumford early in 1935 that the research, which had gone "marvelously well," would be in "final shape" by the fall. It was not. That November, in an article on the Clinic featured in the *Boston Evening Transcript,* he predicted that the book would be published "within a year." Again, he was too sanguine. It was not for lack of effort that things moved slowly. The Clinic was busy day and night with activity, virtually all of it focused on the great book. "There was a lot of talk," Robert White recalled, "a lot of excitement, a lot of argument. . . . Most important, no doubt, was the sense of being launched on a large and significant mission, the development at last of a real way, even though an exceedingly long way, to understand personality." *Explorations* grew larger as additional subjects were brought on board, as new procedures were conceived, and as the theory continued to evolve. It was not ready for a publisher in late 1936, as Harry had hoped it would be. But it was sufficiently complete for consideration by Conant's ad hoc committee. That was the main thing.

The manuscript of *Explorations* was much longer than the published version and must have run to at least 1,500 pages. It needed editing, elaboration in places, and a great deal of pruning. Still, it was not so far from completion that its leading qualities were in any significant way obscured. The members of Conant's committee sat down to what has since been widely recognized as a classic in American psychology, a book among few others belonging on the same shelf with the work of William James. It was, Harry made it clear, the work of many hands. Twenty-seven names—13 Ph.D.s and 2 M.D.s—appear below his own on the title page. A rare triumph of teamwork in the academy, *Explorations* owed its success, Harry often acknowledged, to "the exceptional spirit, character, competence, and imaginative scope" of the Clinic staff. Just as clearly, however, the book's style and distinctiveness were largely the contribution of one man. Harry wrote five of the eight chapters on his own and made substantial contributions to the other three. The ambition of the enterprise, manifest from the start in an Olympian dedication to Prince, Freud, Henderson, Whitehead, and Jung, was also quite obviously his.

Explorations is celebrated both for its bold view of human nature and for the innovative procedures with which it approached its object of study. To an emphatically organismic definition of personality—conceived as an integrated hierarchy of interdependent processes—it brings the answering conviction that human beings must be studied as dynamic, developing wholes. It is a psychology of human motives, giving scant attention to deeds, except as they form a window on the interior life. "Motivation is the crux of the business," Harry insists, "and motivation always refers to something within the organism." At the center of the action is the brain, where motives—or needs, as Harry refers to them—accompanied by emotions and linked to "regnant" physiological processes, have their locus. *Explorations* features a copiously developed taxonomy of twenty manifest and eight latent needs, ranging from abasement and achievement to the repressed desire for succorance. A need is defined as "a force . . . which organizes perception, apperception, intellection, conation and action in such a way as to transform in a certain direction an existing, unsatisfying situation." Needs, which may be conscious or unconscious, are thus geared to a "field" of external objects and persons whose influence is defined as "press"— the power "to affect the well-being of the subject in one way or another." Personality cannot be understood in isolation from its environment. Nor can it be reckoned with outside of time. "The history of a personality," Harry insists, "*is* the personality." His definition of the stages of childhood development, and his emphasis on the infantile complexes, are directly indebted to Freud. The same may be said for his tripartite (id/ego/superego) conception of the structure of personality and his pervasive insistence on the play of unconscious processes. But while readily conceding that psychoanalysis "provides the best orientation for the study of human personality," Harry is hardly passive in yielding to Freud's genius. He finds pansexualism a grievous distortion and highlights what Freud rather minimized in humans—the ego, with its capacity for choice, its striving for mastery, its orientation to the future, and its prodigious creativity. This was a psychology for active, optimistic men and women.

Much of what Harry had to say was new to American psychology. This is not to deny that his needs are reminiscent of McDougall's "instincts," that he was influenced by Lewin's views on the psychological environment or "field," and that he shared Allport's interest in an ego psychology of unique individuals. But it is to claim, following many other observers, that *Explorations,* in its attention to a whole, integrated, developing, creatively goal-directed human nature, brought something distinctive and exciting to the field. "It was indeed a whale of a book," observes Robert White. "It was a tall order for science, but anything less now seemed like nibbling around the edges of personality." For younger students, Harry's work had a unique magnetism. "For me and for many others," recalls M. Brewster Smith, "*Explorations* embodied Murray's charisma and enticed us to commitment to the field that it substantially redefined."

Harry's methods were also highly innovative. His insistence on the intensive study of small numbers of normal subjects was the certain corollary of the belief that personality was to be discovered at depth and in details. "Averages," he wrote, "obliterate the 'individual characters of individual organisms' (Whitehead), and so fail to reveal the complex interaction of forces which determines each concrete event." His attention to imaginal productions—most notably in the TAT but also in an ink blot test, a similes test, a story-completion procedure, and tests of musical reveries and dramatic productions—was also remarkable. "Never before," observes Robert

White, "had such a concerted attempt been made to stimulate a subject's imagination and thus to creep up on the possible shape of his latent needs and unconscious fantasies."

The five-member diagnostic council, modeled—as its name implies—on the staff conferences that Harry witnessed in medical school, was another striking innovation. It was the business of the diagnosticians to rate each subject on all variables. Final scores were settled on at five-hour meetings given to the presentation of reports and the gradual, often heated approach to consensus. From these sessions emerged case histories of individual subjects. Several such narratives were completed, but limited space dictated that only one, Robert White's "The Case of Earnst," would appear in *Explorations*. Organized around a "unity thema"—a repeating reaction pattern rooted in childhood experience—the case histories were, Harry acknowledged, "the proof of the pudding." He defended the narratives as "the factual substance for a true science of psychology," and located them, quite aptly, "somewhere on the continuum between biology . . . and literature." If White's graceful, generous portrait of Earnst, brilliant in its seemingly effortless penetration, is the "proof" of *Explorations,* then it surely vindicates the human promise of the enterprise. We are drawn, by the force of science made supple in fine, generally plain language, to a profoundly enriched perspective on one person's interior life. Pregnant with moral and scientific implications for an enhanced understanding of human nature, this middle ground, defined best perhaps by William James, was what Harry had sought, and surely approached, in his magnum opus.

Explorations is also Harry's book in the sense that it expresses his personality—his values, his needs, an idealized self-image, and something perhaps of his unconscious, or at least unacknowledged, life. Most obviously, Harry's conception of human nature was a reflection of leading elements in his own makeup. Few who knew him failed to observe that he was an extraordinarily dynamic, complexly integrated, striving, consciously discriminating, creative human being. Quite as clearly, he had good personal reasons to suppose that imaginative productions would reveal the deepest, truest self. Harry's attentiveness to the unconscious and his adeptness at deciphering its codes was an oblique index to his fascination with his own interior life. He located the truly human where he found what he took to be his truest self. Little wonder that he preferred the "intraceptive" psychologist, the creative possessor of a "veritable intellectual interest," to the "extraceptive" technician, the quintessentially socialized American, whose horizons are defined by a few well-worn procedures. Harry admired intellectual breadth, the sweep of the gifted amateur, of the generalist, the Renaissance man, master of many disciplines, slave to none. Lewis Mumford fit the profile very well; but so, even more perfectly, did Harry himself. He emerges just as clearly in the declaration that "the greater part of a person's life is private and subjective; much of it is related directly to Nature and much is either casually or informally social or involves only one other person." For all of his attention to the context of personality, to "press," Harry was inclined to view the individual as an island, separate, remote, and generally disposed, as he was, to want to keep it that way.

Explorations is also personally revealing in its insistence on the unfathomable complexity of human nature. Defined as the deepest riddle of all, personality was uniquely adequate to Harry's need to achieve. It was an exhilarating challenge to his wide-ranging talents as scientist, social scientist, and humanist. Only a small elite could even contemplate undertaking the task he set for himself. To construe personality as the remotest *terra incognita* was of course to risk failure. But Harry had no fear of falling short. He was at one level a bold Magellan of the psyche, confident that the goal was within reach; but in another, more deeply characteristic dimension, his pleasure in the continuous, exhilarating play of mind inclined him to hope that the search would never end. Thus, at the same time that it gave Harry's quest great stature, the bottomless riddle of the human soul rationalized the indefinite deferral of closure.

But the idea of insoluble human mystery had another, even more intimately personal attraction for Harry. The idea is potently present to *Pierre,* a novel all about the impossibility of unraveling the tangled skein of human motive. The book took hold of Harry not only because it develops this theme but because it does so in terms

223

of complex romantic involvements that fatefully anticipated his own. It was complicating, of course, that the plot has its outcome in unmitigated disaster. But such fictional woe, Harry insisted, was a species of madness. He had a similar response to the novelist's horror at the mystery of human nature. "Appalling is the soul of man!" Melville cautions. "Better might one be pushed off into the material spaces beyond the uttermost orbit of our sun, than once feel himself fairly afloat in himself!" For Harry, as for many intellectuals, the spectacle of fathomless human complexity was no longer as terrifying as it had been for Melville's generation. Indeed, for the man who endured painful uncertainty and guilt as the price of his persistence in an unorthodox romantic relationship, the vast personal unknown was a secret source of consolation. A part of him believed that the dyad transcended traditional Christian values; another part of him yielded to the old ways. But if the truth of human nature was submerged in mystery, then the dyad, which had its foundation in the remote unconscious, was likely the more authoritative creed. In fact, the enigma of personality gave no foothold to certainty; and that which could not be known could not be judged. The riddle of the soul, as it gave rise to this latter day, secular antinomianism, had an irresistible appeal for one as painfully torn as Harry. That he took comfort from the mystery which consumed Pierre was decisive both in his own life and in the life he planned for Melville.

Even in its unfinished state, *Explorations* should have been enough to carry the day for Harry and his Clinic. But it was not. Nor were the nearly two dozen letters, all but two or three of them overwhelmingly positive, that gathered toward the end of 1936 in support of the cause. Alan Gregg sent a brilliant letter; Alfred Cohn wrote; so did Lewin and McDougall; Jung himself joined the chorus of praise. But even as outside support accumulated, opinion on the inside of the department grew more firmly negative. Lashley advocated the end of all social and psychoanalytic research at Harvard and threatened to resign unless he had his way. Boring professed neutrality but privately gave little weight to the mass of support that had gathered in Harry's corner. His mind was made up. Fortunately, Allport remained faithful. He wrote to Harry in August

1936 to express the view "that any change in the Clinic except in the direction of greater stability would be disastrous for Harvard." He would never warm completely to his colleague's work or personal style, but Allport was supportive nonetheless, in part no doubt because he was the likely heir to Harry's troubles, especially if the Clinic failed. Some such reasoning prompted him to inform Boring that he would resign if Harry lost out.

Conant appointed his ad hoc committee—Boring, Lashley, and Allport from the Psychology Department, Stanley Cobb and Dean Burwell representing the Medical School, and Dean Birkhoff of the Faculty of Arts and Sciences—in early December. He asked that they prepare themselves for a luncheon meeting to be held at his home just two days before Christmas, when he would seek their settled views. There is no absolutely definitive account of the confidential proceedings. But Harry had it on good authority that the discussion began to warm up when Allport compared him to William James, another medically trained innovator in humanistic psychology at Harvard. If that was so, Lashley snapped, then Harry had little to recommend him, for James had done "more harm to psychology than any man that ever lived." Such blasphemy, explicable only as the *faux pas* of a hot-headed newcomer, was offensive to all assembled, not least of all Conant himself, who is said to have rushed angrily from the room. When tempers finally cooled and a vote was taken, the committee divided evenly between Allport, Burwell, and Cobb, who were for promotion and tenure, and Birkhoff, Boring, and Lashley, who were against.

The advisory letter to Conant, drafted jointly by Allport and Lashley, acknowledged that Harry's approach to personality was appropriately complex, and judged that his work compared favorably with research in the same field at other institutions. On the other hand, they faulted him for his terminology, his partiality to psychoanalysis, and his reliance on the diagnostic council—in place of quantitative methods—for the final interpretation of data. In a separate letter written after the committee report had been completed, Allport described Harry as bringing "a more critical mind to his subject than did Charcot, Prince, Freud, or Jung." He urged Conant not to "permit the humanistic tradition in psychology at

Harvard to be imperiled and destroyed. The critical standards of the 'exact sciences,'" he warned, though "admirable in their own right, are not catholic enough in outlook to serve as the norm for the newer science of the human mind." Lashley made just the opposite argument in his own letter to Conant. Offering the case as exemplary of "the conflict between the older humanistic and philosophical psychology and the attempt to evolve a more exact science through an objective and biological approach," he accused Harry of "a sort of intellectual dishonesty" in his "supercilious attitude" toward statistical methods of validating results. Now it was the President's task to resolve the impasse.

Conant was sensitive to the multiple dimensions of the case before him. He was most concerned about the lack of scientific rigor that Lashley and others had criticized in Harry's research. Psychoanalysis was part and parcel with the same problem, and obnoxious to him on personal grounds as well. Perhaps, too, he recognized that Harry's privileges of class and wealth were a source of resentment to other members of the department. Certainly Boring could not conceal his annoyance that as the Clinic controversy wound to its climax, Harry left Cambridge on a vacation cruise to the West Indies. But when at last he squared himself up to a decision in the case, Conant gave most of his attention to the matter of money. If Harry and the Clinic were to stay at Harvard, who would fill the fiscal gap that had grown annually wider since early in the decade? Fortunately, Alan Gregg and the Rockefeller Foundation were willing. In a meeting with Conant on March 12, 1937, Gregg advised that "it was important to reassure Murray by taking action quickly, and to tell Lashley to get used to the decision." Even more crucially, he made it clear that the Rockefeller Foundation would continue to support Harry's work at the Clinic. Five days later Conant announced that he had decided to appoint Harry to consecutive five-year terms as an Associate Professor of Abnormal and Dynamic Psychology. Though the appointment was untenured—a compromise first proposed by Boring—no one doubted for a moment that Harry had won and that the Clinic was at Harvard to stay.

Letters of congratulation poured in. Even Lashley, whose bitterness against the Clinic ran so deep that Conant finally freed him from teaching and administrative duties in the department, sent a word or two. Donald MacKinnon was not alone in observing that "a discontinuation of the Clinic would have been a blow to every center of teaching and research in dynamic psychology while its continuation is a boon to every such center. . . . Every psychologist owes you a profound debt of gratitude." Subsequent observers have amply confirmed MacKinnon's assessment. Thanks to Gregg's timely support, the Clinic, a model for collaborative research in the field, survived to become the training ground for yet another generation of leading American psychologists. The victory all but assured that *Explorations* would find its way into print. In the years since, Harry's theory of needs has been judged a "more widely useful" classification of human motives than any comparable scheme. His pioneering advocacy of psychoanalysis—manifest both in his empirical testing of psychoanalytic concepts and in his ingenious methods for drawing out the unconscious—was to be decisive in bringing Freud home to the American academy. More familiarly perhaps, his bold insistence on the complexity and creativity of the whole person earned him a place among the leaders of the humanistic psychology movement. In short, Harry's "victory" in 1937 was an event of no little significance in the history of American psychology.

The year-end party at the Clinic that June was a memorable celebration. Harry wrote a play for the occasion entitled "Clinicus, or the auto-erotic chronicle of a ten year old orphan of uncertain sex and parentage. A comical tragedy with a sentimental ending in one Act." In the course of a mock-heroic quest after her/his true identity, the young hero, Clinicus, an androgynous foundling, enjoys the mixed blessing of support from an assortment of genial bumblers, including among others Count Von Hamburg (Erik Erikson), "impecunious artist, glorifier of the orifices of Mayflower descendants," the Reverend Sangfroid (Nevitt Sanford), Dr. Lager (Walter Langer), Professor Rosieway (Saul Rosenzweig), Father Divine (Kenneth Diven), and, most notably, Queen Morganatic. "I am the sum of a million incarnations," she declares. "I am a reservoir of living archetypes. I have been here from the beginning. I played post office with Adam before Eve was born, and later, hiding behind a banian tree, saw Eve offer the apple and witnessed the primal scene—and let me tell you . . . it was no trauma." The bad guys include Matron Borley, Professor Lashing "of the Society for Cruelty to Animals and Children," and King Conute, "procurer for an old whore, Harvardiana." The piece ends on a happily raucous note when Clinicus is granted a permanent home at 64 Plympton and discovers that the entire staff at that address are her/his parents.

Still, the play is not unmingled sunshine. There is an abrasiveness to the humor that betrays a certain ambivalence, and even anger, in Harry's feelings about the university. This mood is at its sharpest in his treatment of King Conute's announcement that "Dame Harvardiana" has decided to adopt the foundling. "The venerable old slut has received a legacy from one of her lovers and she can now afford to give Clinicus a playground with the very best equipment." The evident bitterness of the speech culminates in the declaration that the former orphan is at last free to "be as unscientific as she pleases." All the inspired thinking, and all the cooperation among bright, creative colleagues would have come to nothing, it seemed, had it not been for a heap of mere cash. The sentiment was exaggerated, no doubt, and had about it that contempt for money sometimes found in the very rich. Still, the damage to Harry's idealism on the score of the university was deep and permanent. He had been forced to endure a humiliating critical review by men whose professional judgment he could not respect. His best creative efforts had been found wanting; he had been denied tenure. That he rarely discussed these insults to his pride is the best evidence of their gravity. In 1937 Harry completed a decade of teaching and research at Harvard. Of the succeeding eleven years, he gave but two to his alma mater. And when he returned to full-time teaching in 1948, things were not the same. They never would be.

Harry's original plan for a sabbatical year was soon extended, with Conant's approval, to include a second year of leave without pay. Two more years were subsequently added, with the result that he did not return to the classroom until 1941. During his four years away the Clinic continued to operate at a reduced pace under the direction of Robert White. Harry's plans called for the rapid completion of *Explorations in Personality,* to be followed by a long stretch of research and writing on the Melville biography, which he hoped to finish before his return to teaching. During most of the leave he was at home in Boston, though he moved for a while to New York after his mother's death in 1940. There was also time for travel. He crossed the country by train late in 1939, visiting major centers of research in psychology and psychiatry and looking for promising new associates to join him at the Clinic. He toured Germany with his family during the summer of 1937 and wrote home of having had a "close view" of Hitler at the Wagner festival in Bayreuth. "He is an unimpressive, harassed man," Harry reported, "who seems to me to be beyond his depths. He is under the constant care of a Munich psychiatrist of the old school. Symptoms: severe depressions & nightmares (insomnia)—probably of persecution. To think that the peace of Europe hangs on the electro-chemical system in that cranium!"

Harry returned home that fall, in part to hear Jung deliver the Terry lectures at Yale. But by December he was back in Europe, to spend the Christmas holidays with Josephine, who was at school in Lausanne. Just after the New Year he went on to Vienna, where he met for a few hours with Freud. Despite his failing health, the old man seemed anxious to have the meeting. After an exchange of cordial greetings, he led his guest on a brief tour of the house— Harry was especially struck by the dozens of phallic objects on display in the office—but then turned to what really interested him. How was it, Freud wanted to know, that his enemy Jung had been selected to receive an honorary degree at the Harvard Tercentenary, while he himself had not. Harry concealed his shock at this open display of vanity. He explained—quite truthfully—that Freud had been number one on the department's list; concern for his health, reinforced by Erikson's first-hand reports from Vienna, had alone constrained them. This seemed to please Freud, who turned to other matters, including a discussion of *Moby-Dick,* his favorite American novel.

The ominous signs of war in Europe, and the persistence of the Depression at home, were a spur to Harry's comparatively underdeveloped social and political interests. He quarreled bitterly with his sister, Virginia, an unyielding Republican, about Hitler and Nazism, which he attacked, and about Roosevelt and the New Deal, which he defended. There were rather less heated debates with his friend Felix Frankfurter—then on the faculty at the Harvard Law School—who took the offensive against Jung's alleged connections with the Nazis. Harry was sensitive to the evidence of anti-Semitism in Jung's thinking; but he knew as well that the Old Man regarded Hitler as a dangerous paranoid and had refused to take him as a patient. Signs of tension were also beginning to surface in Harry's relationship with Lewis Mumford, whose often rather smug self-absorption seemed especially insupportable during the period of crisis at the Clinic. Harry criticized Mumford for the self-righteous tone that sometimes crept into his commentary on social issues and characterized his authorial manner as "autocratic." The cooling trend in their letters was balanced in Harry's life by a developing friendship with Clyde Kluckhohn, the anthropologist, whose personal warmth and broad interdisciplinary interests were widely known and admired around Cambridge. As the two came to know each other better, they were increasingly watchful for opportunities to teach and write together. "Your suggested project for studying the social structure of Harvard interests me very much," Kluckhohn wrote in 1940. He recognized that the undertaking was "loaded with internal dynamite" but apparently had no objection to joining his new friend in a little blasting.

The work on *Explorations* continued well into the summer of 1937. Harry was himself centrally involved, writing as many as fifty pages in a single week and prodding the laggards on his staff to complete their contributions. He found that most publishers, feeling the pinch of hard times, were very reluctant to risk their scarce resources on his enormous, highly technical opus. But Oxford University Press finally agreed to take the book, on condition that Harry advance $1000 toward the cost of its production. When they insisted that the manuscript was too long, he cut the chapter on statistics, both because it had little interest for him and because he enjoyed "thumbing his nose" at the pseudo-scientists in the field. Harry's determination that the book should succeed was reflected in his close attention to details. He revised carefully, offered advice on likely reviewers, and ordered a load of complimentary copies distributed to friends. As a device for the jacket of *Explorations* he sent his editors a copy of the bronze medallion that had been cast for distribution to all Clinic Ph.D.s at the tenth anniversary celebration in 1937. Designed primarily by Christiana and subsequently adopted as the Clinic's "coat of arms," the medallion represents the unconscious as a vast undersea world of mighty creatures. Just above the water, as if afloat upon it, a human face reposes in sunlight. Harry once explained that the octopus at the bottom of the sea symbolizes the possessive, cosmic mother; a whale near the surface is leviathan, the devouring father; in the middle is a swordfish, representing youth, which strains upward, against the parents, and toward the light of consciousness above. It is an allegory of Jungian individuation, the process of emergence into wholeness which first inspired the dyad and to which it was dedicated. Across the scene appear words that Harry ascribed, somewhat vaguely, to Jung— "Let Not Him Who Seeks Cease Until He Finds, And When He Finds He Shall Be Astonished."

It was to be expected, of course, that Harry's friends would respond with enthusiasm to the long-awaited child of his labor. "This book," declared Raymond Pearl in a brief review, "presents a detailed and technical account of the most original, thoroughgoing, and systematic attempt at a consistently scientific appraisal and understanding of human personality that has yet been made." John Dollard, from the Institute of Human Relations at Yale, confessed in awe that *Explorations* gave him "a considerable feeling of inferiority." Ruth Benedict was equally impressed. "It's the only book I've read that has done the psychological ground-work I need as an anthropologist," she wrote. Jung sent his congratulations and noted with special pleasure what he took to be confirmation of his theory of archetypes. Though grateful enough for the response, Harry secretly doubted that the Old Man had gotten much past the index. A more plausible species of praise came from Conrad Aiken. "How wonderfully you've organized your attack on so slippery and elusive a shadow," he wrote. "I hope it will jolt the harvard grannies, and do for the clinic all you've hoped." The poet made special note of Eleanor Jones' contribution, "a damned good little portrait" of Earnst.

As Aiken seems to have glimpsed, *Explorations* was a maverick performance. Regarded today as a monument to independence and creativity, it was in 1938 a bold challenge to the settled conventions of research and writing in the field of personality psychology. "You will have opponents and derogators," Boring predicted. "The book is too positive and vital not to stir criticism. You must have wanted all that," he observed, quite shrewdly, "in a way at least; and certainly you'll have it." In view of its clear invitation to criticism, it is surprising—and no small tribute to the force of its argument—that *Explorations* fared as well as it did with reviewers. The newspapers were generally very favorable and thus confirmed Harry's view that his approach to psychology had ordinary common sense on its side. Journals with sharply defined perspectives were also generally predictable in their responses. The *Psychoanalytic Quarterly* praised the book for "emphasizing dynamic psychology in academic circles" but faulted it for its "relatively superficial" treatment of individual cases. In similar fashion, the *American Journal of Sociology* condemned Harry for his naiveté "with respect to the social determinants of personality." The reviewer for the *Psychological Bulletin* took a more balanced approach. He wrote with approval of Harry's need theory, his adaptations of Freud, his ingenious methods of assessment, and his freedom from narrow preconceptions. On the other side, he found the book obscure in its terminology, naive at points in the design of experiments, and inadequate in its statistics. Overall, he was impressed, especially with the bold scope of the enterprise. "It has been a gallant attempt," he concludes; "this study might be compared to an attempt to reach the top of Mount Everest."

There is a similar balancing of views in the ten-page critical essay that appeared in the *American Journal of Psychology*. Because of its length, its judicious thoroughness, and the reputation of its author, Richard M. Elliott, a respected experimental psychologist from Minnesota, the review carried great weight in the field. Elliott acknowledged that *Explorations* is "by far the most comprehensive attempt" yet made "to bring Freudian psychology and experimental psychology into line with each other." This is commendable, he granted, but virtually impossible, for psychoanalysis and science simply don't mix. He predicted that the book would please those psychologists who "feel no distaste for psychoanalytic theory and wide horizons in general" but that it would be "trying" for the "larger group" who favor "rigidly controlled experimental methods and carefully used statistics." While Elliott made no bones about the fact that he belonged with the latter, majority contingent, he commended Harry for the courage and the intelligence of his attempt "to correct the prevalent anti-intraceptive bias." *Explorations* is "bold and brilliant," he conceded; it is also erratic in its selection of experiments, gravely deficient in its statistical methods, and fatally infatuated with Freud. "One book like this is enough." But it is a book that all psychologists—and most especially those who hunger after "that far-off goal, the fathoming of *a* man"—must read. The alternative is to risk the taunt that Henry IV of France reserved for his most fearless general: "Hang yourself, brave Crillon, We fought at Arques and you were not there!" Harry knew that he could not have hoped for a more reasoned, thoroughgoing, and generously good-humored response from a member of the extraceptive majority. He said as much in a letter to Elliott, who became a good friend and who regularly apologized in later years for his abuse of Harry's masterpiece.

With *Explorations* successfully completed, Harry turned once again to the project that most pleased and challenged him, the biography of Herman Melville. The work commenced in earnest after his return from Europe early in 1938 and continued, with sundry interruptions along the way, for more than three years. He began at the beginning, with a preface, a prologue, and a chapter on the courtship of Melville's parents. "Now I begin with his first gurglings," he wrote to Josephine in February. He was also busy with background research on the English Romantics and on "the biography of Conscience (the New England variety)," as it descended like a blight from remote antiquity, through Calvin, to its prominent place in the intellectual climate of Melville's America. April found him planning a chapter on "The Oriental Anima & the

Byronic Hero." The work on *Explorations,* he assured his daughter, was "very tedious in comparison with H.M." By October he had a draft of about 400 pages, much of it freshly written, the rest revised and typed versions of handwritten chapters composed several years earlier. He complained to Mumford that he had in all of those pages gotten Melville no further than Tahiti, where the young seaman, then just 23, took a brief break from whaling in the summer of 1842. "I am spending a disproportionate amount of time on youthful influences," he explained, " & am cutting down the last 40 years of spiritual . . . anticlimax to a bare 3 or 4 chapters." Thereafter the chapters on the individual novels came in regular order. *Mardi, White-Jacket,* and *Redburn* filled the summer of 1939, followed by *Moby-Dick* and *Pierre* in 1940.

As he moved forward in the narrative of Melville's life, the pace of Harry's progress slowed. There were distractions, among them his cross-country search for new Clinic staff at the end of 1939, his mother's death the next year, and the rapid spread of war in Europe. Harry was troubled by the conflict between his own advocacy of American military intervention against Nazism and what he took to be Melville's pacifism. His empathic identification with the novelist was so close that their sharp disagreement on a matter of such solemnity shook his confidence. Subsequent research lead Harry to conclude that Melville was not a pacifist after all, but by then his long leave of absence was over. "I haven't been able to write a readable word on Melville since the invasion of France," he wrote to Mumford in December 1941. "Now he is packed away in a file while I rush ahead on a hundred and one other things." Still, at the time of his return to Harvard that September he had put together an enormous manuscipt—three volumes, he estimated—virtually finished in parts but requiring new writing and substantial revision in others. It was a vast, uneven pile. He had ploughed forward to 1852, when Melville, at 33, finished *Pierre.* But there had been neither the time nor the heart to go further. Harry told himself, as he put the biography aside, that he would someday confront the overplus of woe that awaited him in the second half of Melville's life. In fact, he never did.

Harry was initially taken with Melville's life because he saw his own in it. It is one among many reasons for his failure to finish Melville's life that he could not empathize with all of it. Clearly enough, the novelist's later years were an obstacle for him. Harry's Melville was a heroic figure of Promethean defiance, not the failed husband and father, the plodding bureaucrat, the obscure genius bent by adversity into three decades and more of decline. Harry wanted none of this. With Ishmael in *Moby-Dick*—and, we feel, with Melville himself—he looked on "with keenest anguish at the undraped spectacle of a valor-ruined man." But of course dismay at his hero's undoing was tied up with an uneasiness about its implications for his own life. He would share Melville's defiance but not his defeat. This consideration figured with several others in Harry's decision—arrived at in the years just after the war—to abandon the full-scale biography. In its place he published a number of shorter critical studies—most notably the long Introduction to his 1949 Hendricks House edition of *Pierre*—which drew heavily on the now-dormant biography. Unfortunately, one or more of the last chapters of the original manuscript—those covering *Pierre*—were destroyed in the course of revision. Their contents are readily inferred, both from the trajectory of what remains of the biography, and from the *Pierre* edition itself.

The surviving manuscript runs to well over 1,000 pages, and concludes with two long chapters on *Moby-Dick.* Even in its incomplete form, the biography is an extraordinary accomplishment. The story unfolds in long chapters that deal copiously with the novelist's patrician heritage, his mother's pride, the trauma of his father's untimely death, difficulties in securing a livelihood, the years before the mast, and his rise to fame as the author of *Typee, Omoo, Mardi, Redburn,* and *White-Jacket.* The chronological narrative is interspersed with analytical chapters which form the cutting edge of a more general, uniformly brilliant exploration of Melville's interior life. Elaborated in terms of the theory of needs—which is set forth in Chapter 9, "The Personality of Young Melville"—Harry's portrait of the artist is exemplary proof of the theoretical pudding cooked up in *Explorations.* There is nothing in the published scholarship to compare with this richly detailed, fully rounded, and penetrating psychological study. Melville comes plausibly alive here as he does for no other biographer. This is so in part because Harry knew virtually everything there was to know about his subject. It was the rare scrap of evidence that eluded him during fifteen years of hunting and gathering. He was no less diligent in his attention to context. The novelist's life is set within brief histories of Romanticism, whaling, New York politics, Jacksonian ideology, European inroads into the Pacific, American literature, conscience, and much more. Again, nothing in the critical literature rivals Harry's range and command with relevant background materials.

But the true key to the success of the biography is Harry's profound personal identification with his subject. This was the engine that drove him to comb New York and New England for clues; that fueled his interest in the forces that shaped the novelist's world; that sharpened his critical eye; that energized his prose style; and, above all else, that shaped his understanding of Melville's personality. Harry knew his man as intimately as he knew his own mind. He all but says as much in the long Preface that he wrote at the beginning of his labors in 1938. "There is a biographer in every biography," he begins, "a self-appointed guide whose all-too-human particularities pervade everything." He goes on, very much in the spirit of Nietzsche's *Menschliches,* to acknowledge a deep personal involvement in the life that follows. "In order that the reader . . . may make the allowances that seem proper," he cautions, "I shall attempt to set down the circumstances which led to the writing of it, to indicate the extent to which I was absorbed and the means that I employed to disengage and efface myself." The word "attempt" is carefully chosen; Harry makes no promises on the score of objectivity. Rather, he hints at the difficulties which may obstruct our "understanding of that incontestably remote and wilful genius, Herman Melville."

The fateful encounter with *Moby-Dick* on board the *Scythia* is duly reported. In straining to represent the book's potent initial assault on his feelings, Harry is guilty—as he is at intervals elsewhere in the manuscript—of marked overwriting. "It was certain that I was implicated in an event compared to which nothing had ever seemed so moving or so important, and my barbarous blood danced to an archaic rhythm as one crisis after another, met and surmounted, led the mad captain and his crew, I mysteriously and apprehensively felt, ever nearer to an overshadowing remorseless Nemesis. Out of an enormous fecundity of energy Melville was pouring out great floods of barely mastered passion, discharging shocking currents of electric thought, that swellingly burst out in rapturous crescendos succeeded by periods of quivering stillness." There is an excess here of rhetorical froth laid over a bare pittance of content. It is a tendency, everywhere characteristic of the Preface, to set expressions of strong personal feeling in place of an analysis of their sources. Harry makes it indelibly clear that Melville moves him, but leaves the precise why of the matter in doubt. "Despite, or because of, its wondrous irregularities and splendid lawlessness," he writes, *Moby-Dick* "emanated *mana* that was transforming me into something freshly energized, generating density as well as a new perspective." This gets us no closer to the root of the matter than the fervid effusion that succeeds it. "This book, packed with salty episode and dreadfully deep knowledge, was to be the standard for judging life. It was as trustworthy as a clinical thermometer. Living through it had been a full tide experience, to be forever loved, fixed, relived, recreated. Whether the rational intelligence could ever make anything of it, the event of *Moby-Dick* was imbedded in my tissues, never to be reasoned away."

Appropriately enough, Harry declares a preference for what he terms "the affective or artistic" mode of biographical inference, "a 'feeling-in' process called empathy." He is also perfectly straightforward in his embrace of "depth psychology," though he readily concedes that in its penchant for breaking things down, such "analysis is abetted by hate," while "empathy is furthered by love." It is a source of puzzlement, however, that Harry concludes his argument for affect with a claim to personal objectivity. "In the present instance," he writes, "I have worked, as far as I am aware, in a disinterested spirit." The apparent confusion betrays the conviction—as paradoxically firm as his commitment to critical relativity—that his own "feeling-in" to Melville was unique for its depth and breadth and luminous clarity. He could see where others could not, Harry knew, because the chasm that separated ordinary selves from ordinary others had in his very special relationship to Melville been reduced to little more than nominal proportions. The biographer lived in his subject, and his subject lived in him.

That's how it felt to Harry, and never more intensely so than during his first visit to Arrowhead, Melville's home in Pittsfield, Massachusetts, where *Moby-Dick* was written. "I was speeding to the Berkshires," Harry recalls, "where the immense achievement had been wrought, and then, with borrowed key letting myself into the vacant death-bound house, I mounted to old Vulcan's workroom, opened the shutters and stood there in tremulous, holy awe. Here at this window, looking out towards distant, cloud-crowned Greylock, sat mighty Melville, fashioning to his purpose by some inimitable magic the diverse elements that rioted in his brain. Words came to my lips: 'The diver sun—slow dived from noon,— goes down; my soul mounts up! She wearies with her endless hill . . . Oh, life! 'tis in an hour like this, with soul beat down and held to knowledge—as wild, untutored things are forced to feed— Oh life! 'tis now that I do feel the latent horror in thee! . . . Millions of mixed shades and shadows, drowned dreams, somnambulisms, reveries . . . wondrous depths, where strange shapes of the unwarped primal world glided to and fro . . . and the miser-merman, Wisdom, revealed his hoarded heaps . . . Talk not to me of blasphemy, man, I'd strike the sun if it insulted me.'" And so it began, Harry alone in Melville's study, with snatches of *Moby-Dick,* the words formed and uttered now as his own, pouring into the stillness. "Soon I was walking about the countryside," he goes on, "climbing Greylock, following Melville's steps along the Hudson, interviewing old inhabitants, searching frantically through libraries, ransacking attics and pursuing the most improbable clues. Some kind of a book was writing itself in my mind." It was a passionate merging of true minds, utterly extreme in its implied claim to union, and yet borne out remarkably in the compelling fragment of a life that it inspired.

Harry's failure to account for his strong feelings about his subject stands in fascinating juxtaposition to the revelation of complete personal identification dramatized in Melville's workroom. Harry could not say what the episode betrays—that he experienced his tie to the novelist as a unique communion of kindred spirits. But it was true nonetheless. His hold on Melville was not finally a matter of dates and places and books; it was a profound marriage of one soul with another. This is the truth toward which Harry's inflated prose vaguely gestures. It is a truth that he accepted implicitly and yet never put into words, perhaps even to himself. The saying of it, even the clear, bold thought of it, might have broken the spell. Better to know it feelingly. Because he viewed his involvement with Melville in this half-light, Harry could not see that the impulse to reveal his feelings about his subject arose in tension with what he could not say, and indeed only half-knew, about the way he felt. Thus, the scene in the study inadvertently betrays what Harry in a consciously confessional mood can only grope for.

But the ties that bound the biographer to the novelist were unspeakable in the second sense that their full disclosure might have been expected to provoke the moral disapproval of most people in the book's audience. Harry hints at this submerged dimension at several points in the Preface. *Moby-Dick* plunged him downward, he confesses, "to the last limit of ungovernable despair. There was nothing more fearful to be felt or said." The terror that Harry points to is a variety of the *anomie* risked by all deep divers, an encounter with the arbitrariness of human beliefs and values. Melville's heroism lay in his descent to these depths and in his refusal, as dramatized in Ahab's furious defiance, to compromise the dark truths that he had witnessed. "He consumed himself," Harry believed, "for the dawn of a new day. Light could now flash out of darkness." But because of his sweeping subversion of our happiest human assumptions, because he undermined the norms by which people are ordinarily judged, Melville fell "beyond the standard plumb-line of biography. To write of him," Harry declares, "was no work for an entirely good man with a normal, outwardly-directed, cultured consciousness." To make sense of the author of *Moby-Dick* you had to be a little mad and a little bad. Maybe more than a little. Harry admits to having been brought up short by what he learned of his subject, especially of his failures in later life as a husband and father. During one such "spell" of disenchantment, Melville appeared to him in a dream—"as he often did"—and urged that he set the biography aside. The dreamer awakened with the novelist's evocation of the "valour-ruined man" on his lips. In time, however, and in response to Melville's heroic example, Harry abandoned conventional thinking for "a pride and a morality of another sort," a "deeper and . . . more charitable" perspective on the life before him. His eyes opened at last, he recognized as "fact that the creation of prophetic art calls for such self-surrender to the demiurge that the entire rest of a man's life might justifiably be misspent."

It is perhaps not altogether fanciful to suppose that Harry failed to complete and publish the biography because, his protests to the contrary notwithstanding, he could not acqiesce comfortably in the moral position which the justification of Melville's life seemed to require. Too much hangs here on "prophetic art" and "the demiurge." Does the fact that he wrote *Moby-Dick* somehow excuse Melville for his human failings? Or isn't it a matter, really, of his being a great artist and a not-so-great mate and parent? Harry bridled at the "ignominious" blemishes in his hero because they were reminders of similar failings in himself. Just so, the license that he extends to the demiurge is held out at the same time to the dyad. Harry had his own demiurge, and with Christiana he was engaged in what they hoped would be a "prophetic art" of living for their times. Yet he feared that the human price for their passionate experiment was too high. To be sure, he shared with Melville a resistance to "the fixating bonds which held him to his past," the "unconscious attachment to" his mother and "the moral code which chained him to" his wife. "In a society that is hostile to the spirit," Harry wrote of the novelist, "the right sort of a marriage for a creator is none at all, or an elopement by which he and his bride make public what is strictly true: their break with culture." The application of the principle to Harry and Christiana is obvious enough; but so too is the unwillingness—his much more than hers—to make a clear, public break with convention. Harry faltered because he was not as sure of himself as his vigorous prose prescriptions would seem to suggest.

Something of the terms and texture of Harry's uncertainty may be glimpsed in his discussion of *Moby-Dick*. Melville "was disastrously married," he confides; "*that* was the rub, *that* the incommunicable grief, the ever-gnawing pain that he, apostle of chivalry, could neverr confess to anyone." That the biographer shared his subject's sentiments on the score of matrimony, and on its supporting social framework, could hardly be more obvious. Behind "the sacrament and the state of marriage," Harry observes, "was the Church and the great bulk of respectable men and women with their damn rules, customs, formalities, manners, fads, proprieties, pretensions, rites, rituals, decrees, ordinances, laws, taboos, sentiments, beliefs, principles, Catechisms, creeds, and categorical negations." The social fabric arose before Melville like a wall separating him from the fruition of his desires. At their deepest source, the novelist's longings were sexual in nature. "My hypothesis," Harry declares, "is that Moby-Dick stood for Christian Society and its God working through conscience against the sexual instinct, and that the resultant maiming of the instinct evoked the agression which was Ahab." Identified as he was with his monomaniac hero, Melville emerges as "a forerunner . . . of the revolution against sexual oppression." He was, Harry's observes, speaking for the rebels of his own generation, "fighting our battle."

But Melville's war on suffocating convention was doomed from the outset by the oppressive weight of his superego, which made him hostage to the social tyranny he sought to overthrow. The real enemy, in this construction of his dilemma, was mother, Maria Melville, the principal agent of her son's crippling socialization. "Melville had fled half way round the globe to escape his mother only to return and find her influence still powerful. It was she, much more than society, that determined his conscience." But even as he aligns Maria and Christian Society with Moby-Dick, the punishing Leviathan, Harry concedes that "in attacking it with hate in his heart Ahab-Melville, a member of that society, is evil." The mad captain is "undone by a single inflexible bias of the will." The moral to be drawn is "the old familiar one that too much pride is the ruin of a man." In hunting Moby-Dick, Ahab abandons all reason and surrenders to the very vindictiveness that he assaults in his hated adversary. By extension, of course, the moral indirectly illuminates both Melville's decline into obscurity and Harry's decision to abandon the biography. By further extension, it may be applied to the dyad itself, and to what Harry must have sensed was its tragic flaw.

"Ahab brings death upon himself and his brave followers by trusting the transcendentalists' doctrine that no law can be sacred to the individual but that of his own nature." Can Harry have written that sentence without reflecting on the heavy price paid by others that he and Christiana might have their way?

It is sadly paradoxical that the sense of intimate personal kinship responsible for the brilliance of the biography was also the leading obstacle to its completion. Harry's identification with Melville was finally too deep for his own comfort, too compromising to be shared with the world. The novelist, he wrote—in terms that applied equally to himself—"could not sacrifice his pride and acquiesce to the rule of the majority, nor could he sacrifice it by exposing himself on a fundamental issue to moral censure. He was unwilling to open himself to the reproach that he was too weak to resist a libidinous temptation." But while Harry joined Melville in refusing to brave the world's judgment, he made no effort to conceal the elements from which such a judgment might be formed. In fact, the completeness and utter candor of the record that he left behind him is in all dimensions confirmation that he wanted the story told in its entirety. In this, as in so many things, he was like Melville, who set out a complete and unflinching account of his moral and spiritual life in his books, but wrote so darkly at key turnings that the story was for decades buried in obscurity. Both men believed passionately that the truth of the unconscious, which they struggled to fathom and obey, would bear them out in the eyes of the world. Yet for good reasons both also bent under the pressure of that species of doubt defined in the biography as "a sad compromise between accepting oneself and accepting one's society." Melville's "unrelenting opposition to his culture," Harry wrote, was forever in tension with his sense that "rebellion was also a crime, springing out of pride, the first of the deadly sins." His biographer was similarly torn.

It seems unlikely that Harry was ever completely conscious of the extent of his personal stake in Melville's story—empathy, he observes, "is a subconscious process that cannot be directly controlled." Had he recognized fully what drove his identification with the novelist, then he would have retreated from it altogether. Had he seen that his rationalizations on Melville's behalf were the oblique manifestations of his own moral anguish, then he would have been obliged to abandon them. The biography invites interpretation as a sustained but very significantly incomplete negotiation of a delicate, finally untenable moral position. It is a plea, developed obliquely and only half-knowingly, for the ultimate justice of the dyad. Had Harry recognized it as such, he could not have written as much and as well as he did. Had the emergent case succeeded, then the book would have been finished and published. In the upshot, the manuscript is as betwixt and between as the state of mind, the halting moral consciousness, from which it emerged.

It is entirely symptomatic that Harry was slow to share the manuscript with anyone. The worst of his buried fears were realized in November 1939, when Conrad Aiken—who knew something about Melville and about psychoanalysis—delivered his judgment of the two or three opening chapters that Harry had finally given him to read. It was after dinner on Thanksgiving; there had been much drinking and the talk was unrestrained. "You think you've baleened," Aiken sneered, playing on the term for whalebone, "but actually you've ballooned." The poet was "appalled" by what he had read; he declared the manuscript "inflated and overblown," a "piece of gigantism." The criticism was no doubt most stinging in its suggestion that the excesses of the biography could be traced back to an informing "inflation" in Harry himself. What Aiken later described as "a screaming altercation" brought the evening to a close. "It was the beginning of a rift" that never completely closed. "I'm afraid I oversaid my say," Aiken admitted the following February. "I always do." Harry came around in time but never forgot. How could he? Aiken had touched too closely on the hidden agenda of the biography, and Harry recoiled as from an intolerable accusation. He continued to labor at the book for a while, failing to see what is now, a half-century later, perfectly clear—that he would never again risk the painful personal exposure to which the life had made him vulnerable.

The concealed moral agenda of the biography—its plea for the justice of the dyad—is anchored in Melville's discovery of the unconscious. Because of his unprecedented and perilous explorations of his own psyche, the novelist dealt in "experiences that are known

to the insane but never felt by anyone in full possession of himself."
Here, then, in the descent to the depths of the psyche, first inspired
by Jung, undertaken most boldly by Christiana, and described for
both members of the dyad by Melville, was the most important
common link. Harry thought of himself as a deep diver cut from
the same cloth as his subject. They were daring explorers of the
unconscious interior who came back wiser but sadder men.

Life, they both concluded, began in the woe of rejection by
proud, punishing mothers. Maria Gansevoort Melville, in Harry's
rendering, is a haughty daughter of wealth and station who rules
her amiable, pliant spouse by force of will and who weans her son
Herman—not by any means her favorite child—much too early.
The sudden withdrawal of affection is traumatic for the child, who
hungers hopelessly for what he cannot have and who is easily tyrannized by his mother's endless suffering (Harry dubs her "the Mater Dolorosa"). He emerges with a craving for succorance which is
only partly met by his father, a genial soul who is hardly adequate
to his son's needs. Though inclined to seek favor by being docile,
the boy is inwardly resistant to criticism and intensely self-
absorbed. Over time he recoils from the fruitless courtship of his
mother into the compensatory ambition for autonomous superiority
as a wayfarer and explorer, and later as a deep diver into the unconscious. Retreating from the context of his frustration, and armed
with a host of "credulous idealisms," he is outwardly apostate to his
class, though the traces of his patrician background endure. In his
sexual nature, which is formed primarily in response to rejection by
Maria, he is on one side borne down by the guilt arising out of his
repressed oedipal designs, and on the other primed for an encounter
with his anima, a woman alluring in her pain and utterly mysterious.

At the very outset it must be acknowledged that Harry's portrait
of Melville—here distilled from hundreds of pages of detailed elaboration—is a powerful, even definitive rendering. The image, we
feel, is the faithful evocation of a real person. But the portrait is
also a mirror of its maker. This is true to some degree, presumably,
of all biographies; but it is true in a most extraordinary way of
Harry's. For the more we know of Harry, the more we will catch

sight of him in Melville. Both lives, the biographer would have been the first to insist, are constructions; they are narratives stitched together from a myriad of facts, reports, and surmises and designed to persuade, to induce the suspension of disbelief. It is precisely to acknowledge that lives are rhetorical fabrications that Harry refers to himself as "Murr" in his autobiography. Murr is a fictional character, significantly related to Henry A. Murray but emphatically different from, and less than, the real—mysterious and ungraspable—man himself. Nor would Harry have denied that his own story and Melville's shaped themselves dialectically, the one informing and reinforcing the other in his mind. But he was also quite certain that his parallel fabrications had their foundation in an astonishing array of parallel facts, some playfully farfetched (HM/HAM), but most of them pursued in earnest as the marks of a deep personal kinship.

Conrad Aiken caught sight of the connection between biographer and subject and vanquished with drunken ridicule Harry's impulse to lay it, half-concealed, before the public. We are witness to the same connection in "The Case of Murr," a self-portrait that with minor adjustments might pass for a profile of young Melville. It will be recalled that Murr's mother, the proud child of wealth and rank, is the prime mover in the formation of her son's personality. Energetic, "changeable, moody, and susceptible to melancholy," she conveys to her middle child, by abruptly weaning him at two months, and in other ways as well, that "he could count on only a limited, third-best portion of his mother's love." Finding that his appeals for comfort lead "only to frustration and shame," young Murr retreats "into a private, maternal-like claustrum of his own making," where he bathes "in narcissistic self-pity." The outwardly docile child takes some solace in the affection of an equally docile father; but his life is shaped by maternal rejection, which is "tragically experienced" and which in time fosters "emotional self-sufficiency" and a "venturesome autonomy" that expresses itself in admiration for explorers and adventurers. Numerous other personal qualities—among them a responsiveness to tragic themes in literature, an impulse to dive into "the darker, blinder strata of feeling," an attraction to suffering women, prominent needs for succorance, inviolacy, and deference, and rejection of the "prejudices" of his class—all of them shared with Melville, would also emerge. Harry is understandably reticent about Murr's sexuality, though the repressed attraction to mother, with its sequel in marked susceptibilties to guilt and to the anima, are readily inferred. The same may be said for narcissism, which "The Case of Murr" expresses by its imperfect restraint.

It is abundantly clear that the story of his intimate kinship with Melville was one that Harry wanted told, even though he shrank finally from telling it fully and directly himself. It is equally clear that in perfecting an image of the novelist he was also fabricating a self, an *apologia pro vita sua* at one remove. The biography held Harry's attention because in it he caught sight of a rationale for his life with Christiana. Early on in their relationship he discovered that he could neither say no to the dyad nor accept the guilt that came with it. He was in chains at once to desire and to a conscience that condemned his desire as sinful. In Melville, who had been similarly torn, he glimpsed a way out of his dilemma. Errant desire, and a host of other leading personal qualities, were in the novelist's life and work best explained as adult manifestations of the trauma of rejection in infancy and childhood. Not least of all in his susceptibility to the anima, Melville was his mother's son. Harry makes the same case for himself in "Murr," and with the clear implication that fault in the matter may be laid at the offending parent's door. Ahab, he writes in the biography, is burdened with "an insufferable and inconsolable grief, a secret inward bleeding too deep for words or tears." The engendering analogue in Harry's construction of Melville's life, and of his own, is betrayal by mother. This is the dark fountain to which all the tears could be traced. But in Harry's case at least, the grief bore with it a secret consolation, for it explained and justified what was otherwise morally intolerable.

Guilt is in this perspective not denied but displaced. The son's admitted lapse into error is the direct result of parental failure. The impulse to neutralize acknowledged blame is also evident in the argument, previously noted, that Melville's artistic accomplishments somehow justified his failures as husband and father. Harry doesn't pursue this line very far, in part perhaps because he was

246

without a *Moby-Dick* to set in the balance. Of course the highest moral ground lay in arguing for the dyad as a positive good. Harry found support for this position in Melville's rejection of contemporary Christianity as unnatural and spiritually corrupting. Against this background the dyad, with its emphasis on the expression of the whole self, the freeing of the mind and body from artificial constraints, appeared a crusade in the name of human liberation. Again, this position had its ultimate authority in the unconscious, the deep bedrock of human personality, which Melville first witnessed in the lives of the "savages" in the south Pacific and later explored within himself. The unconscious spoke unequivocally against the tyranny of head over heart, against the puritanical shackling of sexuality, against the fear of and subordination of women, against constraints on play and pleasure and beauty of all kinds. The unconscious as Harry found it in books like *Moby-Dick*—"a healing chalice to the Hamletized modern man," he describes it in the biography—was an advocate for life as he wanted to live it.

But to follow where it beckoned, he knew, was to invite—as Melville had invited—the condemnation of the vast benighted majority. The novelist had no illusions on this score. *Moby-Dick*, he wrote to Hawthorne, had been baptized in the name of the Devil; "I have written a wicked book," he later acknowledged, "and feel spotless as a lamb." Harry's departures were in their time hardly as radically subversive as Melville's; nor—thanks in part to Aiken—did he risk the exposure to public wrath that the novelist had suffered. Still, Harry made Melville's cause his own; and it was bracing to imagine himself in a succession of Romantic rebels, tragic in their suffering and heroic in their defiance. With the novelist as his occasion, but with the dyad squarely in mind, he wrote: "Today a merely 'good' man has no mana, which indicates, I think, that people are looking for better modes of living: new ideologies for individual evolution. And for this a merely 'good' man is inadequate. The Devil must have a hand in rejuvenating conscience." The dyad, so regarded, is sinful only to those who lack the wit to see that its departures from convention are the very essence of its moral heroism. In this happiest of all self-constructions, Harry has his mother to thank for the grief that made him what he was, that drew him ineluctably to Christiana, and thence to the dyad itself, a new model for enlightened living.

Harry and Christiana were of course ahead of their times. Much that they stood for in the 1930s became gospel to the generation of the 1960s. Just as clearly, however, Harry was not fully persuaded of the rectitude of his cause. Had he been convinced, Melville's life would have been much easier to complete. But it was not morality alone that gave him pause. The course of his true love, however grand its calling, had never been smooth. In notes toward a new Preface to the biography, written in 1944, Harry offers several reasons for setting the project aside, among them Aiken's crushing critique, the sense that Melville was a pacifist, and the appalling weight of the novelist's years of decline. Finally, he acknowledges a need "to gather my forces for what remained of my own life. If it collapses about my head—pathetic aftermath." This is a reference, it would appear, to the dyad. Life with Jo, though far from perfect, was stable; and the Clinic was for the first time on a solid footing. But Harry's passionate experiment, pursued at great cost to others, and to which Melville and academic psychology were merely adjunct, was not the unmingled triumph that he and Christiana had looked for. In the same years that he labored toward closure with Melville, Harry and Christiana endured a succession of crises in their relationship. There was nothing new or particularly surprising in this; after all, they had dedicated themselves to constant development and change, however painful. Still, it is ruefully ironic that he felt pressured to abandon the biography in order to save the dyad, most especially since the uncertain justice of his renegade love had itself been an obstacle to the completion of the life. But the collapse of the dyad was virtually unthinkable now, for in the wake of its failure all that had been sacrificed in its name would become a pointless waste. That was the "pathetic aftermath" Harry sought above all things to avoid.

By the time of Pearl Harbor, Harry and Christiana had consumed all that remained of their youth together—she was 44, he was 48. This is not to suggest that they had burned themselves out. But the intensity of their shared lives in the years just before the war took them to the endurable limit of contradiction and intensity, pain, passion, narcissism, and joy. It was the old pattern all over again, in even higher relief. Their sexuality blazed as never before; but it became more complex and more violent as its fires reached their peak. Christiana demanded aggressiveness from Harry as the sign that he had passed beyond good and evil to a new level of freedom and creativity. Wona would "go mad," she wrote in 1936, "if her body were not conquered as violently as her spirit had been conquered by his Mana. Her body must be completely possessed—and for that she must break the Christian conscience that made him impotent and tender." Because he was aroused, and also because of her challenge to his manhood, Harry gave Christiana some of the pain that she, in her own grappling with guilt, demanded of him. But there was something more that moved him now—fear. He was indeed afraid that Christiana might "go mad," or that in her frustration she would become self-destructive. He was concerned for her sake, of course; but he shrank as well from the unbearable remorse that her increased suffering held in store for him. Christiana was not unaware of the leverage that Harry's conscience gave her. He was devoted to her and committed to the dyad; but he was also a hostage to his lover's pain. Harry knew exactly what he meant when he wrote that Melville "was afraid of guilt."

The period has as its humorous prologue Harry's decision to commission Gaston Lachaise, the French-born sculptor best known for his grand mammalian evocations of the Earth Mother, to do a figure in bronze of Christiana. Though a bust was originally planned, Lachaise soon warmed to his work and insisted that a fuller rendering was required. Whether the artist was more inspired by cash than his subject's form is not entirely clear. Still, as he moved down, regaling Christiana with his sexual history as he went, the price for the work went up. He wrote in October 1934 with thanks for a check and with assurances "that other forms of beauty have been revealed for me to glorify." Harry and Christiana bent gracefully enough to the exigencies of fine art; she was flattered, he amused. Despite some wrangling over money, the work was finally completed in time for an exhibition at the Museum of Modern Art in January 1935. Harry was pleased with the result, a figure to mid-thigh—graphic in its attention to intimate detail—of a slender woman in her mid-thirties, attractive enough though hardly striking, a little subdued, even a little worn. Whitehead remarked, perhaps evasively, that the piece was not at all "realistic" but true to Christiana's fiery spirit. Harry meanwhile described it to Mumford as "the most living figure I have ever seen in any material—raw, impressionistic, electric—at once serene & violent. We are immensely pleased with it." The blurring about the mouth, he added in a subsequent report, "was what Lachaise saw—a conflict between passion and restraint—expression & reticence."

The statue was the site for multiple acts of possession. Most obviously, Lachaise took over just as much of Christiana's body as interested him, and no more. His interest, measured first in units of her anatomy, was convertible to cash, which he took from Harry. But of course in paying for the work Harry was also taking possession of Christiana. He insisted that only one bronze be cast; and after the New York show the piece was never again displayed in public. The statue was also its subject's to admire and to possess. Christiana was enthusiastic about the project and about its result. It fed her narcissism; it was palpable testimony to Harry's love; it was possession on her own terms. The figure evinces a ready, earthy, experienced sexuality; it shows the real, not the ideal, face of desire. Christiana wanted to be taken in this light. She demanded of her lover that he possess her completely, admitting in so many words that his sexual aggressiveness was the surety of her purchase on his spirit. Harry recognized that he was taken in turn by the extremity of his desire. He once complained to his friend Ina May Greer that he felt ruled by his sexuality.

The theme here is of competition, subtle and not so subtle, for control of the relationship. Harry wanted the dyad, but he also wanted a conventional domestic arrangement and the freedom to pursue his intellectual interests. Christiana's demands were much narrower—she wanted the dyad full-time. Because it was a monument to her archetypal visions, she was willing to give it everything. She expected no less of Harry. Christiana believed that she came first in his life and regarded all else—his family, the Clinic, Melville, even guilt—as a distraction from her primary devotion to

250

her. It was a struggle—as they sometimes viewed it—between the enclosed, feminine, erotic domain of the unconscious and the public, male, rational, and scientific sphere. Harry strained outward; Christiana angled to draw him in. "I'm his ground; I'm his soul; I'm his creativity; I'm his center; I'm his base; I'm it," she told Ina May Greer. Narcissism looms large here; but so does a certain protesting too much in the face of abundant competition for Harry's time and attention. Christiana wanted more of Harry than he could give; Harry wanted more of life than Christiana's narrow dyadic circle could provide. In the difference lay the continuing source of their trouble.

The stages of their journey during this period were regularly marked (in Christiana's copious records) at moments when power or authority were significantly at issue. Most often, the precise distribution of initiative at such intervals is rather ambiguous. For example, during the summer of 1935 Harry and Christiana rooted a granite column several feet high in the lawn outside the Parker River cabin. The authority of the phallus was clearly on display— the Guidance Pillar, they called it—though its control was just as clearly a matter of uncertainty between them. Earlier that year, in April, doubtless in acknowledgment of the accelerated work on *Explorations,* Christiana vowed Submission to Masculine Mana. Her records for the occasion include a number of appropriate quotations—"Horn of my salvation, my high tower"; "Reason shall build a house for the spirit"—including a rather grand effort by Mansol: "Woman, clair-audient to the furtive oracles of Nature, senses a thousand occult rhythms to which man's unaided logic is obtuse. But these mute flashes of enlightenment are lost in obscurities of feeling if not caught and given shapeful body by the fashioning powers of man's reason." As if to restore the dyadic balance, they began that September to concentrate attention on the enhancement of Wona's beauty. Harry gave lavishly of clothing and jewelry— Christiana took an almost child-like delight in presents—and agreed to an annual dyadic holiday, Increase Through Feminine Adornment, first celebrated on January 31, 1936. Swinging carefully to the other side, they added Increase Through Masculine Adornment that summer. Christiana gave Harry an Italian chest for his new clothing, much of it designed for special evenings of ritualized drinking—"soma," or alcohol, a divine gift, was consumed in generous quantities—imaginative play, and sexual experiment.

The creation of holidays, or "annuestas," accompanying rituals of dress, drink, and literary recitation, and private schemes of color and language, were leading elements in the effort—largely Christiana's—to redefine daily life in terms of the dyad. Wona and Mansol were expanding into the spiritual vacuum of modern life, filling it with meaning. Once perfected, their new model for living—complete with myths, rituals, symbol systems, and an elaborate calendar—would be set forth in inspired prose and offered to the awaiting world. This at least was the idea. Yet the more they elaborated their system, the more intensely private it became. The dyad was not so much an answer to the world's need as it was a retreat from the world's poverty of spirit. And who, save for the very rich—in material as well as spiritual resources—could afford to follow Wona and Mansol into their secluded garden?

The contradiction was perhaps nowhere more evident than in dyadic sexual relations, which with time became increasingly complex and idiosyncratic, and for that increasingly remote from the practices of "ordinary" people. Harry and Christiana shared Jung's ambition to free the body from Christian prohibition and to open the way to the fullest possible expression of the components—male and female—of the individual's sexual nature. Thus Christiana sometimes adopted an aggressive male posture, smoking a pipe or cigar as she did so; while Harry on occasion submitted to having his nails painted a flaming red, to symbolize sexual desire. But did the role reversals reflect dimensions of universal human nature, or were they pawns in the complex, sexually polarized play of power within the dyad? Certainly there was little of liberation in The Whip for Slavery, which appears first in the records for October 1936, along with the Nietzschean injunction, "Thou goest to women? Do not forget thy whip!" Sexual pleasure was a first priority with Christiana—"Discovered the power of 2 rings on one finger," she noted on November 12—though it was hardly distinguishable now from humiliation and physical pain. "Discovered that our life was in the whip—the black whip that hurt," she wrote two weeks later. "Without that there is no passion for us now." That same night she began anew the record of the dyad, more than ever assured that "the day would come when Wona's book would be written & these events would be significant." But, again, what audience had she in mind? For whom would her pleasure in pain be significant?

The link between physical pain and the dyadic "book"—"The Proposition," as they now referred to it—resided in what Christiana took to be the meaning of Harry's exertions with the whip. His willingness to inflict pain was the sign that he had passed beyond good and evil and was thus morally equipped to interpret her visions. Because the whipping had its consummation in heightened sexual pleasure for both of them, it was also the instrument of her increased control over her lover. Such control was the key to getting the Proposition written; for the actual writing was Harry's task, and it would take time—time that he had hitherto reserved to himself, for the Clinic and for Melville. The whip thus expressed the enhanced authority of its ostensible victim, which helps to explain why Christiana craved its sting.

Rather more obviously perhaps, the whippings met a need for punishment. Construing her pain as pleasure was likely as close as Christiana could come to rewarding herself for her part as liberating seducer. For Harry, on the other hand, the whip expressed his moral condemnation of his mate, his resentment at her sexual mastery, and his self-contempt for having surrendered to rampant, sinful desire. The latter motive surfaced again toward the end of the year. "This night for the first time," Christiana wrote on December 12, "my lover understood that my word could not be spoken without my tears." Two days later, during a session at Fairfax Hall, she made her intentions perfectly clear: "Write my words." *Explorations* was nearing completion; Melville stood next in line for attention. Me first, Christiana demanded, seizing her advantage. Harry agreed in a general sort of way, but only on condition that she take up the whip herself. "She knew that my writing from her depths meant her submission to my depths," he noted. "There can be no clarity until the lust of the whip has been felt in ecstasy. Wona has said for

253

the first time in her fateful life, 'Write my words.' And she knew that for this she would know cruelty."

Two weeks later Harry got the whipping he had asked for. "Wona was in black," reads the diary for December 31, 1936, "black eyebrows, black velvet dress with train & the strong turquoise ring on her index finger. Her red nails transmitted power that was irrevocable. And she said: 'Again we are at the beginning and again I shall trance. And I shall not care for any forces that in the past have swayed you—your family, or any demands from the world. I shall only know my need and my lust.' Mansol's body knew that this was their truth. Here they were at a new place—uncertain of fate. Mansol's lust knew only obedience—ultimate, sensual submission." Harry could indulge himself completely, but only at the price of taking his pleasure passively—Christiana was in charge and entirely to blame—and as the sequel to punishment. Christiana meanwhile had her way, but at risk of being more vulnerable than ever to Harry's resentment in the next phase. As if to prepare for that turn of events, she explained on January 5 that it was "the World Force, not herself, that was speaking" in her determination to bring the visions to fruition. "Her ego had tried to withstand her trance but the Force was too strong. 'You shall write *my* book, *my* book,' the Force said. There will be hundreds of offers, universities will give you money and slaves, but *my* trance stands between these things and our life. 'You shall write *my* book'."

The next phase commenced almost as the Force's sentiments emerged from Wona's mouth. They had gone too far, for Harry at least; but the initiative, which Christiana had taken to extremes, was now his. He recoiled in righteous anger, announcing his imminent departure for a cruise in the Caribbean. "You had better learn to live alone and like it," he added, cruelly. It was time for a truce; they both saw that now. When Harry returned in February, he came bearing "great beauty and great recognition"—bracelets and rings from Trinidad and a willingness to make peace. Christiana declared her needs.

This is what I, Wona, want before I die.
I want my trances to be known—to be part of the world—to be made manifest through my lover's writing of them.

254

> I want my lover to be strong and aloof—so fortified by my worship
> and utter love that he will dare to do this.
> This means great loneliness for us both.
> This means that we will be unknown in our generation.
> This means a great sacrifice for my lover.
> This is our proposition.

Here was acknowledgement at last of their isolation. The world
would not listen; they must forge ahead in obscurity. Wona's tone
is also noteworthy. She approaches not with commands from the
World Force but in "worship and utter love" and in gratitude for
her lover's "great sacrifice." Harry was no less accommodating in his
"recognition" of Christiana.

> This is what I, Mansol, must know before I die.
> That my loveress was loved enough.
> That from this day she never knows loneliness or forsakenness.
> That my loveress is immortal.
> That I reached down to the sensitive chaos of her trances and
> found out the living word for them so that they would live
> forever.
> That the dark and ultimate love between man and woman
> should be known on this earth.
> That the course of love was forever established through my
> loveress in words and in stone.

Even as he grants the deathlessness of Christiana's visions, Harry
emphasizes that they are the merest "chaos," inert and ephemeral,
without his informing "word." Nor does he shrink from the admission that their love, for all of its archetypal depth and grandeur, is
a thing of struggle and tragic dissolution.

It was no coincidence that Harry's "recognition" came to him
during the last tense weeks of waiting for Conant's decision on the
fate of the Clinic. The dyad at least was secure. Harry made it
securer still on March 8. "He told me," Christiana wrote on that
day, that he had "recognized the longing of my heart," which was
to build a Tower on the Parker River property. It would be the
expression in stone and wood and glass of Wona's fabulous visions,
and a monument to the dyadic union which they had fostered. Jung

had built a tower; so had William Butler Yeats and Robinson Jeffers. Melville had himself contemplated the construction of a towered house at Arrowhead. Harry was inspired by such examples; he was also anxious that Christiana have a place to anchor her unconscious. "Great joy & life came back to me," she wrote. "We drew plans for the Tower—'That the outside shall be as the inside.'" She was swept up completely in the new project—which she equated with their "new life" together. "Our dreams would live again for us," she predicted; "we would *make* our own fate and not be carried by the demands of the world about us." Christiana announced that she would now minimize her work at the Clinic. The Tower would rise in its place as her proper medium.

The work began almost immediately. Kenneth Knight, a sturdy, taciturn artisan of the old school, agreed to take charge of the building. The original cabin, which became the living room, was enlarged on one side by the addition of a kitchen and enclosed porch; on the other by the Tower itself, a massive structure, tapering gently above the house toward a flat roof, and set squarely on a bluff overlooking the river and the marshes below. The circular room at the ground floor was designed as a place for the display of dyadic artifacts and for the celebration of special holidays, or annuestas. Dark, cool, and quiet, it is the womb of the house—the claustrum, as it was called—set aside for meditation and associated in obvious ways with the unconscious. It was to feature symbols of Christiana's power. Just above it, at the midpoint of the stairwell, is the bedroom, dedicated to the pleasures of the body. "The standard of living," Christiana later carved in a small door, "is ecstasy." At the top of the Tower is the smallest and best lit of the three rooms, the study or thalamus. Here, where the symbols of his rational powers were to be displayed, Harry did most of his work. The building was thus conceived as an allegorical construction, a harmonious composite of the elements—mind, body, and spirit—that Harry and Christiana sought to develop and integrate in their union. It expressed the dyadic ideal of human wholeness.

Later that spring, as construction began, Christiana urged Harry to set "his book" aside and to take up work on hers. This he would not do. Instead, he pressed forward with *Explorations,* using the small house just down the path from the Tower—"Councie's House," it was called, after Christiana's son, Councilman—as his study. Christiana's disappointment was soon forgotten, however, for her new project absorbed her utterly. The shell of the building was complete when Harry returned from Europe in October. He was moved by Christiana's exertions to a new "recognition" of her power. "Our conception of life is weak," he wrote, "without the acknowledgement of our Central Truth: That you are the Creator." Wona responded with a number of demands, most notably that Mansol "lose himself with her in the Primitive," that "he commit evil," and that "his writing of Melville be such as to convince her that he can write her books." In effect, she was giving ground on the biography—it would come before "her book"—in return for an increase in sexual aggression. "Before Wona gives her cathexis to the Clinic or to any work she requires that I commit evil," Harry wrote. He confirmed the compromise in a set of demands—"Mansol's Commands"—issued just before his second departure for Europe that December. "Thou shalt be my slave until I have finished Melville to your utter satisfaction," he ordered. "When I have finished a section that excites & satisfies your Thalamus, you will do my fingers. This will give me my pain-power which my soul demands. . . . You, slave Wona, will prepare your soul to be branded by this faith when your Lord returns."

The Tower was habitable when Harry came back in January. It was a memorable homecoming made especially dramatic by a heavy snowstorm. Power was out and the road was closed; but Harry packed in through the woods, pulling a toboggan loaded down with beautiful gifts—symbolic artifacts, rugs and fabrics, clothing—that he had gathered in Europe. Christiana met him at the door, where they wept and hugged each other in the darkness. He made his offerings; she proudly led him through the house and Tower, giving special attention to the new shutters she had carved, to a glorious stained-glass window, and to the heavy beams Mr. Knight had found for the high ceiling in the thalamus. Later that night Harry made good on his promise to be evil. "He told me he loved my cunt," Christiana recorded. "He brought chains, handcuffs, a whip, a knife. He asked me if I was ready for a year of submission. . . . He told me of his blood lust. . . . He told me that I would submit to him as to the God of my trances. . . . He wore the orange shirt and green skirt. Pearl bracelets on his wrists." In the months that followed there was much of Melville and, in return, much of the bruising sex that they both now craved. "I shall reverence as nothing else in the world my God's flaming fingers," Wona declared of her lover's painted nails, and of the passion that went with them. "Could you love anyone but a Sadist?" Mansol asked. "This is what you have been born to teach me. Your masochism. I can only love masochism." And so it went. "Now I could ask you for the whip, my Lord," Wona wrote in August, "so full of joy is my heart. Laughter came when my Lord whipped me."

From the night of Harry's second return, the Tower was home to the dyad. Except during the coldest winter months, when it was closed, Christiana was there whenever she could get away. To her ceaseless regret, Harry was around less frequently; he had more to hold him in town, and he spent half of each summer with Jo and Josephine. When alone at the Tower, Christiana was busy building with Mr. Knight, whose craftsmanship she admired, or in decorating the interior, most notably with hand-carved shutters and panels symbolizing aspects of the dyad. When Harry joined her, their days commenced early with breakfast and work, he in the study, she in the house below. Later afternoons found them in the garden, planting, trimming, or cutting trails through the surrounding woods. After a swim in the river, they enjoyed their "soma" on the lawn in front of the house. Harry would read his day's writing, and the talk, always lively, continued through dinner. There were occasional guests—the Mumfords, the Whiteheads, and a select few others. But most often they kept the place to themselves. Love-making came last. On special occasions Wona and Mansol embraced in the moonlight on the roof of the thalamus.

"The Tower accelerated everything," Harry recalled. In the three years after its completion—the final years of Harry's extended leave—the swing back and forth between the poles of their relationship was as violent as the sexuality to which it gave rise. All of the elements of their complex union—willfulness and surrender, anger, narcissism, rebellion, the resentments flaring up out of pervasive guilt, fear, and equally potent desire, tenderness, the hurt, the joy—wound together to produce unpredictable lurches and spasms of feeling, at times exhilarating, at others very painful, always consuming. In the fall of 1938 Christiana was again overtaken by an impulse to pursue her visions. "She had waited ten years for her creative lover to generate an image that was as strong as one of hers." He had worked prodigiously; but nothing that he produced "stirred the embers of her latent life." Now at last, it seemed, "the time had come. She wanted him to do her work." She brought to mind a "trance image of her lover as a negro with graceful muscles lying prone upon the ground. A deep gash was in his side from which poured his heart's blood, flowing about her feet to nourish her. . . . That was what she wanted now; her lover's blood, and his right hand to produce the fruits of her being."

On the other side, Wona acknowledged a profound dependency on Mansol. "If she insisted on his dedication and he refused, or, accepting, was unable to bend his heart to hers, then all was lost: their magnificent life together was ended,—and hers most disastrously, for she could not carry her trances any further." Nor could she deny that they had scaled a great height together. True, they had not climbed the "blue mountain" of her visions; but their peak was "a beautiful and lofty one," nonetheless. Still, Wona was lonely and desperate—at times to the verge of a breakdown—in her frustration. She continued to press her case, cautioning Mansol that his creativity would languish in her absence. When would he muster the courage to venture "alone regardless of consequences to the outposts of sanity?" She ridiculed him for his "adherence to society, his loyalty to family, friends, clubs & associations. There was a boyishness about him which annoyed her greatly." She threatened him with suicide, then with the tyranny of her suffering. "Your penis has conquered both of these," she conceded. "I give you the morality of a large penis and imperial authority—I want daring, My Mansol—Brutality. Show me the animal in you, so that I can be proud of my lover. I detest your pity and your timorous, tame penis."

At moments the dramatics may have been a bit self-conscious

and even "staged." The records have some of the thoroughness and regularity of a script. There are signs of editing; portions of evidence appear in narrative reconstructions written years after the fact. Clearly enough, the dyad, even in its most exotic and forbidden dimensions, was a construction, a story conceived and elaborated and improvised as its leading elements unfolded in time. This is not to hint at inauthenticity but merely to emphasize the obvious—that Harry and Christiana were bright, imaginative, intensely self-conscious people, driven by an ambition to produce between them something new and distinctive in the world. There was nothing fabricated about Harry's fear, conveyed to Christiana in May 1939, that she "was dragging him down to destruction." He recognized the truth of Wona's desire just as he acknowledged that his need for her was very great. But Mansol was not above reminding his mate that while he could work well enough on his own, she needed him absolutely; for without his mediating voice, the visions would come to naught.

The constant going back and forth demonstrated the potent durability of their relationship. They were in it now for good; that much was clear. It remained to find a way to slow down a little. "O how weary I am of this perpetual pendulum swing," Christiana wrote in December 1939. But it was no simple matter coming to terms. Grievances were old and deep. The visions cried out more urgently than ever for attention as their relevance to the alienated modern predicament drew into sharper focus. But would Harry ever do his part? He had promised—and failed time and again, Christiana felt—to transcend the morality of good and evil. He had promised to give more time to her visions. Again, he let her down. On December 6, 1939, Mansol vowed to become the "instrument" of Wona's will but soon left on his long Western trip with Jo. It was the old story all over again.

Harry failed Christiana not as the result of some fixed resistance to her ambitions but for lack of time—and perhaps, as she claimed, because he had not plunged deeply enough into the irrational. He shared her reverence for the visions and her feeling of urgency about the Proposition. There is no denying that his feelings were complex—that his moods had seasons and his love and desire their light and shade. Something approaching the full complexity of his attitude emerges from two typescripts, one entitled "Written by Mansol" and dated October 1939, the second, "The Way to the Sanctuary," completed on February 1, 1940. Both are biographical narratives; both draw attention to themselves as at once factual and fictional in character. This is to say that they follow *Explorations* in yoking the objective and the intuitive, science and art, in venturing to discover and represent the truth of the human heart. In one case the heart is Harry's, in the other Christiana's, but in both the truth is quite plausibly mingled and elusive.

The story opens with Wona's arrival at Mansol's room. She is all in red—dress, shoes, nails. "Her lips were bright and reached for his with a surplus of palpitating life." She brings whiskey, and her intentions are bluntly and unmistakably sexual. Mansol sets his writing aside as Wona goes on excitedly about her visions, about the pressing modern issues they address—"What is Modern Man?" she asks—and about her need for his intellectual guidance. Her ideas, though vague and general, restore Mansol's faith in their union. They have passed somehow "into a new zone of the spirit, a new togetherness which would be the ground for an excess of creative energy." But both respond to glorious reunion by wishing to be alone—Wona to continue her vision, Mansol to reflect on its significance. He sees her dramatic renewal—it has been ten years since her last trance—as the direct result of his recent recognition of her primacy in the dyad. Now that her power is restored, he welcomes her demands that he set to work on the Proposition. True, she will "give him enough blood to finish Melville"; but she will also demand that he write for her whenever a trance surges up.

Mansol insists that his devotion to the task ahead will depend on Wona's admission that she has always put her own work first, that she has given of herself only to "make his body beat with the fullest agitation" and thereby to win him to her cause. The strategy has always held him, but never as fully as at present. This is because her new vision centers on the condition of modern humanity, a topic to which Mansol warms immediately. "Modern man," he reflects, "is one whose culture provides no significant forms for his heritage of archetypes." Human longings go unrealized; true spirituality languishes for lack of an outlet; technology has alienated men and women from their bodies; social intercourse is shallow and impersonal. As a solution to the prevailing "Ishmaelism," he offers the "completely personal synergy" of the dyad. Sex is "the pathway to this synergy, as well as the sign to the right way of the spirit." He advocates the "release under favorable conditions of all impulses that recent religions suppressed: aggression particularly." Dyadic relations will foster personal creativity and the evolution of positive— healthy, relevant, liberated—human values. This is his message— their message, really, as stirred by Wona's vision—to a world in desperate need.

"Written by Mansol" is revealing in a number of ways, not all of them intended. It is fascinating, for example, that the initial sexual motive is almost immediately sublimated in intellectual excitement. Though Wona and Mansol are "brought together and fused in a single flame," the heat is all in their heads—or, more properly, in his. Mansol is evidently more moved by the thought of Wona's potent sexuality, and by the meanings he attaches to it, than he is by her body. Yet the ideas that excite him in his lover's vision are hardly as fresh as he makes them seem. They have origins in the dyadic critique—largely Jungian in inspiration—of the modern condition; and they are virtually of a piece with the social commentary everywhere at large in the Melville biography. Christiana no doubt shared such views. But they were hardly original with her; nor, in their developed form, did they hold her attention as they held Harry's. Thus, Mansol's seeming conversion to Wona's vision is in fact a kind of fictional cooptation of Christiana to Harry's enduring preoccupations. At the same time, and as a tacit reward for his willingness to "compromise," Mansol wins time to finish the Melville and establishes to his own satisfaction that Wona has been selfish in demanding otherwise. "Written by Mansol" is a tidy little construction.

Obviously enough, Harry was determined to finish with Melville before turning to the visions. That was not in itself an unreasonable ambition, and it is understandable that he wanted to represent it in a manner that would be acceptable to Christiana. He wanted his way, and he wanted peace. By construing the visions as a point of departure for the analysis of the contemporary malaise—and not in the more personal and symbolic terms that Christiana might have preferred—he gestured in earnest toward compromise. He was also concerned, it seems clear, to reposition the dyad in a broad social framework and thus to rescue it from the virtually hermetic secrecy into which it had drifted. We may fault him for insisting on Christiana's selfishness, but then we will have to fault her for the same thing. And while it is true that he provides her with views that she had never quite possessed, it is also true that she came into their possession not long after the fictional narrative was written. Perhaps "Written by Mansol" records an actual transition in Christiana's thinking; more likely it helped to promote the change that it merely imagines. Either way, the little story is more reasonable and generous, and less devious in its subtlety, than it may be made to seem.

"The Way to the Sanctuary" is no less challenging in its ambiguity. It was written as a kind of adjunct to "The Steps to the Sanctuary," a set of new—if familiar—agreements that Harry and Christiana settled on in February 1940. The narrative finds Wona seated before a warm fire on the evening after Mansol's departure for the West. Amply supplied with cigarettes and liquor, she meditates on the dyad, reflecting that "there was something awry about the method of their life." She acknowledges that she has been fortunate—in Mansol's decision to become a psychologist, in his willingness to follow her sexual lead, and in his general readiness to bend to her interests and desires. "In most essentials," she concedes, "I have remade my lover." But vexing problems—Melville, family and society, the burden of guilt, her lover's unwillingness to surrender to the irrational, and his failure to properly comprehend the dark passion of her trances—flood the foreground of her consciousness. She resolves to take complete control of the dyad, shaping Mansol utterly to her will that he may at last become a fit servant of the visions. Even more than in "Written by Mansol," Harry here gives fictional emphasis to Christiana's authority in the dyad. Once again, however, her initiatives, though set forth with great sound and fury, may be read as tacit concessions to Mansol's agenda. In addition to the usual demands for more attention, more daring, less guilt, less family, and an increase in sex and violence, Wona insists that they spend more time in public. The Melville will continue, and they will in due course resume their work at the Clinic. Most crucially, Wona is now cast as the author of the Proposition. The time is approaching, she says, "when I shall want to write." Her lover will be required to "read, listen, criticize," and no more.

In the course of dramatizing Wona's unwitting capitulation to Mansol's desires, Harry gives oblique—and not so oblique— expression to his own reservations about the dyad. These center exclusively on Christiana and emerge, quite ironically, from the very midst of Wona's imagined assault on Mansol. Indeed, it is the first of her faults that she finds so many faults in him. Wona is surrounded by luxury and comfort; she is fortunate in the talent and amiable pliancy of her mate. Yet her gratitude invariably gives way to a familiar litany of complaints. Wona's discontent is linked on one side to her narcissism ("Yes," she muses, admiring her lips in a mirror, "Lachiase had seen them as they truly were"), and on another by the frightening darkness of her interior life (though Mansol "was less terrified of her than any man she had ever met, he was always on the verge of panic"). Her sexuality, equally extreme in its violence and destructiveness, is at once the expression of self-contempt and an instrument of tyranny over her lover. But even as she seizes all authority, Wona insists on being mastered. The contradiction is as complete as it is pervasive. "Understand, my darling," she imagines herself saying to Mansol, "I have no desire to exercise authority. I am looking forward to the day when all the power will be yours and I can rest in my submission. But first I must teach you by example to lead precisely where I wish." Finally, Wona is an alcoholic. "Wine, or Soma," she reflects, is "the good companion of the soul." In fact, Harry makes it perfectly clear that drink is closely tied up with the other excesses at the root of Christiana's misery. "She took another drink," he writes, "and felt the hot blood run through her. Ah! This warmed her. This was what she required—drink and his penis and his fist and his iron heel."

For all of its bite, Harry's list of grievances did nothing to diminish Christiana's enthusiasm for "The Steps to the Sanctuary," the most recent of their dyadic fresh starts. Ostensibly an affirmation of

Wona's authority, the agreement confirms in fact what "Written by Mansol" and "The Way to the Sanctuary" suggest in fiction. "Learn to have your thoughts and ideas spring out of my central feeling," she demands. Yet clearly enough the sense to be made of her inner promptings was her lover's to decide. More than ever before the interpretation of the dyad, the direct formation of the meaning of their lives together, was in Harry's control. His dabblings in fiction are themselves evidence on this score. So are Christiana's records for the duration of Harry's long leave of absence. "Mansol told me that now I am faced by an enormous gap between my experience & my power to formulate it," she reported, without protest, in December 1940. "I don't need to be intellectually critical of something I happen to want to express," she wrote the following January; "Mansol can do that for me." In April she confessed that it pleased her when Harry "began to talk about his plans at the Clinic for next year." That May she was overtaken by an ambition to know her lover's every thought, "to see and understand the world through him, to understand the beautiful shapes that he is constructing." In some part, she had seen the light; she had opted for Harry's way. But the light and the way would not have tempted her just a year or two before. Christiana was ready to change—to capitulate gradually and on what appeared to be her own terms—because she was tired. Life at the pace she set for herself was exhausting; and for all of his gestures of compromise, Harry gave little ground. She surrendered— in many ways to her benefit—because she had to. The swing of the pendulum was killing her.

▼

chapter ten

Chronometricals and Horologicals

"At the age of 51 I acquired a sense of social responsibility." So Harry observed of himself to his daughter, Josephine, then 24, in the early summer of 1945, just weeks before the atom bombs fell on Japan. Thanks primarily to the war, Harry had indeed opened himself to social and political concerns of all kinds. The shift in focus was in some degree thrust upon him. "My office is with the individual & his development & his discovery of value," he wrote to Lewis Mumford in August 1942; "but unfortunately this has come to a dead-end, since the individual can't enjoy much value now, & can only thrive by putting it in the common pot & dedicating it all to the extermination of Satan." But in fact Harry responded to the crisis with the zest of a born extrovert. He hankered after a taste of the glory that had been denied him, and that his brother Ike had so thoroughly enjoyed, in 1917. He flourished as a leader in the global crusade of good against evil, taking genuine satisfaction in the status and activities of the public man. In joining the war effort, Harry became attentive as never before to questions of collective rather than individual moment. He came to feel that in *Explorations* he had cast the personality adrift in a "social vacuum." But he recognized as well that his error was a common one in the period between the wars. The erosion of American values and of the national will was painfully evident to him in the widespread reluctance, especially among the young, to join the struggle against Hitler and the Nazis.

The isolated individual has grown soft and selfish, he wrote to Lewis Mumford. "Now is the time to fashion a new superego," a framework for action at once consistent with traditional beliefs and freshly adapted to present needs. Defining the superego as those "eternal values to which everyone should be loyal," Harry assured his friend that a new moral order could be "arrived at step by step through clear-headed individual & social experimentation . . . led by creators like yourself & checked & verified by social scientists like myself."

The shift in Harry's bearings was radical and permanent. He wrote to FDR in 1941 proposing the formation of a government department of social science, staffed by specialists responsible for the development of public policy and for guidance in periods of crisis. He was of course anxious to serve in such an agency. His passion for deep diving had given way now to a burning interest in what he called "the great social & moral dilemmas of our time . . . the New World & the Education required to be equal to it." Christiana, acquiescent for the present in Harry's direction—"Mansol will know the way," she wrote, "his word will deliver me"—did her best to follow his lead. She wrote to a friend in 1943 of assuming with Harry "our share of the back-breaking effort involved in winning this war." She was also willing to share in the responsibility for what she regarded as the shortcomings of America's young people. "We had given them nothing," she confessed, "neither religion, nor world loyalty, nor love of country, nothing in fact to which they felt that they could dedicate themselves." At Harry's suggestion, she was even willing to consider making the Tower an endowed retreat for creative writers. Her zeal notwithstanding, however, Christiana was simply not made for social action. Harry suggested as much in a letter to Mumford, allowing that his own "centrifugal" spin into public affairs was properly balanced by his lover's "centripetal . . . pilgrimage into her own depths," which Pearl Harbor and its aftermath did little to disturb. Christiana's deeper resistance to the war—rooted finally in her refusal to surrender the dyad and all that went with it—would surface in a terrific rush when the call to public duty finally summoned Harry from her side. Perhaps in his readiness to leave she caught a glimpse of the hateful truth—that the demands of their relationship had become a burden to him.

Harry went to war, as he turned to social and collective concerns in his work, for many reasons—fame and glory, idealism, genuine concern for the welfare of the country, and, less consciously perhaps, to gain relief from what he found suffocating in the dyad. At the focus of his attention was the American character. National morale and morality, he felt, had fallen on hard times. The country cried out for spiritual guidance, for a new, usable, positive creed—a new mythology. Central to the problem as he saw it was the restless, divisive individualism that so crippled the nation's resolve in its hour of need. Harry was the first to admit that his own life had been symptomatic of the disease; he was also determined to cure himself of pride and privacy even as he sought to instill a spirit of unity and communal solidarity among his countrymen. In his class report for 1940 Harry confessed to an interest in rum, romanticism, and rebellion. That formula required but "one correction," he quipped in 1950: "for rebellion I substitute reunion." The social analogue to this personal sentiment turns up in a letter of 1945 to his daughter. Discussing Erich Fromm's *Escape from Freedom,* Harry insists that "there is very little Freedom in the sense of Independence or Self-Sufficiency. We are almost completely *interdependent. . . .* The first thing to realize is our utter dependence upon a certain degree of solidarity in society & be profoundly grateful for the solidarity when we have it." In the broader postwar perspective, he took the view—in another letter to Josephine—"that Modern Man is Obsolete & that National Man must become World Man very quickly if atomic energy is to be held in control." Almost in the same breath he boasted of having "become a politician working undercover to get Congress to pass a Bill establishing a National Institute of Science *including* the Social Sciences with 6,000 scholarships a year and lots of money for research." He would do his part to broaden the American horizon.

For all of his good intentions, however, Harry went public against the strong bent of his nature and training. His forte was a masterful intuitive grasp of individual motivation, a strength grounded in his own intense self-absorption. It was the defect of this virtue that he tended to "psychologize" social issues and failed thereby to recognize the weight of larger economic forces bearing on individual lives. He often admitted to bafflement at the spectacle of American politics and lacked, according to Talcott Parsons, the instincts of a true social scientist. Moreover, reunion with the Class of 1915 was in part a return to solidarity with the old ways, not least of all with Jo, who figured more prominently in Harry's life precisely as that life became more public. She was increasingly visible as his companion at conferences and meetings; they went as a couple to an evening at the White House in 1942; she stood proudly at his side when he received the Legion of Merit for distinguished military service in 1946; she was, in her lifelong commitment to charity and social uplift, a modest example for her more ambitious spouse. For Harry and Jo, all such activities bore the subtle color and accent of their social class—of superiority experienced as an unconscious reflex, evident to all (save perhaps to its possessors) as something distinctive, whether for good or ill. Harry was often slow to pay his associates at the Clinic, not for want of money but because the idea of financial need was utterly abstract for him. More and more after the war he invited his students home for "informal" suppers, never quite recognizing that few of them would feel readily at ease in the opulence he took for granted. And for all of his commitment to social solidarity, Harry was increasingly drawn to the comfort and privacy of home. "My great consolation & joy this year has been our house," he wrote to Josephine of their stylish new residence on Brimmer Street, "the most perfect (for our purposes at least) that I have ever known. It has been especially gratifying recently, since the garden was finished, with the fountain playing & the mock-orange exuding delicious fragrances." This serene Arcadian spot was as remote from the common streets as it was from the more strenuous version of Nature observed at the Tower.

The sheltered garden of home and family was a sanctuary against the vulgarity and hustle of postwar America. In truth, Harry was not as fully reborn into solidarity with his fellows as he sometimes hoped he might be. Nor was he blind to the truth of the matter. In

another of his confessional and self-analytic letters to Josephine—
this one written at the beginning of 1946—he consoles her for
having been born too late to witness his youthful absorption in "the
social organism," when he "enjoyed membership, teams, friends
&c." During most of her lifetime he has been at work on "problems
requiring solitude & introversion. I had my second birth," he explains, "in 1925 (at the age of 32) during the year we were in
Cambridge. This threw me clear out of Society into the Third Dimension & to hold my place there against the constant pressures I
built up some formidable defenses & paid for them." Carefully
avoiding mention of the dyad, he recalls, somewhat contritely, his
rejection of Jo. "You and I ganged up & formed a scarcely moveable
block in opposition to Mummy's Moving Towards People." He goes
on to acknowledge that the habits of solitude formed at the time of
his second birth have been obstacles to the personal transformation
looked for in a third. "I am under the impression *today* that the
central problem of the spirit is managing Disgust—disgust with
American materialism in all its forms, advertising & publicity, blatant vulgarity, hapless raucous fatuous pleasure-seeking, going
places, sickly pallid crooning music, spiritual dearth, emptiness,
motion without meaning &c. &c. All this is a dreadful bolus to
swallow, but I am determined to do it, because I am in the midst
of my Third Birth, & if I can not embrace my own world it will be
an abortion. The conception of our interdependence has helped me
more than anything—if only I can hold on to it."

In hindsight, it is easy enough to see why Harry found it increasingly difficult to sympathize with the culture of the postwar era.
Because the world had taken a course he could neither approve nor
control, it cost him no little effort to "hold on" to his social commitment. Indeed, even as he reasserts that commitment, he grants
himself "a couple of years to make the transition" into the full current of public life. Rather than return immediately to Harvard,
where research and teaching in the new field of Social Relations
await him, he announces plans for "another long dive into [the]
Sargasso Sea" of his independent work on Melville. Harry now regarded the biography as a species of self-indulgence akin to the
errant individualism that he had come to condemn in his subject.

Melville had taken deep diving to a socially profitless and self-destructive extreme; his biographer was determined to avoid a similar fate. But Harry was torn—by his sense of social responsibility, by a recoil from what that entailed, and by the old pull downward into the romantic claustrum of the psyche. The public and the private, conscious and unconscious, science and art, Jo and Christiana—all of these overlapping oppositions widened and deepened for him in the years after the war. More than ever he was drawn in both directions at once, with the result that he moved in neither with complete conviction or satisfaction or success. The best days on all fronts, he must have sensed, were behind him.

Four years earlier, in 1941, Harry's interests had already begun to shift, but there was as yet no trace of uncertainty in his stride. He returned to the Clinic that September, fortified with a $60,000 Rockefeller grant and a plan for 5 years of research on social relations among young people, with Clyde Kluckhohn along as an advisor. It was *Explorations* all over again but with greater emphasis this time on diagnostic and statistical accuracy. Harry's notes for the period include jottings on "Problems to be Studied, 1941–42," which highlight the analysis of the subject's "sentiments," or values, their determinants, comparative intensity, and bearing on political preferences. His interests took rise from a suspicion that American unity and will had eroded, and from a gathering fear of Nazism— which "must be kept out of this country," he wrote, "and if necessary attacked until it is abandoned or wiped out." Harry's teaching was similarly slanted toward public issues. In the fall of 1941 he joined Kluckhohn and the rising young psychologist O. Hobart Mowrer in an ambitious new course on personality and culture, which took "socialization" as its principal topic. Meanwhile, his seminar with Gordon Allport on social and dynamic psychology featured an emphasis on problems of wartime "morale."

The mood at the Clinic was decidedly upbeat. Harry was very enthusiastic about his paid staff, which included Robert White and Daniel Horn—the latter a statistician—Brewster Smith, Silvan Tomkins, and Frederick Wyatt. Thanks apparently to the reputation of *Explorations,* numerous others—Robert Holt, Leopold Bellak, Thelma Alper, Elliott Jaques, Rosemary ("Molly") Pritchard, and Ernest Haggard among them—gathered at 64 Plympton to get in on the action. Jaques recalls being drawn to Cambridge by Harry's rousing essay, "What Should Psychologists Do about Psychoanalysis?" published the year before. Arguing that psychology needs psychoanalysis, and that the university needs both, Harry makes a strong case for the unique brand of research practiced at the Clinic. "Superficiality," he argues, "is the great sin of American personology. It suits the tempo of the times; it suits industry and commerce; it suits our interest in appearances; it suits our boyish optimism. And it suits the good heart of America, its Rotarian solidarity, its will-to-agree, since it is easier to agree about the surface than about the depths. Perhaps there are no depths. Who knows? There *are no* depths. Since truth is a congenial fiction, and *this* fiction is most congenial, *this* is truth." Harry replies to "all this shallowness" with psychoanalysis, which believes in depths, and which opens the way to their exploration. It was this spirit of confident rebellion, of heady breaking away, that made the Clinic so attractive to students in September of 1941.

But the catastrophe at Pearl Harbor in December changed all that. A few of the staff were called away to war almost immediately; others followed, until by the next summer less than half of the original group remained. Those who continued until the Rockefeller grant was formally suspended in September 1943, were of course frustrated in their long-range plans. Still, a number of research papers were completed, most of them elaborating on new methods of personality assessment. Harry's contributions included collaborative work on the revised TAT (which was published by the Harvard University Press in 1943), a pair of book reviews, and an Introduction to Silvan Tomkins' *Contemporary Psychopathology*. But he was increasingly preoccupied with the war. Angling for ways to get more actively involved, he co-authored (with Morris Stein) a brief note on techniques for combat officer selection. "I am not satisfied with psychology now," he wrote to Mumford. The Clinic was too far from the center of things, and likely to stay that way, if the majority of pacifists on the staff had their way. "Tremendous interest," Harry wrote, again to Mumford; "but all of them to the core innoculated with pacifism. It is largely because of this that I must leave—cutting everything off in the middle."

Key dimensions to Harry's mood at the time of his leaving the Clinic are on display in *A Clinical Study of Sentiments,* a monograph co-authored with Christiana in 1942 and 1943. A closely detailed analysis of the values (or "sentiments") of eleven Harvard men, the book was salvaged from the larger research program cut short because of the war. Harry wrote the theoretical and methodological sections of the monograph and its concluding overview, while Christiana joined him in organizing and composing the case histories. Though nominally concerned with attitudes toward war, religion, parents, and sex, they were in fact principally interested in the first topic and thus inclined to treat the other three as adjuncts to it. It is a matter, the reader feels, of religion, parents, and sex viewed in their bearing on the subject's readiness for what is described repeatedly as "the most portentous spiritual and political conflict in Western history." Harry and Christiana acknowledge early on their assumption that "the integrity of American society . . . is worth preserving, and that in the event of war instigated by an aggressor nation one way that an American can be of social value is to dedicate his energies to the war effort." But this puts their position much too mildly. In fact, *A Clinical Study of Sentiments* is charged with muscular commitment to heroic struggle against evil incarnate. It finds America unready for its historic summons to valor and spreads the blame variously among leftist academics ("Perhaps the correlation . . . is negative between socialistic inclinations and fortitude in a fox hole"), the churches, popular social critics, and other contributors to the decadent spirit of pacifism. Young people are chastised for their "disregard of the existence of evil." One subject is handicapped by "his extreme, if not pathological, physical timidity"; another "has no convictions to live or die for"; a third is "not yet the man to keep the sword of conviction sharp and shining in the wet weather of fashionable cynicism"; yet another is faulted for failing to "conceal the fact that a reluctance to run the hazard of dying on the battlefield has got the best" of him. All of which fuels the conclusion that "victorious armies and navies are not welded out of such stuff as these men are made of."

Such barely restrained contempt for the young was at once an expression of genuine concern for the country and a reflex evasion of several rather awkward contradictions. Harry knew nothing of combat, yet adopts the tone of one who has faced bloodshed and death without flinching. He makes small of his subjects as "college intellectuals," never acknowledging that he is a professional model for the type. Complaining that they have "no common enlivening ideology to encourage and sustain them," he says nothing of his lifelong indifference to social issues. He is critical of the insulated "Romantic Genius figure," but keeps Melville, its veritable apotheosis, to himself. Despite his adult resistance to their authority in his own personality, Harry holds out the college athlete and clubman as positive alternatives to the members of his rather brainy sample. "Intellectuals," he observes, are "better fitted for peace than for war." He deplores "the high valuation of individualism" among Americans, never hinting that he has until recently shared their perspective on the matter.

When Harry confessed to Lewis Mumford that "*A Clinical Study of Sentiments* . . . is a fairly mediocre performance," he meant to suggest that the sample was small and not very representative and that he and Christiana had lacked the time to draw out the full potential of their materials. Less consciously, perhaps, he was voicing a sense of personal implication in the very condition that they had so vigorously exposed. A cognate suggestion emerges in their virtual apology for having "failed to do justice to the virtues, talents, and attainments" of their subjects. Harry was as deeply uncertain about these bright, introverted, romantic, peace-loving young intellectuals as he was about the large part of his own nature they mirrored back to him. Worse, his subjects could blame the malaise of their generation on the failure of leadership in his. *Sentiments,* he admitted to Mumford in June 1943, "amounts to an indictment of the education our generation have been giving young people in the period Between Wars." Worst of all, the young pacifists were perfectly consistent in their position on the war, while their judges, for all of their seeming confidence, were not. "Our subjects," Harry observes at the very end of the study, "had an almost compulsive need for voicing criticism . . . which seemed to arise out of a deep barely-articulate *dissatisfaction with the ethos of American culture.*" The students were unwilling to risk their lives in defense of what they took to be the ruthlessness and unrelieved vulgarity of American capitalist democracy. Harry of course shared their estimate of the national culture, yet beat the drum loudly in its support. Were they truer than he to their ideals? Or were they, as men of modest, middle-class means, less the beneficiaries than he of the system's acknowledged inequities? Such questions, rising rather awkwardly from the midst of the many contradictions in *Sentiments,* are never directly posed, let alone answered. Yet they figure decisively in the uncertain tone—and, as Harry seems to have sensed, in the limited analytical value—of the deeply divided document from which they emerge.

Harry had been sharply alert to the threat of war in Europe at least since the summer of 1937, when he observed first-hand the military build up in Germany and scrutinized the face of Adoph Hitler at the Wagner festival in Bayreuth. He wrote to Josephine in early 1938 that "the Hitler regime is another invasion of Huns— this time mechanized & made more hideous by poison gasses, bombs &c. It is the destruction of free inquiry, free speech, free thinking, art, science & everything that is mature & humane." He added that pacifism—"the extreme of Christianity"—makes it "easy for the gangsters to get control." Later that year he raised with Mumford "the question that bothered Melville: what is a man of good-will (a man of Christ, let us say) to do with his endowment of aggressive instinct?" The topic, with its obvious bearing on the war, did not restrain Harry for long. "Can this selfish country be aroused?" he asked Mumford in 1939. A few months later he admitted to "having murder in my heart for everything Fascistic." Harry made it known to the staff at the Clinic that he advocated prompt, decisive American intervention in Europe. He geared his teaching to the war and was "enormously relieved," he told Mumford, "by Japan's attack on us," because he felt sure "it would anger & so solidify the country." The following February he was at Bryn Mawr, urging the students to support the war. That same month he wrote an article for the *Boston Herald,* warning against the complacent assumption "that this war will be a short and jolly one." He urged his readers "to be 'high morale carriers' in speech as well as in deed, to stare realities in the face, to support the government, to abstain from grumbling and criticism, to go into training, physi-

cally and morally, in order to be equal to the setbacks and depriva-
tions that lie immediately ahead of us, and above all to encourage
and honor the men who are destined to save us from the ugliest and
most shameful fate that has ever clouded the horizon of the people
of the United States."

Harry was easily as good as his words. He was active in trying to
raise support for the war. He wrote letters of advice and encouragement to public officials. At the time of his mother's death in 1940
he moved with Jo to New York, where he became an active member
of the so-called "morale seminars" headed by his neighbor Arthur
Upham Pope and attended by dozens of interested social scientists,
including Margaret Mead, Gregory Bateson, and Ruth Benedict.
The group conducted research, often on request from the federal
government, on various aspects of strategy and propaganda—Harry
best remembered trying to develop questions for the crew of a captured German submarine. A year later, Harry joined Gordon Allport in leading a similar seminar at Harvard. Their group circulated
"Worksheets on Morale" covering such topics as psychological warfare, testing programs for combat officers, and studies of the elements contributing to high morale in a democracy.

Harry's proudest contribution in this vein was an analysis of the
personality of Adolf Hitler, requested on short notice by an intelligence agency of the federal government in 1940. Harry completed
a brief profile while still in New York, then continued the work at
Harvard the following year. He and Gordon Allport, working with
graduate students in their morale seminar, developed a profile of
the Fuhrer that appeared in a paper by W. H. D. Vernon in 1942.
A call for a more ambitious study—of Hitler's personality, the
sources of his influence with the German people, and his likely
response to defeat—followed the next spring. It came from Walter
C. Langer, a former member of the Clinic staff who had been placed
in charge of the project by General William ("Wild Bill") Donovan,
head of the Office of Strategic Services (OSS). Expanding on his
original portrait, both through the study of materials provided by
the OSS and through the close textual scrutiny of *Mein Kampf* and
other writings, Harry produced in October 1943 a 227-page "Analysis of the Personality of Adolph [sic] Hitler, with Predictions of

His Future Behavior and Suggestions for Dealing with Him Now and After Germany's Surrender."

Given the complexity of its topic, and the brevity of the time allowed for its completion, the study was a brilliant success. Hitler's personality unfolds as a fabric of extreme contradictions (inferiority/superiority, weakness/strength, love/hate, sadism/masochism) which combine in the galvanizing Nazi ideology and take expression in a reign of heartless terror and cruelty. Harry must have shuddered at those moments when the trajectory of the German leader's interior life seemed to intersect with his own. "Counteractive narcism," he finds, the "reaction formation to underlying feelings of wounded self-esteem," is basic to Hitler's makeup. In his recoil from childhood trauma, mad Adolf—whose "irreal world has become real" and whose "insanity is sanity"—is akin to Ahab, the hero of dyadic defiance, and another potent paranoid schizophrenic. With the captain of the *Pequod,* the Nazi leader is compelled, as "the last resource of an insulted and unendurable existence," to "die, dragging all of Europe with him into the abyss." The Fuhrer's indebtedness to Nietzsche was also a troublesome detail, not least as it fueled his ambition to rise above the constraints of an antiquated Christian morality. Harry must have squirmed a little—even more than a little—both inside his own skin and inside the dyad, as the portrait formed itself in his hands.

The most sensational of Harry's insights fell on the Fuhrer's twisted sexuality, which had at its nadir a masochistic pleasure in being spattered by the urine of a woman squatting above him. This tentative analytic conclusion, based in the "careful study of the three thousand metaphors . . . in *Mein Kampf,*" was verified by a German journalist who "questioned two of the women with whom Hitler . . . had relations." Harry relayed all of his findings to Walter Langer but omitted offensive details from the thirty copies of the report prepared for Donovan and the military brass, fearing that disgust might impede comprehension of the larger argument. "Your report is a humdinger," Langer responded. "I knew that you were a past master at this art but this report convinces me that I had underestimated your talents." It was understood, as Harry recalled years later, that his report would be combined with others in a comprehensive final rendering. Still, he was surprised and upset when news reached him that the copies of his work had been ordered destroyed. Langer had offended other staff members with his overweening ambition to "mastermind" the Hitler project. Was he in over his head? Would he properly represent the contributions of his associates? Such questions went unanswered at the time, as the final report—which Langer did not share with Harry—disappeared into the labyrinth of the military establishment. It was not until 1972, when Langer published *The Mind of Adolf Hitler: The Secret Wartime Report,* that the truth of Harry's original suspicions was confirmed. Langer had indeed taken the best of his ideas, including the sexual analysis and the prediction of Hitler's suicide, without a word of acknowledgment.

Harry had little time in 1943 for dwelling on imagined grievances. Impatient with the pittance of supporting roles that had been assigned him, he was restless for a major part in the war. Though well along in his forties, he made the effort to get in shape, cutting back on cigarettes and alcohol, taking brisk walks, rowing on the Charles. Various leads had come to nothing. In 1940 he put out feelers for a commission in the Naval Reserve. Two years later he tried the Navy again. "I am planning to get my hands dirty with a clear conscience & a good vengeance," he wrote to Mumford in August 1942, "for I think I have found a job that I can perform—Combat Intelligence Officer on an aircraft carrier." Both opportunities fell through. So did a commission as brigadier general with the War Office Selection Board (WOSB) of the British Army. The position finally went to an Englishman. It was not until late in 1943 that Harry finally landed the job he had been looking for. That November he was invited to Washington to consult on a new assessment program for recruits in the OSS intelligence service. The task was to measure the readiness of selected men and women for special, often hazardous duty, much of it behind enemy lines. When asked on short notice to join the senior staff of Assessment Station S (synonymous with "Secret")—the principal testing site, situated on a large country estate outside of Washington—Harry accepted without hesitation. Here was important work for which he was eminently well qualified. Opportunities for leadership and travel, and

the sheer glamor of involvement with spies and special agents, were
additional incentives. Captain Murray reported for duty in December, satisfied now that his investment of time and energy with Walter Langer had finally paid off.

But success in the public sector precipitated crisis at home. For
all of her support in principle of the war effort, Christiana was emotionally unprepared to let Harry go—especially, it is safe to say, as
he contemplated his departure with such evident relish. A routine
physical checkup that fall revealed that she was suffering from extreme hypertension. "Christiana's blood pressure began its upward
course," Harry later wrote to Lewis Mumford, "as soon as she fore-
saw that the war would eventually take me off." Her blood pressure
ran so high—consistently over 200—that her physicians urged immediate and radical surgery, a so-called sympathectomy, the sever-
ing of the sympathetic nerves that lie along the spine. It was a
desperate move. The sympathectomy involved two separate procedures, one for each side, to occur about a week apart. There was no
guarantee of success, let alone survival. Recovery would be protracted, some long-term enfeeblement was inevitable, and the pain
would be excruciating. But there was no alternative. Fortunately,
Jo and Josphine were in Europe, leaving Harry complete freedom
to attend to Christiana. "The affrighting first stage—operation on
the right side—has been achieved," he wrote to Mumford at the
beginning of November. "Christiana has one bad week of pain, &
then another horror on the other side." He wrote again about a week
later to report that the second stage had also gone well. "I might
say *only* the pain, or *nothing but* the pain remains, except that *pain*
can fill the whole world." The crisis brought out the best in both of
them. Christiana was resolute and tough. She complained little,
except when the pain grew so sharp that she cried out in spite of
herself. Harry's extraordinary reserves of loyalty and tenderness were
meanwhile on conspicuous display. "For the first time in my life I
am on the margin of my fortitude," he confessed to Mumford. Still,
he was an observer at both operations and haunted the hospital
corridors once they were over.

Christiana's recuperation was slow but steady. The pain passed,
and much of her physical strength returned. But a measure of the

old vitality had slipped permanently away. The energy that brims up almost palpably in Mary Aiken's portrait of 1939 had ebbed. The operation left her a slower, older woman. She was subject now to sudden fainting spells and to periodic fluctuations in body temperature. Still, she had survived. Her level of energy had dropped, but only to a more nearly normal, livable level. The precipitous rise in Christiana's blood pressure betrayed the dark fatality in her makeup, the furious intensity of the tragic anima, verging in its extremity toward destruction. This was the dyadic implication, they both saw, of Denis de Rougemont's *Love in the Western World,* which they read not long after it appeared in 1940. "Happy love has no history," de Rougemont declares. "Romance only comes into existence where love is fatal, frowned upon and doomed by life itself." The whole deadly trajectory of the Western erotic tradition, he argues, is captured in the myth of Tristan and Iseult, which may be said to operate "wherever passion is dreamed of as an ideal instead of being feared like a dangerous fever; wherever its irresistible character is welcomed, invoked, or imagined as a magnificent and desirable disaster instead of as simply a disaster. It lives upon the lives of people who think that love is their fate (and as unavoidable as the effect of the love-potion is in the Romance); that it swoops upon powerless and ravished men and women in order to consume them in a pure flame; or that it is stronger and more real than happiness, society, or morality." If we investigate "the innermost recesses of their hearts," he concludes, we find that such people are "obeying the fatal dictates of a wish for death."

Harry and Christiana could not fail to see themselves in this dark picture. They were of course disturbed by what they read, not least by de Rougemont's argument that passionate lovers in the tradition of Tristan and Iseult are doomed to unhappiness "because the love agitating them is not a love of each for the other as that other really is. They love one another, but each loves the other *from the standpoint of self and not from the other's standpoint.* Their unhappiness thus originates in a false reciprocity, which disguises a twin narcissism." Wona and Mansol were not blind to the intense self-absorption on the nether side of their professed love for each other; indeed, the transcendent unity ascribed to the dyad was their answer, in more than name they hoped, to just that threat. Still, the yoking of passion with destruction, and both with narcissism, must have seemed particularly apt in the early 1940s, especially in its bearing on Christiana's behavior. In one mood, Harry dismissed *Love in the Western World* as the product of an unsuccessful anima experience. In another he acknowledged the destructiveness in passion but welcomed it as the necessary prerequisite to new growth. Still, something in him had begun to retreat from entanglement in the dyad— something gregarious and optimistic, even conventional, that shrank from the dark fury of Christiana's passion.

Harry's pulling away, though gradual and never expressed in so many words, exacerbated the problem. Christiana's drinking had increased in the years just before her operation; and she was prone, in her cups, to open up about Harry and the Tower, sensing perhaps that making it public would somehow make it secure. But Harry resented her indiscretions, which only reinforced his impulse to retreat. Christiana in turn grew more lonely and more frightened and more angry as Harry pulled silently away. And so her blood pressure rose to perilous heights. The war was to blame, they told each other; it was stern duty that summoned the warrior away. But he would return; he might then consider leaving Harvard, or at least cutting back. At any rate, they would make time, at last, for "her work." Sustained by such vague, happy prospects, Christiana was recovering comfortably at home when Harry left for Washington in late December.

"It was all very good fun," Harry later recalled of his OSS work, "terrifically interesting, terrific fun." World War II satisfied his craving for service in a noble cause; it drew on his very considerable skills as a leader; it provided a modicum of adventure, and travel to far away places; and it occasioned a long interval of separation from the heat and anguish of the dyad. Harry was not long in making his presence felt at Station S. Donald MacKinnon, one of several from the Clinic to join the assessment program, recalled that Harry's preeminence among the senior officers was evident almost from the start. His energy, aptitude for the work at hand, and charismatic personality left no doubt that he was the man to lead the operation.

281

Testing began early in January 1944. Recruits in groups of eighteen arrived twice each week for three-and-a-half days of testing with a senior staff of about seven psychologists, psychiatrists, and sociologists, and about as many junior staff, most of them graduate students in psychology. As Harry later reported in *The Assessment of Men*—his co-authored account of the experimental program—the obstacles to success in testing the fitness of the candidates were legion. There were few precedents for the kind of assessment they had in mind; the recruits were an inexperienced and heterogeneous lot being screened for a wide variety of tasks; the staff were equally inexperienced and quite as varied in their backgrounds and assumptions about personality. Into this vacuum Harry brought what he knew best, the theory and research techniques employed over the past decade or so at the Clinic. The OSS program, he boasts in the Introduction to *Assessment of Men,* "represents the first attempt in America to design and carry out selection procedures in conformity with so-called *organismic* (Gestalt) principles." Assessment was "multiform," which is to say that the "whole person" was scrutinized in numerous and varied settings. There were standardized tests of intelligence and mechanical comprehension; personal history forms and interviews; group problem-solving sessions, some of them "leaderless"; various measures of physical strength and endurance; stress tests, debating tests, even an indirect assessment of the candidates' need and tolerance for alcohol. Using a six-point scale, the staff rated the candidates on eleven variables (motivation for assignment, energy and zest, practical intelligence, emotional stability, and so on). Brief personality profiles were prepared for a culminating staff meeting at which final recommendations were hammered out. It was the Clinic in a nutshell, complete with ingenious procedures, an informal social setting, heavy staff involvement, an expanded Diagnostic Council, and a modified version of the concluding biographical narrative.

Harry's initial inclination to apply what he had learned at 64 Plympton was pleasantly reinforced during a visit to England in March. He was delighted to find, as he wrote to Mumford, that his counterparts in Britain "had read *Explorations* & spoke of it as their Bible & expected me to make speeches & deliver wise judgments on

282

a hundred issues." So fortified, Harry returned to Washington intent on bringing the American program even more fully into alignment with his own ideas. Promotion to Major followed that April, and by June he was confidently in control of operations at Station S. During the weeks that followed he took a hand in setting up new testing programs in the Washington area (Station W) and in California (Station WS). He flew to France in late July, and again in October, to evaluate OSS personnel in the field. Appraisal of the assessment process was also undertaken stateside, at Station F in Potomac, Maryland, set up that fall to evaluate personnel moving from the European to the Far Eastern theater of operations. Harry was himself increasingly concerned with the war in the Pacific. The early Spring of 1945 found him at Georgetown University, taking courses on the economics, politics, and culture of Japan, China, Burma, and India. "I am taking notes, reading books, drawing maps & writing papers," he wrote to Josephine, "just as if I was at college again." He was in regular touch with Josephine during the next few weeks, sending her animated accounts of his long airplane journey via Bermuda, the Azores, Casablanca, Cairo, Karachi, Delhi, Calcutta, and over "the Hump" of the Himalayas to Kunming, in southwestern China. There it was his task to supervise the assessment of Chinese paratroopers for combat, sabotage, and intelligence operations behind Japanese lines. That mission accomplished, he returned home in General Donovan's private plane just as the Japanese finally surrendered.

"I enjoyed myself hugely in China," Harry wrote to Josephine. For him at least, the war had been an exhilarating holiday from business as usual. His subsequent promotion to Lt. Colonel and decoration with the Legion of Merit (for "patriotic zeal and devotion to duty" in the OSS) were just so much icing on the cake. He had been active, independent, and largely successful in all the ways that mattered to him. True, the assessment program had not yielded the kind of statistical reassurances that Harry and his colleagues had looked for. There had been neither the time nor the occasion for a careful, scientific appraisal of their efforts. But they felt obliged nonetheless to acknowledge a lack of "tangible proof" that their work had repaid the time and money expended on it. Confidence in the diagnostic scheme was generally firm, and it was agreed that they had been successful in identifying candidates who were psychologically unfit for service. Moreover, their techniques for the assessment of "normal" people provided valuable direction and encouragement to the rapidly expanding field of clinical psychology. Leonard W. Doob, a Yale psychologist reviewing *Assessment of Men* in the *Saturday Review*, praised the volume for its "very significant and numerous insights into our knowledge of human personality and its measurement." It would prove helpful, he predicted, "to any organization employing large numbers of people which seeks to select fewer square pegs for round holes." Still, there was no concealing a certain disappointment with the outcome of the OSS work. "The picture presented in this volume," Harry conceded, "is not that of a noble building ready for occupancy, but rather of a mass of rubble with many good blocks of granite and marble out of which a substantial edifice can be erected in the future."

But the book was itself the least of Harry's wartime experiences. It was written in the aftermath of the action and in the midst of other, more compelling projects. The pleasure of military service had been in the doing of things, in the constant, bracing challenges to Harry's resilience and creativity in an active, public setting. An old relish for competition took hold of him during the initial struggle for control of Station S, in which he outflanked and finally displaced his predecessor, James Alexander Hamilton. It was intensely gratifying that men and institutions shaped themselves so readily and profitably to his designs. It was in the OSS that Harry established himself as an innovator in modern personality assessment, which "had its start," according to Donald MacKinnon, "at Station S." There had been the excitement of Normandy, a jubilant tour of Paris in a jeep, and then the ride north to Brussels on the heels of the advancing British forces. China was equally memorable. "I liked everything about it," Harry wrote to Josephine—"the climate . . . the landscape, the stolid and enduring peasantry, the binding ties among family members & among friends, the peacefulness, the casual subjective sense of time, the food and the pervading good humor."

Travel had the added benefit of making home more dear. Back in the States, Harry was pleasantly impressed with "the cleanliness, the order, decency and efficiency of all our systems of transportation & communication." Nor could he restrain his pleasure in victory—"a confirmation," he assured Josephine, "that our great sprawling disorderly democracy is basically sound & when confronted by a real emergency can rise to the occasion with a terrific concentration of energy and resolve, and morally—under the leadership of Roosevelt—is capable of influencing other nations to pursue the path of goodwill and lawfulness." Harry had a decidedly mixed feeling about what he called "the GI mind." The virtues of "the Joe culture," he wrote to Mumford, "are goodwill, loyalty to the unit (sticking by each other), humor & courage." On the negative side he observed "dissatisfaction with regimentation," a pervasive contempt for foreign cultures, and a tendency "to gripe about everything." The average GI combines complete irreverence with a marked distrust of ideas. "All of this goes for a kind of decerebrate sincerity—behavior without principles or without passion, but in the right direction, & unpretentious & on the whole generous." Above all else, he emphasized, the GIs value *"unit affiliation & brotherhood. It is worth much more to them than individuality & freedom."*

Harry's portrait of the common soldier bore the traces of his own postwar mood, most especially in its conspicuous display of what he might have called *n Aff,* the need for affiliation. Harry's letters to Josephine are compelling evidence on this score. They mingle paternal pride with an affectionate impulse to share ideas and advice, all of this in the midst of warm evocations of home. "I was in Topsfield 3 weeks ago," he wrote in May 1945, "and the place was calling for you. The apple blossoms were out, the lilacs showing the faintest color and the little patch of dwarf daphnes (next to Sleepy Hollow, on the hill overlooking the Georgetown Rd) raging with feverish fragrance. Juno recognized me after 15 seconds of indecision, and then immediately jumped into the back of the car, & started sniffing round for you, whining when her hopes were unrealized." Jo is also regularly present to the letters. "Mummy came to Washington this week-end," Harry reported in March, for "a memorable char-cooked steak at Harvey's" and two evenings out on the town. They were together again a month later in New York for a round of theater and the opera. During two weeks of waiting for air transportation to China, Harry was with Jo at Topsfield, enjoying the brilliant spring weather. There were rumors at Station S that Harry and Marjorie Ingalls, for years the secretary at 64 Plympton and now his assistant in Washington, were having an affair. Perhaps so. There may have been other wartime liaisons. But such relationships, if they existed, were no impediment to a rapprochement with Jo. Indeed, the warming trend in Harry's marriage was geared both to the gradual cooling of his libido and to the slackening of his ties to the dyad. In some perceptible degree, the war took Harry away from Christiana and brought him home to Jo.

But only to some degree. To say that Harry drew closer to Jo during the war years is not to suggest that he had written Christiana out of his life. On the contrary, his impulse to retreat from the dyad stirred the countering impulse—an amalgam of love, loyalty, and guilt—to compensate Christiana for such suffering as his faithlessness may have caused her. He was similarly divided and uncertain in other dimensions of his life. Harry was tempted by job prospects in the public sector—as the leader of the Psychological Division of the Veterans Administration, for example, or at the head of an Assessment Institute to be funded by the Carnegie Corporation. On the other hand, there were promising changes afoot and plenty of interesting work to be done at Harvard. At the same time, Melville, who had now risen to a "canonical" stature within the literary establishment, pulled Harry away from psychology. So did Christiana, who demanded that he retire from Harvard and join her at last in writing the Proposition. In the short run, *Assessment of Men* stood squarely in the way of all other activities. The book would be several months in the works, Harry complained to Lewis Mumford. But what then? "I can not predict," he conceded. In the years just after the war Harry gave himself in fits and starts to many projects but without settling decisively into one or another groove. "I'm in transition," he wrote to Josephine, "unsure of what I am for the moment." Sharply torn between the public and the private, between

the Clinic and the Tower, he would be in transition for some time
to come.

Harry's fledgling sense of social responsibility was stimulated in
the late summer of 1945 when General Donovan asked him to go
along as a psychological consultant to the war trials in Nuremberg.
His task, Harry wrote to Josephine, would be to represent the proceedings to the German people "in such a way as to facilitate in
them a transformation of attitudes & aims." He confessed to Mumford that the prospect of "watching the reactions of Beelzebub Goer-
ing & Co." tempted him, as did the opportunity to observe "a whole
people suffering a hangover after 10 years of Satanic possession."
Still, he declined, in part for lack of German and in larger part
because he was "more intimately committed" to the work on *Assessment of Men*. He turned down several other opportunities—among
them the Directorship of the Social Science Branch of UNESCO—for
the same reason. This latter was an especially attractive opening; it
was based in Paris, and it dovetailed with Harry's most enduring
postwar cause, the control of nuclear arms. "I was not disturbed by
the atomic bomb," he admitted to Mumford. "It is the logical &
predictable result of the course we have been madly pursuing for a
hundred years. It may help to arouse people to the desperate need
for the reformation of man & of society."

In the months just after the Armistice Harry labored in a failing
effort to convene leading British, Soviet, and American social scientists for a conference on the prospects for global peace. "It is One
World or No World," he wrote to Mumford. Harry had no illusions
about the difficulty of uniting the world against the spread of nuclear arms. "The kind of behavior that is required by the present
threat," he readily acknowledged, "involves transformations of personality such as never occurred quickly in human history; one transformation being that of National Man into World Man." Still, his
optimism was buoyed up by the United World Federalists, an association of liberal-democratic internationalists founded in 1947.
Led by Norman Cousins of the *Saturday Review,* the organization
dedicated itself to the cause of world peace, principally through its
support of the United Nations. Harry wrote to the *New York Times*
in June 1948, advocating congressional initiative in the creation of

a world federation. Later that summer he circulated copies of his letter to influential friends, inviting them to join the good cause. "Individuals can do a good deal," he counseled Mumford, "but when it comes to Congressional action—as it does now—only pressure groups can be effective."

Harry developed his case more fully in a pair of articles for *Survey Graphic*. "Time for a Positive Morality," published in March 1947, argues, as its title suggests, "for a positive ideal of moral development, widely shared, well defined, and inviting." The lack of such an ideal renders the country vulnerable to the divisive scramble for success—"the concept of individualism," Harry cautions, "must be fused with that of social responsibility"—and incapable of leading the rest of the world toward peace. A sequel of sorts, "America's Mission," which appeared in the fall of 1948, elaborates on the idea that "the abolition of war is the supreme goal" for modern mankind. Toward that end, Harry describes and vigorously advocates the program of the United World Federalists. Insisting that "the only way to win World War III is to prevent it," he urges his readers to lobby their representatives for "a world federation that has sufficient power to insure the reign of justice in place of the wilfulness of force." But even as he wrote these words, Harry doubted their power to move the members of his audience. "During the war," he confided to Lewis Mumford, "perhaps for the first time wholly & consciously I felt identified with my countrymen & their destiny. More recently, however, I have become more appalled by their commitment to cynical ruthless materialism and by the general degradation of cultural values—by their lack of appreciation of the ways & beliefs & profounder accomplishments of other societies—by their bantering superficiality, irreverence, & adolescent self-assertion &c.—most particularly, by everything that stands in the way of our immediate commitment to world government."

Harry soon recognized that the great mass of Americans were not ready for new ideas. "The public are largely governed by inertia," he complained; "they run along in the old grooves until some tremendous emergency forces them to change their ways." He was also struck by the widespread "intolerance of any subordination, personal or political," especially within what he referred to as the "GI culture." Faced with such resistance, Harry turned to the universities for help. How, he asked, do people in large groups operate? What can scholars do to better illuminate the dynamics of social change? Characteristically, he looked to the positive rather than the negative side of the register for guidance. "I am pretty much fed up on negative attitudes," he snapped. Let us turn from the abnormal to the normal, from failures to successes, in shaping our future. In his "Proposals for Research in Clinical Psychology," published in 1947, Harry advocates the study of "unusually successful relationships" as the key to "the survival and further evolution of Modern Man." Science has freed humanity from the fear of an angry God but only to replace it with "the unquestionably real threat of atomic bolts from heaven and hell on earth." The options, he insists, are clear and simple—"mutually creative relations between groups and between nations, or widespread annihilation." He closes with an appeal for responsible professional action. "We are world citizens first, psychiatrists and psychologists second. The laws that govern the continuation of trustful satisfying relationships between two persons, or among members of a single group, or between two groups, should be susceptible of discovery by social scientists. This accomplishment might be the most significant contribution to civilization they could make."

Among the "unusually successful relationships" that Harry had in mind, the dyad was surely foremost. We must not dwell overlong on the irony of his assuming, if only implicitly, that his furtive, heavily financed, and troubled love affair might be the solution to the world's problems. Harry was surely not the first of his kind to confuse dyadic blisters with mortal bliss. By Denis de Rougemont's reckoning, after all, love in the West was little more than that mistake writ large. Nor, in fact, was Harry very much deceived. He knew better than to suppose that the dyad was workable as a model for most people. But two decades of intense interaction with Christiana had taught him this much—that peace and harmony between people, even between intelligent, comfortable, well-intentioned people, was not easily achieved. Love, he knew, was precious and mysterious. Its deep foundations were largely unknown; it seemed to come and go in flashes; the expense of time and money and patience and imagination in its service gave no guarantee of a favorable return.

Harry knew all of this better than he cared to admit. But it was also a fixed feature of his thinking on the subject that social arrangements had their beginnings and their ultimate foundations in dyadic units. The inadequacy of this assumption is nowhere more evident, perhaps, than in its application to the processes of change. The emphasis on successful pairs, for example, might encourage a socially retrograde privatism, individualism redoubled in singular, self-serving units of two. Nor, even more basically, is it obvious that what works for the few—especially the very privileged few—will work for the many. Still, the dyad had been at the center of Harry's personal life for more than two decades. However improbably at times, he and Christiana had grown accustomed to thinking of themselves as a model for progress. It is doubtless a measure of real changes in our world that their sense of mission as a couple now seems so hopelessly naive. But again, Harry was not simply self-deceived. The monograph on *Sentiments,* with its attention to social context and values, was a species of research that Christiana could approve and even join. Harry's postwar emphasis on the dyad went even further in this general direction and thus had the great advantage of seeming to incorporate her abiding personal concerns into his professional agenda. Harry's interest in dyads was real; but so was his fear that Christiana would present him with a nonnegotiable demand that he leave Harvard for good. Rather than give up the academy for the Tower, or face the consequences of rejecting his lover's ultimatum, Harry featured the dyad in his research. It was the alternative to having it dominate his entire life.

A compromise so freighted with ironies could bear little realistic promise. Years later, Harry rued his decision to return to Harvard as "a great mistake in my life. That was the biggest mistake, to go back." On one side, he felt guilty for having denied Christiana; on the other, he surely glimpsed what seemed cruelly clear to Robert White, that his research on the dyad had been "a dead duck." And yet when his decision was finally taken, the alternative—private life, the Proposition, and removal at least half-time to the Tower—seemed the lesser of his imperfect options. Harry in fact resigned from Harvard for a brief period, though he did so in a half-hearted way and with an eye to the strategic advantage it afforded him. The university "has barely tolerated me since 1926," he complained to Dean Paul Buck. Had it not been for Alan Gregg and the Rockefeller Foundation, "John Croesus Harvard" would have shown even less interest. It is gratifying, he continues, with bitter irony, that "three fine old friends, Allport, Kluckhohn and Parsons, misguided by personal loyalty, seem to feel that I am competent enough for a job at Harvard. But three eloquent voices in the Legislature don't make a Government. And so I am pretty well convinced that my services, helpful as they might be, are not required." But in closing he shifts his ground slightly, allowing that current discussions of change in the social sciences hold out real promise. For the time being, he is willing to be consulted on planning; "and then, as matters develop, we can see whether you really need me as a part-time lecturer in the future."

Harry's subsequent resignation gave him a chance to blow off even more steam. It was an occasion—he wrote to Josephine—to speak his mind on "what a backwater . . . Harvard had become in the field of the social sciences." It also caught the attention of Dean Buck, who at first refused to accept the decision and later made a special personal effort to bring Harry back into the fold. Indeed, it seems likely that Harry withdrew primarily in order to gain leverage in negotiations bearing on the formation of Social Relations, a new interdisciplinary program taking shape just as the war ended. He notes with pleasure in his letter to Josephine that taking a hard line has forced "a few changes which will allow for some development." Gordon Allport wrote to him on the same day that Dean Buck had finally seen his way to funding the new program. "It occurred on the heels of your visit!" he crowed. "You *are* a statesman!" In fact, the Department of Social Relations was the final flowering of an interdisciplinary impulse that first surfaced at meetings of the "Levellers" during the 1930s. Clyde Kluckhohn wrote enthusiastically in 1940 of "collaboration in research and teaching between you and Parsons and myself." Three years later Harry joined Allport, Kluckhohn, Mowrer, and Parsons in proposing to the administration the establishment of a new department combining anthropology, psychology, and sociology. Frustrated by narrow disciplinary constraints, and by assorted personal conflicts, the members of this brilliant coterie finally had their way after the war. On January 29, 1946, a committee of six, including Allport and Boring among its members, and with Parsons as Chair, won Faculty approval for the establishment of the Department of Social Relations.

"Soc Rel," as it soon came to be called, has been compared with Yale's Institute of Human Relations and the graduate program in Social Psychology at Michigan as a successful experiment in interdisciplinary education within the social sciences. The Harvard program featured an undergraduate degree, along with doctorates in Clinical Psychology, Social Psychology, Social Anthropology, and Sociology, and a separate research facility, the Laboratory of Social Relations, under the direction of Samuel Stouffer. Parsons was Chair. Harry had good reasons for wanting to join company with this ambitious group. The interdisciplinary study of social issues was at the top of his professional agenda. It was a relief to be free at last of Boring and the other experimental psychologists, who had moved to the basement of Memorial Hall. He looked forward to lively intellectual exchanges with colleagues whose work he could respect. He was stimulated by the challenge of helping to develop a new, innovative program of study. And his own work was beginning to make a real mark. *Explorations,* described in 1945 by Richard Elliott as an "epoch-making book," was reissued in response to wide demand. The TAT was on its way to becoming a household word. And the OSS work showed real promise. President Conant requested a tour of Station S in September 1945 and came away very much impressed with what he saw. Accounts of the assessment program were also frequently featured in newspapers and magazines. *Time* ran an article in January 1946. A much longer piece— in which Harry appears as "a unique combination of thinking machine, dreamer, two-fisted drinker, and scientist, whose inner driving force suggests a band of Scotch Presbyterians rising from their knees to do the will of God"—turned up in *Fortune* just two months later. Harry quietly relished the attention. It was no small pleasure to be recognized as a bold, brilliant innovator at the apex of the professional establishment.

Harry was reappointed half-time Lecturer on Clinical Psychology in April 1946. A professorship was offered, but he declined, insisting that the lower rank would free him from unwanted administrative responsibilities. There may have been a trace of bitterness in his apparent modesty, an ironic refusal to make peace with "John Croesus Harvard." He advanced to a full professorship in 1948, when he returned from the two-year leave of absence that had commenced with his reappointment. Dean Buck was happy enough to grant the time off, agreeing with Parsons that Harry had "a very legitimate desire" to get on with several writing projects. Still, the demand for a long leave in advance of his return to teaching was yet another sign that Harry's resentment had not yet cooled. There were others. He made it clear at the outset that he wanted no part of service on committees; he held himself back at department meetings, leaving the floor, the initiative, and all responsibility for leadership to others. He would be just as marginal, he seemed to be saying, as Harvard had made him feel. The Clinic was an especially sore point. During the period of Harry's resignation, Robert White was offered a permanent lectureship in Social Relations and asked to head the new program in Clinical Psychology, to be housed at 64 Plympton. Assuming that Harry had been consulted, and that his resignation left the door open, White took the job. Later on, when he decided to return to Harvard, Harry gave signs that he resented the loss of his old building and that he had not favored White's appointment. Relations between the two men remained outwardly cordial—White actually invited his old mentor to join him at the Clinic—but were never again warm.

Things were little better with the others in Soc Rel. Chairman Parsons seemed begrudging of support, possibly—Harry speculated—because he was secretly envious of his colleague's conspicuous personal advantages. Allport had been a faithful supporter over the years but kept a certain social and intellectual distance. He was a man of caution, control, and conventional decency. Harry must have seemed a little irregular and intemperate to him—even a little dangerous. From the other side, there was enough of the fussy "old woman" about Allport to discourage a man of Harry's temperament. Their contrasting styles were on public display at consecutive meetings of the Social Relations proseminar, held at the end of 1946. The now celebrated "confrontation" was organized by Talcott Parsons, who invited Harry to join Allport and Kurt Lewin in the classroom for a frank exchange of ideas. The first two stole the show, Allport by espousing a psychology of conscious, voluntary, rational endeavor, Harry by taking the part of the id, the child, the involuntary, the unconscious. "If love were an ego process," he observed, "it would be planned and rational. But it is not." According to Brewster Smith, who remembers the meetings as "a joust of Olympians," Harry was "playfully provocative" in his "id-like" assault, while Allport, the advocate of restraint, turned "progressively deeper shades of red in response." Little wonder that their relationship, though friendly enough, was never intimate.

Clyde Kluckhohn was Harry's only close friend in the new department. Drawn together over the years by shared interests, among them a strong literary bent and designs on interdisciplinary research and teaching, they drew closer still with the formation of Social Relations. Kluckhohn had his own carefully guarded secret life, which made him a sympathetic and trusted confidant. He was also perfectly open in his attachment to Harry. "Your friendship is the only fulfillment in personal relations that has come to me from being at Harvard," he wrote in 1944, "and I am grateful both to God and to you." Kluckhohn confessed to feeling "no barriers" with his friend. "I think part of what binds me to you is the richness and depth of your personality—in contrast to the flatness I feel in too many of our countrymen. Most of all, though, it is because you are the great humanist—which is what I want to be."

Kluckhohn followed Harry in defining humanistic social science as the systematic study of "the whole man." This elusive figure was their principal subject in the co-edited *Personality in Nature, Society, and Culture,* a collection of readings by a dazzling assortment of leaders in the field (Mead, Parsons, Fromm, Allport, and Benedict among them). The volume, which was completed in the late spring of 1947, opens with paired introductory chapters—the first, "A

Conception of Personality," largely Harry's, the second, "The Formation of Personality," largely Kluckhohn's. Much in Harry's section—the emphases on process, childhood, the unconscious, regnancies, personality as life history—is familiar. But much else, thanks in part to Kluckhohn's influence, is new. There is greater attention than in *Explorations* to the dynamic integration of the organism and its environment. The individual and society, personality and culture, are not polarized but rather recognized as constituting a single "field." The concept of need makes an appearance but in a context of "tension reduction" geared to learned, or "culturally determined," goals. "Positive need-tensions," a leading characteristic of healthy organisms, also give rise to expressive behavior enjoyed for its own sake, and not merely as the means to some larger end. More generally, however, the individual is inclined by nature to strive; from early childhood on we are engaged in active negotiations with the ideals and prohibitions of our social environment. "Human personality," Harry sums up, "is a compromise formation, a dynamic resultant of the conflict between the individual's own impulses (as given by biology and modified by culture and by specific situations) and the demands, interests, and impulses of other individuals." These words were themselves a kind of compromise, balancing Harry's earlier emphasis on individual autonomy with his more recent interest in context. Kluckhohn, in a formulation that his co-editor never wearied of repeating, said it best for both of them. "Every man," his sections begins, "is in certain respects like all other men," in certain respects "like some other men," and in certain respects "like no other man."

There was less of compromise in Harry's decision to take his leave of absence in New York. Work on *Assessment of Men,* which was to drag on for nearly two years, kept him in Washington for several months after the war's end. But once he was released from the army early in 1946, it was to be expected that he would return to Boston and Cambridge, where his life and work had their center. Instead, he joined Jo and Josephine in a Manhattan apartment at 72nd Street and Park Avenue. "Don't bring up those awful things," he once lashed out, when asked to explain the move. He had his reasons, of course. Josephine was at school in New York; Jo could have her fill of theatre; and he would be at a comfortable remove from the demands and distractions of Harvard. Still, the subject provoked him because it was a reminder of his refusal in 1946 to return to the dyad on a full-time basis. That decision came freighted with guilt that never left him. He had knowingly betrayed Christiana, who was desperately lonely after more than two years of separation. The sympathectomy had been permanently enfeebling; menopause was upon her; she felt old, tired, and emotionally unsure of herself. Her drinking had increased. And yet Harry stayed away.

Though his remorse spoke volumes, Harry was never willing to elaborate on what prompted his defection. The subject was too painful for that kind of scrutiny. We may surmise that he was influenced by the dramatic changes in Christiana's physical and psychological condition. His own advancing years, and restored intimacy with Jo, were also no doubt at play. Characteristically, however, his motives were mingled. Even as he contemplated the retreat to New York, Harry confided to Josephine that he regarded "creative activity—that is, imagination, knowledge & will—applied to the living out of an intense human relationship" as the "summit of experience." He had no wish to sever ties completely. During two years of residence in Manhattan, he made regular trips to Cambridge and to the Tower. The dyad was still vitally important to him, though he held it now at arm's length, except during intervals scheduled in advance. Christiana seems to have acquiesced in this arrangement. There is little in the record of complaint. Still, Harry's remorse was real—as real as the grave lapse in faith which first gave it rise.

The dyadic letters of the period, written during more than four years of separation, do not entirely dispel the mystery of Harry's behavior. In this they reinforce the impression that he was imperfectly aware of the forces that moved him. But the letters are nonetheless a source of light. It is of some interest, for example, that Harry and Christiana took pains to preserve the correspondence as an integral unit and to enhance its overall "look" and coherence. The collection is preserved on uniform binder paper, and there is evidence of minor editorializing. Unposted drafts are included. A few items, originally composed as diary entries rather than actual letters, appear as supplements to the unfolding story. Harry held on to the correspondence until the end of his life, when he turned it over—reliving his grief as he did so—to his good friend Edwin Shneidman. Clearly enough, Harry and Christiana wanted their wartime story preserved and told in full, even though the prospect of the telling must have caused them to wince.

The letters commence in late October 1944 but make constant reference to a crisis that occurred earlier in the year. Christiana's recovery from the sympathectomy had been predictably slow. I am "staggering from chair to chair," she wrote to Mumford, "& spending most of my time on the sofa." According to Ina May Greer, who became a close friend during the war years, Harry's visits and letters did little to mitigate Christiana's loneliness and deepening self-absorption. She turned during the long, solitary days and weeks to a thorough review of the dyad. It was a record, she found, of deferral and distraction, of recognitions without results, of a Proposition that had gone unspoken, of Wona's work forever taking back seat to Mansol's. "For twenty years their life had been provisional," she wrote. Christiana confronted Harry with her frustration during a visit to Washington at the end of May. He bowed to the weight of her complaints, confessed that his pride had been responsible for their failures, and promised yet again to prepare himself for major changes once the war was over. "This day is also our D-day," Wona wrote on June 6. "Our time of preparation is over. This [is] the very crisis of our life. The period of *Actual* Moral Transformation has begun. From now on I will be your conscience. I shall decide what is right and what is wrong." Harry went along willingly enough. "It is possible," he wrote to Mumford, "that when the war is over [Christiana] will want me to give the larger share, if not all, [of] my energies to collecting material as background for the things which she feels that she must say before we die." The initiative was hers; but could she hold on to it?

Harry knew very well that she could not. They had been over this ground many times before, and always with the same result. "Lead me, my Superior," Mansol prayed. "I cannot find my way without your word. I put my whole life in your hands. . . . Teach me what it means to lead the spiritual life. Teach me to view things in a large frame as you do." But he knew at some level, just as she

297

did, that he was asking for more than she could possibly deliver. Mansol was the Logos in their relationship; it was—and always had been—his role to put words to Wona's feelings, to give rational shape to her vivid but elusive visions. In fact, Wona demanded power only that she might be mastered on her own terms. She seized the initiative as leverage on Mansol's attention and commitment but relinquished what she could not wield once her equanimity had been restored. It was a kind of dance, the old swing back and forth between extremes, in which there was much motion and scant progress. But repetition did little to ease the pain. Indeed, it hurt more as they got older and as youth and passion, Wona's surest allies in love, slipped away.

The dozens of letters written during the first year of the correspondence—between October 1944 and October 1945—may be said to trace two large movements or developments. In one, the more familiar, Christiana collapses in the face of Harry's superior will. At first she claimed him as her "Instrument." But within a few weeks he was again her "Master," demanding "unquestioning & unquestioned power." Dropping all pretense to spiritual and intellectual preeminence, Wona accepted that she was helpless without Mansol's "beautiful conceptual clarity" to guide her. To his demand for guidance through the trances, she confessed in frustration that she could not decide on her own "what the hell they are about." By the following January her subjugation was complete. "There is no life in me unless I am on my knees to you," she confessed. "Mansol, Master, you know everything."

But Harry would give no quarter. Refusing to accept Christiana's surrender, he demanded the impossible, that she produce the energy and clarity she had promised. She was too passive, he complained; she had no "zest," no interest in ideas, in writing, in the form of the Proposition. "Unless Wona can change," he threatened in May 1945, "the Synergy is dearth." Here was a chilling variation on the usual pattern. Rather than seize the initiative, as he had in the past, Harry hurled it back to Christiana, insisting that her failure to take hold would spell the end of the dyad. As he must have seen, she could neither meet his demand nor accept the price of failure. Instead, she made concessions, hoping thereby to bring him around to his old self. She granted that she had been making too much of her visions. "The work of the trances is done," she wrote. It was time to turn from her own interior life to Harry's, to nourish the Logos as it formed itself in him. "Unless I can do this," she went on, "I will be holding Mansol to an unliving bondage."

At the beginning of June, on the eve of his departure for China, Harry capitalized on his advantage. "An hour before leaving U.S.A.," he declared, "I wrote to Conant, the lab boy, and presented my resignation from the Faculty. As a *substitute* I expect a good rich centre to enter when I return. It is up to you to provide it." Again, as if to punish, he was asking the impossible. Christiana was hardly deceived. "Wona, Wona, your season of creation is done," the voices at the Tower seemed to tell her. On June 6, one year exactly after D-day, she confessed to feeling "sad and submerged ever since Mansol left—and so frightened by his saying 'That unless you change the Synergy is dearth' that I have been trying very desperately to be as he conceived it should be. But when I try to do this . . . I have the sense of being driven and at the same time lost and unhappy—just sheer blind effort without inner peace or joy." Thus cornered and distraught, she took the step toward which Harry, in some shadowy region of his will, seems to have been pushing her. "My passionate desire is to nourish and make live our spirit which is now in Mansol," she wrote. "I will give all my passion and all my love to that in him *wherever* it goes. For I find that it is that in him which I love more than any Proposition plan that we have ever conceived of. If the wayward creative spirit in him turns to the writing of my books I will be glad. If not—he is my God and I will follow him—will follow his spirit wherever it may lead." So long as she was included in his plans, Christiana was content now to tag along. Her capitulation was complete.

And yet Harry was not ready to relent. The initiative was now entirely his, but something in Christiana still eluded him. The second major movement in the year's correspondence records the emergence in Wona of a sociable, gregarious, even fun-loving strain. For years she had been reclusive. She was close to her sisters but otherwise had fews friends outside the orbit of the Clinic and the dyad. Harry was her conduit to the larger world. Thus his absence—in combination with her very limited physical mobility—reduced Christiana's already straitened social life to a virtual nullity. At first she was content enough in her isolation. "No medieval monk has been more apart from the world than I," she wrote to Lewis Mumford in September of 1944. Two months later, however, she began to doubt her ability to "endure such loneliness and isolation." It was natural enough under the circumstances that she should begin to reach out to other people. She wrote on a regular basis to Mumford, to find that they had much in common. Her friendship with Ina May Greer, Harry's faithful research assistant, grew closer. She also socialized with the Whiteheads and with Mr. and Mrs. Ananda K. Coomaraswamy, who encouraged her new interest in Eastern art and religion. At the Tower Christiana enjoyed the company of Kenneth Diven, a Ph.D. from the Clinic who was regularly around after Harry's departure for Washington. A skillful craftsman, Diven accepted modest wages and shelter in return for his work, most notably elaborate symbolic carvings in doors, panels, shutters, and furniture. He and Christiana enjoyed working together during the day and drinking together in the evening.

Company, Christiana discovered, was good for her spirit—as good, in fact, as solitary work on the Proposition was bad for it. She had a wonderful time, and "many good belly laughs," at her son Councilman's wedding in June 1945, just weeks after giving up altogether on her futile dyadic labors. It helped, she found, to share her work with friends. Mumford was fascinated with what she revealed to him of her life with Harry. Diven was also brought in on the secret. Christiana asked Mrs. Coomaraswamy to comment on the evolving mythology and symbolism of the dyad, as it took shape in the artifacts and decorations accumulating at the Tower. She was even more candid with Ina May Greer, who readily agreed to lend a hand in the interpretation of the visions. Harry was not pleased. He cautioned Christiana against opening their "Irrational life" to Evelyn Whitehead; intimacy of that kind, he noted, had already complicated their relationship with Kenneth Diven. There were no assurances, he conceded uneasily, that the story of the dyad would have a uniformly "*good effect* on the *right people*." Hence the necessity to guard their secret, even from well-meaning friends like Ina May

300

Greer. "I did not tell you to show her the trances," he snapped. "I do not want her close to our life or to know about us."

Harry's insistence that she forge ahead in solitude with her work ran directly against the grain of Christiana's strongest desires. "I need Hansi [Greer]," she insisted, "just as I need Mrs Coomaraswamy—just as I need Evelyn [Whitehead] who will listen in love and understanding to my first halting steps. Whatever I do now with any living soul comes out of my own need for help, for nourishment, for understanding." She drew back from the Proposition during the spring of 1945, to find that her health and spirit, thanks to "the devotion of friends," lifted with the season. Harry was pleased for her, of course. But during a week's leave at the beginning of May he complained of her passivity and indolence in the face of the Proposition. Where was her trust in him? What had become of her promise to submit? She had failed utterly in her obligation to elaborate their story with "illustrations, experiences— *New Ideas.*" She was, he declared, "a *traitor to the cause.*" Christiana did not deny the charges; nor, at least in the short run, did she buckle under the weight of her lover's reproach. "Life is indeed strange & wonderful," she wrote at the end of the summer. "My mechanic writes that I have changed his life—Vivi writes that I am her ideal—Hansi writes that I am the only person who has ever had a deeply healing quality for her. Clyde comes for lunch today & says that without me now . . . he would never dare his own soul. . . . I see Altie [Whitehead] this morning and he brings me his best." Cultivation of the world outside had repaid Christiana with a harvest of comfort and love. Her happiness, she began to recognize, was tied in unanticipated ways to Harry's absence and to suspension of work on the Proposition. "I feel now today that my effectiveness is the effectiveness of *Eros working well,*" she wrote in October of 1945. "And just at that point where it becomes perfected in life— it isn't where we are. Today I felt close to you because I knew that you would not have loved this. *You* would have said—'Give this up'—just as I said to you 'Give up the Clinic' at exactly that point when we really began to function well. So I learn of the sacrifice that I have asked of you—and that you now ask of me. Help me, now, my Master."

Here, perhaps for the first time ever, Christiana gave signs of disenchantment with the dyad. She was happy in spite of Harry's absence—even, she suggests boldly, because of it. Work on the Proposition, once her passion, she had now come to regard as a "sacrifice" to his demands. "I am your slave," she went on to add, but Harry was not convinced. In her clarity and independence of judgment, in her impulse to negotiate, even perhaps in her happiness itself, he caught sight of rebellion. His response was a relentless reassertion—often subtle, never fully conscious—of his own will. He was concerned, he wrote, that her drinking and general lassitude were obstacles to his sexual pleasure. "I have the strange feeling, Master," she wrote back, not without an edge of resentment, "that for the last year all of your interpretations of me . . . have been just *slightly off*." Harry in turn expressed his fear that working on the Proposition together might now be impossible. "And this all seems to come down to some change in you," he added, "rather than any change in me. . . . I feel that it is a diminution of zest, interest, and faith in you towards me, the synergy, the proposition & life in general." Was it the operation? menopause? or had she lost touch with their dyadic religion of love? "If you have no faith," he went on, "no religiousness, then the Synergy is the greatest Love Affair of all time but it is *not* the salvation of man." In place of their religious vocation, he groaned, she seemed to want nothing more than "closeness"—"not for the Synergy, not for the Proposition, but just Closeness."

He was right; and he would have none of it. When he protested that her backsliding would provoke him to reconsider his resignation, Christiana gave ground. "I cannot live without the Proposition," she wrote, but then confessed that she was in a very bad way. "I am physically breaking under the stress of it all," she complained at the end of November. "Oh Mansol—I am so broken down into fragments now—that I can only write you a little each day," she reported just after Christmas. A few days later she cried out for a truce. "I am profoundly—interiorly used up," she pleaded, "exhausted—drained dry." Still, Harry persisted. Christiana was the victim, he suggested, of an unconscious death wish. She had sacrificed their dream to a "passive succorant narcism that wants to *re-*

ceive All, All, All." In time his anger turned to fascination with the analysis of her putative condition. "All this is *necessary* & so I push you deeper & deeper down," he explained. "O my sweet, I'm not being sadistic." Reminiscent in his cruel detachment of Hawthorne's Rappaccini, Harry had his way completely with the now defenseless Christiana. She was to blame for the breakdown in their work on the Proposition—which Harry was in truth quite content to abandon—and that in turn justified his going back to Harvard. Thanks to the leave of absence, he would have time for *Assessment of Men* and Melville before returning to academic psychology.

It was a triumph of will but at great price, both to Christiana, who would never completely recover, and to Harry, who would never forgive himself. Again, a satisfactory explanation for his behavior is not easily constructed. There was an unsettling extremity in his response, a cruelty disproportionate both to the provocation, which was slight, and to his final objectives, which might have been gained with much less cost in suffering. It is probably fair to speculate that Harry's reserves of love and pity gave way before a multitude of frustrations, real and imagined, that found focus in Christiana's resistance to his will. His behavior was extreme because it was vastly overdetermined. On one side, and most obviously perhaps, he bridled at the renewed pressure to devote himself to the Proposition and thus angled for excuses to return to Harvard, to psychology, and to Melville. On another side, he resented the libidinal lag that came with aging but contrived to blame it on Christiana's understandably diminished "zest." It was chastening to discover that in the waning of passion the dyad lost much of its allure. It was expensive and durable and unique; but it was a love affair, after all, and no revolution. Thus, Harry's extreme resistance to intrusions on his secret life may be taken to express the fear that others might judge it a tragic mistake—or, worse, a specimen of folly. His apprehensions on this score took confirmation in Mrs. Coomaraswamy's observation—relayed to him by Christiana—that the evolving dyadic mythology, with its eclectic assortment of rituals and symbols, was "childish, something to be outgrown." He was equally upset at Kenneth Diven's penetration into the significance, often sexual, of the carvings he was asked to complete at the

Tower. But who, then, had lost faith in synergy? Was it Christiana, as Harry claimed, or had he glimpsed in her a reflection of his own uncertainties?

Though he was much too proud to say so, Harry also feared that he was losing control of Christiana, that her devotion was wearing thin in his absence. In time he became suspicious of her friendship with Diven and took a part in bringing it to an end. He tried to hold her to the Proposition not for love of that project but because the work served to preserve her isolation. As her contacts on the outside grew more numerous, he saw, her independence of judgment did too. The prime offender in this regard was Lewis Mumford, whose friendship with Christiana deepened dramatically while Harry was away. They exchanged warm letters during her convalescence. Mumford fueled Christiana's determination that Harry should resign from Harvard. She responded gratefully—"I have always told Harry that if I hadn't fallen in love with him I surely would have with you." Christiana insisted that Mumford be included in the planning for her work on the Proposition. Harry complied but with evident resentment at the curb on his autonomy. Early in 1945 he asked her to restrain the impulse to confide in their mutual friend. But Christiana persisted. "I feel very close to you now," she wrote to Mumford in April, complaining of her "desperation of loneliness." That summer she outlined the entire history of the dyad for him. Harry would not permit himself an open display of hurt feelings. But his reiterated criticism of *Green Memories*—Mumford's biography of his son, Geddes, who died in combat—though perfectly reasonable in itself, touched too roughly on a sensitive subject. A subsequent reference to Mumford's "autocratic, Mount Sinai" tone in developing ideas, again though apt enough, was hardly calculated to please. Real intimacy between the old friends was now a thing of the past.

His own frustrated plans, the depredations of time, diminished desire, a general loss of control, and the perception of multiple betrayals—these were some of the elements that fused in Harry's cruelty toward Christiana during and just after the war. As her resistance became compliance, and as Harry, released now from concern about the Proposition, became more fascinated with his new projects, Christiana found that less of the dyad was not necessarily a bad thing. She was delighted that Harry had put off returning to Harvard until 1948 and took the maximum pleasure from his periodic visits to Cambridge and the Tower. As the Proposition fell into the background, life became steadier and warmer for both of them. "I know absolutely and finally now that our labors of Synergy are done," Christiana wrote in November 1946, and "that we don't need any new concepts or any further revelation." Harry came back occasionally to her lassitude, or to thoughts of renewed deep diving, but for the most part wrestling with the recalcitrant *Assessment* manuscript kept him busy and distracted. Christiana's self-confidence continued to revive. "I feel for the first time in my life an absolute responsibility for myself," she wrote. "I am waiting upon no revelation, no trance." Her physical health was equally responsive to the reduced pressure. "Philosophies can well rest now for a little time, my darling," she suggested playfully. "Let us, as Rilke said—'collaborate with the sap.'" Their time together at the Tower during the summer of 1947 was as good as it had ever been. They were at ease with each other; love-making was good again. "Wore the white dress with fringes," Christiana recorded of her fiftieth birthday party. "Mansol said I looked beautiful." There had been enough of analysis and soul-searching for a while. "We have to find the way to be light-hearted together," she counseled, and to "find renewal in ease and joy. There is no renewal to be found in sweat anymore. Indeed, I am willing to affirm that anything we cook up together now which demands great effort from either of us—may well end in sickness."

▼

chapter eleven

I Will Gospelize the World Anew

Those who knew Harry in the last decades of his life were familiar with the litany of self-criticism that invariably rose to his lips at the mere mention of his writing. The list of unfinished books—on Melville, aspects of psychology, the dyad—grew longer as he grew older. He complained that he had spread himself too thin; that he lacked the writer's gift; that his education was somehow deficient; that his mental powers were in premature decline. Yet by any reasonable standard Harry was extremely productive in the years between his return to Harvard in 1948 and his retirement in 1962. During that period he published the co-authored *Assessment of Men* and *Personality in Nature, Society, and Culture,* a major edition (featuring a 90-page Introduction and 75 pages of scholarly notes) of Melville's *Pierre,* a justly celebrated issue of *Daedalus* on "Myth and Mythmaking" (later produced in expanded form as a book), more than two dozen articles—several of them very long and substantial—on a variety of subjects, and numerous introductions, forewords, reviews, and sketches. For a man with a demanding personal life, an active commitment to teaching, and a heavy travel schedule, Harry in fact flourished as a writer during his years of ostensible decline.

This is not to deny that he left many tasks unfinished. The source of more ideas, more plans, and more actual projects than he could possibly complete, Harry was chronically overextended. He was also at points frustrated by untoward circumstances and various breakdowns in cooperation with associates. Composition was at times an effort (such was the price of his reputation as one of the premier prose stylists among American psychologists). True, because articles sometimes had to stand in place of unfinished books, there is a certain breathless haste to much of his writing. But the loss in girth has its compensation in pace and compression. Harry is rarely superficial or obscure, seldom repetitious, and never dull. The ever-increasing latitude of his conception of personality was itself a daunting obstacle. "I have come to think," he declared in 1959, "that no theoretical system constructed on the psychological level will be adequate until it has been embraced by and intermeshed with a cultural-sociological system."

Although Harry spread his attention over a wide field of interests, he was in his writing not so much diffuse or dispersed as divided. His commitment to social issues, for example, was enduring. "I have come to believe," he assured Edward R. Murrow in 1953, "that nothing is of signal significance today save those thoughts and actions which, in some measure, purpose to contribute to the diagnosis and alleviation of the global neurosis which so affects us." "World Concord as a Goal for the Social Sciences," the title of his paper for the 1951 International Congress of Psychology in Stockholm, amply represents his general objectives. As elements in this larger concern, he gave continuing attention to world government, American ideals and moral values, the decline of religion, and the need for a new, post-Romantic mythology of human nature. In all such endeavors he emphasized interactions between people in groups, especially in pairs, and the necessity for "the constant vision of the Ideal. A negative orientation," he insisted, following Whitehead, "is inadequate. A man cannot discover truth merely by attacking error, or achieve fellowship by condemning hate or security by repressing fear."

But in direct tension with such social concerns was Harry's unflagging fascination with Herman Melville, the possessor of "an insurgent Id in mortal conflict with an oppressive cultural Superego." In the creator of *Moby-Dick* he found continued focus for his rebellion against vulgar America, materialistic America, and the eros-crippling influence of Calvin's God on one side, and of mother on the other. "As I see it," he wrote to Mumford, "Americans of all ages constitute one great Youth Culture of mediocrity, with a profound aversion to moral excellence & authority." He labored consciously to cultivate a feeling of greater solidarity with his countrymen. "It will take a couple of years to make the transition," he explained to Josephine in 1946, "& I must rid myself of Melville in the process." But the novelist, and the defiant individualism he stood for, would not go away.

The competing strands in Harry's thought form a dialectical unity accessible not so much in individual essays as in patterns of tension and opposition emergent from the larger aggregate of his writing. Thus the interplay of separate and apparently unrelated ideas may be said to constitute the meaning of much of his work. "The final goal of personality," he lectured Lewis Mumford in 1947, "is to create a philosophy of life and *become* the incarnation of it." Harry's personal philosophy of life was rooted in the dyad, and in the wide range of ideas about sexuality, the unconscious, creativity, religion, myth, and the social and world order that attached to it. General systems theory—that "perilous practice of discovering analogies among events at different levels" which he first encountered in Henderson, Pareto, and Whitehead—became increasingly useful to Harry as his areas of interest multiplied. The various dimensions of his thought were loosely unified as parallel expressions of a modified evolutionary scheme featuring prominent physiological processes—the alternating systole and diastole of the heart, for example, or the recurrent anabolism and catabolism of the metabolic system—as metaphors for the creativity to be found at all levels (biological, psychological, intellectual, social) of human experience. "Zest" was a talismanic term with him. It described the bright spark of energy and optimism overflowing in people properly attuned to the abundance and boundless creativity of their world. It expressed itself in sexual and social and artistic endeavors; but above all else it was manifest in the exuberant analogical play of mind across horizonless interior spaces. Zest was the abundant life in all things but most emphatically in consciousness itself, expanding outward like the Logos, the informing Word of God, to give shape and light to creation.

Harry was the first to concede the slipperiness of arguments by analogy. It may be that reservations on this score contributed to his difficulty in bringing projects to completion. Still, the constant multiplication of interests fueled the exhilarating play of mind and at the same time deferred indefinitely the narrower integration of ideas, and the reckoning with enabling metaphysical premises, that would have ruined the game, either by wrapping it up or, more likely perhaps, by exposing the arbitrariness of its leading assumptions. It was zest that Harry craved, not closure. Quite ironically, however, his brilliantly expansive intellectual enterprise, with its prevailing emphasis on interpenetrating systems, "whole" persons, and, above all else, on procreative dyadic relations, was in fact a critically and quite consciously diminished thing. Nowhere in the hundreds of pages he produced during this period does Harry refer directly to Christiana; nowhere does he acknowledge that virtually all of his leading ideas have their *fons et origo* in her visions, in the Proposition, the Tower, and in a quarter century and more of bold, purposive, passionate interaction. The omission is of course painfully telling, for it makes palpable the gap at the very center of Harry's metaphysics of creativity. He might complain that the world was not ready for the dyad; but if this was so, then why persist in the advocacy of ideas premised directly on his own dyadic experiences? It is the unavoidable irony of Harry's omissions that they betray his own uncertainty about the solutions he advanced so vigorously for others. He professed too little and too much all at the same time. He shrank from the barricades of his own revolution; he was first apostate in his own church.

This is of course to exaggerate. Harry was intensely loyal to Christiana and to the dyad. He believed, quite properly, that their vision of wholeness, process, equality, sexual liberation, global solidarity, peace, and exuberant human creativity held out something new and valuable to future generations. Nor was he deceived in the belief that people might mistake the human imperfection of his love—its catabolic phase, he might have said—for its whole truth. And of course he was constrained by concern for Jo's feelings, though Harry and Christiana both knew—what time would make painfully clear—that his scruples on this score served to rationalize the deeper misgivings that stood in his way. Harry's loyalty to the dyad was real; but so were his doubts. In Christiana's eyes most especially, Jo was not so much an obstacle to candor as a cover for Harry's resistance to "going public" with their religion of love. In refusing to step forward as the incarnation of his own philosophy, Harry denied a part of himself. He also denied Christiana. The contradiction was damaging to both of them; and it was always there, as painfully evident to him, and to her, as it was invisible to his admiring audience.

Time and again in his writing, Harry approaches the spiritual center of his life's work only to shrink from the living truth before him. In a speech at the Signet Society in December 1955 he offered himself as the mouthpiece for a chorus of prominent commentators (Freud, Tillich, Melville, and others) on the human condition. Toward the end of the talk, the voice of a "Mysterious Woman" is heard, complaining that "men—men without women—have made a mess of things for long enough." She goes on to protest the subordinate place of her sex in Christian thought and to offer the dyadic philosophy in its place. "Come to me," she beckons, "and I shall make you whole—not perfect, but complete. And we can evolve together and create a saving myth for this despairing world." Here, to be sure, was Christiana's voice. But it was a "mysterious" voice, nameless, disembodied, and, most crucially, without an obvious connection to the speaker. Christiana is a similarly shadowy presence in "Preparations for the Scaffold of a Comprehensive System," where Harry draws an analogy between the metabolic system—his "basic model" for creative activity—and "the emotional, verbal, and actional participations of two lovers." Again, the allusion, though vital to the larger implication of the argument, is oblique and immediately abandoned. There is a virtually identical gesture in "The Possible Nature of a 'Mythology' to Come," a paper published in 1960. For the most part a rather arid exercise in defining terms, the essay postpones until its final paragraph any mention of the topic to which its title refers. We are a godless generation, Harry here observes; the old mythologies are either dead or obsolete. In their place, he asks, "what would our instincts say to a procession of myths in which there were never less than two chief

characters—two leaders meeting amicably at the summit, two nations settling their disputes, rituals cementing international reciprocities and concord; and, on the personal level also, never less
than two chief characters, man and woman, in a creative, mutually
self-developing relationship?" And so he ends, quite abruptly and
obscurely after all, at the outer door to the temple of his new religion.

What is truth? Harry asked again and again, and just as regularly
drew back from a direct answer. Glancing references to Christiana
were not new with him in the 1950s. In "What Should Psychologists Do About Psychoanalysis?" an essay published in 1940, she
appears as a nameless but influential "woman" in his life. Just so,
in "The Case of Murr," which appeared in 1967, she figures mo-
mentarily as a Jungian visionary on the staff at the Harvard Psychological Clinic. But the references, always brief, always anonymous,
and always framed by his advocacy of the dyadic philosophy, multiplied dramatically in the years after the war. They were the issue
of competing compulsions to reveal and to conceal the same thing.
Harry protested too much about his failures as a writer. He had not
lapsed into premature senility; his associates had not abandoned
him; he wrote more and better than he was willing to admit. But
his protests were real, nonetheless; and they had their hidden source
in his mute disenchantment with Christiana and the dyad. It was
the Proposition, the vital soul and center of his thought, that he
could not complete. Here was the secret failure from which much
of his frustration derived. Christiana labored valiantly, but with
considerable frustration, over the manuscript—now entitled, without ironic intent, *What Joy!* And Harry found other things to do.
But the want of zest at the center spread into the larger circle of his
creative life. Nothing—his own work, Christiana's, his staff's—
could dispel the mood of failure that gathered, like a dark cloud out
of nowhere, over his endeavors. He was not deceived; nor was Christiana, who knew, intimately and bitterly, that Harry's real failure,
and hers too, was part and parcel with their secret. It was as though
he had refused to be seen with her in public.

Harry had from the first long dive into *Moby-Dick* made his life
out of Melville's. The novelist served him as model and as an *apolo-*

311

gia pro vita sua. But life in the Melville mold had its drawbacks, not least among them the fact that the writer's problems with mother, wife, and anima—in which Harry was astonished to recognize his own—had their issue in denials and silence. Such is the inescapable drift of "Bartleby the Scrivener," whose title character starves himself to death, all the while refusing to reveal the woes that are killing him. "I would prefer not to" is his response to all requests that he speak out. It is equally the message of *Pierre,* where a mingling of idealism, rebellion, and infatuation inspire the hero to "gospelize" the world anew but leads instead, and quite ironically, to mute frustration and an early grave. The living sequel to *Pierre* was Melville's own decline, first into fictions designed on purpose to mislead and baffle the reader and then to the virtual end of writing for publication. Disenchantment, concealment, denial, silence. Harry acknowledged early on that getting past the middle of the novelist's life was a problem; yet he expressed no related apprehensions about his own. Melville was his Fate, yes. But he would avoid the novelist's mistakes. Things would be different for him and Christiana.

But would they? That question was always at the back of Harry's mind—and sometimes, especially at moments of decision, it was foremost in his thoughts. What he took to be Melville's pacifism gave him pause as he sought entry into the war. Later on, having had his fight, he found cause to conclude that the novelist was not a pacifist after all. Harry was just as determined to agree with his leader in other matters of conscience. In "Personality and Creative Imagination," an essay published in 1943, he allied himself with Melville in eschewing the American cultural mainstream. "There has been a breach for a hundred and fifty years," he observes, with more than a hint of pride, "dividing the artists, indeed all intellectuals, from the acclaimed and favored leaders of the nation." In the years during and after the war, however, as he grew into a leadership role himself, Harry's relationship to Melville became more ambiguous. In one mood he drew back from the self-absorbed Romantic rebel as from an irresponsible former self; in another, he looked to Melville as the supreme embodiment of creativity and zest. The tension between perspectives, which mirrored cognate tensions in his feelings about Jo and Christiana, Harvard and the Tower, psychology and the dyad, resurfaces in "In Nomine Diaboli," his acclaimed interpretation of *Moby-Dick,* published in 1951. Melville, he argues, was of Ahab's party in his opposition to that dominant species of American Calvinism, represented by the Whale, which "blocked the advance of a conscience beneficent to evolutionary love." At the same time, however, the novelist was intolerant of the heroic captain's furious nihilism—his selfish incapacity to rise above vengeful outrage and to think constructively about the world around him. Thus, even as he identified with Ahab, Melville was compelled to bring him down. But in condemning his hero, Harry asks—reflecting, it is now clear, on his own life—had Melville in fact capitulated to that oppressive "compound of puritanism and materialism, of rationalism and commercialism, of shallow, blatant optimism and technology," which had proved so crushing to his creativity and which he had set out in his masterpiece to oppose? In a sense, yes. "With his ideal drowned," the artist's spirit collapsed, and he endured "a martyrdom of forty years" until the time of his death. But in another sense, no. For while his outer self languished, his "embattled soul refused surrender and lived on, breathing back defiance, disputing 'to the last gasp' of his 'earthquake life' the sovereignty of that inscrutable authority in him."

Fair enough; though it should be added that Melville's undying resistance had its counterpart for Harry in uncertainty, denial, and the outward incapacity to be well-pleased. Where the novelist held on defiantly to a "sovereign" individuality, his admiring biographer labored fretfully between incompatible public and private identities. But Harry was perhaps not so sure of Melville as "In Nomine Diaboli" suggests. Defiance may have been a kind of wish—for both of them. A truly defiant Melville would have been fit subject for a complete biography; and a truly defiant biographer would have written it. Here, indeed, was another unfinished book—two lives, as it were, awaiting completion. "I shall return to Melville with renewed excitement," Harry wrote to Josephine in April of 1946. But almost in the same breath he launched into an examination of pride, that fatal aloofness from ordinary life which he had struggled, half-successfully, to overcome in himself. He differs in this, he trusts, from the unfortunate Melville, who was exemplary "of all the weaknesses & failures & sins of pride & the final defeat to which it leads its victims." Harry wrote to Josephine again a month later, this time to argue that "the role of the creator is no longer to destroy"—as Melville had in *Moby-Dick*—"but to build one edifice of truthful beauty after another, until the foundations for a rejuvenated culture have been established."

In spite of his evident ambivalence, however, Harry pressed forward. That same year he arranged with officials in Pittsfield, Massachusetts—the novelist's home when he wrote *Moby-Dick*—to underwrite and develop a Melville Memorial Room in the local Athenaeum. He was also actively supportive of the fledgling Melville Society, whose founding just after the war was yet another sign that the novelist had at last arrived. Most crucially of all—at least so far as his personal identification with the artist was concerned—he accepted an invitation to edit *Pierre* for a major new collection of Melville's complete works. Howard P. Vincent, who was in charge of the project, appealed to him as "the one man above all others who should prepare the introduction and the necessary notes for this edition." Harry was in a mood to comply. "Needless to say," he wrote, "all this interests me immensely." Perhaps here, in the tortured sequel to *Moby-Dick,* and the gateway in fiction to Melville's long personal decline, he might find the clarity he sought, in the artist's life, and in his own.

Harry regarded his work on *Pierre* as a first step toward the completion of the Melville biography, which he now envisioned in two volumes, the first ending at the novelist's marriage in 1847 and the second at the onset of his decline in 1852. *The Development of Herman Melville* might serve well enough as a title, he wrote to Christiana in February 1946. Since the research and the majority of the writing on this portion of the novelist's life were already well advanced in 1941, it was not unreasonable to expect that the momentum of the *Pierre* edition would carry him through to the completion of the biography before his return to Harvard. He made little at the time of his decision to draw the curtain over the long second half of Melville's life and attended instead to clearing his desk of other projects—most notably the interminable *Assessment of Men*—before turning at last to *Pierre* in the summer of 1947. Viewed initially as an editing chore to be dispatched in a few weeks, the edition was more than six months in the making. Not that Harry minded. He labored with especial care over the Introduction, which had stretched to well over 100 pages in manuscript by the time he submitted it to Howard Vincent in January 1948. "I have fitted it together as if I were making a stone pier into the Atlantic," he wrote. The metaphor was a peculiarly apt one. "Pierre," as Melville well knew, was the French for "stone." His usage involved a complex allusion, at once backward to the "rock" upon which Christ had constructed his church and forward to the shambles of Christian values in contemporary America. The Pierre of the novel is a fallen hero, whose belief system has come down in the storm of a wayward passion. Against this background of broken idols and collapsed values, Harry's intact "stone pier" is unique. It is the rock foundation of a new faith, erected on the ruins of the old, and grounded in the evolutionary creativity of the dyad. Melville lost his "Joy"—his zest—in *Pierre,* Harry observed years later. The novel expressed his feeling of total defeat and a readiness to be "annihilated." "When I first read *Moby-Dick* I was sympathetic with the brooding grief," he acknowledged; "but then I discovered it wasn't necessary." That discovery dawned gradually during the 1940s and rose into the clear light of day as Harry worked through *Pierre.* "It was the woe that drew me to Melville," he conceded; "but I didn't want to end up there."

For all of his modesty—he questions his editor's sagacity in asking "a professing psychologist to join his élite circle of scholars"— Harry knew that his Introduction to *Pierre* was something special. Howard Vincent assured him early on that there would be no complaint about its length. "It is a superb piece of work," he wrote, "the finest essay in the Melville field that I have yet read." Mumford found it "the most colossally compact and compactly colossal summation of scholarship and human understanding anyone has brought forth in our generation." Poet and Melville enthusiast Charles Olson sang its praises to Merton M. Sealts, a scholar of American literature, while Aiken described it as "marvelous, surely the best ever on the old Night-Eater." Even Jung professed to like it. The Introduction, buttressed by 75 printed pages of original (and still useful) explanatory notes, has since become a classic, both in Melville studies and in the field of psychological criticism. It argues persuasively that the novel is Melville's "spiritual autobiography," an expression of his idealistic commitment to "dedicated love" and therefore indispensable to the study of his development. *Pierre* is compelling testimony, Harry insists, to the novelist's discovery of "the Darkest Africa of the mind, the mythological unconscious," and of his yielding to its "racing tide." In this Melville allied himself with those "forces, antithetical to the contemporary cultural compound of puritanism, rationalism, and materialism, which were lurking, barbarized by repression, in the heart of Western Man, biding the moment for their eruption."

It is hardly possible to exaggerate the extent of Harry's personal immersion in what he took to be the meaning of *Pierre*. His Introduction is at once an authoritative critical argument and, as he privately acknowledged, "the most personal thing I could possibly say." "Even though the book is a fantastic version of reality," he wrote to Christiana, "it is nearer to our spiritual experience than any book which has ever been written." *Pierre* is the record of Melville's attempt to reconcile the Galilean *caritas* of the New Testament with the hypocritical distortion of Christian values prevailing in mid-century America. The novelist's moral crisis, a vertigo of ambivalence bearing him to the verge of personal annihilation, is dramatized in young Pierre's failing effort to negotiate conflicting personal commitments to his mother, his conventionally virtuous fiancée, Lucy Tartan, and the mysterious, alluring Isabel, his half-sister. The latter, a "perfect example of the dark, or tragic anima," is the object of immediate and intense fascination to Pierre. His love for her is tantamount to "a declaration in favor of the unconscious as the directing influence in his life." Though Harry does not say so, the fictional transformation that he attributes to Isabel's influence on Pierre duplicates in stunning detail the actual changes that Christiana prompted in him. Melville's young hero exchanges his Christianity for an immanent religion of love; he renounces his mother, his class, and his marriage, all for Isabel; his adolescent superficiality gives way to "the knowledge that is woe"; he turns his back on conventional values and espouses in their place views generally considered "immoral, impious, or insane." Thanks to her chance appearance, and to Pierre's prepared mind, Isabel is an inspiration to her half-brother's suppressed creativity. She leads him, as Christiana led Harry, to "the threshold of a saving evolutionary way through relationship."

But here, Harry insists, the numerous and close similarities end. For from this point forward in the narrative Pierre commits "a long series of fantastic errors of judgment and treacheries of the heart" that plunge the principals toward a tragic catastrophe reminiscent of *Hamlet.* Harry faults the book for this chilling descent into destruction. It was symptomatic of the novelist's personal decline that he could imagine no "elevating substitute for Christian ethics." "Melville's moral is that there is *no* moral, no satisfactory solution." Although his potential as a "creative religionist"—one "whose function it is to conceive of myths and validate them in action"— is on display in *Pierre,* the novel's promise is finally squandered on its hero, who is sadly "deficient in heroic substance." But Pierre's deficiency is Melville's as well. Both succumb to narcissism. Each is illuminated by a journey into the unconscious, but neither has the creative zest or maturity to rise from his deep dive, a minister to the needs of a spiritually depleted world. "Both the best and the worst features of this novel are consequences of one thing," Harry concludes—"Melville's unconditional surrender to the forces of the unconscious."

It was one thing to criticize the novelist and his hero; it was another to succeed where they had failed. The Introduction leaves little doubt that Harry was uneasy about the dyad and about the prospects for bringing the Proposition—his and Christiana's long-deferred testament of love—to fruition. His problem, like Pierre's, had its source in the unconscious and erotic dimensions of the dyad itself. To properly understand *Pierre,* he wrote to Christiana in February 1946, one must first understand Isabel. "What is her nature as anima? Why does Pierre focus all his love on her? What are her virtues & defects as target of his energies? To answer these questions one must review once more the entire Anima problem, that is to say *our problem.*" Why is it that "intense Tristan-Isolde love," he goes on to ask, "has death as its unconscious end? . . . It seems to me that we must solve these problems before we can go ahead ourselves & before we can finish Melville." Christiana was properly upset by Harry's remarks, as she was by his gathering reluctance to tell the whole truth about the dyad. Should the Proposition be "a book that adheres to the exact facts," he mused, pointedly, "or one that somewhat symbolically transforms them to a more ideal conception." "*If* you can even conceive or dare to write" such a book, Christiana replied, "*we* are through—*finished*—*Our* life lived in vain. I won't give a damn from here on what you write." She was especially incensed by the suggestion that it was her recent loss of zest that had given him pause. "Mansol—Mansol—What kind of talk is this?" she cried. Harry promptly relented.

But his impulse to scrutinize anima love as the possible symptom of some deeper pathology—both inside and outside Melville's novel—resurfaces in the Introduction to *Pierre.* The consuming intensity of dyadic love, Harry implies, especially as it is informed by the inward and downward thrust of the anima's energy, works as a drag on the outward, world-embracing energy requisite to success in the final, gospelizing phase. True, he is attentive to the hero's defects of character, and not least to his emotional desertion of Isabel. But the reproach is duly tempered by the acknowledgment that Pierre recoils instinctively from the enveloping "death wish at the bottom of [Isabel's] nature." Her lack of vigor contributes indirectly to his narcissistic surrender to the unconscious and in turn to the "complete repudiation of the world" that results. However "unwittingly," Isabel lures Pierre "away from an enviably happy life to engage in a Quixotic experiment for which both of them were almost wholly unequipped."

Let us acknowledge that intimate personal revelations are not ordinarily to be looked for in scholarly places. That being the case, it remains to ask why Harry elected to infuse his commentary on *Pierre* with oblique allusions to matters that the context barred him from discussing openly? What was the payoff on such enforced obscurity? It may be that he was attempting to sow the seeds for some future vindication of the dyad. These were the obstacles to our success, he may have been suggesting; this is how we went wrong.

318

Rather more obviously, it was a way of talking publicly, but in virtual privacy at the same time, to Christiana. She was, after all, the only audience to his covert commentary on the dyad. Why he chose to address her in this way is not entirely clear. Messages in print have a certain finality about them, to be sure; and Christiana was without the means of responding, at least in kind. Nor is the message itself a clear one. On one side, Harry appears as an exponent of the "saving evolutionary way through relationship." On the other, his commentary on Isabel is oblique evidence of uncertainty about the future of the dyad. Was he hinting at a desire to break from the small, closed circle of their love? Was it his plan to abandon the Proposition for Harvard and the larger world beyond? Or was it merely a retreat from deep diving that he had in mind? Was he now aiming to succeed—where Pierre had so miserably failed— at gospelizing the world anew? It was impossible to say.

In its covertly autobiographical trajectory, Harry's Introduction recapitulates the strategy of *Pierre.* Both novelist and critic obey a paradoxical impulse to appear very personally, and yet almost as secretly, on the public record. Melville concealed his revelations under the mantle of fiction, while Harry folded his into the fabric of ostensibly "objective" critical commentary. It was the predictable effect of this strategy that it further obscured the complex personal questions it covertly opened to scrutiny. Ambiguity was not reduced but compounded. And that, at least in Harry's case, appears to have been the point. The enforced restraint of the Introduction permitted such decorous advocacy as he could comfortably sustain, yet plausibly rationalized his unstated impulse to conceal far more of the dyad than he revealed. It was a decidedly mixed message; a modest concession but hardly a rousing show of confidence. Harry was no more ready to reveal the intimate truth of the dyad than he was to divorce Jo and marry Christiana. The Proposition was evidently in doubt; but so was almost everything that mattered in Harry's life. In the midst of his ambiguously revealing concealments, that much at least is clear.

Harry's uncertainty about the Proposition was mirrored in his increasing hesitation over the Melville biography. He shrank from the "exact facts" of the dyad because they spoke of recent decline;

and he shrank from the novelist's life because, in its oblique but penetrating commentary on his own, it augured more of the same, only worse, for the future. It was a matter now of parting ways with Melville or of risking his long dive into moral confusion and misery. Harry thus drew back from the books that told his story, even as he had once rushed to complete them. The cooling trend is manifest in the *Pierre* edition—directly so in the portrait of the artist's failing genius and less directly in its sheer volume of biographical detail and analysis. As the Introduction grew under his pen, Harry found himself drawing more and more on materials that he had originally planned to feature in his much longer rendering of the life. It was not quite a conscious decision, perhaps; yet the effect of such disclosures was to reduce the pressure to complete the biography. It was "just as if I'd taken a little cream out of here," Harry observed years later, and a little "cream out of there." Some of the material turned up "In Nomine Diaboli," but most of it was routed into the discussion of *Pierre*. "That took some of the steam out of" the biography, he acknowledged in retrospect. "I'd already told the main things."

Harry's wavering commitment to Melville's life was further complicated by the advent of Jay Leyda, a former student of Sergei Eisenstein, the Russian film director. Leyda's interest in Eisenstein's use of color symbolism led him to *Moby-Dick* and thence, just after the war, to an interest in Melville's life that grew rapidly into a major biographical undertaking. It was inevitable, of course, that the enthusiast's hunting and gathering would lead him to his principal predecessor in the field. Harry was not pleased to learn that he had a competitor; he was unhappier still when it became clear that the newcomer was active, resourceful, and very determined in his pursuit of all there was to know about the novelist. Still, he assured himself that his main source of information, Melville's great-niece Agnes Morewood, would honor her promise to give him first priority on all the materials in her possession. But Leyda found Miss Morewood in the spring of 1947 and apparently seduced her with a pleasing fiction about his interest in her family history. Harry was at first furious to learn that his secret hoard had been discovered. He and Leyda had a heated meeting in Stockbridge at which the guilty interloper agreed to delay his own work that Harry might have time to finish first.

But as the *Pierre* project drew to a close, Harry's approach to Leyda began to reflect his divided feelings about the biography itself, which he was now free to complete. On one side, he complained of delays in progress, thus obliging Leyda to slow his own pace. As time passed, however, Harry gave increasing signs of a willingness to cooperate, allowing that Leyda's industry and insight deserved no less. He offered financial assistance when it seemed appropriate and psychiatric advice when his competitor—who was prone to breakdowns—asked for it. Then, in June 1948, having put Leyda deeply in his debt, Harry threw up his hands in defeat. "I have not been able to bring myself back to Melville since seeing you," he wrote. "I am satisfied that your book will be an outstanding landmark & that further labors on my part would be a waste of time." Leyda responded remorsefully to the "cruel announcement," pleading with Harry to reconsider. "I'll always blame myself more than you can blame me," he claimed.

Leyda in time overcame his guilt sufficiently to finish his omnium-gatherum of biographical lore, *The Melville Log,* which finally appeared in 1951. Relief came in good part from a reading of the Introduction to *Pierre,* which was so extraordinarily good, he wrote, that it belied Harry's complaints about having been robbed of Melville. "My wounding of you has taken a backfiring revenge that could satisfy any feudist—but your self-inflicted wounds do no more than tickle you & make you more satisfied with your cozy retreat into spiteful silence." He continued in this vein, hardly denying his own portion of guilt but angling quite shrewdly at the same time to shift some of its weight on to Harry's shoulders. "I feel sure," he wrote, "that if you came to your senses & got down to tough, scheduled work on the job of saying *everything* you have to say about HM . . . much good would come of it. While if you continue to enjoy the sensations of being deprived & cheated by a shark-pack of rivals, nothing but harm will come of that."

The jousting continued on and off for years, though neither antagonist gave much ground. Harry privately condemned Leyda for his dishonest, "cut-throat" methods and blamed him—and the other Melville "hounds" who followed him—for the demise of his great work. On the other side, Leyda's conscience continued to bother him, but he was sure nonetheless that Harry had used him as an excuse for his own mysterious failure to follow through. "I think that was what griped me most," he wrote in 1971—"Harry's accusation that I had killed his greatest work." There was more than a little justice on both sides of the dispute. Leyda stood self-condemned for his methods. But his hunch about Harry's moral posturing, however self-interested, was also shrewdly on the mark. Christiana touched indirectly on the real source of the trouble in a letter of May 1947. "That Morewood business is a bitter blow," she agreed. "But, my blessed, it may be the Lord's hand on us—because *our* Melville now will have to live by the way we shape it and by the way we interpret it. It's twenty years of living that we want to have in it more than twenty years of research." She was right, of course. Leyda was never a serious threat to the heart and soul of the Melville biography, to the novelist's story as it moved in secret union with their own. The real obstacles, which began to surface as Harry studied *Pierre* during the summer of 1947, were in Melville's abrupt turn toward darkness and in the shadows that his decline cast over the dyad. Leyda's offense was a chance that some half-conscious part of Harry's mind could not refuse. The loss of the biography was very real; but Harry embraced it willingly, because it spared him both the pain of facing himself in Melville and the blame for his failure to finish what he had started.

It was symptomatic of Harry's ambivalence about the dyad that his relations with Jo continued to grow warmer during the 1950s. Life at home was increasingly satisfying to both of them. They entertained students and colleagues on a regular basis and appeared to many a perfect, perfectly happy pair. They were often seen together at professional meetings and at such elite gatherings as the Eisenhower inaugural in 1953. Jo was steadfast in her devotion to charitable work, though she also continued to enjoy occasional contacts with the likes of Paul Robeson and Katharine Cornell. Leisurely cruises to Europe every year or two were another shared pleasure. Josephine sometimes joined her parents in their travels. Friends often commented on the extraordinary similarities in the looks and mannerisms of father and daughter. After years of delay and uncertainty, Josephine had settled at last on a medical career. She was even less decisive in love. Suitors appeared in the usual numbers, but the magic was never complete with any of them. Harry loomed large—too large, perhaps—in his daughter's life.

Christiana had her own enduring objections to the course of dyadic love. As the years wore on she grew steadily more resentful of work that drew Harry away from their life together. He was given to defining the dyad abstractly as a social unit of two and to construing it as an object for clinical study. His impulse, clearly, was to build a bridge between the private and the public spheres and then regularly to cross it. Christiana was not pleased. She avoided the term "dyad," with its binary emphasis, and stressed instead the unifying absorption and interpenetration of their lives. She urged Harry—increasingly against the tide of his inclinations—to complete the Melville biography; once finished, they had agreed, it would form the gateway to the Proposition. But Leyda had ruined all that, Harry complained, and veered off into other interests. They both drank heavily; but where Harry kept control, Christiana lost it. Her drinking problem was by now well known to other members of the staff. Her breath gave it away; so did her weaving down the sidewalk late mornings on her way to work. She got drunker than the others at parties. She appeared old and haggard. Her general health had perceptibly declined.

Still, there was enough love and loyalty between them, and enough of the old pleasure in their shared life, to keep the dyad afloat. They were at their best during the spring and summer, when they were together for weeks and months at a time. On her own at the Tower, Christiana was susceptible to deep depressions. "In my reveries," she wrote in July 1950, "it seemed to me that since the time of the trances life must have been a down hill process in spite of all the joy and wonder—because then I felt alive and now I feel dead." But "then Mansol arrived. . . . The moment we met I knew that we were one—I knew that he knew all that. . . . The first kiss—and the feel of his body before he even spoke—was an answer of joy and power." Within two days Harry was at work designing their answer to Christianity, the religion of "Synergy—taking into oneself the highest potential of the other and giving to it." It was understood that he would labor to perfect the "theory" of the dyad, the Proposition, now tentatively entitled *Challenge,* while Christiana would take responsibility—in *What Joy!*—for recording its history. During the mornings and early afternoons Harry worked in the Thalamus. Later on they gardened together, swam, enjoyed their soma (when Harry read his day's writing over drinks), then turned to dinner and bed. They made it a habit to take a snack together in the middle of the night—fruit, crackers, and milk consumed amidst merry recitations from Pepys's *Diary.* "He told me how this was his Paradise," Christiana noted on July 17. She was excited about Harry's writing, which featured an attack on the Christian suppression of women and sexuality. "I saw that he was saying what *I* truly believe," she reported; "I saw that he was expressing the essence and the meaning of my life." Their unity was seemingly complete, their identities interchangeable. Christiana referred to herself as Mansol and praised Harry for being "a superb Wona . . . so beautifully feminine in his receptivity" to her energy and ideas. And so it went, perfect bliss, until the month was over. Harry then returned to Jo; and Christiana, between intervals of reflection on the unfinished manuscript he had left behind, resumed her struggle with the "perpetual problem of loneliness." At summer's end she inscribed their "golden words" from Congreve over the porch door:

> Life without love is load; and time stands still.
> What we refuse to him, to death we give;
> And then, then only, when we love, we live.

Their love had many other bright seasons. "For the last days I have had a sense of wonder about our life," Christiana wrote in February 1952. When Harry arrived a few minutes later, they rushed into each others arms, "whispering of the 'mysterium' of the new life" they felt within them. True to pattern, such intervals of confident affirmation alternated with periods of loneliness and reproach. Christiana's inspiration waned during long months of virtual separation. She put off the writing of *What Joy!,* finding it more agreeable to carve or paint. Harry complained of her "passivity"; she replied that her art was an enduring contribution to their history. They had a fine July together in 1955. "It was one of those 'spelled' months without any interruptions," Christiana wrote, "when ideas came pouring out even faster than I could type." Though Harry was at work on assorted articles and lectures and thus made no headway with *Challenge,* she was content; they were together. There were other good summers. And Christiana took pleasure from her small practice in Jungian analysis and, intermittently, from her work at Harvard. Moreover, she had grandchildren now. They were a delight during short visits. Best of all, perhaps, was travel with Harry. There were trips to Mexico and Hawaii and, beginning in the mid-1950s, regular spring junkets to the West Indies.

Harry made little direct progress with *Challenge;* instead, he spread the dyadic gospel in brief installments scattered here and there in his published writing. It was a faint enough blast from the trumpet of salvation; but it sufficed to appease Christiana. Ironically, she was finally responsible for most of the sustained writing on their relationship. Her journals, dairies, chronologies, and illustrated records were legion, though often sporadic and almost never complete. Inspiration was recurrent with her but satisfaction with the results was not. Nor was Harry easily pleased. At times, in fact, he was brutally frank in his criticism. Still, beginning in about 1950 Christiana labored faithfully for more than a decade on the manuscript of *What Joy!* The result is a long fragment of several hundred pages. A prologue and an epilogue were composed as the frame for more than two dozen chapters, some virtually complete, some rough, a few apparently never written. The dyadic narrative, with almost exclusive emphasis on the early days—Jung, the visions, the construction of the Tower—alternates with sections outlining their philosophy, rituals, and symbols and others that recall friends and meditate on recent experience. Most of the writing is Christiana's, though Harry's voice is clearly perceptible in sections given to the development of ideas. The style is uneven. Generally rather stiff, sometimes clumsy and unfinished, it is at points fluent, supple, at once penetrating and subtly expressive.

What Joy! has its center in the Tower. "If we didn't write a single word," Harry once observed, the dyad "would be represented there," in the building, its contents, and in surrounding gardens, pathways, and woodlands. Not that the meaning of things falls open naturally to the uninitiated. "The chief feature of this whole place," Christiana wrote, "is that everything—pretty nearly everything, inside and outside—is symbolic. Symbolic in a new sense, symbolic of the interior forces, the states, the episodes, the achievements, which have marked the course of our evolving synergy." In its largest significance, the Tower expresses a commitment to a comprehensive, evolving, and creative religion of love. A section of *What Joy!* entitled "Points of Religion" sets out the articles of dyadic faith that Harry and Christiana strove to embody in their lives and varied works and with which they hoped to gospelize future generations. Their creed features pairs, not individuals, and gives special emphasis to "the *Potential for Growth* in the other person." In place of fixed beliefs and a "final perfect state," they advocate "progressive *change*" and "the idea of development"—in Harry's words, "the continuous creation of approximate perfection." They eschew rigid Christian dichotomies, preferring an evolutionary approach to values, the freeing of sexuality, and provision for the "catharsis of evil." God is neither male nor transcendent nor eternal but the construction of human beings impelled by "influxions of feelings and images" from their "deeper, unconscious strata." For all of their humanism, Harry and Christiana proudly proclaim their belief system a religion—"because it is based on *faith*—*faith* in the everlasting potentiality for good in the other; *Faith* in intuitive revelations in the course of development; *Faith* in love as a creative force; *Faith* in the possibility of spiritual growth."

In addition to their creeds, religions have elaborate systems of myth, ritual, and symbol. *What Joy!* is amply provident on this score. It sets out a eclectic Pantheon of gods and goddesses assembled from the religions of the world and renamed within the dyadic scheme. Male and female sexuality are unified in "Dyle," the god of Synergy (the name links "Dy," an ancient Chinese figure of a ram, with "Le," the figure of a beautiful Chinese woman, who stood together by a pool in the garden near the Tower). "Viv" is the goddess of beauty, color, vitality; she was manifest in the statue of a graceful dancer from Angkor. Nature itself, or "Co," the god of composition, combination, and creation, was embodied in the La-chaise statue of Christiana; "Vu," or exhibition and self-expression, in portraits of Wona and Mansol by Mary Aiken; and "Crue," the god of Philosophy, in bookshelves dedicated to the works of Freud, Jung, Nietzsche, Murray, and others. The building, the land, and all possessions fell under the care of "Sted," while "Hola," the ori-entation and highest aim of dyadic love, was symbolized by a golden sunburst at the center of the ceiling in the living room. And so it went—more than twenty-five gods and goddesses represented in dozens of statues, paintings, carvings, tapestries, and other dec-orative objects scattered through the house and grounds. Dyadic rituals are also mentioned, most prominently "soma," or the con-sumption of alcohol, "Walpurgis," the periodic release from sexual and other inhibitions, and the "annuestas," a dozen holidays cele-brated annually in honor of the major actors and institutions of the dyadic religion. These last, quite elaborately choreographed with costumes, music, readings, and libations, were staged in the claus-trum and included tributes to friends and teachers and reminders of "recognitions" and other major turning points in love's creative evo-lution.

The guidance pillar, a phallic shaft of granite set in the lawn, was only the most eye-catching of the symbolic sites on the exterior of the Tower. It gave way on one side to the lovely Pool of Cyane and on another to Goethe's Brow, a prominent rise in the slope of the land. Nature figures very prominently in the dyadic philosophy, as an affirmation of the "natural" in men and women and as an abundant symbolic resource. Harry and Christiana were especially lavish in their indulgence of "the pathetic fallacy," hailing trees and prominent shrubs by name as they strolled through the grounds. Christiana's records pay close attention to annual plantings, move-ments of wildlife, the loss of trees to storms and disease, the moods of the marsh, and the patterns of the weather. Her writing was frequently at its best when she turned to natural subjects. She loved working in the garden and gave time nearly every day to the gath-ering and arrangement of flowers. For years she worked with Harry to complete the "Via Sacra," a pathway through the woods marked at regular intervals by symbolic renderings—carvings, statues, inscriptions—of leading dyadic ideas. Their version of the traditional *via crucis,* or stations of the cross, was designed as an answer to the Christian renunciation of nature and the body.

The omnipresence of dyadic symbols in and around the Tower served at once to express and to reinforce the sense, reiterated in *What Joy!,* "of participation in a greater order of things, elemental and historical." Thanks to the visions, and to deep diving with Melville, Harry and Christiana were confident that they had access to archetypal images, the primordial elements from which abiding myths and religions take their rise. They were of course sustained in their mission by such assumptions, just as Christiana was renewed in her faith by Whitehead's occasional benedictions. "I have found out something about you," he said, after one of his many friendly visits to the Tower. "Everything that you have made here tells me that you are a creative person. This place represents more than individuality and uniqueness. It is more than you. It must go on." Somewhat ironically perhaps, the impression of genuine inspiration, so palpably manifest in the dyad and its harvest of creativity, is most evident in *What Joy!* at moments where it is least intended. The something "more" that Whitehead caught sight of at the Tower was first visible to him, we must suppose, in Christiana herself. Yet it was hardly a matter of metaphysics with her. She took hold of inspiration in the sight and smell of natural things and in surges of feeling for which she rarely found words. But something of Christiana's intense engagement with life surfaces in her descriptions of quotidian routines at the Tower, especially as they involved Harry.

How beautiful to me are his strong and shapely hands, which I delight to look on while we have our quiet breakfast, watching the sun win the river from its mists, and from the shadows of its tall grasses, and seeing the softly drooping fronds of the willow tree beginning to stir with the day's first breathing. In the tip of the tall cedar the Towhee bird, having found his full song after his tentative practice in the dawn, sings as though, like Narcissus at the pool, he were about to die for ecstasy of his own discovered loveliness—while

328

now and then a chipmunk rushes with pert daring across the stone threshold outside the door.

Then Mansol, all gathered into brooding silence, big with the burden of thoughts as yet unwritten, heavy with his impending labor, and the dread of defeat by deep fatigue, but with the fresh morning joy of all his senses persuading him to hope, goes up to his desk. Some days I hear him whistling as he mounts the stairs, blithe in confidence of spirit, and that little snatch of song, that unfinished tune, is to me an offering which he is laying at my feet, because out of me has come this grace.

This song of delight in simple things expresses a real and enduring dimension too easily lost sight of amid the ironies and anguish of the dyad. Indeed, *What Joy!* must be valued as a supplement to our understanding of how Harry and Christiana managed to carry on. Profound devotion, especially on her side, was obviously a key. So was their shared pleasure in creativity of all kinds. They believed in the generative power of the unconscious and "dedicated themselves to the proposition that woman could make a life-myth." They never seriously doubted that "between them a god was being made." And it helped immeasurably that both of them knew how to laugh.

Yet *What Joy!* is also a conspicuously incomplete account. From the title on, the manuscript sustains its illusion of creative fulfillment as much by what it omits as by what it includes. True, there is brief mention of conflict here and there along the way; toward the end Mansol actually complains that Wona has not said enough about their "tribulations and difficulties." A chapter is duly assigned to "the magic word and concept, 'Manahata.'" The neologism, as it is defined in *What Joy!*, combines elements from "Manipura" and "Anahata," terms which in Tantric Yoga describe opposing psychological "centers" or states of unconsciousness and consciousness, subjectivity and objectivity, irrational feeling and rational judgment. An evening of "Manahata" was the occasion for venting wayward and aggressive emotions, no matter how potent or potentially destructive. Such periodic purges cleared the air and inured Harry and Christiana, we are assured, to taking "the irrational on the chin without flinching." But there is no reckoning in this account of conflicts that would not go away. There is no mention of Jo and Will, of Ike, or of Josephine and Councilman. Or of Eleanor Jones. There is an almost prudish reticence in sexual matters and not the slightest hint of anything unusual or eccentric in the dyadic repertoire. The impracticality of their religion—its prohibitive costs in time and money and its remoteness from the everyday—is not acknowledged. There are no children in paradise; nor is their place in the scheme of things discussed. And Christiana's loneliness is barely touched upon.

What Joy! closes on a mingled note. On one side, Christiana proclaims the dyad a triumph. "Right here and now," she concludes, "we are living day by day at [the] utmost reach of our most exuberant imaginations." On the other, she registers regret that their book of love will not appear in print. To an extent they are constrained by their own "limited literary powers," which are inadequate, she allows, to the task they have set themselves. But there is a greater obstacle in their prospective audience, a youth culture given over, they fear, to self-indulgent rebellion. "The genuine Beats of our generation," Christiana complains, "are prepared for hardly anything but a spiritual hand-out—Heaven on a platter." Such people lack the reserves of imagination and endurance necessary to success in the dyadic discipline. Christiana knew better, of course, and so did Harry. Few in their audience were "genuine Beats"; and prose style had relatively little to do with the shortcomings of their manuscript. The gravest obstacle to the publication of *What Joy!* was the truth—the hard truth about dyadic love that they could not escape but that they could not bear to face either, not even in their fragmentary and unpublished manuscript. Once again, the most telling story was the one left untold.

To judge by his publications at the time of his return to Harvard, Harry was anxious to get back to research. He was confident, thanks to the rapid spread of programs in clinical psychology, that the study of personality was on the rise. His reviews, most notably of Gardner Murphy's *Personality,* were positive evidence on the same score. He retained a lively interest in the development of projective testing, especially the TAT. And his rather copious published observations on research planning indicate that his interest in moral and social issues and in the social dimension of personality development had not diminished. "Personality abstracted from cultural forms and cultural forms abstracted from personality," he wrote in 1949, "are errors of misplaced concreteness." In the same essay he lobbied for "the formulation and pragmatic validation of a regenerated system of morality and the discovery of the means by which the system can be represented to the growing child." Still, for all of his ideas and enthusiasm in print, Harry was torn by misgivings about Harvard. The dyad pulled him the other way. So did Melville. His warm feelings for Kluckhohn did not extend to the other members of Soc Rel. Nor can it have pleased him that 64 Plympton was now the headquarters, under Robert White, of the new program in Clinical Psychology. He would be starting all over.

The uncertainty, compounded no doubt by guilty concern for Christiana, surfaced in chronic headaches that first came on in New York in 1947 and continued for about two years. In this light, it was a happy accident that possession of the house assigned to the new clinic, or "Annex," originally scheduled for the fall of 1948, was delayed for a year by legal complications. This made resettling in Boston more leisurely and left time for a trip west in search of promising research associates. Harry commenced teaching for Social Relations in 1948, offering Dynamic Psychology (or Personality) to undergraduates and graduate courses on Projective Techniques and, later, on Methods and Problems in Clinical and Social Psychology. He also took a hand, with Parsons and Kluckhohn, in the graduate proseminar. The delay was useful as well in making it possible to fit out the new clinic, at 48 Mt. Auburn Street—just around the corner from 64 Plympton—in proper style. Again, antique furniture, rugs, a library, and assorted decorative *objets,* many of them of Melvillean origin or purport, were installed. Gardens were carefully landscaped and fenced during the summer of 1949. They formed an elegant backdrop to the psychodrama theatre, which Harry— thanks in part to the urgings of J. L. Moreno—ordered built at the same time. The remodeling more or less complete, Harry designated his new quarters "the Baleen," adopted a spouting sperm whale as his personal logo, and opened for business in September.

Things got off to a promising start. Harry's grant from the

Rockefeller Foundation—$18,000 per year for three years begin-
ning in 1949—made provision for three research fellowships, secre-
tarial assistance, and other essentials. He proposed to use the money
to expand on the theory and practice of personality assessment de-
vised in *Explorations,* to analyze and classify imaginal productions
(as derived from the TAT and other sources), and to launch his
dyadic research with an investigation of "factors which facilitate and
factors which impede the development of mutually satisfying interpersonal relationships (friendships)." Subjects would be few in number—about twenty Harvard undergraduates at a time—but testing
and analysis would be both intensive and extensive, involving dozens of procedures closely monitored over a period of three years. It
was emphatically the spirit of Harry's "scientific humanism" to resist the "predominantly negative" orientation of most contemporary
social science. His interests lay not in human weakness but in creative striving after "health, fellowship, cooperation, and content-
ment." Gardner Lindzey was his able right-hand man, while Henry
Riecken served as a half-time research associate. Another young
Ph.D., Anthony Davids, joined them the following year. Christiana
was in and out, there to preside at the served luncheons, especially
when distinguished guests made an appearance. Robert Wilson, a
graduate student with literary interests, signed on as Harry's assistant in a special TAT study of prominent American poets and
writers. Meanwhile, a host of other graduate students and volunteers—Goodhue Livingston, Mortimer Slaiman, Esme Brooks,
Bert Kaplan, Richard McCann, Philip Lichtenberg, Josephine Murray, and others—gathered at the Baleen to assist in various capaci-
ties.

Still, by 1952 Harry's initial ambivalence about returning to
Harvard had tilted almost completely to the negative pole. That
spring he requested a terminal two-year grant from the Rockefeller
Foundation and announced—confidentially—his intention "to retire from active participation in Harvard affairs in about two years."
He observed that competition from the Veterans Administration,
with its ample budgets, "made it difficult to get first-rate research-
ers at the salary that Harvard permits us to pay men in this
bracket." In fact, he was very discouraged with his staff, who oper-

ated, he complained to Josephine, "on a rather dull & desultory level of cortical activity." Morale at the Baleen was not high—certainly not to be compared with the exuberant *esprit* of days gone by. Harry could not fail to see that many of his younger associates felt uncomfortable at the luncheons, which they found too formal, even pretentious. It pained him that people in some quarters regarded the Baleen as an eccentric indulgence paid for out of a rich man's pocket. And he sensed—accurately enough—that his popularity as a teacher had fallen off, especially among undergraduates. It was less apparent to Harry that his personal and intellectual style were often confusing to his associates at 48 Mt. Auburn. He was quick to pick people up with his interest and enthusiasm, but just as quick to put them down again as his mood, or busy schedule, dictated. His views on most subjects were in constant flux; he loved to ruminate in company, to feel the rapid rush of new ideas rising into consciousness. But such zestful play was often a burden to junior colleagues, who felt the need for clear, consistent guidance in their work. Many of the best prospects among the new graduate students allied themselves with other Soc Rel faculty members. Meanwhile, members of the staff began to drift away. A disenchanted Henry Riecken left the Baleen in 1951; that same spring Robert Wilson declined Harry's offer of continued support in favor of a job at Cornell.

"It has *not* been a noteworthy year for the Baleenians," Harry wrote to Josephine in April 1952. "In general they depress me a little, & I prefer to stay away." In retreating from the site of his frustration, he found relief from the growing fear that his research was for the most part an uninspired rehash of old ideas. It was a great "mistake," he reflected years later, to undertake another of those longitudinal "studies involving a big staff and quite a few observations." His co-workers, caught up in the GI spirit of rebellion against authority, were incapable of cooperative effort; worse, his ideas had worn thin. "It was time to turn to something else." Getting away with Jo to conferences was increasingly a source of pleasure, especially as audiences away from home were generally lavish in their approval. Thanks in part to the *Pierre* volume, Harry was now much sought after at meetings of Melville scholars. "In

Nomine Diaboli," which he delivered at the 1951 *Moby-Dick* centennial celebration in Williamstown, was a stunning success. "A great moment," recalled Howard Vincent. Lewis Mumford declared it "the very best thing anyone has written on Melville." Aiken was of like mind. "The best short analysis I ever seed," he quipped. Even Charles Olson, whose contempt for the burgeoning "Melville industry" was well known, sent congratulations. "This piece proves again what I have always insisted," he wrote, "that you have . . . the pieces of [Melville's] heart in your hand."

But nothing repaid Harry's time away from the Baleen more generously than his participation in the highly publicized trial of Alger Hiss. "The whole thing was very enjoyable," he later reflected. He was called upon late in 1949 by Claude Cross, Hiss' defense attorney, to provide a psychological assessment of his client's accuser, Whittaker Chambers. Harry was properly chastened by the hard fate of his old friend, Carl Binger, whose psychiatric testimony had been reduced to a humiliating shambles by Chambers' very shrewd lawyer, Thomas F. Murphy. When he was finally summoned to the stand in mid-January 1950, Harry was very well prepared. He had asked the students in his graduate seminar on the TAT to assist him in the analysis of samples of Chambers' published writing. Cross coached him carefully, paying special attention to the traps that had brought poor Binger down. Certainly Harry's testimony was effective—"far more adept," in one expert's judgment, than Binger's. He declared boldly that Chambers was a "psychopathic personality" and then held on to that judgment through several sessions of strenuous cross-examination. Hiss's subsequent conviction was a disappointment, of course, though Harry was neither surprised nor very much moved by the news. He had meant what he said about Chambers, but at the same time he found little to admire in the defendant, whose professions of stainless innocence struck him as obtuse. Harry's undiminished pleasure in the case derived from having held his own on the witness stand—without so much as a trace of stammering—against the formidable Murphy. "What a clean, honest, brilliant job you did in all your testimony," wrote Mumford. Nationwide attention from the press was also flattering, of course. Best of all, Harry was intensely stimulated by the task of developing the case against Chambers. "The conditions under which my head worked best of all at any time were those preparing for the Hiss trial," he later recalled. "Three weeks in New York, preparing for the questions they might ask me. And thinking 12 hours a day on this one topic."

The fall of 1952 brought with it a welcome lift in Harry's attitude toward the Baleen. We "started the new year with a bang last week," he wrote to Josephine that October—"better crowd, better problems, better prospects. I am in a better mood about it than I have been for sometime." He was especially pleased with Gertrude Chang, "a peculiarly gifted *classifier,*" who would for several years assist him in the elaboration of what he once referred to as his "preposterous value-vector analysis of all possible human actions." Their work together centered on the classification of behavior at points of intersection between need-based actions and value-based objectives. The research and writing continued for several years, but a projected book—tentatively entitled *Behaviors of Men*—was never completed. Archival records suggest that the conceptual scheme grew to unmanageable proportions as Harry continued to dilate on its social and evolutionary significance. Work on what he called the "Icarus complex," undertaken during this period with the assistance of Ina May Greer, had a more positive outcome. Again, a co-authored book was planned—Harry liked *Glory in the Highest* as a title—and again it was never completed. But the Icarian type or hero, with his characteristic narcissism, love of fire, unique sexual disposition, and craving, both literal and figurative, to ascend, was the subject of numerous talks and two published papers. Embodied variously in Christopher Marlowe, Freud, Antoine de Saint-Exupéry, Merrill Moore, and in Harry himself, the Icarus figure lost definition as its manifold implications continued to suggest themselves. It was yet again the problem of thought expanding beyond workable—or even conceivable—boundaries, of zest forestalling closure. Little wonder that Harry admired Gardner Lindzey for his ability to bring projects promptly to completion.

It is noteworthy that Harry was able to pursue the value-vector analysis and his Icarian typology in relative separation from ongoing work at the Baleen. He was happiest and most successful during the 1950s in activities that could be pursued at a comfortable distance from his ostensible home base. He made an effort to improve his teaching, most especially in courses co-taught with faculty from other disciplines. Working closely with Clyde Kluckhohn, he helped to develop an ambitious, often successful undergraduate course on "Natural Man and Ideal Man in Western Thought." And for several years he joined Harry Levin in offering a comparative literature seminar on recurrent themes—Faustianism, the Devil, Paradise—in Western literature and legend. The 1958 American Academy of Arts and Sciences symposium on myth, for which he served as Chairman, drew heavily on his time. So did editing the symposium papers for *Daedalus* in 1959, and again for an expanded book version, *Myth and Mythmaking,* which appeared a year later. Harry served the Academy a second time in the planning for its 1960 conferences on evolutionary theory and human progress. He was paired with B. F. Skinner as a keynote speaker for the final meeting, on evolution and the individual. Chairman Hudson Hoagland thought so well of Harry's paper, "Unprecedented Evolutions," that he sent a copy to President Kennedy. The 1961 International Congress of Applied Psychology in Copenhagen was equally stimulating. Harry's talk, later published as "Prospect for Psychology," features a highly literary rendering of a psilocybin "trip" that he took with Timothy Leary a year earlier. Reports on the original experience suggest that Harry was not especially impressed with the controversial hallucinogen; his deep diving had prepared him, he claimed, for the journey on "acid." But for the purposes of the conference, where Leary and Aldous Huxley were on prominent display, the visionary mode served him well as a vehicle for his own ideas on religion, mythology, and world government. A brief brush with Huxley, who was somehow offended by the simulated hallucination, did nothing to dampen Harry's pleasure in the occasion. "The newspapers described it as the report of a drug-induced vision," he wrote to Mumford, with obvious delight.

Harry's mood on the subject of the Baleen continued to fluctuate. During the summer of 1956—a brief interregnum just after the departure of the old staff and just before the arrival of the newcomers who would initiate the final, six-year phase—he betrayed no signs of eagerness or optimism. But his spirits had risen dramatically by the following February. "The winter has been good at the Baleen," Christiana wrote to Lewis Mumford. "Five extraordinary PhD's have come to work with Harry. They are so good that they take a large part of our time, and challenge us to do our best for them." She added that 48 Mt. Auburn Street was scheduled for demolition later that year—to make way for Quincy House, a new undergraduate residence. Thus the Baleen was forced to move, first to temporary quarters on De Wolfe Street, and thence to a permanent home at 7 Divinity Avenue. The staff responded well in adversity, appealing good-humoredly to President Nathan Pusey for a reprieve but then accepting their fate with grace. To Christiana's eye at least, the quality of social and intellectual life at 7 Divinity continued at a high level. She wrote to Lewis Mumford late in 1960 that Harry was pleased with the newcomers to his staff. Her report was even more glowing in 1961. "We have a *very* fine group at the Baleen now—a real joy—since this is our last year."

It is certainly true that research took a firmer hold on Harry's attention during the late 1950s than at any other time during the postwar years. Working with a new federal grant, a new staff, and a new cohort of subjects, he turned to the close study of interactions between people in pairs under conditions of stress. Testing was intensive, covering a wide range of psychological processes observed in various settings, by numerous means (questionnaires, interviews, life histories, projective tests, filmed interactions) and by different members of the staff. The first objective, as Harry described it in an early research plan, was to "discover all that can be known (more than has ever yet been known) about 20 or more stressful, dyadic episodes" of a specified type. From this base, and for the duration of the three-year testing period assigned to each group of subjects, a variety of other questions about dyadic interactions—centering on perception and recall of self and other under stress—were studied. Harry made ample provision as well for the assessment of research techniques and for the refinement of relevant theoretical systems. In its fullest elaboration, as it was administered between 1959 and 1962, the stressful dyadic situation took the form of a debate between the subject and a well-prepared "stooge." As instructed, the unwitting subject attempted to represent and to defend his personal philosophy of life. Invariably, however, he was frustrated, and finally brought to expressions of real anger, by the withering assault of his older, more sophisticated opponent. The carefully staged episode, as Harry describes it in his "Studies of Stressful Interpersonal Disputations," was tracked from start to finish on audiotape and film, while fluctuations in the subject's pulse and respiration were measured on a cardiotachometer. All subsequent inquiry revolved around the records and memories of this intense experience.

Christiana's very favorable reports notwithstanding, however, Harry's last years at the Baleen were neither harmonious nor productive. In his published reflections on the period he describes the research project in a single, rather weary sentence. As to publications, he can boast of "no substantial accomplishments"—excepting his "sketch of the icarian personality and an article on . . . stressful dyadic disputations"—as the yield on his investment of time and energy. Referring to his "many collaborators," he mentions only three by name—"the disciplined and effective Gardner Lindzey," wondrous "Gerhard Nielsen of Copenhagen," and "the contagiously zestful and productive Ed Shneidman." The others—Kenneth Keniston, Arthur Couch, David Ricks, Paul Gross, Alden Wessman, Leo McNamara, Bernard Rosenthal, and Ted Kroeber among them—found no warm place in his memory of the 1950s. It may be that Christiana's sanguine sense of things mirrored her own approval of Harry's increased attention to dyadic research. Perhaps, too, she was moved to put the best possible face on his Harvard finale. Whatever the case, she had it wrong. Harry's last years at the Baleen were an ordeal, both for him and for most of his associates.

From Harry's point of view, the trouble had its principal source in the intractability of the young men on his staff. He complained of reduced funding and of competition for the best students; he faulted his co-workers for their sloppiness, lack of imagination, and failures to follow through on assignments. A cooperative volume, to be entitled *Aspects of Personality,* languished because several chapters were never completed. "They left me holding the bag," Harry grumbled. But at root it was "the GI mentality"—resistance among the rank and file to authority—that made life at the Baleen so unprofitable. Harry was accustomed to the ready compliance of the students who flocked to the Clinic during the 1930s. They had shared his excitement in ideas; they had been moved and shaped by his charismatic leadership. Less obviously, perhaps, they were also utterly dependent in hard times on his support. The mood was decidedly different in the 1950s. The gap between generations was of course wider and therefore much harder to bridge. But Harry gave scant attention to his own advancing years, focusing instead on what he regarded as a national epidemic of insubordination. He was thinking of the Baleen when he wrote, in 1956, that "frequent, indignant objections to the statements or decisions of a superordinate are, in most cases, no more than an equalitarian masquerade, or cover, for neurotic narcism or for narcism plus a frustrated and repressed dictator complex." Such symptoms were locally manifest in the behavior of "The Three Musketeers"—Keniston, Ricks, and Wessman; "they had their muskets out to do away with me," Harry recalled, only partly in jest. By contrast with Nielsen, who was respectfully cooperative in all things, and Shneidman, who went out of his way to please, the rebellious threesome conspired to undermine their leader's authority. Or so it seemed to Harry. They shunned his advances and ignored his advice; they did not include him in their meetings; they showed little respect for his accomplishments, little delight in his company.

The situation had a different face, but hardly a happier one, when viewed from the other side. Even Edwin Shneidman, the most warmly dedicated of his former students, admits that Harry was "terribly difficult" to get along with. Shneidman is quick to add that it was "worth it 50 times." Others were less disposed to be pleased. Arthur Couch, though himself an admiring and sympathetic observer, notes that Harry's aristocratic style was offensive to the egalitarian sensibilities of the young, middle-class research associates who came his way in the 1950s. Social-class tensions, though unnoticed as such by Harry, thus had a part to play in the rebellious mood of the staff. "He used to talk about the 'G.I. Culture' and hatred of officers among enlisted men," recalls David Ricks. "It showed our comparative status in his eyes." Ricks was the most deeply ambivalent of Baleenians. While readily admitting that his four years with Harry "were probably the most intense learning years" of his life, he is quick to recall the "tremendous sense of relief" that swept over him in 1960 when he finally broke away. "I think he wanted sons," Ricks reflects, "and he treated us with the closeness, and the willingness to freely criticize and praise, that a father might have for a son. I resented the assumed closeness, and I hated the praise, which seemed manipulative and condescending."

It was the ironic corollary to Harry's fretting about authority that he so little exercised his own. Too little, at any rate, for many of his junior colleagues, who looked to him for more intellectual leadership than he was willing to provide. "We spent a lot of time trying to figure out what it was that Harry wanted," recalls Leo McNamara. "I never saw him," Kenneth Keniston adds; "he was always off on other projects." Like Ricks, Keniston was impressed with Harry's energy and imagination. In 1956, when the new team was first forming, the prospects were "terribly exciting." But they were not far along in the first year, Keniston reports, before Harry "announced that this GI culture was forming, that it was based on antagonism against him, and in some way we were subverting—unconsciously, of course—the project." It was not authority, after all, that Harry most wanted. It was the respect and cooperation and loyalty and love that he had enjoyed in the making of *Explorations* and that he could no longer inspire. "Harry felt betrayed and abandoned," Keniston recalls, when several of the staff moved on in 1960. Ted Kroeber was warned away from the Baleen that year— "you get set up for adulation and then destruction," he was told. But he found Harry weary and half-hearted, even in his anger. Clyde Kluckhohn's sudden death in July weighed heavily on him. In paying tribute to his rare friend's "once-vibrant being," Harry no doubt reflected on his own waning powers. He was as hard on himself, Kroeber observed—on his diminished imagination, his failing energy, and his baffled inability to write—as he was on his colleagues. Edwin Shneidman was his brightest stay against the shadows. "Hallelujah!" Harry exclaimed in May 1961 when the young Californian announced that he was coming to the Baleen for a year. But a more sober tone soon overtook him. "Perhaps we should be more wary and not cheer too loudly at this point," he cautioned. "As you know, I am very difficult to get along with (at least *some* people have come to this conclusion)." Shneidman's reply was characteristically warm in its partiality. "Respecting you as I do," he confessed, "I find the prospect of working with you an extremely thrilling one. Whatever those hostile bastards feel about you (or about me, for that matter) is of little interest to me."

Harry's grousing about premature senescence accelerated as 1962 drew nearer, but so, happily enough, did his production of first-rate essays. Indeed, much of his best postwar writing was published on the eve of his retirement. But little of this work sprang directly from his exertions at the Baleen. When Harry complained "that his brain was deteriorating etc. etc.—you know"—as Christiana wrote to Mumford in 1960—it was because he felt blocked in his ambition to complete the grand sequel to *Explorations in Personality*. For years he had subordinated all else to the promise of that undertaking; now how bitter the prospect of failing again, as he had failed with Melville and with the dyad. The problem was most painfully evident in his unavailing struggle to properly complete his "Preparations for the Scaffold of a Comprehensive System." Undertaken on request from Sigmund Koch, who wanted it for his massive *Psychology: A Study of Science* (1959–1963), the essay was planned as a discussion of Harry's theoretical system, to be divided into two parts—the first covering relevant autobiographical background and the second setting forth "a logically articulated skeleton" of his mature, fully developed scheme. Part one of the assignment "was easier than I anticipated," Harry observes in his prefatory remarks; but part two was impossible. "I was unable to arrive at a satisfactory set of basic propositions before the date line," he concedes; "I proved unequal to the set standard."

We may be grateful that Sigmund Koch saw his way to publishing "Preparations" in its incomplete form. The essay is indispensable, both as a detailed guide to Harry's intellectual development and as a window, thrust open here and there along the way, on his

341

more private selves. He takes arms in his own defense, insisting, with scarcely concealed disdain, that theoretical precision is fine for "exclusively experimental specialists, observers of closely restricted animal activities, peripheralists, and positivists" but premature for wide-ranging "naturalists, generalists, and centralists" of his own breed. He cautions personologists against the "perfectionistic rituals" and "hair-splitting fussy Conscience" of the pseudo-scientist in the field. Still, it was not for lack of trying that Harry failed to put his theoretical house in order. He agonized over the essay for nearly two years—"I sweated gum drops on it," he once declared. He sent a draft of the theory section to Conrad Aiken, who found it impenetrable. "You wade in so fast and so deep," he replied, "and in so many directions and on so many levels, that your reader (this one, anyway), loses the thread." Once set in motion, Harry's theorizing—as he describes it at the very end of "Preparations"—was boundlessly expansive. "I was led on," he concedes wearily, "from complication to complication," until "the produce of variables had reached an unmanageable degree of refinement and of magnitude."

Harry borrowed the title for his essay from a strange pamphlet on "Chronometricals and Horologicals" that turns up toward the middle of Melville's *Pierre*. The first in a series of no less than "Three Hundred and Thirty-three Lectures" projected by one Plotinus Plinlimmon, the discarded "paper-rag" is "not so much the Portal, as part of the temporary Scaffold to the Portal of" the deluded author's "new Philosophy." Harry's allusion appears to be a humorously glancing acknowledgment that he had been undone yet again by his own prodigious zest. It is of some interest, however, that the assorted theoretical ruminations which he elected to include in "Preparations" terminate abruptly with his definition of the "dyadic system"—"the interplay of two personality systems, each of which is given equivalent attention." Harry drew up short not because he had reached a point of theoretical closure but because he was unwilling to say more—unwilling, in fact, to say anything at all—about the formative role of the dyad in his intellectual background. "Preparations" is thus most incomplete not in its acknowledged shortcomings but in its failure to mention Christiana Morgan, who was far and away the most important single "influence" on his de-

velopment. That omission, irresistible evidence of Harry's disenchantment with the dyad, was surely symptomatic of what ailed
him as a theorist. True, his subject, human nature, is impossibly
complex; and it may be that he was handicapped by an overplus of
ambition. But his frustrated wandering beyond all ordered bounds
was also—and perhaps principally—the result of his wavering faith
in the now diminished center of his life and thought.

Harry's theory went unfinished because he could not find his way
back to its true point of departure, let alone its culminating vision
of dyadic union. It did not follow that he was similarly blocked in
his writing on other psychological subjects. His "Commentary on
the Case of El," published in 1961, is a brilliant—imaginative,
nimble, shrewdly self-aware—analysis of a homosexual whose id
has all but emptied itself into "two contrasting, fully conscious
overt personalities." Harry's fascination with the knowing but secret
appropriation of a once-buried self is readily understood. But it was
in most respects his personal "distance" from "El" that enabled
Harry to write comfortably and well about him. The case was remote in its concerns from the research in progress at the Baleen. It
was theoretical only by implication. Harry and "El" were antipodal
in their sexual natures. "Commentary" was written for delivery in
Los Angeles, at a continent's remove from Cambridge. And it had
nothing to do with dyads.

Harry often claimed that he shied away from telling the dyadic
story because of his limitations as a prose stylist. "I wasn't talented
enough to say what we had to say," he insisted; "that was the crux
of it." Few of Harry's readers would accept his self-estimate. He is
justly respected among psychologists, and among scholars and writers in other fields, for the supple strength—the energy, color, imaginative range, allusiveness, and elegant fluency—of his prose. The
psychologist Frederick Wyatt speaks for many in proclaiming Harry's style "one of his great contributions." Moreover, it is evident
that Harry's confidence as a writer reached a peak during the decade
or so before his retirement. He was eloquently at ease in more settings, and on more subjects, than ever before in his career. The
pace, sure-footed compression, analytical mastery, and incisive good
humor of his tour de force, "The Personality and Career of Satan"

(1962), find him in full flower as an essayist. It is integral to our pleasure in this piece, as in most of Harry's best writing during the period, that it moves brightly and briskly along, rarely pausing to develop ideas fully but always darting off, at quick imagination's prompting, in new directions. Having applauded this conspicuous feature of Harry's writing as "witty, charming, [and] flexible," Wyatt goes on to suggest that it may be the positive manifestation of a certain defect. Harry "cannot always say no to a clever idea and to a clever topic. To a little joke, to a little sideline, he diffuses his style, he departs too much." This is "the child in Harry," Wyatt goes on, "who has to do his little bit of prancing and displaying." True enough. But let us allow that the impulsive child in Harry's style may also conceal a half-fretful adult, who is not showing off so much as constantly shifting ground, for fear of landing squarely and all unawares on some forbidden terrain. So viewed, Harry's diffuseness, his evident reluctance to "get into a groove," may express nervous resistance to the pull of the dyad, the main source of his inspiration. It is not mere boyish ebullience that we witness in Harry's style, then, but a kind of reflex refusal to settle fully into focus, an unwillingness, in so many words, to say what he really meant.

Harry never came closer to revealing the whole, saving truth about the dyad than he did in "Vicissitudes of Creativity," published in 1959. Yet for all of its comparative directness, the essay retreats—in a perfectly knowing and intentional way—from full candor into partial, glancing revelations. It is inherently the nature of his subject, Harry insists at the outset, that this should be so. Creativity is mysterious in its workings; it moves "toward an unknown destination by countless digressions and irrelevancies, decompositions and altered recompositions" and sometimes fails to reach its goal. What better description than this of his own brilliantly diffuse style? And what better explanation of the fact that "Vicissitudes" unfolds in brief, incomplete surges of thought, no sooner unveiled than abandoned to the reader, who is invited to finish them "in any way *his* creativities dictate." Harry insists that this "renegade" structure directly reflects the vagaries of his own creativity, which left him, as the deadline for the completion of "Vicissitudes" approached, with an assortment of "roving cerebrations," and not the "capsule of neatly articulated sentences" he might have hoped for. Thus, "in the very act of writing about the fortunes of creativity," he observes, "I shall be illustrating one of its misfortunes."

Still, it was the great virtue of imagination's putative defect that it rationalized in an apt and even charming way Harry's impulse to represent the dyad to a world in need but without claiming it personally as his own. Thus, both his theorizing about creativity and the fitful play of imagination in his writing were directly geared to his ambivalence about life with Christiana. "Creativity," he declares, following Whitehead, "is of the very essence of reality." This broad affirmation opens on a host of familiar themes—the metabolic model for creativity, an emphasis on the importance of unconscious processes, and the demand for a broadly interdisciplinary approach to the study of human nature. Because "space is short," however, none of these topics is developed; just so, a number of dyadic "variables"—Go, Co, Va, Na, Ro, Hola—are introduced but with scant attention to their meaning and provenance. Harry instead hustles along to the dyad itself, which he defines abstractly as "two interdependent regions of imagination operating as a single system." He goes on to stress the importance of sexuality in creativity and the need for regular "exchanges of nourishing, gutty thoughts or feelings." As illustration, he offers the example of "two ardent lovers—hereafter to be known as Adam and Eve," whose life together, thanks to Adam's "zest for communication," is well known to Harry. But no sooner has he begun to expand on their "unique dyadic enterprise" than he finds that "space is running short" and so reins in abruptly. He makes room for a description of "Walpurgis"—regular exchanges, energized by eros and soma, of deep, often disruptive feelings between the members of the dyad. Such "complete emotional expression" is offered as a corrective to "the traditional Christian doctrine of repression of primitive impulses" and to "the psychoanalytic notion of the replacement of the id by the ego (rationality), which results so often in a half-gelded, cautious, guarded, conformist, uncreative, and dogmatic way of coping with the world." With that bold generalization, Harry stops, beckoning the reader to "carry on from here."

345

In a brief, final movement Harry offers the experience of Adam and Eve as the "germ" of a possible new mythology, a modern credo designed to do away with both the childish dependence enforced by the patriarchal Judeo-Christian scheme and the destructive adolescent rebellion fostered in turn by the Romantic myth of individual freedom and self-sufficiency. The new "phase of spiritual manhood and womanhood, the era of Brahma," he writes, will feature a "mythology of creativity, fundamentally derived from that period of life when a man and woman participate in the formation of a dyad, of a home, of offspring, and of a new family culture. This spiritual phase, this symbolism, might be exemplified . . . on all levels: an embracement and reunion of the opposites: man and nature, male and female, conscious and unconscious, superego and id, reason and passion, rational and irrational, science and art, enjoyable means and enjoyable ends, upper class and lower class, West and East." And so, having ventured this fleeting glimpse of his brave new world, Harry urges the reader, one last time, to "go on happily from here."

There was a vast difference, obviously, between the blissfully expansive family of Harry's imagining and the furtive, failing love affair to which it corresponded in his own life. That painful gap is explanation enough perhaps for his refusal to go further in setting the dyad before the world. The waning momentum of his utopian dream carried him forward into brief, oblique disclosures, but no further. "One of the distinguishing marks of a culturally creative person," he announces in "Vicissitudes," is "a continuing, hopeful commitment and allegiance to a selected aim." Harry and Christiana can hardly have been proof against the sharp irony of that claim. Yet amid much strain and frustration they *were* faithful, both to each other and to the vision of transcendent union that they had shared for so many years. But carrying their story to the world was nonetheless beyond them.

Harry was surprised that the response to "Vicissitudes" ran to no more than a couple of letters. In fact, he had given his readers too little of the dyad to go on. He gave them even less in his other writings of the period. In his essay on Conrad Aiken, "Poet of Creative Dissolution," he declares that Western civilization is "entering

346

the last phase of spiritual disintegration" but ventures nothing personal in describing the "fundamental reconstruction" which he envisions for the future. Contemporary American society suffers "from want of a kindling and heartening mythology to feel, think, live, and write by," he observes in "Beyond Yesterday's Idealisms," his Phi Beta Kappa Oration, delivered at Harvard in 1959. As a partial cure, he limns out the "micro-sketch of a macro-sketch of a book for a new age"—as ever, time was short!—a volume featuring "a mythology of adulthood, something that is conspicuous for its absence in Western literature, a mythology of interdependence and creation." But he came no closer than this to identifying the dyadic source of his new gospel. In "Two Versions of Man," finally, he argues vigorously for a secular religion to be based on the spontaneous visions of some inspired prophet. He numbers Socrates and Nietzsche among his models but makes no mention of Christiana, whose example was surely foremost in his mind. He goes on to enumerate leading elements of the dyadic creed—sexual liberation, creative evolution, the overthrow of repression, and the development of appropriate myths and rituals—in his outline of the new religion, but again without reference to the personal source of his ideas. It is ironic, in this light, that he should have settled in closing on Santayana's evocation of the modern "European races," bereft of their traditional faith and incapable therefore "of uttering the ideal meaning of their life."

The decade or so before his retirement in 1962 was an uneven period for Harry. The mingled pattern of success and failure is exemplified best perhaps in the dyad itself, which continued, amidst no little evidence of decline, to provide intervals of gratification and renewal. It was a love affair dependent in its flourishing on enormous reserves of youthful energy and optimism. As these fell into short supply, a certain deflation was all but inevitable. It is thus tribute to the truth of the dyadic vision that it sustained its bearers through these often difficult years. Harry's psychological research was for the most part a disappointment, though Edwin Shneidman's arrival in 1961 helped to enliven the final months at the Baleen. There were many other compensating sources of pleasure and pride. Harry was a featured speaker at the tenth anniversary of the founding of Social Relations in 1956. "Three sore and seven years ago," he began, in a speech made memorable by its biting juxtaposition of Clyde Kluckhohn, who studied "Witchcraft in New Mexico," and his wife, Florence, who practiced "Bitchcraft in New England." Harry was on much better behavior the following May, at the gala thirtieth anniversary celebration of the Clinic. It was a two-day affair, with reunions at both 64 Plympton and 48 Mt. Auburn, speeches by White, MacKinnon, Sanford, Tomkins, Holt, Smith, Lindzey, and others, and a festive dinner at the Harvard Club of Boston. "Gosh, that was a party," Harry recalled. In 1958 a large handful of former students put together a special TAT issue of the *Journal of Projective Techniques,* which they dedicated to Harry on his sixty-fifth birthday. Later that year he traveled with a small contingent of American social scientists to the USSR, where he learned something of Soviet theory and practice in psychology and enjoyed a reunion with his old friend A. R. Luria. The following June brought the invitation to deliver the annual Phi Beta Kappa Oration at Harvard and thereby to join such immortals as John Quincy Adams, Ralph Waldo Emerson, Woodrow Wilson, and FDR. There were old friendships with Aiken and Kluckhohn and Mumford to be grateful for and warm exchanges with Gordon Allport and Felix Frankfurter. And though he declined when Sanford and Tomkins offered to nominate him for the Presidency of the American Psychological Association, Harry was nonetheless touched by their gesture of respect.

Despite much outward show of buoyancy, however, Harry's mood during the 1950s shifted by imperceptible degrees to the negative side. He was brought back, in his review of Philip Rieff's *Freud: The Mind of the Moralist,* to Melville's persuasion that "that mortal man who hath more of joy than sorrow in him, that mortal man cannot be true." It was telling perhaps that the Icarus complex, with its emphasis on "the inevitable fall of over-reaching aspiration," should have figured so prominently in his thinking during the period. The Baleen, Christiana's drinking, and Kluckhohn's death weighed most heavily on his spirit. Deepening discouragement with the hustle and glitter of postwar America was also a factor. And despite his very considerable productivity, he was increasingly fretful about his writing, most especially about his inability to finish books. The fear that his mental powers were failing grew sharper as retirement drew near. It occurred to him that all the years of heavy smoking and regular drinking had begun at last to take their toll.

But all such lingering complaints were as nothing to Harry's grief on the evening of January 14, 1962, when Jo died quite suddenly of a heart attack. They had just returned from New York. She complained briefly of discomfort on the train but made little of it; she would see a doctor in the next day or two. Upon their arrival at 37 Brimmer Street, Jo put in a call to Josephine, who was completing a medical internship at Duke University Hospital in Durham, North Carolina. After an animated exchange with her daughter, Jo gave the phone to Harry and withdrew to the next room. When he called to her a few minutes later, there was no reply.

Jo died too soon. She was only 67 and apparently in very good health. As all the newspapers observed, she was still very active in a wide variety of social and civic activities. Her life with Harry was as good as it had ever been, and getting better. But there had not been time enough for the kind of healing they both required. Perhaps that was asking too much. In any case, Harry was deeply shaken. He missed Jo and their newfound life together. And the weight of his guilt, now as irredeemable as her long years of suffering, brought him low. Carl Binger recognized the burden of remorse in his old friend's grieving. It is also manifest in Harry's letter of January 22 to Lewis Mumford. "You and Sophy know this incurable desolation," he wrote, alluding to the Mumfords' wartime loss of their son, Geddes. "You have been given few reasons, however, to suspect to what extent the affections and purposes of the three Murrays became, as time went on, inextricably interwoven, with Jo the indispensable warp of the fabric evolving in the loom of time." Harry's prose was no more strained perhaps than the sentiment it voiced. He needed to believe that his wife had accepted her life and that she had come some way toward forgiving him his part in it. He evoked for Mumford "Jo's noble nature, moulded with divine cheerfulness and courage out of disillusionments until it reached the peak of its perfection. Your confirmation of my own (untrustworthy) assurance that Jo had achieved a state of inward peace and genuine serenity constitutes the most consoling, strong support that could be given me for my ascent, if ever, out of the abyss."

The funeral gave evidence of a similar straining amidst contrary emotions. Harry arranged everything. He wrote the service, brought the Groton School Choir in to sing Jo's favorite hymns, and summoned 91-year-old Karl Reiland—Murray family friend and retired rector of St. George's Church, New York—to preside. Harry was in church early—well before the fashionable crowd of six hundred who gathered to pay their respects—attending nervously to last-minute details. There were "enough flowers," Christiana observed, "to make it look more like a wedding than a funeral." But having seen to the grandeur and decorum of the affair, Harry fell into a posture of nerveless bereavement. He refused to wear an overcoat as he stood in the freezing cold outside the church, making his farewells to the last of the mourners. He was determined, it seemed, to suffer publicly. Edwin Shneidman came upon Harry at the Baleen a few days later. He was alone, seated on a bench, in tears. Jo "had tasted the horrors of life," he sobbed, "the horrors." It was emotionally touch-and-go that way for months.

▼

chapter twelve

The Oozy Weeds about Me Twist

Jo's death was a sudden, perverse-seeming stroke of chance for which Harry was completely unprepared. No one close to the dyad expected Christiana to outlive Jo. Borne down by loneliness, frustration, and poor health, Christiana had grown more boozy, more emotionally erratic, and more frail as her sixties wore on. Jo, on the other hand, was robust, active, full of life. She was comfortable with herself, stable, predictable, and happily attentive to her husband's wishes. In a memorial sketch written for the *Radcliffe Quarterly,* Harry noted that the more than six hundred people who came to Jo's funeral were drawn there by "green memories of her inexhaustible good-will and humor, her nobility of character, and her limitless generosity." Here was the ideal companion for old age. And her health, which contrasted so visibly with Christiana's frailty, made it perfectly reasonable to assume—as many did—that Harry and Jo would draw together, undistracted, fully reconciled, as their lives came to a close.

That happy scenario seemed as natural and inevitable as the alternative was unthinkable. The prospect of marriage to Christiana, once longed for as the highest unattainable bliss, was an embarrassing burden to Harry when it fell finally within his reach. There could be no doubt about Christiana's feelings in the matter. They would be married, she assumed, in due course. Their friends made the same assumption. "Hold fast, have faith, and quietly wait!" Lewis Mumford advised Christiana, not long after Jo's funeral. "In some ways this is a greater ordeal than Harry's: but you will in the end share the same reward, all the more fully because you've not tried to snatch it." But Harry showed "no inclination at all," Mumford later observed, to move toward marriage. Inwardly, he grieved for Jo and drew back in guilt and bewilderment from his depleted mistress. Christiana held on desperately; she would not—she could not—let him go. Harry relented but refused to consider marriage so long as she continued to drink. He insisted that they keep their relationship a secret, assuming—quite against the evidence by now—that the insiders to the truth were a known few. Nor was he willing to give much time to the dyadic writing. Not surprisingly, Christiana's resolve gave way under the strain. She went on the wagon for a few months but returned in earnest to the bottle before the year was out. And so the grave pattern of their lives was formed—his retreat fueled her collapse, which in turn reinforced his impulse to back away.

Harry welcomed his retirement—which was duly noted in *Time* magazine—as an opportunity to get on with his writing. He moved from Boston to a large, comfortable house on Francis Avenue in Cambridge, just a short walk from Harvard. A Japanese houseman cooked for him and kept the place in good order. It was a relief to be free of formal obligations to students—"No more experiments, no more co-workers, no more promising projects," Harry wrote to Alvan Barach—though he met regularly with his staff at the Baleen and circulated an ambitious outline of *Aspects of Personality*. Keeping busy was a partial antidote to grieving. He worked on a paper for a conference in Los Angeles; he gave a series of talks in St. Louis; and he delivered the Elliott Lectures at Minnesota, offering up a renewed attack on scientism in psychology. Still, his spirits flagged. In February 1963 he complained to Mumford of "senescent mental paralysis, or pervasive fatigue and staleness, with 10 half-finished books in my files." Among his unfinished projects he included a life of young Melville (to be drawn from the now abandoned full-scale biography), a study of imaginative "themas" in Western literature, his book—*Glory in the Highest*—on the Icarus complex, an analysis of Merrill Moore's poetry and personality, a technical survey of methods for interpreting the TAT, a comparative critical study of

Melville and Aiken, a theoretical inquiry into "The Activities and Wants of Men"—which he described as "a comprehensive classification of the functional activities and aims of human beings, according to a biological model"—and several volumes of collected essays. His frustration would grow even sharper with time, as the futility of his labors became more painfully evident. Despite the prodding of interested publishers, not one of his major works-in-progress would find its way into print.

Harry fared better with less ambitious projects. In 1963 he published reviews of Clyde Kluckhohn's posthumous *Anthropology and the Classics* and Avis Dry's *The Psychology of Jung*, along with a foreword to Frances Wickes' *The Inner World of Choice*. His pleasure in such restored productivity spills over in a letter to Lewis Mumford, in which Harry makes note that he is at work on a paper, "Dead to the World: The Passions of Herman Melville," scheduled for delivery at a conference in October. The essay, which features an analysis of the self-destructive impulses that overtook the novelist during the second half of his life, may be read as an oblique reconfirmation of the decision to abandon the biography. With its emphasis on suicidal woe, it might also seem to offer itself as a window on the critic's mood in troubled times. But even as he brilliantly chronicled Melville's decline, Harry experienced a brief resurgence of energy and optimism. It was an excess of grief on one side, a temporary cresting of the "sanguine surplus" on the other. Never had the essential difference between the two men emerged in such bold relief.

Still, Harry was slowing down. Though he found the time to apply for a renewal of grant support for *Aspects of Personality*, he failed—where he might have succeeded years earlier—to inspire his co-authors with enthusiasm for the task before them. Only two chapters—by Shneidman and McNamara—had been submitted by January 1964; a few more trickled in, but by the summer of 1965 it began to appear that the project would have to be scuttled. Harry was left feeling, as he wrote to Alvan Barach, that he had "wasted the greater part of the last eleven years" at Harvard. He was of course gratified to be invited—by his old antagonist, E. G. Boring—to contribute a chapter to *A History of Psychology in Autobiog-*

353

raphy, a collection of reminiscences and reflections by the elite in the field. "For you this is indeed a *must,*" Boring urged; "you have become the elder statesman in psychodynamics in America." Harry responded with "The Case of Murr," surely the most brilliantly illuminating of his late writings. He was also pleased by the very positive response to "Bartleby and I," his essay on Melville's best-known short story. Cast as an imaginary conversation between the story's leading characters, an array of critics, and Melville himself, the characteristically supple and imaginative analysis yields a portrait of the artist as a man walled-in by bitterness and hate—a man that a feeling biographer might prefer to avoid. It was a "distinguished" critical performance, as Howard Vincent was quick to observe. So was Harry's long, carefully measured review of Frederick Crews' *The Sins of the Fathers: Hawthorne's Psychological Themes.* "That is criticism! That is writing!" exclaimed Jacques Barzun.

But there were disappointments, too. A gathering of humanistic psychologists at Wesleyan in December 1964 was a letdown. Though he respected the leading figures in the movement—Abraham Maslow, Rollo May, and Carl Rogers among others—Harry found the emergent program of the "third force" (in opposition to behaviorism and psychoanalysis) at once strident and confused. Nor was he very much pleased with his own contribution to the proceedings—a dialogue between psychologists of competing "schools," which he thought better of publishing. "I have been in a bad way for a year or more," he wrote to Leo McNamara the following February. He felt drained "to the point of exhaustion & staleness—maybe with no renewal possible." It scarcely helped that his Harvard headquarters had been uprooted yet again. "Last week," he complained to McNamara, "we moved from our cozy, memory-packed Baleen to the top (15th) floor of the hermetically-sealed, air-conditioned, mechanized William James Hall—a white sepulcher of former hopes." In April he declined an invitation to contribute to an issue of *Daedalus* on religion in America. Though the topic intrigued him, he was restrained by doubts about his ability to produce. "I was beginning to have trouble writing," Harry recalled, "putting things down in sentences that suited me." His health was an additional burden. Emphysema was detected in 1965, for which

354

Alvan Barach—a pulmonary specialist—recommended oxygen treatments and regular supplements of vitamin B$_{12}$. The year 1966 saw the onset of a chronic sciatica. A year later it was viral pneumonia. The pace and trajectory of social change in America also weighed heavily on his mind. "*Here,*" he wrote to friends in England, "there is nothing but explosions—of nuclear and human energy, of genes and population, of affluence and autos, of white and black ghettos, of robberies & violence, of the city into the country, of advertising and ugliness, &c, and in all this rage the gentle plea of beauty is not heard."

The dyad was scant consolation. To be sure, there was little outward sign of discord. "Have you read Jung's autobiography?" Christiana inquired of Lewis Mumford during the summer of 1963. "I was deeply impressed with a life so well devoted to subjective experience in all its confusion and loneliness and ambiguity and finally understood in terms that he could live with. I bless him with every breath I draw for had he not been through *his* experience *we* could never have had ours." Work on her masterpiece, the Tower, was virtually completed in 1966 with the installation of stained glass windows in the Claustrum. Drawing directly on the imagery of the visions, the large triptych in glass—designed by Christiana and executed by Clare Leighton, the celebrated English artist and illustrator—sets forth in colorful symbols the steps toward individuation. "We have been waiting 30 years for these," Christiana reported; "I think it is the last great creative effort for the house." Harry was no less affirmative about their relationship. He had the dyad in mind when he reminded his audience—at a conference in January 1965—of the familiar "conflict between conventional morality" and individual values. "The most critical experiences in my life," he declared, "were those in which individual moral judgments were decisive and had beneficent results." They even held on to the hope that they might one day get back to their dyadic writing. "*Our* book remains as the real thing," Christiana assured Lewis Mumford in 1965, "but must wait."

Still, the months and years passed without a wedding. Christiana persisted in her heavy drinking. She was a familiar figure around Cambridge, bent, frail, making her way almost daily across Brattle

Street, through the Common, and slowly past the Law School toward Francis Avenue. She carried a folding campstool and stopped regularly to sit and catch her breath. Torn between compassion and repulsion, borne down by remorse, Harry groped for answers. He did what he could to help Christiana control her drinking. But she craved oblivion. She drank secretly, insisting against all the evidence on her sobriety. She was often dizzy with sherry or gin when she arrived at the house; most evenings she drank to the point of quiet incoherence and collapsed early into bed. She was much more in control of herself when they were at the Tower or on their frequent junkets to the West Indies. Sun, exercise, regular meals, plenty of sleep, and having Harry to herself, away from the grasping, distracting world—on such terms Christiana usually found her way to a measure of serenity.

Usually. But not so on their visit to St. John, Virgin Islands, in February 1967. They had been to the tiny island before, as guests of wealthy friends who provided them with a private beach house, plenty of time to themselves, and the run of beautiful, isolated stretches of sand. It was, as Christiana once wrote to Lewis Mumford, like going "to live in the Garden of Eden for a time." But their departure for paradise was clouded that February by an ominous quarrel. During the weeks before they left Christiana engaged a lawyer in Cambridge to make adjustments to her will. She was especially concerned about the disposition of the Tower. She consulted with Harry, and with her son, Councilman, but neither was happy with her decision to leave the building and grounds to Governor Dummer Academy, on condition that they remain Councilman's for the duration of his life. Both expressed fears about the fragile integrity of the Tower; both felt deprived. "That's the goddamnedest idea I've ever heard of," Harry raged when Christiana showed him the revised will, just hours before their flight to the West Indies.

Three weeks later, in circumstances that made Harry suspect suicide, she was dead. There is no direct evidence that Christiana's unwonted attention to the will was part of a plan to end her life. Nor, apparently, did her behavior on St. John betray a self-destructive bent. Still, her drinking had hardly abated. It appears that she drank heavily on the night before her death. There was more of the same the following morning on the beach, until her intoxication became painfully evident. "You're disgusting," Harry lashed out, little suspecting that these would be his last words to Christiana. He had not yet fully recovered from the extraction of an abscessed tooth and decided that a nap might help. As Christiana retreated across the sand toward the water, he fell into a light sleep. Minutes later, as he jerked suddenly back to consciousness, Harry sensed that something was not right. The beach appeared abandoned. But then, rising to his feet, he caught sight of a body face down in the water. He knew at once that it was Christiana. She showed no signs of life as he carried her to shore. Still, he labored desperately at mouth-to-mouth resuscitation for more than an hour. But it was no use. Christiana was gone, drowned in less than two feet of water.

The Certificate of Death, issued that same day—March 14, 1967—makes no mention of suicide. Christiana's personal physician thought it likely, as Harry wrote to Alvan Barach, that she had suffered "one of her occasional heart attacks or fainting attacks as she was stepping down the steep slope of the soft coral sand" and had then "fallen under water and drowned before regaining consciousness." This account appears even more plausible in the light of Christiana's intoxication—she vomited alcohol in some quantity as Harry attempted to revive her on the sand—at the time of her death. Still, Harry could not put the thought of suicide from his mind. Christiana's last-minute adjustments to her will seemed to point in that direction, especially when viewed against the background of her deteriorating physical and emotional condition. She was, it could hardly be denied, a woman out of love with her life. Even if her death was in some technical sense accidental, it was obvious that years of loneliness and frustration had weighed heavily in her descent to the grave. Harry accepted his part in that sad drama and suffered terribly for it.

Characteristically, he kept his guilt to himself. Yet it was not pride alone that moved him to secrecy. He was restrained as well by the unbearable pathos of the truth. In his letters to friends he put the most positive face possible on Christiana's last days. "We had

had three beatific weeks together, despite a few bodily frailties," he wrote to Edward and Elizabeth Handy. "As it happened, Monday, March 13, marked a high point in our life this year. My sciatica was almost gone, and Christiana, sun-tanned as a Polynesian, seemed to be at her peak of healthfulness and radiance; and both of us were looking forward to being married, for comfort's sake, with the blooming of the flame azaleas in the Spring." This was the first that anyone had heard of wedding plans, and few were persuaded by the belated announcement. It was a fiction interposed in desperation against an intolerable reality. "The description you've given of your last weeks together," wrote Lewis Mumford, "makes me feel that . . . this was the perfect ending of the life you shared together—herself in good health, aglow with the beauty of nature, united not only in the memory of your past life but in anticipation of the formal acknowledgement of its deep reality. What more at that moment could life offer her?" What indeed! Harry must have groaned, aghast at the irony of Mumford's happy surmise. But he continued nonetheless to circulate the story, trusting perhaps that in the repetition of the telling he might somehow make it all true.

Harry had good reason to grieve. For more than forty years Christiana had been at the center of his life. They had shared everything; and now, suddenly, she was gone. Worse, the circumstances of her passing seemed to confirm that their extraordinary experiment in living, purchased over the decades at great human cost, had been a failure. Had Jo's life, and Ike's, and Will's, been sacrificed in vain at the altar of the dyad? It must have felt that way in the months after Christiana's death. Here, in the parched aftermath of great plans and great passion, in Harry's loss of faith, and in the desperate, self-destructive pattern of Christiana's drinking was more perhaps than the tragic sense of life had bargained for. Nor was this the end of it. Harry would have nothing to do with the memorial service arranged by Christiana's family at a Unitarian church in Newburyport. Councilman in turn refused to attend the ceremony that Harry was planning at the Tower later that Spring. "The strong sense of rejection suffered in earlier years [has] continued to plague me," Councilman wrote. "I would certainly not have called Mum either a 'happy mother' or, indeed, a happy woman," he added, sharply, in a subsequent letter. Having spoken his mind, he decided to attend the Tower ceremony after all.

It was a lovely occasion, held on a fine day in mid-May, with copious readings by family and friends from some of Christiana's favorite works. "In beauty it is finished," Harry recited from a Navaho chant; "In beauty it is finished." But in fact it was not. Councilman's bitterness grew deeper when his mother's lawyer—either through scheming or bungling or both—lost the entire cash legacy of more than $400,000 to bad investments. Harry was to blame, in the son's eyes, because in his desire to keep the dyad a secret he had failed to provide Christiana with reputable, "establishment" legal counsel. Bereft now of both his mother and his inheritance, Councilman abruptly relinquished the Tower to Governor Dummer Academy. Better to be done with it, he concluded, than to possess it on borrowed time. Councilman's bitter sense of betrayal made Harry's emotional burden all the heavier. "I find myself surviving my own death," he wrote to an old friend at year's end.

It is possible that there was an additional strand to Harry's guilty fear that Christiana had committed suicide. Not long before their departure for the West Indies, Christiana complained to Ina May Greer that Harry had succumbed to an infatuation with "a young divorcee." How Christiana obtained this information, and whether or not she shared it with Harry, are not clear. But there was a substantial measure of truth in what she told her friend. At 46, Nina Chandler Fish was young—or at least younger, by some 27 years, than Harry. And though not yet divorced, she was in process of parting ways with her second husband, Elliot Fish. Nina came—as Jo and Christiana had come—from a wealthy, upper-class background. Her father, Alfred DuPont Chandler, was a genial inventor who gave much of his time to managing the family fortune. The mother of five children, Nina had recently completed an Ed.D. at Boston University, where she was an Assistant Professor of Special Education and Co-Director of the Psychoeducational Clinic. She was attractive, articulate, and very much alive to psychology—especially to the work of Piaget—when she and Harry first met, through a chance family connection, the year before. Infatuation it was. There were notes and flowers and tea, lively exchanges on professional subjects, a gradual approach to more personal revelations (though Harry said nothing of the dyad), and the arousal on both sides of dormant libido.

In April of 1967 Harry felt compelled at last to fill out the picture of his personal life. "Precious Nina," he wrote, "I must explain my silence—in the simplest, coolest terms, and leave the depth dimension to your imagination. I spent three beatific weeks in the Caribbean with my all-the-world, at the end of which she was drowned in two feet of water on a solitary beach of the island of St. John. . . . We were to be married in May." After an interval during which Harry was emotionally consumed in mourning, the romance resumed at a brisk pace. Nina soon restored her suitor to his gusto for life. "Now that I am keen to live as long as possible," he wrote to Alvan Barach, "I am beginning to pay serious attention to your various prescriptions." His sexual energy returned, and with it his old charm. "I am a species of Pagan, or polytheist, who can't bear to think of a male-monopolized heaven," Harry announced in an animated 1968 interview for *Psychology Today*. At a party some months later he bellowed out joyously, "I'm 76 years old, and I'm in love." The wedding, planned originally for March 1969, was abruptly set back when Nina fractured two lumbar vertebrae in an automobile accident near Harvard Square. Harry canceled their honeymoon plans, which had included a stop in Oslo for an honorary degree, and gave himself night and day to the care of his beloved. Though slow and initially quite painful, Nina's recovery was virtually complete by May 17, when they were married at Francis Avenue.

Isabelle Kendig, an old friend and former student, spoke for many when she observed that Harry's union with Nina was *"the* successful relationship" in his life. Comparisons in such matters are notoriously difficult, but inevitable just the same. Certainly Harry's second marriage was the most balanced and stable of his romantic attachments. It could hardly compete with the dyad for intensity; nor could it match his marriage to Jo for endurance through adversity. But there can be no gainsaying Harry's extraordinary good fortune in Nina—nor, for that matter, hers in him. She brought him youth, beauty, energy, and a supple readiness to bend when necessary to the rather fixed habits and expectations of a much older man. He responded with unquenchable enthusiasm, abundant material and professional support, a world of intriguing friends, and a limitless fund of knowledge and wisdom. They shared intelligence, zest, charm, and all conceivable shades of good humor. Perfectly content to be alone together, they were equally delighted in gatherings of good company. They enjoyed traveling, especially for rest and recreation to various spots in the West Indies.

Marriage was not without its vicissitudes, of course. Nina wisely resisted Harry's attempts to cast their relationship in the pattern of the dyad. She knew enough of Christiana's fate to wish quite another for herself. Nor, it followed, could she rise to her new husband's level of admiration for the ideas of Jung. Here, in time, they learned to compromise—he soft-pedaled on the Old Man, and she in turn cut back on her references to Piaget. Nina was also quick to perceive that working on a book together was the surest avenue to grief. Harry's frustration with his own writing, she saw, would almost certainly spill over on to her own. Her very sensible restraint in such matters cost Harry an occasional twinge but spared them both much heavier abrasions. Nina's steady good sense, administered with love, tact, and unfailing humor, was the ballast and keel in their marriage. Bereft of Jo and Christiana, and laboring in vain to revive his powers, Harry was surely vulnerable at 73 to the chill of loneliness and self-accusation. It was the final blessing of his long, charmed life that for its last twenty years Nina was his stay against that dark side of himself.

For all of its potency in his life, the magic of new love was powerless when it came to Harry's writing. "Components of an Evolving Personological System," which appeared in 1968, was an attempt to formulate an up-to-date version of his personological scheme. It was an uphill battle, against advancing years, limited space, and a virtually boundless theoretical vision. "An itch for comprehensiveness," Harry warns at the outset, "has resulted in such a multiplication of *idenes,* or basic gene-like ideas—stolen goods for the most part—that at this juncture I find myself utterly incapable of packing them coherently into an essay of this length." He hardly exaggerated. Though formed out of familiar elements, "Components" is so densely and dryly compacted as to be unreadable. His discussion of "Need," first formulated in English for the German *Lexikon der Psychologie,* is much more lucid, though utterly devoid of Harry's usual energy and rhetorical color. The same may be said of "Indispensables for the Making, Testing, and Remaking of a Personological System," a brief, breathlessly condensed outline of his assessment procedures and goals, published a few years later. Just at the time of his courtship and wedding Harry was also laboring to complete a multivolume collection of his papers in psychology. It was his hope, according to his assistant, Barbara Du Bois, that immersion in the earlier work might lead to the formulation of "a fleshed out and updated" theoretical statement. But distractions, indubitable senescence, and the daunting pattern of previous failures to finish were insurmountable obstacles to his ambition.

Harry was similarly frustrated in his attempt to complete *Options,* a novel of ideas undertaken years earlier and revived, with the thought of publication clearly in mind, during the early 1970s. The idea for the book first crystallized in the spring of 1952. Discouraged with the quality of staff endeavor at the Baleen, Harry made time for other interests. "At present I am trying to deal with the World's Problem," he wrote to Josephine, "but am uncertain of the proper form. This week I am casting it as a series of dialogues which, in the hands of most authors since Plato, have failed miserably. We shall see." The project—originally entitled *Dialogues in Search of a Path*—took life almost immediately and occupied much of Harry's time that summer. By the beginning of the fall term he had outlines or rough drafts for more than a dozen of about eighteen projected chapters. The narrative unfolds from the point of view of an American intellectual and writer, one Dr. Mann, who has embarked on a walking tour of Italy. Quite evidently cast in the image of his creator, Mann meditates deeply on the history of the countryside through which he is passing. "The continuity of culture," he reflects, "is achieved through periodic transformation—dissolutions, dissections, re-evaluations, eradications, corrections, and reconstructions." Even as they emerge into consciousness, such thoughts are echoed in the words of a bearded old man who appears suddenly on the scene, discoursing out loud about the "seeds" of cultural renewal. "Seeds are in the wind—hints, clues, signs, portents, revelations—for all who will receive them, for all who are open, without pride and without dread." The nameless sage gives voice to Harry's conviction that the revival of a depleted Western Civilization will have its necessary point of departure in visions arising from the unconscious. "Brood upon the waters," he urges, in a manner reminiscent of Melville's Ishmael, "upon the incoming tide of gliding shapes, shapes for a world to be created. Await the unforeknown. Expect the unforeseeable. Welcome the improbable. Dive. Dive until you find. Plunge into the mazes of your being, and into the mazes of other beings."

A student of Vico, Spengler, Pareto, Mumford, and Toynbee, the old man is an American expatriate who has abandoned his homeland—"a good-hearted, kid-centered nation, with a kid's love of baseball, thriller movies, mechanical power, and quick, tangible results"—for an environment more conducive to his creativity. He is principally concerned to discover and represent the chief determinants of the rise and fall of civilizations, with a special eye to "the causes of the decay of Western culture." His reading and reflection have brought him to "the very simple, and by no means original idea, that the cement of every society—the stuff that binds it and sustains it as a system—consists of principles and practices, ethical in the broadest sense, which derive their authority from an accepted faith, or vision of the ideal, religious in the broadest sense." He makes a special place for visionary women in the creation of such saving cultural forms but laments that Americans, in their preoccupation with the specter of the Soviet Union, are blind to the enemy that attacks them from within. Here, then, in radically condensed form, is Harry's own analysis of "the World's Problem," and his considered program for its amelioration, grounded in Christiana's visions, driven by creative evolution, in conflict with the dominant American cultural ethos, and culminating in the formation of an inspired new mythology for present and future generations. "The salvation of our world," he concludes, "hangs on whether some vision of a better world—a credible and approachable ideal—is born out of the turmoil and torment of our Free World, and so compellingly represented that peoples of all lands will trustfully repair to it."

The old man's broad general perspective serves as the prophetic prologue to the chapters that follow, in which Dr. Mann engages in dialogue with the proponents of various, more narrowly conceived responses to the perceived decline of Western Civilization. Cyril Ober, a Christian scholar at Cambridge University, insists that the widespread loss of religious faith has unleashed anarchy on the world. In response, Dr. MacGregor, a London psychiatrist, argues that "the sciences, especially the psychological and social sciences, should serve the purposes of religion." Noval, a Romantic artist in the tradition of Shelley and Blake, takes the view that "art-works—the best of them—are crystals in which gifted gazers can perceive the future." A Harvard sociologist, George Henson, denies that the Western world is in decline. By contrast, Ronald Whitridge's study of pervasive social pathologies has brought him to the verge of despair. "I . . . have pretty much made up my mind to be annihilated," he admits. Several of the characters had real-life models. Cyril Ober was based on Harry's old friend Joseph Needham, the brilliant student of Chinese civilization at Cambridge. There is something of Conrad Aiken in Noval and of Melville in Whitridge. Harry's personal investment in most of the chapters is even more conspicuous. "Nansen" summarizes his position on the need for world government; Louis Buxton, a biologist-turned-philosopher, advocates social change guided by an "attainable image of the ideal"; and Ben Bridge insists that Americans must surrender their individualism to the values of interdependence and mutuality. Harry's ideas are manifest as well in a section advocating research on conflict between individuals and groups, and in the description of an institute for the study and cultivation of erotic relationships.

Harry was very much stimulated by his work on *Dialogues in Search of a Path*. "It went off just as fast as I could write it," he later recalled; it was "almost the last time where writing just took care of itself." Still, he was unable to finish what he had started. With the beginning of classes that fall, he consigned his manuscript—an assortment of rough drafts, outlines, and notes—to a drawer, where it would gather dust for more than twenty years. Why Harry abandoned so promising an undertaking is not readily explained. He may have recognized that the work lacked dramatic interest. However heady the play of its ideas, *Dialogues in Search of a Path* was no novel. Virtually without plot or depth of characterization, it had unfolded as a series of monologues loosely organized around the subject of Western (or American) Civilization. The audience for such writing was certainly not large. It is also perhaps telling that Harry set the manuscript aside just as the chapter on dyadic love began to shape itself in his hands. Was it a case of his shrinking yet again from disclosures about his personal life? Possibly so.

Such constraints were evidently much less binding in 1974, when he was struck with the idea of reviving the project. Jo was now safely beyond hurt, and the dyad, viewed in the aftermath of the 1960s, had little about it to shock or surprise. Indeed, it may have occurred to Harry that he and Christiana, like the speaker in Donne's "Canonization," had earned a place among the forerunners of love's bold new "pattern." He was also mindful, it appears, of the literary shortcomings of the work. For in weighing its potential for publication, he at once recognized his need for expert assistance. He wrote, therefore, to John Parke, a skilled essayist, poet, editor, and an old friend with whom he had in years gone by shared both his passion for Melville and the secret of the dyad. Complaining of his "10 half-finished books" and "a senescent brain," Harry outlined the story—now tentatively entitled *Options*—and offered to pay for help in bringing it to completion. Parke agreed to the arrangement and set to work, reading what Harry sent to him and developing ideas for chapters on the likes of R. D. Laing, Thomas Merton, Mother Teresa, Timothy Leary, and others. But even as Parke gathered momentum in the work, his collaborator began to waver. In July Harry expressed disappointment at the discovery that none of his original chapters was "anywhere near finished." Worse, he was strapped for time until the summer of 1975. Still, he encouraged Parke to "experiment with a dialogue or two—at the rate of $10 an hour up to 2 Grand." But the signs were even more ominous a month later, when Harry wrote that he would not be able to make much headway on the project until 1977. By October he had decided that very few of the original chapters were "of real interest and relevance today." He was ready to give up. Harry was 81. He was tired. *Options* needed more time and energy than he could summon. Parke was good, but it would not do for him to carry the entire load himself. And so they settled their accounts, and *Options* went back in the drawer to stay.

Harry was defeated by time, self-doubt, and inexperience in the art of fiction. He was also mindful that the level of discourse he most enjoyed, and the social and political transformations he sought to advance, were remote from the real standards and expectations of his countrymen. In matters of beauty, creativity, cooperation, and peace he expected too much. This was brought home to him quite painfully during the 1960s and early 70s, when the rebellion of the nation's young people gave a new edge to his disenchantment. "To-day—when reverence is at its lowest ebb," he wrote to Lewis Mumford in 1967, "the USA is fast becoming a breeding ground of young emancipated criminals—freedom *ad absurdum.*" He made the same point a year later, in his interview for *Psychology Today.* "You could regard these explosions as one of the countless symptoms of the breakup of Western culture," he observed gravely. "Anarchy may get rid of a lot of the objectionable impediments to freedom, but it doesn't *create* anything." Harry found something to applaud in the widespread clamoring for sexual liberation. "Here," he acknowledged, "the hippies have a message for us." But he hastened to add that "the love-ins are outnumbered by the hate-ins, and America is becoming a breeding ground of killers." Though he was firmly opposed to the war in Vietnam and supportive of demonstrations against it, he had no patience with the occupation of university buildings. That, he felt, was "stupid and unjustified." In his review of Lewis Feuer's *The Conflict of Generations: The Character and Significance of Student Movements,* Harry approvingly summarized "the author's major conclusion, or message: all full-fledged student uprisings end disastrously." Though he drew back from the sweeping Oedipal bent of Feuer's analysis, Harry was quick to acknowledge an alignment between the book's general drift and his own sense that American universities were verging toward "a giant plunge into the educational abyss of another Dark Age." "I have spent lots of time thinking about possible ways of stemming the tide," he wrote to Alvan Barach; "but I don't go round preaching, because, for one thing, I am too happy with Nina."

Harry's mood of disenchantment with the course of American life lifted only slightly during his last years. To be sure, he shared the general sense of relief when the war finally ended. But he was dismayed at its terrible costs in life and spirit and at the ignominious finale of Richard Nixon. The subsequent advent of Ronald Reagan—"the apotheosis of silver-screen reality"—only confirmed his sense that there was something fundamentally awry in the culture. But blessed as he was by the "sanguine surplus," Harry was constitutionally immune to prolonged depression. He was right, too— Nina gave added lift to his native buoyancy. Thus spared the dark, suffocating melancholy that overtook Melville in his later life, Harry was also spared the irony of becoming himself what he could not abide in the novelist. It is for this reason, among others, that his interest in Melville lost none of its edge as he settled into old age. Harry continued to give amply of his time, money, and knowledge to the Melville Society, where he was properly venerated both as a scholar and as a leading figure in the Melville revival of the 1920s. He was equally dedicated to the Melville Room, which had grown up under his care at the Berkshire Athenaeum in Pittsfield, Massachusetts. In recognition of his eminence in the field, the 1985 PBS documentary on Melville's life and work, *Damned in Paradise,* was dedicated to Harry. The director of the film, Robert D. Squier, took him up in a helicopter over Pittsfield for a bird's-eye view of Melville country. Harry is one of several expert commentators featured in the production. He appears at numerous intervals—once without his false teeth—to reflect on the novelist's personality and achievements.

Harry's research and writing on Melville fared less well. Though he labored intermittently on the novelist's early life—*Melville in the Making,* as he referred to it in 1973—he was unable to improve significantly on what he had written more than thirty years before. "I think I am approaching the end of everything I once thought I had to say," he wrote to his old nemesis, Jay Leyda. This was, characteristically, to confuse biographical facts with critical commentary. Of the latter, Harry left great riches unpublished. As to the former, he worked until the end of his life on what he called the Melville "Morsels," brief snatches of information and insight that he wanted to add to the scholarly record. One such "Morsel," entitled "Allan Melvill's By-Blow," co-authored with Harvey Meyerson and Eugene Taylor and published in the *Melville Society Extracts,* sheds valuable light on the biographical background to the suggestion—in *Pierre*—that Melville had an illegitimate half-sister. This was much the most substantial of Harry's late publications, and it would be the last of any real significance.

Beginning with the American Psychological Association's Distinguished Scientific Contribution Award, which was conferred in 1961, the recognition and celebration of Harry's achievements came thick and fast during the last quarter-century of his life. A 1963 gathering in Philadelphia to celebrate his seventieth birthday—along with the twenty-fifth anniversary of the publication of *Explorations*—was the most memorable of numerous reunions. Old friends turned out in large numbers, and a Festschrift of enduring merit, *The Study of Lives,* was produced for the occasion. Harry was so delighted at the prospect of the party that he composed a volume of verse portraits—*Leaves of Green Memories*—in honor of his former students. He had a wonderful time. There was an APA symposium in honor of his eightieth birthday in 1973, another—on *Explorations*—in 1978, and a third, in Atlanta, ten years later. At the 1978 meeting the Henry A. Murray Award for achievement in personology was established. That same year the first of the Henry A. Murray Lectures in Personality were held at Michigan State University. In 1981, at the APA meeting in Los Angeles, a distinguished panel of former students offered new elaborations on Harry's personological system. A year later, the first annual meeting of the Society for Personology, coordinated by Rae Carlson and inspired by Harry's contributions to the field, was held at Princeton.

Lawrence College granted Harry the first of his honorary degrees in 1964. Others followed, from the University of Louvain in 1966, the University of Oslo in 1969, Kent State University in 1971, and Adelphi University in 1973. Harry was inclined to make light of such awards, though it gave him pleasure to observe that his work on Melville figured prominently in their conferral. He was a long-time member of the American Academy of Arts and Sciences, the recipient of a Gold Medal Award from the American Psychological Foundation, and a Fellow of the American Association for the Advancement of Science. He was also recognized for his achievements by the Society for Projective Techniques, the Massachusetts Psychological Association, and Columbia University. In 1979, thanks in good part to the prodding of Radcliffe President Matina Horner, Harry agreed that the Radcliffe Data Resource and Research Center might be renamed in his honor. A locus for the multidisciplinary study of the life experiences of American women, the Henry A. Murray Research Center is dedicated to scholarship in the tradition of *Explorations in Personality.* Harry's intellectual legacy is also well represented in *Endeavors in Psychology,* a copious selection of his most important writing, very ably edited by Edwin Shneidman. Meanwhile, commentary on the life and work, taking rise from the chapter on "Murray's Personology" in Hall and Lindzey's influential *Theories of Personality,* has steadily accumulated.

It was the price of his great longevity that Harry witnessed the passing of many good friends. Jung died in 1961. His "life and works have given all mankind multiple causes for wonder, gratitude, and homage," Harry wrote. For Felix Frankfurter, who succumbed four years later, he observed that the transcendent had little attraction. "For him, the magnetism has resided in the stuff of the ideal incarnate in human character, in the very best that operates in man, especially when stretched and tested in face-to-face engagements here and now." Gordon Allport died in 1967, as did Frances Wickes, a good friend over the years to both Harry and Christiana. Harry remembered Frances as "one of numerous gifted, 'Delphic' Women for whom Jung's personified abstractions, his metaphorical and mythic modes of speech, were wholly captivating." Conrad Aiken followed in 1973, Carl Binger in 1976, loyal Alvan Barach a year later, and Edward ("Ned") Handy in 1980.

Harry died just a few weeks after his ninety-fifth birthday. Among the old friends of his own generation, only Lewis Mumford survived him. Though he bore up under the discomfort of emphysema and sciatica for many years, Harry's health was tolerably stable until late in 1978, when a massive stroke laid him low. Recovery was slow and painful. His appetite failed—"that fine chiseled face sharpening as he eats less and less," Nina wrote—and he was prone to dangerous falls. His mind wandered over the past; dark rages alternated with periods of genial sociability. But by the following April he was alert between regular naps, talkative, able to get around on a cane. His condition stabilized at that level—sometimes a little better, sometimes a little worse—for the next several years. Harry bridled resentfully at his decrepitude; Nina held on.

The pitch of Harry's decline grew steeper during the first months of 1988. Robert Penn Warren, a warm friend in later years, wrote to say goodbye. "Damn it, why didn't I (we) know you all many years earlier," he groused. Brewster Smith was also moved to make a grateful farewell. "More than any other psychologist I have known," he reflected, "you have shown us—shown me—the excitement of what human psychology can be at its best." Still, rather cruelly, life lingered. "He is just bones, hasn't eaten for two months, is bleeding heavily from the kidneys, has horrid bed sores, congestive heart failure, etc. etc.," Nina wrote. "He is just about incomprehensible and in far away worlds all the time. Yet he *does* go on . . . and on . . . and on." Harry was certainly willing to be done with life, though never to the point of losing his sense of humor. "I am dead," he announced to his nurse. "No," she replied, pinching him gently on the cheek; "see, you're alive." "I'm the doctor," Harry snapped back, not without the hint of a smile— "I'm the doctor; you're the nurse; and I'm dead." Just days later, on Thursday, June 23, he had his way.

▼

chapter thirteen

The Case of Murr

"He was undoubtedly one of the outstanding psychologists of his time," ventured Robert Holt in a *New York Times* article marking Harry's death. "He was one of a small number of leading theorists in the study of personality, and his work was known worldwide to psychologists and psychiatrists." The *Boston Globe* obituary, featuring comments by Edwin Shneidman, was equally laudatory. "He was the most important American psychologist alive," Shneidman observed. Praise of a more personal cast was heard at Harvard's Memorial Church on October 3, 1988, when a large audience gathered in celebration of Harry's life. He was "as remarkable a human being as any of us are likely to know in our time here," observed Howard Gardner, a close friend and human development specialist at Harvard. "This measurer of men and women was himself one who set standards by which men and women will be measured for many years. His strength, his humor, his wisdom, his graciousness, his generosity, his charisma were equaled by few, and the propitious combination of these traits by none that I have encountered. Even in death, Harry remains larger than life."

Many of those closest to Harry ranked charisma and charm among his leading qualities. "He has a tremendous . . . romantic charm that nobody can deny," declared Harvard psychologist David McClelland. "When Harry Murray enters a room," observed his old friend Hiram Haydn, "there may be a man or two so intent on someone else (or on himself) that he does not notice the arrival. I have as yet to see a woman fail to look up." Haydn evokes vividly a morning in Washington when he "came into the lobby of a hotel to find [Harry] awaiting a cab. There he stood, legs spread, hands on hips, snap-brimmed hat tilted back, confronting the world." The humanistic psychologist Rollo May was impressed with the effortless regality of his friend's bearing. "He always struck me as born into royalty," May confessed. Councilman Morgan, who saw Harry first and foremost as a rival—"we were engaged in a fierce competition for the affections of my mother"—remembered his old foe as "a master manipulator" who could "charm you to death." Harry was brilliant in conversation; he was engaging, witty, penetrating, a fund of insight and information. He loved to laugh, and at all registers, from the furtive chuckle to an expansive guffaw. He was also a great listener; you came away from an encounter with Harry feeling full and satisfied, at the top of your personal form. He was notably tender with patients and with those in distress, especially women. His qualities as a leader were widely acclaimed, perhaps most vigorously by those who worked at his side during the 1930s and 40s. True, he had a reputation for cooling off on people after warm initial encounters. He was too busy or too distracted to follow up; he lost interest; he had more prospective friends than he could possibly please. He was also possessed, as Harvard's literature scholar Daniel Aaron observed, "of a certain fastidious reserve, a distaste not for the earthy and common (quite the contrary) but what might be described rather as a vulgarity of spirit. His response to persons he called 'fools' was rather like Henry James's. That is to say, he faulted them not so much for their silliness but because of their insensitiveness to human vibrations, their want of tact, their inability to enter imaginatively into another's mind—to love."

Harry's zest was legendary. Kenneth Keniston judged his old mentor "the most imaginative and creative person I've ever known." David Ricks concurred, ranking Harry as "the most creative of the psychologists who studied creativity." His prodigious playfulness of mind lost none of its brilliance in later life. "This is an impish man," wrote Nathan Cobb, a reporter for the *Boston Globe* who interviewed Harry just after his ninetieth birthday. Zest had its correlative—its source, one might argue—in the vast breadth of his interests. Describing Harry as "a Renaissance man" and "a legendary figure," psychologist Joseph Adelson highlights "the protean nature of his talents and achievements. He has been . . . an athlete, an undergraduate student of history, a playboy, a physician, a surgeon, an embryologist, an anatomist, an orthodox psychoanalyst, an unorthodox psychoanalyst, the co-inventor of the Thematic Apperception Test, the director of Harvard's Psychological Clinic, one of the fathers of the experimental study of personality, our Government's chief selector of undercover agents during World War II, the prime developer of complex assessment methods in the study of personality, an adoring student and scholar of the life and works of Herman Melville." And consider that Adelson knew nothing of Harry's co-partnership—for more than forty years—in the dyad! Nor does the list, however impressive, properly convey the potent synergy between the diverse elements in Harry's makeup. "The most striking thing about Henry A. Murray's thought as a psychologist," argues Leo McNamara, "is not that he was a student of history turned physician and surgeon turned anatomist-physiologist-biologist-embryologist turned psychologist, but that he turned from none of these without taking with him what was of value for the next endeavor. . . . Nothing needful was lost or thrown away; all was shaped to the new task."

It was this rich diversity that stood out in Harry's personal and intellectual profile. He was a scientist, a humanist, an aristocrat, a rebel, a deep diver, a sage, a lover. He spoke with equally great authority against "scientism" in psychology, for Melville's preeminence in American literature, and about such matters as mythology and comparative religion, evolution, the need for world government, and the history, present condition, and future prospects of dyadic love. Harry carried his vast learning with grace and humility. Quite obviously, he was not exempt from selfishness, self-delusion, and other varieties of human folly. Yet these were finally integral to his wisdom. It was one part of Harry's calling to rescue psychology from those so dazzled by science as to lose sight of the "merely" human. He won that point most emphatically in *Explorations in Personality,* his myriad, ambitious, irreverent, stylish masterpiece. Here, in the light cast by Prince, Jung, Whitehead, Henderson, and Freud, guided by bold interdisciplinary principles, equipped with a stunning array of innovative techniques, and in an abundant literary language like nothing in American psychology since James, he made his most indelible mark on the field. *Explorations,* as Edwin Shneidman has insisted, is Harry's *Moby-Dick.* It is one of a small handful of giant books in American psychology. Take it away, and its author is a relatively minor figure in the annals of the discipline.

American psychologists are inclined to view the century-long history of their field as a struggle between the scientists—the experimentalists, quantifiers, and behaviorists—on one side and the humanists and philosophers on the other. The first group is most familiarly represented by Wilhelm Wundt, Edward Titchener, John B. Watson, and—at Harvard—by Münsterberg, Boring, Lashley, Stevens, and Skinner; the second by the likes of Freud, Jung, Adler, and, in this country, by Prince, McDougall, Allport, Murray, Erikson, and others. Of course the preeminent American in this latter category is William James, whose *Principles of Psychology,* first published in 1890, was a kind of Bible for those determined to keep the complex interior experience of the individual at the center of attention. Theirs has been an uphill battle, especially within the university, where the hegemony of science and the pressure to produce publishable results in rapid order have been obstacles to research in the style of *Explorations.* Harry had the energy and the determination, the brilliance, the charisma, and the financial independence to keep the Clinic afloat in a hostile institutional environment. But he was an inspired maverick in what has remained a maverick branch of psychology; and there have been none quite like him since.

The close likeness between William James and Henry Murray has been noted by many but never more fully or persuasively than by Howard Gardner, one of the speakers at the memorial service in 1988. "Both men," Gardner observed, "were New Yorkers, trained as physicians, attracted initially to physiology and the 'tough minded sciences,' but finding psychology increasingly compelling as they neared middle age. Both had a strong attraction to literature, which colored not only their writing styles but also the topics

374

that piqued their interest. Both dared to range over the full terrain of the human condition, refusing to be restricted or pigeon-holed by a single method, principle, or field. Not surprisingly, both were a trifle impatient with their narrower colleagues. Perhaps most important," Gardner continued, "both men sensed that the center of psychology lay not in perception, not in sensation, not even in cognitive processes—but in the individual self, will, and consciousness."

Harry of course recognized his kinship and common intellectual purpose with James. He recalls in "The Case of Murr" that as a newcomer to the Harvard faculty he was shocked to find "the majority of academic psychologists . . . militantly engaged in a competitive endeavor to mold psychology in the image of physics." Harry was natural scientist enough to know that what interested him about human beings—their elusive interior lives—might not be susceptible to precise measurement. Something more—imagination, empathy, expressive language—was requisite to meeting the challenge. Almost inevitably, William James became one of Harry's "major exemplars" during this period of trial, and he "found himself agreeing with almost everything his hero had to say—completely, for example, with the heretical statement that 'Individuality is founded in feeling; and the recesses of feeling, the darker, blinder strata of character, are the only places in the world in which we catch real fact in the making, and directly perceive how events happen and how work is actually done." This was a perilous creed at Harvard in the mid-1930s, with Conant at the helm, Boring in charge of the department, and Lashley—who believed that James had "done unparalleled harm to psychology"—just coming aboard.

Yet for all of his success in that struggle, Harry was never fully secure in his achievements. "This is one long confession of failure," he wrote on the copy of "Preparations for the Scaffold of a Comprehensive System" that he gave to Gordon Allport. To no small degree, he was being unfair to himself. It was the leading liability of Harry's style that ideas poured forth in defiance of closure. His was an abundant and exhilarating but often untidy habit of mind. He had no illusions on this score; indeed, he made a virtue of his own excess. "Nothing for Harry was ever finally done," remarked Edwin

375

Shneidman at the memorial service. "His major written contributions . . . were entitled explorations, preparations, scaffoldings, prolegomena. Harry's rule was that one can have only the latest clarifications, never the final one. Life, the world, the universe is an open system." Still, he went on chastising himself for his failure to accomplish the impossible. The contradiction, as Brewster Smith has observed, expressed the tension between the scientist and the humanist in Harry's intellectual makeup. "I suspect," Smith writes, "that Murray the ex-biochemist would have loved to have left as his legacy a system of needs and press, actones and themas, which would do for personality what Mendeleyev's periodic table did for 19th-century chemistry." Such an enterprise, he goes on, taking a position that Harry never quite accepted, "no longer makes sense."

This is not to suggest that Harry is likely to be forgotten. Even as he makes his point about "grand systems," Smith credits his old teacher and friend with having "essentially launched the modern psychology of personality." The study of individual lives is avidly pursued by scholars in this country and abroad, most visibly perhaps by the members of the Society for Personology. Granted, clinical research of the ambitious variety that produced *Explorations* has not been widely emulated. The Murray tradition in personality assessment, as it evolved in the OSS, flourished for years under the leadership of Donald MacKinnon at the Institute for Personality Assessment and Research (IPAR) at the University of California, Berkeley. Versions of the multiple measurement scheme have also been successfully adopted at centers within the business world. But Harry's style of "exploring personality the long way" (Robert White's apt characterization of the approach to research at the Clinic in the 1930s) has never been duplicated.

Still, the impress of Harry's achievements is prominently on display, not only in psychological circles but also in the field of literary studies, where his work on Melville is unsurpassed for its learning, critical penetration, and elegance. The TAT has been of enduring utility, both as a research tool and in clinical practice. The study of creativity has continued to reflect his influence; so has work on the interplay between mental and physiological events. Harry's emphasis on systems has retained its currency, as has his close attention to interactions between the individual and the environment. Kenneth Keniston has meanwhile spoken for numerous others in stressing "the personal side" of Harry's legacy. "He provided a model, a style, the possibility of in-depth" research on individuals. "He convinced a whole lot of people that this was really an interesting, valid, fruitful kind of study." It was not charm or charisma or force of personality alone that brought students and colleagues around to Harry's point of view. But knowing him personally, feeling his potent magnetism, observing his mind at play, made all the difference for many. Harry was parent to no single school of psychology; he was much too various for that. But for great numbers of students and admirers he was in himself the surest evidence that human nature—evolving, creative, various, mysterious—exceeded the measure of mere science.

The comparison with William James extends to a shared preoccupation with values, though in this domain Harry's concerns were surely the more urgent. Addressing the Harvard chapter of Phi Beta Kappa in 1959, he observed that Emerson—"that tall, angular, gentle, blue-eyed mystic, who saw evil at such a distance that he could dismiss it and condone it"—once spoke for most Americans on the subject of human nature. But the optimism of Man Thinking had withered up in the terrible heat of modern warfare—in "the blights and blasts," as Harry put it, "of more than forty lurid years of enormities and abominations." In such a world, he went on, "the darker vision of the once-rejected Herman Melville resonates with more veracity" than ever before. Likewise the chilling analysis of mankind advanced by Sigmund Freud, "who, on the question of innate, potential evil, concurred with St. Augustine," and who "marks the great divide that separates us irrevocably from the benign atmosphere of the untempted, unhurt, and unmolested sage of Concord." Freud dove deep into the unconscious, and he found there "what Puritan and Victorian morality suppressed as Sin, spelt with a captial." Time now, Harry admonished his auditors, to face squarely what Freud and two world wars had revealed—that humans, driven by powerful unconscious impulses, are "still capable of surpassing all other species as callous and ferocious torturers and killers of their own kind." We may of course ignore this "unflattering knowledge," but only at the price of failing to recognize "that the present degree and aim of certain of our dispositions and certain states and aims of our various societies are definitely out of date, unsuitable for survival. It looks to me," Harry concluded, "as if we must transform or fall apart."

That same year another concerned American, moved by the gravity of recent history "to re-examine the classic assumptions about the nature of politics and about the political character of human nature," arrived at strikingly similar conclusions. "The development of weapons of destruction makes our present dilemma plain," wrote Norman O. Brown, "we either come to terms with our unconscious instincts and drives—with life and with death—or else we surely die." Harry's social vision was neither as fully formed nor as widely broadcast as Brown's. But even had Harry's ideas found their way clearly and copiously into print, it is highly unlikely that his impact would have equaled Brown's, especially with young people. In its urgent, prophetic tone, its utopianism, its flight from science to the senses, from logic to intuition, from adult self-discipline to playful, infantile self-indulgence, in its rejection of history, culture, and all established authority in the name of human freedom, and in its clarion call to sexual liberation, *Life Against Death* perfectly anticipated the dominant mood of the so-called "sixties generation." Harry was by contrast quite imperfectly sympathetic with the ideas, aims, and methods of insurgent youth. Though in general alignment with Brown on most key issues, he was characteristically moderate where the younger man was inclined to "go all the way." Harry had his own quarrel with science, but he was hardly tempted to jettison what he considered a precious human resource. Nor did he share Brown's rage for "abolishing the reality-principle and its unreal distinction between public and private, between head and genital." Harry would have agreed that "freedom is poetry"; but it did not follow for him that "freedom is violence." And while he might well have acknowledged the element of truth in Brown's declaration that "all metaphors are sexual; a penis in every convex object and a vagina in every concave one," the formulation would have struck him as extreme. It smacked of Freud's pansexualism, and for that it left too much of the human out.

Harry was at least outwardly more upbeat and optimistic than Brown. He regarded *Civilization and Its Discontents*—which directly informs *Life Against Death*—as excessive in its pessimism, and characterized his own approach to personality "as a health-oriented extension of, and complement to, the illness-oriented Freudian system." Nature, including human nature and culture, is inherently creative. Harry's emergent social vision entailed a major overhaul of inherited values; but it was evolution, and not revolution, that he had in mind. "The picture," he once declared, "is one of continuity through change." His was a vision of gradual human betterment, a process involving "cycles of creation, conservation, decay, or induration—tending, in the long run, toward the fulfillment of that dream of human fellowship which centuries of deep and loving people have recommended to our hearts." He was above all things impressed with the creative authority of the unconscious, though he did not share Brown's persuasion that "the boundary between sanity and insanity is a false one." Melville had crossed that line, and Harry thought better of following. A little chaos went a long way with him.

"The alternative to dualism is dialectics; that is to say, love." Brown wrote these words, though Harry could have. But love (Eros) for Brown strains instinctively against all boundaries, and seeks total union—or reunion—with the world. "We are all members of one body," he argues, "an androgynous or hermaphroditic body, containing both sexes." The *principium individuationis* is likewise illusory in the matter of minds. "Since the true psychic reality is the unconscious," we read in *Love's Body*, "the true psychic reality is collective; there is only one psyche, a general possession of mankind." The solution to "the problem of identity," it follows, is to "get lost." Brown's construction of Eros, featuring the dissolution of difference in all-consuming union, though attractive to many in the 1960s and after, did not describe love as Harry understood it. His was a biological model, with an emphasis on mergings in the midst of multiplicity, on new and creative combinations of separate, distinct entities. Harry had no craving to abolish difference; he was too much in love with variety and originality for that. "Evolutionary love" on his plan bore with it the obligation to "embrace the opposite." This rule had a wide application, "to opposing groups and nations, and to opposing theories and ideologies, just as well as to opposing individuals." Thus in "Unprecedented Evolutions" he lays stress on what he calls "synthesism"—"the production and continuation of a synthesis (combination, creation, integration, union, federation, procession of developing reciprocities or trans-actions) particularly of opposites (positive and negative, male and female, contrary or antagonistic entities, groups or principles)."

Here, then, by contrast with Brown's cosmic body, dwelling un-consciously, out of history, in the timeless gratification of its poly-morphous sexual instincts, was a world of numberless contending forces, individual personalities among them, merging in new com-binations, growing, dying away, processing creatively through time. "Synthesism" is most easily defined, Harry observes, "when it refers to the formation and perpetuation of a *dyadic system,* that is, a unity of *two* interacting and in some ways antithetical compo-nents." In its application to the larger public arena of the 1960s, synthesism bore with it the implication that the antagonists in the Cold War, and the parties to the equally bitter domestic feud over the justice of American involvement in Vietnam, should give much less of their energy to defending narrow points of view and much more to finding solutions to their differences. Habituation on all sides to rigid, pseudo-rational oppositions of right and wrong, good and evil, formed an obstacle to empathic, cross-cultural under-standing.

The admonition to "embrace the opposite" stood little chance of being heard or heeded in a political climate of unbending moral dualisms. Harry drew attention to this grave fact of life in his Phi Beta Kappa Oration and in other essays of the period. Yet he was not as vigorous as he might have been in presenting his counsel— the distillation of his views on myth, creative evolution, dyadic interactions, and world government—to an embattled humanity. Advancing years and increasing difficulty with writing were factors here; so were the deaths of Jo and Christiana and the much happier distractions of new love. But Harry was also unsure of his own best solution to the world's problems. That solution had its foundation, after all, in the dyad, the most rudimentary of social units. Harry staked his hopes for the future of the race on a proliferation of sharing, zestful, procreative adult pairs. In attempting to define "the highest ideal for our time," he settled on "sexual love, sexual conjugation, pregnancy, and deliverance" as "the very best paradigm." The model dyad "proceeds like the Hegelian dialectic," he wrote; "the male thesis embraces the female antithesis, and the result is genetic synthesis and the development of a new and unique being." Or so he claimed in his essay, "Two Versions of Man," published in 1960. "Mutual erotic love, erotic adoration," he insisted, thinking of the dyad, "is the most natural religion." Harry believed what he said, of course; he had grounded his entire adult life in the creative authority of dyadic love. And yet in some way he knew better; he recognized, without quite saying so, that the dyad—his own experiment in "mutual erotic love, erotic adoration"—had not in fact been a model for mankind. That recognition registers obliquely in Harry's half-hearted advocacy of his professed social ideal.

Harry knew from personal experience that theories about the nature of reality reflect the private, frequently unacknowledged, often unconscious wishes and impulses of those who construct them. It followed in his view that theorists should give attention to "the distorting operation of their own preferences and ambitions." It was precisely because of his "conviction" on this score that Harry took pains—as he explains in "Preparations for the Scaffold of a Comprehensive System"—"to expose my inborn and acquired bents and biases, rather than to make a great to-do about my exemplary scientific objectivity." Such reflections are entirely relevant to an understanding of Harry's social theory, which expresses in an oblique way his frustrated dyadic ideal. The link between the public and private was hardly lost on him, though he was not finally willing to expose his intimate "bents and biases" in the matter. Still, Harry did what he could to abide by the spirit of his advice to theorists. "Vicissitudes of Creativity" describes the dyad at one remove. And "The Case of Murr" may be read—most directly in those sections dealing with childhood—as an oblique analysis of what went wrong between Harry and Christiana. Basically, it was his mother, Fannie's fault. Her refusal of nurture and affection produced an answering independence in her son, who as an adult gave more of his time and energy to ideas than to the emotional needs of those close to him. The dyad failed, in short, because Harry's head prevailed over his undernourished heart.

In the very brevity and obliqueness of his account, Harry seems to invite skepticism; there is much more to the story, he suggests. Still, the commentary is telling, both for its indirect acknowledgment that a problem existed and for the signs of willingness to shoulder some of the blame. Withal, it is a characteristically ambiguous gesture—as ambiguous, say, as Harry's Postscript to the *Vision Seminars,* in which he concedes that his relationship to Christiana was "personal" (in what precise sense he does not say) and suggests that "love" (for whom it is not clear) figured in her decision to cooperate with Jung in his "search for truth." Or as mingled as his disposition toward the dyad after Christiana's death. On one side, he was keen to have the visions published, and he made substantial contributions to the maintenance of the Tower; on the other, he consigned the dyadic narrative, *What Joy!,* to the trash.

Harry's ambivalence toward Christiana was there from the beginning, and it ran deep. He lived in his mind, she in her body; he craved zestful thought more than sexual passion. Christiana ridiculed him for being guilt-ridden and repressed. The pleasures of the body, Harry had learned early in his life, were an invitation to sin, sickness, and death. Desire was thus geared to the idea of degradation. Christiana aroused Harry, where Jo did not, because of her wanton allure; her demeanor hinted rather openly at a taste for dissipation. It followed in love's logic that women—especially desirable women—needed saving, that the approach to true union ran in cycles of conflict and crisis leading to healing resolution administered by Harry. The evidence of suffering triggered desire, which moved in step with compassion. The pattern is clear in Harry's "really astonishing" dream of his mother, reduced to helplessness in his arms; it persisted variously in his marriage and in a lifetime's quarreling with his sister, Virginia, whom he first subdued when he was 9. Alice Henry, fallen, pitiful, and doomed, was the dark precursor to the quintessence of the erotic type, Christiana herself, whose need for suffering was apparently commensurate with Harry's need to feel pity. She was at once fit object of desire and disgust.

Witness her role in "Clinicus," Harry's play for the triumphant year-end party at Plympton Street in 1937. Christiana is Queen Morganatic, by name designated an inferior to her regal mate, by characterization a lusty, boozy, rather worn veteran of the amorous wars. She is a figure conjured up out of extremes of attraction and repulsion. Little wonder that Harry and Christiana settled into a fixed pattern of alternating crisis and resolution; little wonder, really, that they ended as they did—Christiana drunk and desperate, Harry drawn back in reproach.

Once again, this is to exaggerate, to isolate the dark strands in what was, it should be obvious, a complex, durable fabric. It is to highlight what went wrong in the dyad, most especially in the later years, when the waning of youth and passion threw dominant tensions out of balance. No doubt, there were seasons of disenchantment, seeming betrayal, and remorse; but there was an abundance as well of love, laughter, and creativity. There was nothing safe about the dyad; but nothing dull, either. It was conceived along high romantic lines. Harry and Christiana experienced one another as archetypal figures out of literature and myth; he was Mansol, Siegfried, Pierre, she was Wona, Brunhilde, Isabel. Dante and Shakespeare, Goethe and Byron, Wagner and Melville were the life-breath of their union. The costumes and rituals, the Tower, the codes and records and proliferating symbols, the furtive trysts, the deep diving, the fascination with madness, the plangent partings and ecstatic reunions, the overriding sense of religious mission, the pervasive embracements of fate, and the inevitable descent to a tragic denouement—here was life and love on the grand Olympian scale. It was folly, of course; but what a ride!

From the beginning Harry and Christiana took to tragic models. She was drawn as an adolescent to Dante's *Inferno;* he could not get enough of *Moby-Dick.* They knew they were in for trouble; indeed, they cultivated trouble; they were, they saw, each other's best trouble. That was the point, after all—to blaze like Icarus above the mortal shallows. They had no illusions about the trouble in Jung—the hedging with morality, the narcissism, the grandiosity, the subordination of the anima—but it gave them little pause. On that long night during the summer of 1925 in St-Jean-de-Luz, when they went back and forth about "the devious-cruising *Rachel*," it was Christiana who took Ahab's part. Be a man, she urged; leave wife and child behind; embrace your fate and accept the guilt that goes with it. She was surely the bolder of the two. It was her own fate, she had decided, to be torn; that was inevitable. She was strong in the face of Will's death, and Ike's, and Billy's, and Ralph's. Harry gave more thought than she did to De Rougement's linking of passion, narcissism, and destruction. Christiana moved through her life as through a journey of some lofty and tragic but obscure design. The visions moved her greatly, but never to sense; that was Mansol's business.

All of which attracted Harry. Christiana liberated his libido, nerved his resistance to guilt, ennobled his narcissism, and at the same time amply vindicated his countering impulse to draw back from the surfeit of sinful self-indulgence. The dyad made it easy to have things both ways. Christiana's visions were at once a gateway to wisdom and an errand into insanity. Just so, Melville was a model of heroic resistance to the repressive tyranny of conscience and Christianity but also an example of the woe that comes to those who deviate too strenuously from the norm. The dyad was at first premised on the scornful rejection of traditional domestic arrangements; later on it served as a blueprint for "that period of life," as Harry wrote in the late 1950s, "when a man and woman participate in the formation . . . of a home, of offspring, and of a new family culture." Harry was hardly deceived in such contradictions. He had no more illusions about consistency than he had pretensions to objectivity. Nor did he romanticize "the distorting operation" of his buried "preferences and ambitions." His adult burden of guilt—for Jo and Will and Christiana and Josephine and all the others—was heavy tribute to the hidden tides of his nature. "The Case of Murr" was at first entitled "Narcism Re-exhibited." That essay, we have observed, is among other things a kind of oblique grappling with Harry's failures in love. He recognized, it goes almost without saying, that any attempt to represent the dyad would be a fiction, just as he recognized, and emphasized, that his autobiography was a semific-tional narrative about a fellow named "Murr." This was acknowledgment on one side of the profound immersion of his life and personal identity in literature. He was almost literally "made" out of books. But it was also to concede that objectivity had little part in personal renderings of the self and beloved others. All such accounts, he would have argued, are fabrications—not baseless, to be sure, but constructions subject to myriad distortions.

In the Prologue to "The Case of Murr" Harry gives attention to the "sanguine surplus," his tendency to envisage "every new, appealing undertaking in the most voluminous dimensions, huge and teeming with every possibility of adventure and achievement." As a curb on this expansive disposition, he invokes "the corrective maxim: limitation of aim is the secret of success" and resolves that "the functionally autonomous governor of my conscious ego system (the little self)" will "ostracize theory and the sanguine surplus (from the larger Self)." But such good intentions come to naught, primarily because Fannie Babcock Murray expands outward from the center of her son's narrative, dominating his interpretive focus and disturbing the balance of his presentation. Quite in spite of the corrective maxim, Fannie steals the show and thereby prompts Harry to concede that "there was more functional autonomy in the Self than in the self: the legs of the portrait came out too long and lanky, the belly of childhood memories was too bloated, and I had hardly stretched above the eyebrows when I found myself simultaneously at both the ordained space limit and the time limit. Down came the blade of the editor's guillotine, and my last section, the forehead and crown of the portrait, which contained whatever retrospective bits of wit and wisdom Murr could muster, rolled into the basket with a thud." The concluding figure of the conscious ego, the head, being overpowered by the rebellious, unconscious Self is wonderfully telling. The image has its general frame of reference in the history of the French Revolution. But it is more specifically an allusion to Nathaniel Hawthorne's account, in "the Custom-House" chapter prefatory to *The Scarlet Letter,* of being removed from his post as Salem Surveyor of Customs in 1848, when Zachary Taylor and the Whigs took over from the Democrats. "My own head was the first that fell!" Hawthorne complains. "Keeping up the meta-

385

phor of the political guillotine," he goes on to compare his subsequent literary exertions, including *The Scarlet Letter,* as the "Posthumous Papers of a Decapitated Surveyor."

Harry was closely familiar with Hawthorne's works, and there can be little doubt that he had "The Custom-House" in mind as he brought "The Case of Murr" to a close. At the level most available to scrutiny, his identification with Hawthorne was grounded in a shared inclination to conceive of individual identity as an unstable fabrication. Hawthorne labors the image of himself in his "decapitated state," only then to emphasize that it is a fiction ("like Irving's Headless Horseman"), and to contrast this "figurative self" with "the real human being . . . with his head safely on his shoulders, [who] had brought himself to the comfortable conclusion, that everything was for the best." Such maneuvers have the net result of eroding rather than reinforcing the distinction between the imagined and the actual. Hawthorne's self, as *The Scarlet Letter* well illustrates, is no more substantial or real than the selves of the manifestly fictional characters with which it keeps company in the novel. "The Case of Murr," with its comical array of large and small selves, its mockery of pretensions to scientific objectivity in the study of lives, and its constant reminders that "Murr" is a fiction by Henry A. Murray, has a similar point to make.

But the connection with Hawthorne goes deeper still. "Be true! Be true! Be true!" the novelist exclaims in the Conclusion to *The Scarlet Letter.* "Show freely to the world, if not your worst, yet some trait whereby the worst may be inferred!" As Harry understood it, Hawthorne's "worst," his remote coolness of heart, could be traced back to his mother's withdrawal of affection at the time of her husband's death, when her son was just a child of four. The adult novelist's notorious aversion to intimacy, his chilling detachment, his resistance to Melville's passionate appeal for friendship, and his artistic preoccupation with "the unpardonable sin" of indifference to the claims of the human heart—all of these had their deep source, according to Harry, in traumatic maternal betrayal. "Having your mother turn you away like that," he once remarked of Hawthorne's experience, "might ruin your life." But if it was mother who decapitated the Salem surveyor, then just as surely it was mother who separated Murr's heart from his head and thereby shaped long in advance the emotional idiosyncrasies that would later cripple him in love. When it came to Jo and Will and the others, but most importantly when it came to Christiana, Harry could not help himself. Or so the story goes.

If we balk at this account, it is because we are meant to. For it is integral to the meaning of "The Case of Murr" that Harry is in control even when he most protests that he is not. Thus the acquittal, because it is so manifestly a fabrication, is also a kind of reindictment. Fannie made her son what he is; but, just as obviously, the son constructs the portrait of his mother with his own moral vindication deeply in mind. More generally, "The Case of Murr" may be read—as *The Scarlet Letter* may be read—as a dramatization of just that doubling impulse to acknowledge one's guilty failings, and at the same time to argue them away, that Harry's characterization of his mother betrays. Hawthorne had a different, much graver story to tell; he shared Harry's penchant for tragic themes but enjoyed little of his sanguine buoyancy—perhaps because it never occurred to him that the fault for his shortcomings might be laid at his mother's door. Still, it is the all-important link between the two that they recognized their narcissistic urge to show their "worst" to the world as a call to fiction-making in the face of impenetrable mystery. They were both fixed by that most consuming of riddles—themselves. Like Hawthorne and Melville before him, Harry was a brilliant explorer of personality who believed—largely as the result of his own prolonged self-scrutiny—that individual identity is best caught and represented in the shifting terms and tone and tempo of its own ongoing self-invention. Thus, in "The Case of Murr" he advances contradictory constructions of his own behavior, yet clearly implies that he is bound by neither. The truth of the matter, he suggests, is in no single point of view but rather in the exuberant play of mind between multiple perspectives, in the zestful and unending process by which he fabricates and refabricates himself.

But of course the idea of personality as process, as a series of shifting negotiations, was itself a construction, an "interested" choice among multiple options. It was an especially happy choice for a man of strong conscience like Harry—or like Hawthorne—who wanted above all else to avoid getting cornered with his dogged sense of guilt. The trade-off, at least potentially, was to suffer the anomie that comes with having so many selves as to have no self at all. Hence perhaps the fate of Melville's Narcissus, "who because he could not grasp the tormenting, mild image he saw in the fountain, plunged into it and was drowned." It was Ahab's heroism to be so singular; and it was Melville's immitigable woe. But Harry knew who he was, even as he allowed that he was many people. He came to the shimmering image in the fountain—"the ungraspable phantom of life," in Melville's description—as one self among many possible selves, to be invoked at need, or at worst endured, but not to die for. His way, he saw, was not for everyone. It was not Melville's way; nor, alas, was it Christiana's. She lived and died so absolutely "in" the tragic anima, her sole self. Harry, by contrast, was at liberty to invent and reinvent himself as will and circumstance seemed to require. This is not to suggest that he was an entirely free agent. It was imperative from early on that he achieve a workable balance between "the marrow of misery and melancholy" on one side and his "sanguine and expansive buoyancy" on the other. And there was dread conscience to deal with. Guilt was never far from the foreground of consciousness, though Harry managed—by means eminently on display in "The Case of Murr"—to hold it at bay.

Harry's mind was irrepressibly—one is tempted to say constitutionally—active and playful. It was the great advantage of his élan that he was able to inhabit many roles, to live numerous lives, but to spring free of the "worst" in all of them. He was blessed in this, and he knew it, as the long, concluding sentence in "The Case of Murr" makes clear. Reiterating the distinction between "Murr and myself, the viewed and the viewer," Harry comes back to a "residual query" about the painful eye operation that his mother lured him into when he was still a boy. "Would I not have been capable of contributing more substantially to my profession," he asks, "if that eminent ophthalmologist had left my right eye focusing on something just beyond my nose which I could seize and scientifically contain in the hollow of one hand, instead of allowing his own sanguine surplus to take hold of his scalpel and send me off with a right eye that was bound to wander, joyfully but wastefully, beyond the standard circumference of healthy vision?" Would it have been better to rest comfortably at the breast, with nourishment and a stable reality securely in view? Or wasn't it after all a happier fate to have endured the fragmentation of self and world that came with rejection but that opened the way to a wonderful, wall-eyed revel in contradiction? "The Case of Murr" is not so much an argument for the latter condition as it is a dramatization of how such a state of mind might express itself. Harry plays brilliantly at playing. Christiana and the dyad are obliquely but unequivocally affirmed; Fannie is forgiven; so, himself, is Harry. He looks on, as we do, absorbed, admiring, warmly acquiescent in the bright face he bends to the world.

Notes

For permission to cite and quote from materials in their collections, I am grateful to the Harvard University Archives, The Special Collections Library at the University of Pennsylvania, the UCLA Department of Special Collections, and the Rockefeller Archive Center. Unless otherwise indicated, all cited materials are to be found among Harry's papers at the Harvard University Archives. For convenience, I have abbreviated Henry A. Murray (HAM) and Christiana Drummond Morgan (CDM).

1. Loomings

Page

1 "grateful to all of us." Sir John Bland-Sutton to HAM, 19 December 1924. Bland-Sutton was very distinguished. Born in 1855 of humble origins, he was knighted in 1912 and created a baronet in 1925. He rose to great eminence in medicine and served as president of the Royal College of Surgeons from 1923 to 1926. He died in 1936.

2 "unheralded American novelist." Melville's regard for "the great Hunter" and the anatomist's place in *Moby-Dick* are well documented in Howard P. Vincent's *The Trying-Out of Moby-Dick* (Boston: Houghton Mifflin, 1949), pp. 218–219, 252–253, and 294–295.

— "shock of recognition." The passage from "Hawthorne and His Mosses" appears in the Norton Critical Edition of *Moby-Dick,* ed. Harrison Hayford and Hershel Parker (New York: W. W. Norton & Co., 1967), p. 547.

— "surgical friend." This was Ned Haggart, who was rewarded with a full, colorful account of Captain Prothero's ordeal. He replied: "I am truly relieved that you have come to recognize the truly great quality of Moby Dick. I agree heartily with all your praises" (Ned Haggart to HAM, 15 October 1924).

391

— "rediscovery of Herman Melville." For a useful overview of the Melville revival, along with copious extracts from the early criticism, see *Moby-Dick as Doubloon,* ed. Hershel Parker and Harrison Hayford (New York: W. W. Norton & Co., 1970).

4 "threshold of his life's work." Murray's initial response to *Moby-Dick* is also amply described in his essay on Melville, "In Nomine Diaboli," *New England Quarterly,* 24 (1951), 435–452.

— *Pierre or, The Ambiguities,* ed. Henry A. Murray (New York: Hendricks House, 1949), p. xiii.

— "The book changed me." "In Nomine Diaboli," p. 437. He once declared that in reading the novel he was like Paul "on the road to Damascus" (interview with Robert Penn Warren, 3 August 1980).

5 "chance and the prepared mind." From an address Pasteur delivered at the University of Lille in 1854: "Dans les champs de l'observation le hasard ne favorise que les esprits préparés."

6 "plunged into it and was drowned." *Moby-Dick,* p. 14.

2. Call Me Harry

8 "for succeeding generations." *New York Times,* 15 September 1902, p. 1; "Henry A. Murray" (autobiography), in *A History of Psychology in Autobiography,* vol. 5 (New York: Appleton-Century Crofts, 1967), p. 296 (hereafter referred to as "The Case of Murr").

— "lived happily ever after." "The Case of Murr," p. 296.

9 "That counted, yes." Interviews with HAM, 27 March 1970 and 7 July 1972.

— "so far away." Interview with HAM, 31 March 1970.

10 "business, culture, and the state." Alan Trachtenberg, *The Incorporation of America: Culture and Society in the Gilded Age* (New York: Hill and Wang, 1982), p. 217.

11 "we deny them." William Dean Howells, *A Traveller from Altruria* (Bloomington: Indiana University Press, 1968), pp. 40, 59–60, 67.

— "Charities organized." From notes among Harry's papers in the Harvard University Archives.

12 "sanitary arrangements." Rudyard Kipling, *Letters of Travel,* as cited in Bayrd Still, *Mirror for Gotham* (New York: New York University Press, 1956), p. 250. For my brief portrait of New York, I am indebted to such illustrated histories as Mary Black, *Old New York in Early Photographs 1853–1901* (New York: Dover, 1973); John A. Kouwenhoven, *The Columbia Historical Portrait of New York* (Garden City, NY: Doubleday, 1953); and Barbaralee Diamonstein, *The Landmarks of New York* (New York: Henry N. Abrams, 1988).

13 "susceptible to melancholy." "The Case of Murr," p. 297.

14 "not my fault." Ibid., pp. 299–300.

15 "stuttering, which had persisted." Ibid., pp. 301–302. Harry's recall of the details bearing on the operation and on his stuttering was understandably uncertain. In one interview (27 March 1970), for example, he said that he began

to stutter when he was four or five, at about the time of his brother Cecil's birth. In another (29 July 1972), he remembered that the aquarium was a reward for accepting a local rather than a general anesthetic. In a third (18 July 1972), he ventured that his stuttering had started out as an imitation of an especially funny classmate but then "stuck" later on.

— "splurge of anger," "The Case of Murr," p. 297.

— "peace." Interviews with HAM, 27 March and 31 March 1970.

16 "interest in books." Interview with HAM, 20 August 1971.

— "vibrant shock of recognition." "The Case of Murr," p. 297.

— "No bona fide intellectual." Ibid., p. 298.

— "Mt. McKinley." Interview with HAM, 5 July 1971.

— "terrier." Interview with Mrs. Byron Thomas, 3 August 1980.

— "enough muscle to subdue her." "The Case of Murr," p. 298.

17 "fragile in her company." Interviews with HAM, 2 April 1970 and 10 June 1982; and with Josephine Murray, 16 February 1989.

— "run your life." Interview with the Rev. Michael Murray, 7 August 1980.

— "Fannie would have none of it." Interviews with HAM, 31 March 1970, 2 April 1970, and 20 August 1971.

— "M-M-M——Ike." Interview with the Rev. Michael Murray, 7 August 1980.

— "intuitive disposition." "The Case of Murr," pp. 297–298.

18 "analytic interest." Ibid., p. 288; interview with HAM, 6 June 1970.

— "educated in the faith." Interviews with HAM, 27 March 1970; and with Mrs. Byron Thomas, 3 August 1980.

19 "when he gave the signals." "The Case of Murr," pp. 302–303. The records of Harry's years at Craigie School are among his papers at the Harvard University Archives.

— "Horatio Alger novels." Interview with HAM, 20 August 1971.

— "ashamed of the house." Interview with HAM, 4 August 1980.

— "pretend he was an Indian." "The Case of Murr," p. 298.

20 "scandalized by what went on." Interview with HAM, 4 August 1980.

— "more deeply felt." A. Walpole Craigie to Endicott Peabody, 31 May 1906.

— "in kind with full interest." Theodore Roosevelt, "The Manly Virtues and Practical Politics," in *American Ideals* (New York: Putnams, 1901), p. 42. Peabody is faithfully remembered in Frank D. Ashburn's *Peabody of Groton* (New York: Coward McCann, 1944), which gives brief attention to Harry Murray. Louis Auchincloss' *The Rector of Justin* (Boston: Houghton Mifflin, 1964) is a fictional portrait.

21 "evil pays to goodness." Interview with HAM, 2 April 1970.

— "admit him to the second form." The correspondence bearing on Harry's admission to Groton is among his papers at the Harvard University Archives.

— "did not mean much in our case." Personal communication from Grafton Minot, 27 April 1970.

22 "toward graduation." Harry's Groton report cards are among his papers at the Harvard University Archives.

23 "regular family summer retreat." Interview with HAM, 31 March 1970. Har-

ry's correspondence with his father is preserved at the Harvard University Archives.

— "ran their strange victim down." Interview with HAM, 28 March 1970.

24 "discourage the performance." Interview with Nina Murray, 2 August 1971.

— "not, after all, very bright." Interview with HAM, 28 March 1970.

25 "died of suicide." Ibid.

— "a fuss about his confirmation." Interviews with HAM, 28 March 1970, 31 March 1970, and 29 July 1972.

— "become a Unitarian." Interview with HAM, 21 August 1971.

— "willing Christian soldier." Interview with HAM, 2 April 1970.

— "cultural breadth." Personal communication from Dean Acheson, 3 April 1970.

3. Harry Just Emerging from His Teens

27 "the three Rs." Interview with HAM, 3 April 1970.

29 "eschew originality." Samuel Eliot Morison, *Three Centuries of Harvard, 1636–1936* (Cambridge: Harvard University Press, 1946), p. 422. My rendering of Harvard life in Harry's time is broadly indebted to Morison's more detailed survey, especially pp. 416–438.

— "steady progression of Cs." Interview with HAM, 17 April 1970.

31 "What follows." Harry's college diaries and scrapbooks—the source for much of the detail bearing on his Harvard years—are the possession of his daughter, Josephine Murray. I am grateful for her permission to use them here.

— "the friendship was never the same." Interview with HAM, 4 August 1980; and with Nina Murray, 12 August 1988.

— "refusal to relinquish control." Interview with HAM, 7 July 1972.

32 "ethical society rather than a religion." Ibid.

— "prominent figure." Interview with Lawrence S. Kubie, 19 August 1970.

— "Executive Committee of the Harvard Varsity Club." Interview with HAM, 3 April 1970.

36 "impeccably bred, and rich." Interview with HAM, 17 April 1970.

37 "coming out at the Copley Plaza." Ibid.

— "talked at the seashore." Interview with HAM, 3 April 1970.

— "kept his feelings to himself." Interview with HAM, 9 August 1971.

41 "the varsity crew won." Interviews with HAM, 3 April 1970, and 9 August 1971.

— "bow seat of the varsity eight." Unless otherwise noted, the details on Harry's rowing career are drawn from his Harvard diaries and scrapbooks.

44 "made a great deal out of it." Interview with HAM, 17 April 1970.

— "Newfoundland." Ibid.

49 "three weeks before each race." A copy of the printed essay appears among Harry's crew records but without reference to its place of publication. Contrary to the author's memory, the piece does not turn up in *Vanity Fair*. Where it was actually published remains a mystery.

50 "nocturnal agenda." Interview with HAM, 4 August 1980.

— "but a trifle." See note to "three weeks before each race," p. 394, above.

— "defeat you in an emergency." Interview with HAM, 9 August 1971.

— "disastrous defeat in New London." Interview with HAM, 1 August 1972.

4. Misgivings and Preparatives

52 "valid bridges of communication." "The Case of Murr," p. 303.

53 "read widely in medical history." Interviews with HAM, 20 May 1970 and 12 July 1972.

— "between 9th and 10th Avenues." Interview with HAM, 31 March 1970.

54 "crazy about medical school." Interview with HAM, 28 March 1970.

— "election for class president." Interview with HAM, 16 July 1971.

— "good sense of humor." Interview with Edwin P. Maynard, 25 August 1970.

— "privileged upbringing." "The Case of Murr," p. 303.

55 "very ashamed of it." Interviews with HAM, 8 July 1972; and with Alvan Barach, 2 July 1970.

56 "costly pieces of jewelry." *Boston American,* 18 July 1915.

— "date of the wedding." *New York Times,* 16 July 1915.

57 "pray may be seldom." From a box of "Engagement Letters" among the Murray papers at the Harvard University Archives; Lucy Rantoul to HAM, n.d.

— "en route to New York." Details from Jo and Harry's wedding and honeymoon scrapbook.

— "Harvard Medical School." Interview with HAM, 8 May 1970.

— "incapacity for stereoscopic vision." Interview with HAM, 27 June 1984.

58 "American ambulance service." Elliot C. Bacon to HAM, 1 February 1915; Charles Codman to HAM, 2 June 1915.

— "fighting with a sword." Interviews with HAM, 8 August 1974 and 27 June 1987.

— "This was discouraging." Interview with HAM, 9 August 1971; additional details from Harry's diary for the years following 1915.

59 "Naval Cross." Interviews with Michael Murray, 7 August 1980; and HAM, 1 July 1971.

— "night bombing." Cecil Murray to HAM, n.d.

— "the best 3 of my life." Cecil Murray to HAM, 22 August 1918 and 31 July 1918.

— "poet of some note." Interview with HAM, 21 July 1970.

— "difficult diagnostic problems." Interview with Edwin P. Maynard, 25 August 1970.

60 "she recovered fully." Interviews with HAM, 6 June 1970 and 27 June 1984.

— "set forth by W. H. Sheldon." "The Case of Murr," p. 288. Some of Draper's leading ideas appear in three essays—"Human Constitution: Its Significance in Medicine and How It May Be Studied"; "The Influence of Sex in Determining Human Disease Potentiality"; and "The Patient and His Physician"—

which were published as a collection entitled *Human Constitution* (Detroit: Williams and Wilkins, 1928).

— "sympathetic observer." Interview with HAM, 6 June 1970.

61 "assent to its basic message." Dean Acheson to HAM, 24 April 1919.

— "nodded his approval." Ellery Sedgwick to HAM, 2 May 1919.

— "on the field of action." "Groton and Adaptation," *Grotonian*, 35 (1919), pp. 405, 407, 411, 415, 419.

62 "slip the essay in." Interview with HAM, 4 June 1970.

— "So much for Emerson." Endicott Peabody to HAM, n.d. Harry and the Rector continued to share books and to debate educational and religious questions for the next several years. The graduate gave little ground in his demand for change and individual self-development, while Peabody persisted in his emphasis on tradition and the group. "The Christian religion," he made clear, "is a social thing": Endicott Peabody to HAM, 9 December 1922. Their correspondence is fully represented in Frank D. Ashburn's *Peabody of Groton*, pp. 242–247.

— "I suffered in those rounds." Interview with HAM, 6 June 1970.

63 "dying the whole way." Ibid.

64 "pull of the dying woman." From an untitled narrative in a folder on Alice Henry.

— "simple, doomed girl." From the "History of Alice Henry," in the same folder.

65 "Ellis Island and the Tombs." A. Woods (Police Commissioner of the City of New York) to HAM, 10 November 1914.

— "convicted sex-offender." Harry's association with Gandy continued for several decades. He sent letters and money, and they met when Gandy was released from prison in 1926. The grateful ex-convict seems to have done well on the outside and was still in touch with his benefactor in 1949. There is a file of letters from Gandy among Harry's papers at the Harvard University Archives.

— "paid her funeral expenses." Interviews with Edwin P. Maynard, 25 August 1970, and HAM, 9 August 1971; Edwin P. Maynard to HAM, June 1918.

66 "a great deal more analysis." "The Case of Murr," pp. 299–300.

— "oedipus hunting season." Ibid., pp. 297, 299.

67 "modest study." "What Should Psychologists Do About Psychoanalysis?" *Journal of Abnormal and Social Psychology*, 35 (1940), 152.

— "what everybody in New York wanted." Interview with Carl Binger, 15 April 1970.

— "medical journals." "The development of the cardiac loop in the rabbit, with especial reference to the bulboventricular groove and origin of the interventricular septum," *Journal of Anatomy*, 26 (1919), 29–39; and "Two unusual cases of melanocarcinoma," *Proceedings of the New York Pathological Society*, 19 (1919), 28–37. The first article was the final result of research undertaken at Harvard during the summer of 1916; the second arose directly from Harry's M.A. work at Columbia.

— "Studies in calcium metabolism." Interviews with HAM, 16 June 1970 and 25 July 1972.

68 "teleological principle." L. J. Henderson, *The Fitness of the Environment: An Inquiry into the Biological Significance of the Properties of Matter* (New York: Macmillan, 1913), p. 308.

— "contrast of mechanism with teleology." L. J. Henderson, *The Order of Nature, An Essay* (Cambridge: Harvard University Press, 1917), p. 209.

— "similar trends were evident." John Parascandola, "Organismic and Holistic Concepts in the Thought of L. J. Henderson," *Journal of the History of Biology,* 4 (1971), 63–113. I am indebted for my summaries of Henderson's ideas to Parascandola's valuable exposition and analysis. I have also consulted Walter B. Cannon's survey of Henderson's life and work in the *Biographical Memoirs* of the National Academy of Sciences (Washington: National Academy of Sciences, 1945), vol. 23, pp. 31–58.

— "always the systematist." Crane Brinton, "Lawrence Joseph Henderson," in *The Saturday Club: A Century Completed 1920–1956,* ed. Edward W. Forbes and John H. Finley, Jr. (Boston: Houghton Mifflin, 1958), p. 209.

69 "He encouraged his brother." Interview with HAM, 9 August 1971.

— "analysis of blood." In letters of 10 October and 4 November 1919, Henderson encourages Harry in his work on "the calcium problem." No doubt he is referring to questions on calcium metabolism that come up for discussion in Harry's M.A. thesis and in a paper co-authored with Alvan Barach, "Tetany in a case of sprue," *Journal of the American Medical Association,* 74 (1920), 786–788. A technical note co-authored with George King on "A new blood coagulometer," evidently a product of the same research, appeared in the *Journal of the American Medical Association,* 74 (1920), 1452–1453.

— "Grand Challenge Cup." Interview with HAM, 20 May 1970; also Harry's "Rowing Season 1920 & Diary of Union Boat Club Crew."

— "Harry's most memorable duty." Interview with HAM, 17 April 1970.

— "The variable acidity of hemoglobin." *Proceedings of the Society of Experimental Biology and Medicine,* 17 (1920), 180–182.

70 "Cartesian nomogram." Parascandola "Organismic and Holistic Concepts," pp. 91ff, provides a detailed, illustrated account of the nomogram's development and use.

— "We rowed as well as ever." Interviews with HAM, 20 May 1970, 16 June 1970, and 10 August 1971; Harry's diary for the years following 1915.

— "organismic, or organismal, proposition." "Preparations for the Scaffold of a Comprehensive System," in *Psychology: A Study of a Science,* ed. S. Koch (New York: McGraw-Hill, 1959), vol. 3, p. 17.

— "most sophisticated scientific theorists." I am guided in my outline of mechanism and vitalism by Garland E. Allen, *Life Science in the Twentieth Century* (New York: Wiley, 1975), pp. xx–xxiii and 102–103, and by G. J. Goodfield, *The Growth of Scientific Physiology* (London: Hutchinson, 1960).

71 "a poor physical specimen." Interview with HAM, 20 May 1970.

— "retreat in Vermont." Interview with HAM, 10 August 1971.

— "an old chum from college days." Interview with HAM, 21 July 1970. The meeting with Robinson was "a disappointment," Harry recalled in a letter of

11 March 1981. "Henderson's presence there inhibited me, partly, I suppose, because I never had the slightest intimation of any poetry in Henderson's make-up. . . . Perhaps Robinson was craving a good slug of whiskey, but the circumstances were not conducive to taking the occasion for that kind of conviviality." Harry and the poet met on a few other occasions, and they exchanged letters.

— "surgeons as glorified plumbers." Interview with HAM, 20 May 1970.

— "opportunity to revise it." L. J. Henderson to HAM, 10 February 1923. Henderson returned Harry's high regard. "I was told the other day," he wrote in October 1922, "that your class at P. and S. had a spirit quite different from that of any other within the memory of man, and that this was due in large part to your own attitude."

72 "fragment of Farragut's cap." Interviews with HAM, 22 June 1970, 12 July 1972, and 27 June 1987.

— "five additional research papers." A. B. Hastings, C. D. Murray, and H. A. Murray, Jr., "Certain chemical changes in the blood after pyloric obstruction in dogs," *Journal of Biological Chemistry*, 46 (1921), 223. Hastings was a chemist with the U. S. Public Health Service; C. D. Murray was Harry's brother, Cecil ("Ike"). A. B. Hastings and H. A. Murray, Jr., "Observations on parathyroidectomized dogs," *Journal of Biological Chemistry*, 46 (1921), 233–256; H. A. Murray, Jr., "The bicarbonate and chloride content of the blood in certain cases of persistent vomiting," *Proceedings of the Society for Experimental Biology and Medicine*, 19 (1922), 273–275; A. R. Felty and H. A. Murray, Jr., "Observations on dogs with experimental pyloric obstruction. The acid-base equilibrium, chlorides, non-protein nitrogen, and urea of the blood," *Journal of Biological Chemistry*, 57 (1923), 573–585; and Henry A. Murray, Jr., M.D., "The chemical pathology of pyloric occlusion in relation to tetany," *Archives of Surgery*, 7 (1923), 166–196.

— "References to the *milieu intérieur*." These appear in the first of the articles, "Certain chemical changes," and in the last, "The chemical pathology." Henderson helped to make Bernard's ideas available in America by promoting the English translation of *Introduction à l'étude de la médecine* in 1927. On Henderson's adaptation of Bernard's ideas, see the differing accounts in Parascandola, "Organismic and Holistic Concepts," pp. 97–99, and Reino Virtanen, *Claude Bernard and His Place in the History of Ideas* (Lincoln: University of Nebraska Press, 1960), pp. 84–87.

73 "Hans Zinsser and Raymond Pearl." Interview with HAM, 10 August 1971.

— "outrageous thing for him to say." Interviews with HAM, 4 August 1970 and 12 July 1972. Harry allowed that Watson's irresponsible remarks may have been a factor in his later very pronounced aversion to behaviorism.

— "greatest psychologic *phallus-y*." Courtney to HAM, 9 February 1921. The characterization of Courtney, along with Harry's account of his early dismissal of Freud, appears in "What Should Psychologists Do About Psychoanalysis?" p. 152.

— "downtown doings and uptown dreams." "What Should Psychologists Do About Psychoanalysis?" p. 152.

74 "Harry said no to both." Harvey Cushing to HAM, 19 March and 29 March 1921; interview with HAM, 10 August 1971.

75 "lessons on loyalty." Interview with HAM, 4 June 1970.

76 "a week or so after the New Year 1919." Except as otherwise noted, the details bearing on Harry and Jo's sexual difficulties are drawn from their correspondence at the time of Jo's sojourn in Florida.

79 "Relative fertility." Edward Reynolds, M.D., and Donald Macomber, M.D., "Relative Fertility: Small decreases in the fertility of two individuals may result in a sterile mating," *Boston Medical and Surgical Journal*, 186 (1922), 383–384.

— "all a good joke." Interview with Lawrence S. Kubie, 19 August 1970.

80 "conceal his identity." Harry's impatience with Reynolds and Macomber is easily understood. In a similar vein, however, it is a good question why he was so evidently willing to allow his revealing correspondence with Jo to rise into the clear light of day. The answer, it seems just as clear, is that he wanted the story told. In one letter he asks Jo to destroy what he has written. Sections of other letters have been excised, probably, but not certainly, by either Harry or Jo. The fact remains, however, that in reviewing his papers toward the end of his life, Harry chose to preserve the intimately revealing letters that he exchanged with his wife in January 1919.

— "parents' uncertain marriage." Interview with HAM, 4 June 1970.

5. From My Twenty-Fifth Year I Date My Life

81 "unfolded within myself." *The Letters of Herman Melville*, ed. Merrell R. Davis and William H. Gilman (New Haven: Yale University Press, 1960), p. 130.

82 "fall to the mould." Ibid., p. 130.

— "key to it all." *Moby Dick*, p. 14

— "a different equilibrium." Henry A. Murray, "Preparations for the Scaffold of a Comprehensive System," in *Psychology: A Study of Science* (New York: McGraw-Hill, 1959), vol. 3, pp. 17–18.

83 "quenchless spirit of man." HAM to Lewis Mumford, 17 June 1945.

84 "chance and the prepared mind." "The Case of Murr," p. 290.

— "as it related to heart disease." Interview with HAM, 12 July 1972.

— "memorial sketch." Untitled tribute to Alfred E. Cohn (1957), p. 5.

85 "allegory of life itself." Interview with HAM, 4 June 1970.

— "flattering letters." Henderson's letter of recommendation is included—with others from William C. Clarke, Hugh Auchincloss, Walter Palmer, and Alfred Cohn—in a box of family letters among Harry's papers at the Harvard University Archives.

— "He had no trouble." Interviews with HAM, 20 May 1970, 11 August 1971, and 12 July 1972.

86 "In reporting on such experiments." Henry A. Murray, Jr., "Physiological ontogeny. A. Chicken embryos. II. Catabolism. Chemical changes in fertile eggs
during incubation. Selection of standard conditions," *Journal of General Physi-
ology,* 9 (1925), 1–37; Henry A. Murray, Jr., "Physiological ontogeny. A.
Chicken embryos. III. Weight and growth rate as functions of age," *Journal of
General Physiology,* 9 (1925), 39–48; Alfred E. Cohn, M.D., and Henry A.
Murray, Jr., M.D., "Physiological ontogeny. A. Chicken embryos. IV. The
negative acceleration of growth with age as demonstrated by tissue cultures,"
Journal of Experimental Medicine, 42 (1925), 275–290; Alfred E. Cohn, M.D.,
"Physiological ontogeny. A. Chicken embryos. V. On the rate of the heart beat
during the development of chicken embryos," *Journal of Experimental Medicine,*
42 (1925), 291–297; Alfred E. Cohn, M.D., "Physiological ontogeny. A.
Chicken embryos. VI. Differentiation in the chicken embryo heart from the
point of view of stimulus production," *Journal of Experimental Medicine,* 42
(1925), 299–310; Henry A. Murray, Jr., "Physiological ontogeny. A. Chicken
embryos. VII. The concentration of the organic constituents and the calorific
value as functions of age," *Journal of General Physiology,* 9 (1926), 405–432;
Henry A. Murray, Jr., "Physiological ontogeny. A. Chicken embryos. VIII.
Accelerations of integration and differentiation during the embryonic period,"
Journal of General Physiology, 9 (1926), 603–619; Henry A. Murray, Jr., "Physiological ontogeny. A. Chicken embryos. IX. The iodine reaction for the
quantitative determination of glutathione in the tissues as a function of age,"
Journal of General Physiology, 9 (1926), 621–624; Henry A. Murray, Jr., "Physiological ontogeny. A. Chicken embryos. X. The temperature characteristic for
the contraction rate of isolated fragments of embryonic heart muscle," *Journal of General Physiology,* 9 (1926), 781–788; Henry A. Murray, Jr., "Physiological ontogeny. A. Chicken embryos. XI. The pH, chloride, carbonic acid,
and protein concentrations in the tissues as functions of age," *Journal of General Physiology,* 9 (1926), 789–803; Henry A. Murray, Jr., "Physiological
ontogeny. A. Chicken embryos. XII. The metabolism as a function of age,"
Journal of General Physiology, 10 (1926), 337–343; Alfred E. Cohn and
Henry A. Murray, Jr., "Physiological ontogeny. I. The present status of the
problem," *Quarterly Review of Biology,* 2 (1927), 469–493. An additional,
very brief paper, "Correlations between growth, differentiation and metabolic
rate in the chicken embryo," appeared in *Journal of Physiology,* 60 (1925),
xx. References, respectively, are to I, 469; III, 46; IV, 289; VIII, 603; and
VII, 428.

— "totality of the organism." "Physiological ontogeny. I. The present status of
the problem," pp. 470, 482, 486, 488.

— "my whole life plan." Interview with HAM, 5 July 1970.

87 "key theoretical issues." Henderson reviewed *Science and the Modern World* in
1926 and refers to it favorably in *Blood: A Study in General Physiology* (New
Haven: Yale University Press, 1928), p. 17.

— "organic mechanism." Alfred North Whitehead, *Science and the Modern World*
(New York: Macmillan, 1925), p. 76.

— "creativity." Charles D. Laughlin, Jr., in his "The Influence of Whitehead's Organism upon Murray's Personology," *Journal of the History of the Behavioral Sciences,* 9 (1973), observes that "Murray follows Whitehead in his conception of a creative universe and in his consideration of man's place in it" (p. 254).

— "angel perching on a pin point." "Preparations for the Scaffold of a Comprehensive System," p. 13.

88 "Keynesian economics." I am indebted to Allen, *Life Science in The Twentieth Century,* pp. 106–111, for this brief overview.

— "respect for such humanistic virtuosity." HAM to John Jay Chapman, n.d. This letter, along with several others in a series with Chapman, are in the Houghton Library at Harvard. Harry goes on to claim "spiritual lineage from the Prophet—in Ecclesiastes—i.e. mystical mechanism." Though the relevance of the biblical allusion is not entirely clear, "mystical mechanism," a curious anticipation of Whitehead's equally oxymoronic "organic mechanism," would appear to elevate the humanist-scientist to the status of a visionary—critical, skeptical, but transfixed nonetheless by the mysterious order of God's creation.

— "Carl Binger recalled." Interview with Carl Binger, 15 April 1970.

89 "My principal interests." *Harvard College Class of 1915 Decennial Report* (Cambridge: Harvard University Press, 1926), p. 196.

— "scientific consultant." Sidney Howard to HAM, August 1924.

— "sort of a witch." Interview with HAM, 16 June 1970.

90 "he drew away." Ibid. On Sheldon's life, see Eric Wollencott Barnes, *The Man Who Lived Twice* (New York: Scribner, 1956). Harry's complimentary letter, and an equally flattering telegram from Sheldon, appear on pp. 126–128. Barnes notes (p. 298) that Sheldon was very kind to Harry's daughter Josephine when she was a child.

— "Paul Robeson entered Harry's life." Interviews with HAM, 16 June 1970, 13 August 1971, and 15 June 1985. See also Martin Bauml Duberman, *Paul Robeson* (New York: Knopf, 1988), pp. 34–35, 37–38.

91 "referred him to Alvan Barach." Interviews with HAM, 16 June 1970, 10 August 1971, and 20 August 1971. Harry recalled that O'Neill found ample confirmation for his understanding of human nature in Jung's *Psychology of the Unconscious.* On Harry's recommendation of Barach, see *Selected Letters of Eugene O'Neill,* ed. Travis Bogard and Jackson R. Bryer (New Haven: Yale University Press, 1988), p. 252.

— "bust of Jo." Interview with HAM, 10 August 1971.

— "Essie Robeson." Interview with HAM, 13 August 1971.

— "Archibald MacLeish." Interview with HAM, 10 August 1971.

— "favorite composers." Interview with HAM, 16 June 1970.

— "Thomas Hardy country." Interview with HAM, 20 August 1971.

92 "leading literary lights." Interview with HAM, 16 June 1970.

— "explosion from within." Ibid.

— "outside the husk of his contemporary world." "The Case of Murr," pp. 290–291.

93 "I began to wonder." "What Should Psychologists Do About Psychoanalysis?" pp. 152–153.

— "irreconcilable interpretations." "The Case of Murr," p. 288.

— "the pecking order of the sciences" Ibid., p. 291.

94 "Murr's first spurt." Ibid., pp. 288–289.

— "hot soil of my Southern soul." Herman Melville, "Hawthorne and His Mosses," in the Norton Critical Edition of *Moby-Dick*, p. 548.

— "framework of the idea." C. G. Jung, *Psychological Types, or The Psychology of Individuation,* trans. H. Godwin Baynes (London: Pantheon, 1923), pp. 442, 481.

95 "No sooner had he arrived." Interview with HAM, 2 Aug 1971.

— "the antithesis becomes ever sharper." *Psychological Types,* p. 484.

96 "without much of a struggle." Interviews with HAM, 4 June and 16 June 1970.

97 "a sort of symbol." "The Case of Murr," p. 291; interview with HAM, 16 June 1970.

— "just a 'little blaze'." Interview with HAM, 16 June 1970; "What Should Psychologists Do About Psychoanalysis?" p. 153.

— "Christiana Morgan was born." Harry composed his description of Christiana as a biographical "Supplement" to Jung's *The Vision Seminars* (Zurich: Spring Publications, 1976). Large sections of what he wrote appear in that publication, though much was excised by the editors. The passage quoted here, and all subsequent quotations, are from the complete manuscript of this document. Harvey Cushing's portrait of Christiana's father, William Thomas Councilman, appears in *The Saturday Club,* pp. 60–72. Chaim Weizmann was a leading figure in the World Zionist Organization and the first president of the State of Israel. Christiana sympathized with his cause and surrendered to a brief infatuation in the early 1920s when they met in New York and later when their paths crossed at a resort hotel in Switzerland.

98 "her sister recalled." Interview with Mrs. Frank Wigglesworth, 1 May 1970. This interview, and another on 14 May 1970, yielded a fund of valuable information about Christiana's childhood and married life, along with numerous insights into her character.

99 "rapt spectator to her own inner drama." Interviews with HAM, 23 and 30 June 1970 and 7 July 1972.

— "beautiful, and she knew it." Interview with Ina May Greer, 15 June 1970. Miss Greer was for years Harry's friend and trusted research associate. A Jungian in her own right, she was also very close to Christiana.

— "He first met Christiana." Details and quotations are drawn from Christiana's chronological and topical file covering the early years of her relationship with Harry. A few of the entries are in his hand, though most, including some adopting Harry's point of view, are in hers.

100 "They soon met again." Interviews with HAM, 3 August 1972; and with Mrs. Frank Wigglesworth, 4 May 1970.

101 "evening course on nineteenth-century thought." Interviews with HAM, 22 June 1970 and 10 August 1971.

— "transparently Jungian questionnaire." The results of the questionnaire are preserved with Harry's other papers in the Harvard University Archives.

103 "he would not, or could not, turn back." Interview with HAM, 4 June 1970.

— "his privilege as a self-creator." Introduction to C. G. Jung, *Psychology of the Unconscious,* trans. Beatrice M. Hinkle (New York: Moffat, Yard and Company, 1916), pp. xlii–xliii.

104 "must be overcome." *Psychology of the Unconscious,* pp. 82, 85.

— "gave him a copy of Bergson." Christiana's chronological and topical file.

105 "Ontogenesis." *Psychology of the Unconscious,* p. 28.

— "Harry made this idea his own." HAM to John Jay Chapman, 1924?

— "Harry's concluding overview." "Long ago it became evident that the Biogenetic Law, which states that ontogeny follows phylogeny, was untenable, for it was noted that each new development or emergence could not be forecast from the very beginning and that each ontogeny showed variance in every stage. The two series, phylogeny and ontogeny, stand nevertheless as crudely analogous phenomena, and, lacking a complete paleontological record for any one species, ontogeny may be taken to present the best record that we possess of racial trend" ("Physiological ontogeny. I. The present status of the problem," p. 489).

106 "grandiose self." Peter Homans, *Jung in Context* (Chicago: University of Chicago Press, 1979), pp. 195–196. Homans summarizes: "Jung's writings, both autobiographical and formal, provide the most detailed and systematic account I have found in modern intellectual history of the struggle of an individual who was unable to accept the Christianity in which he was reared but at the same time unwilling to let it completely pass him by" (p. 196).

— "something powerful had them in its grip." Interview with HAM, 20 June 1983.

107 "Harry was a godsend." Christiana's chronological and topical file.

— "narcissism *à deux.*" Interview with Ina May Greer, 15 June 1970.

108 "do something about it." Christiana's chronological and topical file.

6. He Crosses the Rubicon

109 "I have recently read Moby Dick." HAM to John Jay Chapman, September? 1924.

— "E. L. Grant Watson." From "Some Bytes of Info from Sixty or So Years Ago," Harry's reminiscences of his early Melville research. This essay is one of many unpublished "Melville Morsels"—biographical and critical pieces, generally rather short—that Harry labored over, with the help of his assistant, Eugene Taylor, until the end of his life. Watson, Harry reports, "confessed to me that he had been involved in an experience similar to Pierre's, and so found that what was mysterious to other readers of the book was plain to him."

110 "I had never taken a course." HAM's unpublished talk for the Harvard Social Relations Society, 1956.

— "Truth is forced to fly." Herman Melville, "Hawthorne and His Mosses," in the Norton Critical Edition of *Moby-Dick,* pp. 541–542.

111 "it is only the heart." Ibid., pp. 548, 541

— "one of the greatest of all imaginative writers." Viola Meynell, Introduction to the World's Classics edition of *Moby-Dick* (London: Oxford University Press, 1920), pp. v–viii.

— "the entire cast turned up." HAM's unpublished talk for the Harvard Social Relations Society, 1956.

112 "a drama written out of grief." Ibid.

— "the greatest depth psychologist." Interview with HAM, 1 August 1972.

— "everything this side of love." HAM's unpublished talk for the Harvard Social Relations Society, 1956.

113 "Eros was depravity." Henry A. Murray, "In Nomine Diaboli," p. 447.

— "an incompatible marriage." Ibid., p. 448.

— "egressions." Henry A. Murray, "Dead to the World: The Passions of Herman Melville," in *Essays in Self-Destruction,* ed. E. S. Shneidman (New York: Science House, 1967), p. 23. These egressions occurred, Harry is careful to note, before Melville "got himself married and tied down at the age of twenty-eight."

— "dictated by his daemon." Henry A. Murray, "Bartleby and I," in *Bartleby the Scrivener,* ed. H. P. Vincent (Kent, OH: Kent State University Press, 1966), p. 494.

— "a being of the land of dreams." Herman Melville, *Mardi* (Evanston, IL: Northwestern University Press, 1970), p. 158.

— "explorer of the unconscious." Henry A. Murray, Introduction to Melville's *Pierre* (New York: Hendricks House, 1949), pp. lxiv and xxv. On marriage in *Mardi,* see "Bartleby and I", pp. 17–19.

— "fixed as fate. "*Mardi,* p. 638.

114 "unselfish devotion. *Pierre,* p. xli.

— "gospelize the world anew." Ibid., p. 321.

— "greatest and purest written thoughts." Ibid., p. 399.

— "Jungian anima." For Jung's definition, see *Two Essays in Analytical Psychology,* trans. R. F. C. Hull (Princeton, NJ: Princeton University Press, 1966), pp. 188–211.

115 "one of those faces." *Pierre,* p. 49.

— "drowning in her unconscious." Ibid., p. li.

— "the personification of Pierre's unconscious." Ibid. p. liii.

116 "Fixed Fate and Free Will." Ibid., p. 214.

— "claim is incontestable." Ibid., pp. xlix–l.

— "the center of Melville." E. L. Grant Watson, "Melville's *Pierre,*" *New England Quarterly,* 3 (1930), 233.

117 "This is the case for Isabel." Ibid., pp. liii–lv.

— "gazed on the promised land." Ibid., p. lv.

— "some inevitable ill." Ibid., p. 49.

118   "too painful for words." Interview with HAM, 1 July 1971.

——   "who could fail to see." Interview with HAM, 9 August 1979.

——   "a close eye on things." Interview with Ann McDonald, 28 July 1972. Miss McDonald returned with the Murrays to the United States in 1925 and continued for several years as Josephine's governess. She was well into her eighties when I interviewed her in Edinburgh but still remarkably full and clear in her memories of the Murray family.

——   "He explained to I. A. Richards." Interview with I. A. Richards, 27 March 1970.

119   "so much overlap." HAM's interview with Gene F. Nameche, 4 November 1968, p. 6. This unpublished document is part of the C. G. Jung Biographical Archive in the Countway Library of Medicine at Harvard Medical School. It is a valuable supplement to my own interviews with Harry on his relations with Jung.

——   "but never out of control." Interview with Ann McDonald, 28 July 1972.

120   "plans for a year abroad." Interview with HAM, 23 June 1970.

——   "occasional visits over the years." Ibid.

122   "template of Harry's destiny." Ibid.

——   "in his autobiography." C. G. Jung, *Dreams, Memories, Reflections* (New York: Random House, 1961). See especially chapter 6, "Confrontation with the Unconscious," pp. 170–199. I am guided through the details of Jung's life by Gerhard Wehr, *Jung: A Biography* (Boston: Shambhala Publications, 1987), and Barbara Hannah, *Jung: His Life and Work* (New York: G. B. Putnam's Sons, 1976).

——   "*this* world and *this* life." *Dreams, Memories, Reflections*, p. 189.

123   "enter the unconscious." Hannah, *Jung: His Life and Work*, pp. 118–119.

——   "achieve wholeness, or individuation." I am guided here by Wehr, *Jung: A Biography*, p. 188, who in turn takes his lead from Toni Wolff herself.

——   "proper, unbending Zurich." Interview with HAM, 25 June 1970. Jung's tie to Toni Wolff was still relatively little known in 1964 when Lewis Mumford, in "The Revolt of the Demons," an essay on the lives of Freud and Jung in the *New Yorker* (23 May 1964, pp. 155–185), revealed the truth. Though Jung, his wife, and Toni Wolff were dead by that time, the revelation reportedly scandalized some people in Zurich and was the cause for upset among many of Jung's followers.

——   "shy and quiet." Interview with HAM, 9 August 1979; HAM's interview with Gene F. Nameche, pp. 22–26. Gerhard Wehr, in *Jung: A Biography*, pp. 188–190, following Barbara Hannah, is equally sanguine about the success of the triadic relationship.

——   "an extraordinary way." Interview with HAM, 25 June 1970.

124   "inadequate to the experience." "Nobody can really understand these things unless he has experienced them himself," Jung wrote. "I am therefore more interested in pointing out the possible ways to such experience than in devising intellectual formulae which, for lack of experience, must necessarily remain an empty web of words." *Two Essays on Analytical Psychology*, p. 211.

— "making excuses for it." Interviews with HAM, 23 and 25 June 1970.

125 "a good impression of him." HAM's interview with Gene F. Nameche, p. 5.

— "You take your life into your hands." Interview with HAM, 27 June 1987.

— "the more Harry favored them." Interview with HAM, 25 June 1970.

126 "a world of changes." "What Should Psychologists Do About Psychoanalysis?" p. 153; interviews with HAM, 23 and 25 June 1970.

— "the psyche's hinterland." *Memories, Dreams, Reflections,* pp. 223–226; interviews with HAM, 23 June 1970 and 9 August 1979. On Jung's self-absorption, see Homans, *Jung in Context,* p. 111.

— "exemplary in work and love." Interview with HAM, 25 June 1970. Harry's use of "spherical" to describe Jung echoes Melville's complaint that Hawthorne lacked "the plump sphericity" desirable in an ideal friend. By the logic of the allusion, Jung was for Murray what Hawthorne failed to be for the frustrated Melville.

127 "and possibly expendable." See *Memories, Dreams, Reflections,* pp. 182, 187–188. Once "the anima's ideas" have become conscious, Jung writes, "I can read their meaning directly from my dreams, and therefore no longer need a mediator to communicate them."

— "give rebirth to a man." Jung to Carol Jeffrey, 18 June 1958, in the *C. G. Jung Letters,* 2 vols. (Princeton, NJ: Princeton University Press, 1973), vol. 2, p. 455.

— "she was a woman." Interview with HAM, 30 June 1970.

— "spirit of eternal youth." See Hannah, *Jung: His Life and Work,* p. 117.

— "personal experiment." "The Revolt of the Demons," p. 166.

128 "a reborn man." "The Case of Murr," p. 287.

— "as soon as the time was right." Interviews with HAM, 25 June 1970 and 9 August 1979.

— "jealous of each other's mate." CDM's chronological and topical file.

129 "a young woman." Jung to HAM, 2 May 1925. A portion of the letter appears in the *C. G. Jung Letters,* vol. 1, p. 42.

— "welcome always." Jung to HAM, 31 August 1925. Harry had this letter framed with Jung's picture and kept it on display in his gallery of good friends.

— "a picture of her husband." Emma Jung to HAM, 16 May 1925.

— "Harry warmed to it." Interview with HAM, 20 May 1970

130 "just fingers and toes." Interviews with HAM, 23 and 25 June 1970 and 9 August 1979, and CDM's chronological and topical file. These same materials are the sources for the remainder of the chapter.

7. Mardi Behind, an Ocean Before

133 "biography of Herman Melville." Interviews with Ann McDonald, 28 July 1972, and with HAM, 30 June 1970.

134 "mad, moody Melville." Interviews with HAM, 5 and 27 August 1971; and "Some Bytes of Info from Sixty or So Years Ago."

— "alone, apart." CDM to HAM, 26 October 1925.

— "a sacred place." Interview with HAM, 14 July 1970.

135 "evidence of paternal frailty." George Eustis Corcoran wrote to Harry on 3 June 1926: "An old friend of mine, who is dead now, knew Herman Melville & told me that H.M. told him that 'Pierre' was a true! story & very closely connected with him!" Corcoran was the grandson of the eminent philanthropist William Wilson Corcoran, founder of the famous art gallery in Washington, D.C. The "chair portrait," which was in the possession of Charlotte Hoadley, the daughter of Melville's sister, Catherine, comes up for discussion in "Some Bytes of Info from Sixty or So Years Ago." Harry expended great time and ingenuity in solving the riddle of the novelist's illegitimate half-sister. Toward the very end of his life, and with the help of Harvey Meyerson and Eugene Taylor, he finally revealed what he knew in "Allan Melvill's By-Blow," *Melville Society Extracts*, 61 (1985), 1–6.

— "not enough of a poet." Julian Hawthorne to HAM, 27 April 1926.

136 "from several angles." CDM to HAM, 24 September 1925, winter 1925/1926, 3 February 1926.

— "you are in danger." Van Wyck Brooks to HAM, 27 March 1926, and another to HAM, n.d.

— "wandering in the deep." These observations are drawn from the unpublished fragment, "Melville and Personology," another of Harry's "Morsels."

137 "special angle on things." Eleanor Metcalf to HAM, 12 May 1926 and 30 June 1928.

138 "Melville's literary work." Lewis Mumford to HAM, 14 and 26 August 1928.

— "If there is anything left." HAM to Lewis Mumford, August 1928.

— "not entirely purged." Lewis Mumford to HAM, 26 August 1928; HAM to Mumford, 21 September 1928; and an interview with Mumford, 25 March 1970. Harry discussed Brooks' breakdown in an interview on 30 August 1971.

139 "limited by his thought-cage." Lewis Mumford to HAM, 16 May 1929.

— "listener to the end." *New England Quarterly*, 2 (1929), 525–526. The second review, entitled "Timon of America," appeared in *Hound and Horn*, 2 (1929), 430–432.

— "innocence and superficiality." Interview with HAM, 5 July 1970.

140 "light on Melville." Raymond Weaver to HAM, 17 April 1929.

— "trap door to my own." Lewis Mumford to HAM, 7 July 1929. He continues: "It is amusing to look back and see how, despite my awareness of what ought to be done, I tricked myself into this; how in part it was due to my animus against Weaver's melodramatics, an attempt to take the same facts and explain them by the hypothesis of normality instead of that of 'insanity,' and how in part it was due to the fact that I appropriated Moby-Dick to serve as a vehicle for my own philosophy, and so, though conscious of the turmoil, kept it limited and in hand—like a fireman with a hose, coolly spraying the flames of Mt. Etna."

— "all the promising friendships." Mumford to HAM, 21 April and 7 July 1929; HAM to Mumford, [May] 1929.

141 "I want no other monument." Henry A. Murray, "Dr. Morton Prince, a

Founder of Psychology," *Harvard Alumni Bulletin*, January 23, 1930, p. 495.
A shorter, rather milder version of this original tribute was published as "Morton Prince: Sketch of His Life and Work," in *Journal of Abnormal and Social Psychology*, 52 (1956), 291–295. The definitive study of the Clinic's founding and early years is Rodney G. Triplet's "Henry A. Murray and the Harvard Psychological Clinic, 1926–1938: A Struggle to Expand the Disciplinary Boundaries of Academic Psychology," unpublished Ph.D. dissertation, University of New Hampshire, 1983. In my understanding of the Clinic and of its intellectual and institutional context I am indebted to Triplet's thorough and judicious commentary.

— "high-hushed finaglings." "The Case of Murr," p. 287.

— "Efforts will be made." L. J. Henderson to HAM, 3 March 1926.

— "dinner meeting." L. J. Henderson to HAM [March 1926?].

142 "amused and impressed." Interviews with HAM, 17 April 1970 and 8 August 1974. McDougall, Boring, and Prince, along with others on the Harvard faculty, became involved in highly publicized investigations of Margery the medium. All is revealed in Thomas R. Tietze's *Margery* (New York: Harper & Row, 1973). Harry later sat in on one of Margery's sessions, during which she conversed with her dead brother, Walter. Harry was unimpressed. Walter was a "dumb bunny," he recalled, whose interests from beyond the grave didn't get much past baseball.

— "another glorious instance." "The Case of Murr," p. 291.

— "head of the department." Morton Prince to HAM, 19 April 1926, and to Virginia Bacon, 26 April 1926. "I infer that Morton Prince has grown colder as a result of signs of independence on your part," wrote Henderson on 7 February 1926. Sources of "possible irritation," he counseled, "can quite honorably be left unventilated."

143 "eruption of the unconscious." Interview with HAM, 16 July 1970.

— "leave him alone." Interview with Ann McDonald, 28 July 1972.

— "No Hawkers." Interviews with HAM, 31 March 1970 and 11 August 1971.

144 "once classes were over." Interviews with HAM, 3 July 1970 and 13 August 1971; Morton Prince to HAM, 26 April and 28 May 1926.

— "more charming." Interview with Donald MacKinnon, 1972.

145 "heated medical controversy." Harry summarizes the psychological side of the argument in "A case of pinealoma with symptoms suggestive of compulsion neurosis," *Archives of Neurology and Psychiatry*, 19 (1928), 932–945. In an interview on 13 August 1971, he emphasized that he was satisfied with the outcome of the case.

— "I am somewhat discouraged." Morton Prince to HAM, 26 September 1928, and interviews with HAM, 3 and 5 July 1970.

146 "the life of the mind." I rely here on Joseph L. Moses' interview with Donald MacKinnon, taped in the Pioneers in Assessment series in April 1982. But virtually all those who passed through the Clinic had clear memories of its distinctive style and of the marvelous noontime gatherings. See, for example,

Advance copy from

Harvard University Press
79 Garden Street
Cambridge, MA 02138

LOVE'S STORY TOLD

A LIFE OF HENRY A. MURRAY

FORREST G. ROBINSON

PRICE: $29.95

PUBLICATION DATE: 9/28/92

Please send us two copies of
any review you may publish.

Nevitt Sanford, "Murray's Clinic as a Place to Learn," in *Learning after College,* ed. Craig Comstock (Orinda, CA: Montaigne, 1980), p. 112.

— "are largely excluded." Triplet, "Henry A. Murray and the Harvard Psychological Clinic," pp. 90–91.

— "such nourishment." "What to Read in Psychology?" *Independent,* 118 (1927), 134.

— "the principle of Eros." Ibid.

148 "new dynamic psychology." Interview with HAM, 2 September 1971.

— "was little heard from." I have general debts here to Triplet, "Henry A. Murray and the Harvard Psychological Clinic," and to Ernest R. Hilgard, *Psychology in America* (New York: Harcourt Brace Jovanovich, 1987). On Freud's early reception in this country, see John Chynoweth Burnham, *Psychoanalysis and American Medicine: 1894–1918* (New York: International Universities Press, 1967), and Nathan G. Hale, Jr., *Freud and the Americans: The Beginnings of Psychoanalysis in the United States, 1876–1917* (New York: Oxford University Press, 1971). The details on journal publications are from James William Anderson's insightful essay, "Henry A. Murray's Early Career: A Psychobiographical Exploration," *Journal of Personality,* 56 (1988), 151–152.

— "brilliant, erudite." The quote is from Boring's tribute to his mentor in *Psychologist at Large* (New York: Basic Books, 1961), p. 246. Boring's *A History of Experimental Psychology* (New York: Appleton-Century-Crofts, 1929) is well known.

149 "Boring's preference in colleagues." On Boring, see Triplet and especially Hilgard, pp. 105–108, whose anecdotes are most telling. Boring describes his personal background in "Edwin Garrigues Boring," an installment in *A History of Psychology in Autobiography,* ed. Boring et al. (New York: Russell and Russell, 1952), vol. 4, pp. 27–52. In a letter of 5 October 1927 to G. F. Arps, Boring observes: "Henderson has many strong points, but he seems to me a bit visionary at times." His enthusiasm for the Lashley appointment brims over in a letter to the candidate dated 13 January 1928. His views on Harry's membership in the "local aristocracy" appear clearly in a 13 February 1929 letter to H. Austin Aikins. These materials are to be found in the Edwin G. Boring Papers at the Harvard University Archives.

— "decidedly second-rate." Interview with HAM, 25 June 1970.

150 "naive, juvenile perversity." "The Case of Murr," pp. 292–293.

— "eye, ear, nose and throat psychology." Interview with HAM, 7 July 1972.

— "more dead than alive." "The Case of Murr," p. 305.

— "thoroughly original and authentic contribution." "Dr. Morton Prince, a Founder of Psychology," p. 491.

— "transform our most axiomatic propositions." Ibid., pp. 491–495.

— "insufficiently dynamic." Jung's observations appear in a critical review of Prince's "The Mechanism and Interpretation of Dreams," as cited in Homans, *Jung in Context,* p. 59; Freud comments on the same essay are in *The Interpretation of Dreams* (New York: Basic Books, 1965), pp. 559–560.

151 "claims for the technique." Interviews with Jerome Frank (who took Prince's course in abnormal psychology), 6 August 1970; Robert White, 18 February 1989; Donald MacKinnon, 1972; and HAM, 11 July 1970.

— "hypnosis behind him." Herbert Barry, Jr., Donald W. MacKinnon, and Henry A. Murray, Jr., "Hypnotizability as a Personality Trait and Its Typological Relations," *Human Biology,* 3 (1931), 1–36.

— "Boring could not be relied upon." Interviews with HAM, 13 and 26 August 1971 and 7 July 1972; Isabelle Kendig, 23 July 1970; Robert White, 16 April 1970; and Donald MacKinnon, 1972. Details on research activities at the Clinic are available in Boring's contributions to the annual *Report of the President of Harvard College.*

152 "ashamed to acknowledge it." HAM to Alvan Barach, [1929?].

— "there is no end to it." "Professor Murray Describes Department of Abnormal Psychology," *Harvard Crimson,* 12 January 1929, p. 4. Riesman had the feeling that he had discovered the Clinic, which was "absolutely buried" away along the Charles in those days. He came away with the impression that Harry was "an undiscovered great man" (interview with David Riesman, 25 August 1971). Morton Prince was not similarly impressed. "I thought at first I would send your Crimson article to the anonymous founder," he wrote on 28 January 1929. "But I think it would give him a shock. He would say, is that all I gave $100,000 for?"

— "completion of the self." Jung to HAM, 11 January 1929.

— "his buried self." Interview with HAM, 15 June 1985.

153 "Narcissus gazing into the pool." CDM's notebook, labeled "Cambridge England 1925–1926."

154 "if wreck I do." A copy of the letter, dated 12 September 1925, appears in CDM's "Cambridge England 1925–1926" notebook. The passage quoted is from chapter 169 of *Mardi.*

155 "wisdom that is woe." *Moby-Dick,* p. 425.

— "Christiana locates her problem." CDM's "Cambridge England 1925–1926" notebook. In a "Further description of HAM & Myself," Christiana observes that "Harry wants me because I represent his *inferior* function *feeling.* I want H. bec[ause] he represents my inferior function *thinking.* Thus our inferior functions were motivated by the subconscious—so we spoke in terms of Melville (the primordial image, the whale etc.) the significant thing being that to H. *Ahab was feeling*—to me Ahab was *thinking.*"

156 "Christiana wrote excitedly to Harry." CDM to HAM, September 1925.

— "Jung has made great strides." CDM to HAM, 24 September 1925, as copied in CDM's "Cambridge England 1925–1926" notebook.

157 "There are big things in the air." Ibid.; interview with HAM, 10 July 1971.

— "shortcomings as wife and mother." Interview with HAM, 30 June 1970.

— "be taken possession of." CDM to HAM, "Winter, 1926," as copied in CDM's "Cambridge England 1925–1926" notebook.

— "weight of the head." CDM to HAM, "Fall 1925," as copied in CDM's "Cambridge England 1925–1926" notebook.

— "appallingly vacant as vast." *Pierre*, p. 335.

158 "very kernel of the tragic sense of life." CDM to HAM, 3 February 1926, as copied in CDM's "Cambridge England 1925–1926" notebook.

— "In April she announced." CDM to HAM, 20 April [1926]. A version of the letter appears in CDM's "Cambridge England 1925–1926" notebook.

159 "He can't bear to hurt." CDM's notebook entitled "Analysis June 8 '26–July 8 '26."

160 "she goes on at length." CDM to HAM, 20 April [1926]. A version of this letter appears in CDM's "Cambridge England 1925–1926" notebook.

— "she brought it up in a letter." CDM to HAM, 17 June 1926, as copied in CDM's "Cambridge England 1925–1926" notebook.

— "When he and Jo arrived in Zurich." Interview with HAM, 3 July 1970.

162 "In early July." CDM's notebook entitled "Analysis June 8 '26–July 8 '26." On "active imagination," see *Memories, Dreams, Reflections,* pp. 170–199; and Barbara Hannah, *Encounters with the Soul: Active Imagination as Developed by C. G. Jung* (Cambridge, MA: Sigo Press, 1981).

— "a lifetime's work." *Memories, Dreams, Reflections,* p. 199.

— "Here is my Olympus." Interview with Mrs. Frank Wigglesworth, 14 May 1970.

— "You are always a living reality." Jung to CDM, 28 December 1927, *C. G. Jung Letters,* vol. 1, p. 48.

— "he pronounced them 'very fine.'" Interview with HAM, 3 August 1972.

163 "make you into a woman." CDM's notebook entitled "Dreams, Analysis June 2, '26–Oct 26."

— "the apartment had been home." Interviews with HAM, 30 June 1970, 3 and 5 July 1970, and 11 and 13 August 1971. Andrew Turnbull reports that Raisbeck invited Wolfe to the apartment not long after the young writer arrived at Harvard in 1920 (*Thomas Wolfe* [New York: Charles Scribner's Sons, 1967], pp. 48–50). The fictionalized version of the same meeting appears in Chapter 8 of *Of Time and the River.*

164 "Let me thank you most sincerely." Jung to CDM, 28 December 1927, *C. G. Jung Letters,* vol. 1, p. 48.

— "finally more than one hundred." Harry calculated—in his postscript to C. G. Jung, *The Vision Seminars,* vol. 2, p. 517—that Christiana completed "well over a hundred represented [illustrated] visions."

165 "subject matter for Jung's Vision Seminars." The last of the visions to appear in *The Vision Seminars* occurred on 10 December 1926. It was the 75th of a total of 119 visions (as they appear in my catalogue) that emerged between July 1926 and January 1928. In her chronological and topical file Christiana notes that the visions ended on 14 June 1928. It appears that she stopped writing them down in January of that year. Most of the early visions appear in Jung's *Vision Seminars.* The rest are preserved in various forms and places. There are two volumes of nearly finished—carefully hand-printed and beautifully illustrated—visions in the Houghton Library at Harvard University. These are dated 9 July 1926–7 April 1927 and carry the speaker to the foot of the blue

mountain. A more complete but much less finished collection appears in a series of three notebooks, entitled "Visions July 16, 1926–Nov 31 . . . 1927," "Visions Nov[ember] 17, [19]26 . . . May 1, [19]27," and in a volume of visions, reflections, and dreams with the word "Record" inscribed on its spine. My discussion of the visions is based entirely on these three notebooks.

167   "Will's health began to fail." Interview with Mrs. Frank Wigglesworth, 1 May 1970.

168   "didn't know she had anything else." Ibid.

—   "lonely in her own home." Interviews with Josephine Murray, 9 August 1988; and with HAM, 1 July 1971.

—   "complete physical expression." CDM's chronological and topical file, 5 December 1927.

—   "Earlier in the year." "Creation of the Star," in CDM's "Cambridge England 1925–1926" notebook.

—   "First Great Recognition." Dated September 1927, the written account of Harry's recognition appears in CDM's "Cambridge England 1925–1926" notebook. Christiana took a similar view of the need to broadcast the dyad. "Now we are ready to write upon the parchment," she wrote in the last of her vision journals. "We must see ourselves reflected in many facets now, as we have seen ourselves reflected in each other."

169   "in the wake of the crisis." An account of the crisis and its resolution appears in a nine-page manuscript entitled "Olenka," written—almost certainly by Harry—in 1938.

—   "a training ground." From CDM's "Cambridge England 1925–1926" notebook.

8. No Return through Me

170   "You are the center of my world." CDM's "Cambridge England 1925–1926" notebook.

—   "founders of a new religion." Interview with Lewis Mumford, 15 July 1970.

—   "Christiana now referred to herself." Christiana thought of "Wona" as derivative from an old word for wish, desire, or soul (interview with Ina May Greer, 15 June 1970). "Mansol" echoes the title of a meditative epic poem, *Mansoul or The Riddle of the World* (1920), by Charles Doughty, author of *Travels in Arabia Deserta,* with which Harry was familiar.

—   "epigraph to Christiana's visions." From the two-volume collection of the visions in Houghton Library.

—   "Ina May Greer, a veteran Jungian." Interview with Ina May Greer, 27 June 1970. In her characterization of Christiana, Miss Greer drew on the Jungian typology elaborated in Edward C. Whitmont's *The Symbolic Quest* (New York: Putnam, 1969).

171   "By her own urgent admission." CDM's chronological and topical file.

—   "he wrote to his friend." HAM to Alvan Barach, n.d. fragment.

—   "I'm not aware of anxiety." Interview with HAM, 4 June 1970.

172 "I am utterly terrified." From a volume of visions with "Record" inscribed on its spine.

— "playing at what she most feared." Ibid.

173 "My aim." Interview with HAM, 1 July 1971.

— "humanistic psychology." HAM to Lewis Mumford, [April 1930].

— "high marks." *The Crimson Confidential Guide to Freshman Courses and Fields of Concentration,* 1 September 1936, p. 42. Boring was respected as a scientist but nonetheless generally dismissed as a poor teacher. During the 1940s he seems to have tried his hand at humor, but "failed in this as well as in teaching effectively," reported the *Confidential Guide* for 1949. The report on Psychology 1 the year before was brutally succinct: "Boring was."

175 "give as good as he got." Nevitt Sanford, "Murray's Clinic as a Place to Learn," p. 107. I draw here more generally on interviews with Sanford, 15 and 17 January 1971; Erik Erikson, 12 August 1970; Jerome Frank, 6 August 1970; Silvan Tomkins, 28 June 1971; and Robert White, 16 and 22 April 1970.

176 "A more emphatic endorsement." "Researches conducted at the Harvard Psychological Clinic during the year 1933," pp. 2–7.

— "Far and away the most famous." Ibid., pp. 8–12; and Christiana D. Morgan and Henry A. Murray, M.D., "A Method for Investigating Fantasies: The Thematic Apperception Test," *Archives of Neurology and Psychiatry,* 34 (1935), 305–306. Ernest Jones comments on the essay in a letter to Harry of 9 November 1934. He praises the TAT as "an important link in the chain that must one day bind analysis and academic psychology." But he also chides Harry for failing to acknowledge the earlier projective techniques of Ferenczi, Klein, and Jung and for overstating the TAT's value as a tool for "investigating the unconscious." Harry in several places acknowledges that Cecilia Roberts (later Mrs. Crane Brinton) had a role to play in the original development of the TAT (interview with HAM, 1 July 1971; Robert Holt to HAM, 17 October 1949).

— "keys to the unconscious." According to Donald MacKinnon, the earliest subjects at the Clinic were recruited from among the unemployed (interview with Donald MacKinnon, 1972). This practice was soon abandoned. Subsequent subjects were all Harvard undergraduates selected with an eye to possible neurotic trends. Though narrowly defined in terms of class and gender, most members of the sample displayed no striking psychological abnormalities. Albert Guerard, a subject at 50 cents an hour in 1934–1935, found going to the Clinic both restful and enjoyable. It was "fun to fantasize, be indulged, tell stories, and so on," he recalled (interview with Albert J. Guerard, 11 April 1971).

— "Years later he observed." Interview with HAM, 16 July 1970.

— "In a study designed to demonstrate." "The Effect of Fear upon Estimates of the Maliciousness of Other Personalities," *Journal of Social Psychology,* 4 (1933), 310, 324–327.

177 "Two papers on humor." H. A. Wolff, C. E. Smith, and H. A. Murray, "The Psychology of Humor. 1. A Study of Responses to Race-Disparagement Jokes," *Journal of Abnormal and Social Psychology,* 28 (1934), 345; and Henry A. Mur-

ray, Jr., "The Psychology of Humor. 2. Mirth Responses to Disparagement Jokes as a Manifestation of an Aggressive Disposition," *Journal of Abnormal and Social Psychology,* 29 (1934), 79.

— "Boston Psychoanalytic Society." Interviews with HAM, 23 and 31 August 1971 and 11 and 18 July 1972; and with Sanford Gifford, 23 July 1972. The history of the Boston Psychoanalytic Society is set forth in *The Birth of an Institute,* ed. Ives Hendrick (Freeport, ME: Bond Wheelwright, 1961).

178 "Harry's chief complaint." "Preparations for the Scaffold of a Comprehensive System," p. 37.

— "a black despair." Harry reviewed *Civilization and Its Discontents* for the *Atlantic Monthly,* 146 (1930), 14. He went on to trace the darkness of Freud's vision to "his own present most grievous physical state, and also to a disenchantment of a deeper sort which I shall not attempt to analyze. In the presence of misery we stand with bowed heads. But it is to our peril if we allow such instances of private suffering to color our entire philosophy."

— "his accounts of the experience." "What Should Psychologists Do About Psychoanalysis?" p. 155; "The Case of Murr," p. 302; interviews with HAM, 16 July 1970, 16 August 1970, 29 July 1972; and with Nevitt Sanford, 21 January 1971.

179 "She really gave it to him." Interview with HAM, 16 July 1970. Christiana wrote to Jung about her experience with Sachs. In reply, he observed of Freudian analysis that it is characteristically Jewish in its intellectual detachment. Like the Jews themselves, psychoanalysis operates from the outside. This is not the case, he goes on, with the Aryan mind, which generally finds itself in familiar cultural surroundings. Jung to CDM, 12 August 1933 (Special Collections, University of Pennsylvania).

— "Time and time again." "What Should Psychologists Do About Psychoanalysis?" p. 156.

180 "simultaneous variations." L. J. Henderson, *Pareto's General Sociology: A Physiologist's Interpretation* (Cambridge, MA: Harvard University Press, 1935), p. 13. An abbreviated version of the book appeared as "Pareto's Science of Society" in the *Saturday Review of Literature,* 25 (May 1935), 3–4, 10. It is reprinted in *L. J. Henderson on the Social System,* ed. Bernard Barber (Chicago: University of Chicago Press, 1970), pp. 181–190.

— "the great rationalizer." H. Stuart Hughes, *Consciousness and Society* (New York: Knopf, 1961), p. 82.

— "hardly lost on the members." The conservative political views of Henderson and Homans are well documented in Barbara S. Heyl's essay, "The Harvard 'Pareto Circle,'" *Journal of the History of the Behavioral Sciences,* 4 (1968), 317.

— "in his book on Pareto." George C. Homans and Charles P. Curtis, Jr., *An Introduction to Pareto* (New York: Knopf, 1934), p. 5. As an illustration of what they take to be the irrationality of human beings, Homans and Curtis refer to the widespread belief that a Republican presidential administration is necessarily "the 'tool' of 'Wall Street' or specifically of J. P. Morgan" (p. 7).

— "events at different levels." "Preparations for the Scaffold of a Comprehensive System," p. 50.

— "Homans was pleased to report." *An Introduction to Pareto,* p. 15.

181 "at Henderson's bedside." Interviews with HAM, 20 May 1970 and 5 August 1974.

182 "rare beef." HAM to Lewis Mumford, [April] 1933. In his "Henry A. Murray's Early Career: A Psychobiographical Exploration," James William Anderson observes that Harry "had a need to find a man whom he could admire and after whom he could model himself. But his need to be independent and special was even greater and his heroes eventually had to fall" (p. 157).

— "seek outside support." "Researches conducted at the Harvard Psychological Clinic during the year 1933," p. 22; Triplet, "Henry A. Murray and the Harvard Psychological Clinic, 1926–1938," pp. 113–118.

183 "the deliberate forces of History." Edwin G. Boring, *Psychologist at Large* (New York: Basic Books, 1961), p. 44.

— "second autobiographical essay." "Edwin Garrigues Boring," *A History of Psychology in Autobiography,* vol. 4, p. 30.

— "I don't suppose." Edwin G. Boring to Professor H. Austin Aikins, 13 February 1929 (in the Edwin G. Boring Papers at the Harvard University Archives).

— "Harry's relationship with Christiana." Interviews with HAM, 12 July 1971; and with Robert White, 16 April 1970 and 18 February 1989.

— "plans for the tercentenary celebration." Triplet, "Henry A. Murray and the Harvard Psychological Clinic, 1926–1938," pp. 245–246.

184 "Henderson shared Conant's viewpoint." Interview with HAM, 11 July 1971; and James B. Conant, *My Several Lives* (New York: Harper & Row, 1970), pp. 87–90. Henderson and Conant were related by marriage.

— "To make matters worse." Interviews with HAM, 12 July 1971 and 18 July 1972.

— "According to Boring." "Edwin Garrigues Boring," *A History of Psychology in Autobiography,* vol. 4, p. 45; see also Triplet, "Henry A. Murray and the Harvard Psychological Clinic, 1926–1938," pp. 237–238.

— "when push finally came to shove." Interview with HAM, 7 July 1972.

— "Harry's recent article." Entitled "'Pack of Hounds Attack Gill' Prof. Murray Says in Protest," it appeared—with a picture of Harry—in the *Boston Herald* on 30 January 1934. Harry followed up with another supportive essay in the *Christian Register* on 15 February 1934. Gill was the husband of Isabelle Kendig, a graduate student at the Clinic.

185 "uncertain future at Harvard." Interviews with HAM, 21 July 1970 and 31 August 1971.

— "Boring was ready." Edwin G. Boring to HAM, 23 January 1933.

— "The Clinic staff responded." Triplet, "Henry A. Murray and the Harvard Psychological Clinic, 1926–1938," pp. 235–236. Harry's essays, on fear and humor, are discussed above; Rosenzweig's are listed in Triplet's notes, pp. 262–263.

— "Harry let it be known." "Researches conducted at the Harvard Psychological Clinic during the year 1933," p. 6; and HAM to Alan Gregg, 5 November 1934 (Rockefeller Foundation Archives). In a letter of 3 November 1934 to

Harvard Dean Kenneth B. Murdock, Boring indicates that Harry has two books in the works, one to be published the following spring and the second possibly in the summer of 1936 (Edwin G. Boring Papers).

— "Harry moved just as vigorously." HAM to Alan Gregg, 6 February 1934 (Rockefeller Foundation Archives).

186 "Freud . . . in the flesh." Alan Gregg, "An Oral History," an unpublished autobiographical fragment excerpted in *The Birth of an Institute*, pp. 71–73.

— "His notes indicate." Alan Gregg's diary for 27 April 1934 (Rockefeller Foundation Archives).

— "Just days before." Stanley Cobb to Alan Gregg, 24 April 1934 (Rockefeller Foundation Archives). "Two weeks later." Alfred E. Cohn to Alan Gregg, 7 May 1934 (Rockefeller Foundation Archives).

— "Harry pressed for a decision." HAM to Alan Gregg, 26 September 1934 and 9 October 1934 (Rockefeller Foundation Archives).

187 *"Atlantic Monthly."* Ellery Sedgwick to HAM, 1 October 1934; interview with HAM, 18 August 1971.

— "It was finally published." Henry A. Murray, M.D., "Psychology and the University," *Archives of Neurology and Psychiatry*, 34 (1935), 803–817, passim.

188 "Boring didn't." Interview with HAM, 21 July 1970.

— "in such good hands." Alan Gregg to HAM, 31 October 1934 (Rockefeller Foundation Archives).

— "a certain amount of enmity around." Interview with HAM, 11 July 1971.

189 "reason to believe." "Psychology and the University," p. 803.

— "He took his appeal." "The Harvard Psychological Clinic," *Harvard Alumni Bulletin*, 38 (1935), 142–149, passim.

— "a hateful person." Interviews with Robert White, 18 February 1989; and with HAM, 11 July 1971.

190 "brief glimpses of the dyad." "Psychology and the University," p. 817; "The Harvard Psychological Clinic," p. 145.

— "He wrote to Mumford." HAM to Lewis Mumford, [August, 1931?].

— "he confessed in an earlier letter." HAM to Lewis Mumford, [April, 1930?].

191 "Christiana was not happy." CDM's chronological and topical file.

192 "truly creative person." All details are from CDM's chronological and topical file for 1928–1930, and from "STED," her two-volume, beautifully decorated and hand-lettered chronological record of the dyad and of the Parker River property, covering a period of nearly forty years.

— "in the crisis that finally broke." Ibid.

— "December 2, 1929." Ibid.

194 "two brief poems of mortal sacrifice." Ibid.

195 "I am very much occupied." HAM to Lewis Mumford, [February?] 1930.

196 "Read them to Mansol." CDM's chronological and topical file.

197 "Meanwhile, Harry was fascinated." Ibid.

— "Become the Lord." Ibid.

— "She responded in kind." Ibid.

198 "the volume is a compilation." CDM's illustrated volume of quotations.

199 "hand of destiny." Review of *Pierre, or the Ambiguities, New England Quarterly,* 4 (1931), 334.
— "Anguish and anguish." CDM's chronological and topical file.
200 "stunned by her genius." Interview with Robert White, 18 February 1989.
— "Ina May Greer once observed." Interview with Ina May Greer, 4 July 1970.
— "one of a very small handful." Interviews with HAM, 4 August 1970 and 7 and 26 August 1971; and with Donald MacKinnon, 1972.
— "Aiken was pleased." Conrad Aiken to HAM, 10 and 29 November 1930.
201 "I feel like a devourer." HAM to Lewis Mumford, [March 1931?]. Harry's letter to Jung has not survived, but the tone of his remarks may be inferred from Jung's reply of 21 September 1931.
— "No Margin," *Atlantic Monthly,* 134 (1924), 735, 736.
— "The identical message." E. Clement Jones, "The Basket," *Harper's Magazine,* 163 (1931), 575–583.
— "Isn't she a seraph?" Conrad Aiken to HAM, 23 February 1931.
202 "so hauntingly terrible." Interview with HAM, 18 August 1971; and Ellery Sedgwick to Mrs. E. Clement Jones, 30 March 1931. The Sedgwick letter, along with typescripts of two other characteristically somber stories—"The End of the Quarrel" and "Cyprus Place"—are housed among the Murray papers in the Harvard University Archives.
— "Finally, Harry was wrong." Interview with HAM, 26 August 1971; and CDM's chronological and topical file.
— "you've saved her life." Conrad Aiken to HAM, 23 February 1931.
— "He supported Aiken." Harry and Aiken first met at a Signet Club meeting in 1927. Later that year Harry gave the poet $1000, the first installment on support that continued for decades. As one gesture of gratitude, Aiken dedicated *Preludes for Memnon* (New York: Charles Scribners' Sons, 1931) to his benefactor. Aiken's second wife, Clarissa M. Lorenz, was working at the Clinic when she met her future husband. Her *Lorelei Two: My Life with Conrad Aiken* (Athens, GA: University of Georgia Press, 1983) casts useful light on the friendship between the men. Lorenz suggests, for example, that she "was supposed to be the unfaithful wife and Harry Murray the lover in both *Great Circle* and *King Coffin,*" two of Aiken's novels (p. 177). A few of Aiken's many letters to Harry appear in *Selected Letters of Conrad Aiken,* ed. Joseph Killorin (New Haven: Yale University Press, 1978). Kenneth Patchen was another of the artists to whom Harry gave substantial financial support.
203 "Lewis Mumford complained." Interview with Lewis Mumford, 15 July 1970.
— "a narcissist." Nevitt Sanford ("Murray's Clinic as a Place to Learn," pp. 109–110) is very shrewdly insightful on this point.
— "He went out of his way." Harry met with Powys on several occasions, and they corresponded. Harry and Christiana were also very much impressed with Powys' *The Meaning of Culture* (New York: Norton, 1929).
— "The whole category of evil." HAM to Mumford, 24 September 1929. Henry, Sr., was no keener on the book. "Powys is very poetical," he wrote, "but indulges in a good deal of slimy talk—'dung' and such like, which seems to me

unnecessary, & almost as if he liked filth. Hardy is much to be preferred in my humble opinion" (HAM, Sr., to HAM, 6 August 1929).

— "Christiana was deeply stirred." CDM to HAM, 26 October 1925 and Winter 1926.

204 "best university novel." Interviews with HAM, 20 August 1971; and with George Weller, 28 October 1975. HAM to Lewis Mumford, [April 1933?]; and Conrad Aiken to HAM, 24 July 1933. Harry's reviews appeared in the Harvard *Crimson,* 22 April 1933, and in the *Harvard Alumni Bulletin,* 35 (1933), 729–730.

— "he observed in later life." Interview with HAM, 24 July 1970.

205 "The Wisdom of the Body." CDM's chronological and topical file and CDM's illustrated volume of quotations.

— "Fear of gossip." Interview with HAM, 21 August 1971.

206 "in a letter of 1931." C. G. Jung to HAM, 21 September 1931.

— "little room for thoughtful women." Interviews with HAM, 23 June 1970, 27 July 1970, and 3 August 1972.

— "which open to a portrait." *The Vision Seminars,* vol. 1, p. 1.

207 "the transcendent function." Ibid.

— "It wasn't in his being." Interview with HAM, 21 August 1971. Christiana spoke critically of Jung and *The Vision Seminars* to her friend Cleome Wadsworth. "Harry and I feel that he missed the whole point," she complained. Wadsworth also reports on Christiana's annoyance at Jung's manner as an analyst. (Interview with Mrs. Cleome Wadsworth in the C. G. Jung Biographical Archive at the Countway Library, Harvard Medical School.)

— "In his 'Postscript.'" A draft and a final version of Harry's "Postscript" to *The Vision Seminars* are among the Murray papers at the Harvard University Archive. I quote from the final version.

— "the key to it all." "Postscript" to *The Vision Seminars,* vol. 2, pp. 517–520.

— "In objecting to Jung's conformity." Claire Douglas, "Christiana Morgan's Visions Reconsidered: A Look behind *The Vision Seminars,*" *San Francisco Jung Institute Library Journal,* 8 (1989), 16, 7–8.

208 "Jung was 'vexed.'" Interviews with HAM, 21 August 1971, 5 August 1980, and 3 August 1972; and the "Postscript" to *The Vision Seminars,* vol. 2, pp. 519–520. Harry included Morton Prince (and Sally Beauchamp) in the group and laid emphasis on the leading role of the men in making sense of the unconscious productions of their female associates.

— "Douglas goes on." "Christiana Morgan's Visions Reconsidered," p. 24.

— "that was the crux." Interview with HAM, 13 July 1972.

— "that went back and forth." Interview with HAM, 2 September 1971.

209 "rhythm of dyadic life." In her chronological and topical file for 1933, Christiana refers to *The Rhythm of Living. Systole-Diastole.* The idea of ceaseless dialectical variations was a constant in the dyadic vocabulary.

— "limitless need for control." CDM's chronological and topical file.

— "It fell to Harry." Eaton returned from Zürich in very unstable condition and in time required special care at a "rest home" that Harry found for him in

Topsfield. After a few days Harry received a call that Eaton had disappeared. He rallied a group from the Clinic, who helped to find the body. Interview with Nina Murray, 2 May 1970. See also Kuklick, *The Rise of American Philosophy,* pp. 458–459.

— "He destroyed himself." Interviews with HAM, 21 July 1970 and 11 August 1971. Billy Richards' father was Theodore William Richards, the noted Harvard chemist and Conant's mentor. Conant married Grace Thayer Richards, the professor's daughter, in 1921 (see Conant's *My Several Lives,* pp. 27–34, 54).

— "Will's personal anguish." Interview with Mrs. Frank Wigglesworth, 1 May 1970.

210 "Ike's passing." Interviews with HAM, 1 July 1971, 23 and 30 August 1971, and 7 August 1972; and with Rev. Michael Murray, 7 August 1980.

9. The Pequod Meets the Rachel

211 "Christiana took a different view." The Rachel episode makes regular appearances in Christiana's notes and journals. In Harry's "The Way to the Sanctuary," a dyadic manuscript produced in 1940, he acknowledges Christiana's "having to explain to him the Rachel incident in Moby Dick. . . . The test was this: how much guilt (as society would name it) can a creator carry?"

— "didn't change anything." Interview with HAM, 27 July 1970.

212 "much bitter dying." CDM's illustrated volume of quotations.

— "great advances in the dyad." CDM's chronological and topical file.

— "Harry complained." HAM to Lewis Mumford, March 1935.

— "bayonet in my hand." Interview with HAM, 21 July 1970.

213 "looking for a mechano-set." HAM's videotaped interview with Eugene Taylor, Countway Library, Harvard Medical School.

— "Lashley's opposition." Boring to HAM, 24 October 1936 (Edwin G. Boring Papers); and the diary of Robert A. Lambert of the Rockefeller Foundation, 12 October 1936 (Rockefeller Foundation Archives). Conant reported to James G. Miller that at a personal meeting Lashley became more and more heated in expressing his opposition to Murray and finally burst into tears (interview with James G. Miller, 9 August 1980).

— "he shared with Allport." Edwin G. Boring to Gordon Allport, 11 September 1935; and to K. S. Lashley, 12 January 1937 (Edwin G. Boring Papers).

214 "everything treacherously twisted." HAM to Edwin G. Boring, [May 1936?] (Edwin G. Boring Papers).

215 "the dawn never came." Edwin G. Boring, "Was This Analysis a Success?" with a "Comment by Hanns Sachs," in Boring, *Psychologist at Large,* pp. 129–130, 137, 139, 141.

— "coiling for a strike." Edwin G. Boring to HAM, 3 August 1935 (Edwin G. Boring Papers).

— "so dependent on Sachs." Interview with HAM, 30 July 1971.

— "What a hell of a state." HAM to Edwin G. Boring, [August, 1935] (Edwin G. Boring Papers).

216 "how things really stood." Interviews with HAM, 30 July 1971, and Erik Erikson, 12 August 1970; Edwin G. Boring to Gordon Allport, 11 September 1935 (Edwin G. Boring Papers). Despite his angry condemnation of psychoanalysis, Boring later asked Harry to review a revealing psychological self-study. "I have written without reserve," he said, "but of course I know that the MS has its latent content as well as its manifest content" (20 November 1935, Edwin G. Boring Papers).

— "pipsqueak of a chemist." Interview with Nevitt Sanford, 19 January 1971.

— "Harry did his best." Interview with HAM, 21 July 1970.

217 "he asked Alan Gregg." James B. Conant to Dr. Alan Gregg, 24 April 1936 (Rockefeller Foundation Archives); Triplet, "Henry A. Murray and the Harvard Psychological Clinic, 1926–1938," p. 246.

— "When word spread." Interview with HAM, 31 July 1970.

— "several such papers." "Basic Concepts for a Psychology of Personality," *Journal of General Psychology,* 15 (1936), 241–268, appears in *Explorations* on pp. 49ff; "Facts Which Support the Concept of Need or Drive," *Journal of Psychology,* 3 (1936), 27–42, on pp. 54ff; "Techniques for a Systematic Investigation of Fantasy," *Journal of Psychology,* 3 (1936), 115–143, on pp. 388ff; and (with Richard E. Wolf) "An Experiment in Judging Personalities," *Journal of Psychology,* 3 (1936), 345–365, on pp. 262ff.

— "build, tear down." HAM to Lewis Mumford, March 1935.

— "Two others." See preceding note.

218 "conference honoring Kurt Lewin." Interview with HAM, 31 August 1971.

— "series of six seminars." Interviews with HAM, 30 August 1971 and 15 June 1985; Boring to HAM, 27 July 1936; Boring to Lashley, 28 July 1936 (Edwin G. Boring Papers).

— "Jung and Conant." Triplet, "Henry A. Murray and the Harvard Psychological Clinic, 1926–1938," pp. 245–246. At the luncheon Jung made fun of Piaget's interest in babies—"les enfants, les petites bébés," he cooed—and offended Allport by flirting with Christiana. Jung was interested in women, not babies, Harry observed. Harry reports fully on the tercentenary in his 1968 interview for the C. G. Jung Biographical Archive at the Countway Library, Harvard Medical School, pp. 94ff.

— "Levellers." Interviews with HAM, 11 July 1971; and with Talcott Parsons, 31 July 1972; and personal communication from HAM, 8 May 1973.

— "preliminary proposals." HAM to Boring, January 1934 (Edwin G. Boring Papers); and the diary of Robert A. Lambert at the Rockefeller Foundation, 2 April 1936 (Rockefeller Foundation Archives). Harry elaborates on his proposal in "Psychology and the University," pp. 10–11.

— "Eva Goldbeck." Interviews with HAM, 24 July 1970; and with Lewis Mumford, 15 July 1970. There are numerous references to Goldbeck in the Murray/Mumford correspondence for 1935–1936. See also Eric A. Gordon's treatment of Goldbeck in his biography of her husband, *Mark the Music: The Life and Work of Mark Blitzstein* (New York: St. Martin's Press, 1989).

— "brief study of dreams." H. A. Murray and D. R. Wheeler, "A Note on the Possible Clairvoyance of Dreams," *Journal of Psychology*, 3 (1936), 313.

— "a cogent discussion." Henry A. Murray, "Visceral Manifestations of Personality," *Journal of Abnormal and Social Psychology*, 32 (1937), 184.

219 "He assured Mumford." HAM to Lewis Mumford, [February] 1935. Harry repeated his prediction in a letter to Mumford in March of the same year.

— "article on the Clinic." Magazine section, *Boston Evening Transcript*, 30 November 1935.

— "Robert White recalled." Robert W. White, *Seeking the Shape of Personality* (Marlborough, NH: The Homestead Press, 1987), p. 17. White's remarks on Harry and the Clinic appear in an earlier version, "Exploring Personality the Long Way: The Study of Lives," in *Further Explorations in Personality*, ed. A. I. Rabin et al. (New York: John Wiley & Sons, 1981), pp. 3–19.

— "widely recognized as a classic." M. Brewster Smith's retrospective, "Personology Launched," *Contemporary Psychology*, 35 (1990), 537–539, is the most recent of numerous tributes to the influence and historical significance of *Explorations*.

220 "the exceptional spirit." "The Case of Murr," p. 303.

— "Motivation is the crux." Henry A. Murray et al., *Explorations in Personality* (New York: Oxford University Press, 1938), p. 251.

— "unsatisfying situation." Ibid., p. 124.

— "well-being of the subject." Ibid., p. 121.

— "history of a personality." Ibid., p. 604.

221 "This is not to deny." Harry is scrupulously attentive in *Explorations* to his intellectual debts and to major points of difference with those whose views he shares. See especially his commentary (pp. 711–716) on Allport's recently published *Personality* (1937) and his numerous references to McDougall and Lewin. Saul Rosenzweig's essay, "Converging Approaches to Personality: Murray, Allport, Lewin," *Psychological Review*, 51 (1944), 248–256, is a lucid exposition of major similarities and differences. M. Brewster Smith ("Personology Launched," p. 538) emphasizes that "Murray's *needs* have the psychological characteristics of McDougall's *instincts,* or *propensities."* Lashing out at the "damned mechanists," McDougall warmly acknowledged a "near affinity" with Harry (undated letter [1936?]).

— "whale of a book." White, *Seeking the Shape of Personality*, pp. 7 and 10.

— "recalls M. Brewster Smith." Smith, "Personology Launched," p. 537.

— "Averages." *Explorations*, p. viii.

— "Never before." White, *Seeking the Shape of Personality*, p. 14.

— "proof of the pudding." *Explorations*, pp. 604–607.

223 "veritable intellectual interest." Ibid., pp. 98–101.

— "only one other person." Ibid., p. 721.

224 "fairly afloat in himself." *Pierre*, p. 335.

225   "he would resign." Allport to Boring, 21 January 1937 (Edwin G. Boring Papers). I draw here, and in subsequent paragraphs, on Triplet's excellent treatment of the final phase of Harry's case for promotion. See "Henry A. Murray and the Harvard Psychological Clinic, 1926–1938," pp. 245–260.

—   "Harry had it on good authority." Interviews with HAM, 21 July 1970 and 12 July 1971; HAM's videotaped interview with Eugene Taylor, Countway Library, Harvard Medical School.

—   "In a separate letter." Gordon W. Allport to James B. Conant, 5 January 1937, quoted by Triplet, pp. 255–256.

226   "multiple dimensions of the case." HAM to Lewis Mumford, 8 February 1937; Edwin G. Boring to Gordon Allport, 18 February 1937 (Edwin G. Boring Papers). Triplet's analysis of the elements involved in Conant's decision is especially helpful.

—   "In a meeting with Conant." Alan Gregg's diary for 12 March 1937 (Rockefeller Foundation Archives).

—   "no one doubted." Boring wrote to Allport on 15 May 1939 that while Harry had been "reappointed for five years," it was "plain that the President meant ten. After ten years it would be impossible to discontinue the appointment until he reaches retiring age" (Edwin G. Boring Papers).

—   "Even Lashley." Karl Lashley to HAM, 24 March 1937; and Boring to Allport, 1 April 1937 (Edwin G. Boring Papers).

227   "profound debt of gratitude." Donald MacKinnon to HAM, 24 March 1937.

—   "more widely useful." Calvin S. Hall and Gardner Lindzey, *Theories of Personality,* 3rd ed. (New York: John Wiley & Sons, 1978), pp. 235–236.

—   "humanistic psychology movement." See Salvatore R. Maddi and Paul T. Costa, *Humanism in Personology: Allport, Maslow, and Murray* (Chicago: Aldine, 1972); M. Brewster Smith, "Humanistic Psychology," *Encyclopedia of Psychology,* ed. Raymond J. Corsini, 4 vols. (New York: Wiley, 1984), vol. 2, pp. 155–159; and Floyd Matson, "Humanistic Theory: The Third Revolution in Psychology," *Humanist,* 31 (1971), 7–11.

—   "Harry wrote a play." In his brief reminiscences about "Clinicus," Nevitt Sanford speculates that it "was produced at Christmas, 1935," when "its hero was only eight years old" ("Murray's Clinic as a Place to Learn," p. 105). But the title of the play indicates that Clinicus is ten, and its action explicitly celebrates his/her achievement of a permanent home at Harvard. Harry wrote to his daughter, Josephine, on 25 May 1937 that the Clinic staff were making preparations for a grand 10th anniversary party. It seems probable, therefore, that the play was written and produced *after* Conant's momentous decision of March 1937.

228   "During his four years away." Boring to Allport, 22 March 1937; HAM to Boring, 23 March 1937; HAM to Boring, 15 April 1938 (Edwin G. Boring Papers). See also HAM to Alan Gregg, 23 March 1937 (Rockefeller Foundation Archives). Robert White—personal communication, 22 February 1989—has been very helpful in the shaping of this survey of the years just before the war.

229 "looking for promising new associates." Alan Gregg's diary of 19 September 1938; HAM to Alan Gregg, 9 December [1939] (Rockefeller Foundation Archives).

— "close view." HAM to Boring, September 1937 (Edwin G. Boring Papers).

— "met for a few hours." Anna Freud to HAM, 28 December 1937; and interviews with HAM, 11 July 1970 and 30 July 1972. Harry elaborates on the planning for the Tercentenary in a long letter to Walter Kaufmann, 20 November 1975. An account of the Freud visit appears in Paul Roazen's *Freud and His Followers* (New York: Knopf, 1975), p. 296.

— "quarreled bitterly." Virginia Murray (Mrs. Robert Low) Bacon to HAM, 16 July 1938.

230 "Jung's alleged connections." Felix Frankfurter to HAM, 10 March 1938. During Harry's brief visit to Zurich in September 1937 Jung explained that he had been asked by Hitler's doctors to examine their leader, who had developed worrisome symptoms. The Old Man wrote rather frantically in late 1938, asking for assistance in tracking down the source of rumors that he was a frequent visitor to Berchtesgaden. Jung had somehow heard about Harry's visit with Freud and suspected, quite mistakenly, that the gossip began there. "I don't think that I have paranoic delusions about persecution," he complained. "The difficulty is very real. Whatever I touch and wherever I go I meet with this prejudice that I'm a Nazi and that I'm in close affiliation to the German government" (Jung to HAM, 6 October 1938). Jung's other letters to Harry on this subject are dated 29 August, 21 November, 12 December, and 19 December 1938, and 6 March 1939. See also my interview with HAM, 25 July 1972.

— "autocratic." HAM to Lewis Mumford, n.d. [1939?].

— "internal dynamite." Clyde Kluckhohn to HAM, 9 April 1940; and interviews with HAM, 4 June 1970 and 14 July 1971. Mumford recognized in retrospect that Kluckhohn had taken his place in Harry's affection (interview with Lewis Mumford, 15 July 1970). Kluckhohn's homosexuality was no secret to many in the Harvard community. He was truthful with Harry on this score and promised to respect his friend's very decided heterosexual orientation (interview with HAM, 15 July 1985).

— "Harry was himself centrally involved." HAM to Josephine Murray, July 1937.

— "thumbing his nose." Interviews with HAM, 11 July 1970 and 15 July 1972.

231 "Harry once explained." Interview with HAM, 13 August 1970; and HAM's interview with Alan Elms, 23 August 1978.

— "Harry's friends would respond." Raymond Pearl, review of *Explorations in Personality, Quarterly Review of Biology*, 15 (1940), 505. Pearl also wrote personally to pronounce that *Explorations* was equaled by "very few books of the last quarter of a century" (Raymond Pearl to HAM, 23 September 1940). John Dollard to HAM, 7 December 1938; Ruth Benedict to HAM, 30 July 1940; Jung to HAM, 21 November 1938; and Aiken to HAM, 25 November 1938.

232 "Boring predicted." Boring to HAM, 25 October 1938 (Edwin G. Boring Papers).

— "Newspapers were generally very favorable." See, for example, the *New York Times Book Review,* 5 March 1939, which represents *Explorations* as "a great advance in the right direction" (p. 12). An unidentified clipping filed in Harry's papers registers "pleasure that the authors take as their study the real living man enmeshed in his environment and showing ambition, frustration, rage and joy. . . . This has been the aim of all great psychologists from Aristotle to the present."

— "Journals." Milton R. Miller, *Psychoanalytic Quarterly,* 8 (1939), 391; Kingsley Davis, *American Journal of Sociology,* 45 (1939) 130; and Carney Landis, *Psychological Bulletin,* 36 (1939), 288–291.

— "ten-page critical essay." Richard M. Elliott, *American Journal of Psychology,* 52 (1939), 453–462.

233 "abuse of Harry's masterpiece." Interviews with HAM, 20 July 1971, 30 July 1972; and Richard M. Elliott to HAM, 24 Oct 1939.

— "biography of Conscience." HAM to Josephine Murray, 26 February 1938.

234 "he assured his daughter." HAM to Josephine Murray, 3 April 1938

— "complained to Mumford." HAM to Lewis Mumford, [October] 1938.

— "Thereafter the chapters." Harry's progress with Melville's novels figures prominently in handwritten notes, apparently composed during the late 1940s, on his personal and professional development during the decade beginning in 1937. I am indebted to Eugene Taylor (interviewed 2 March 1989), who was employed as Harry's assistant for several years during the 1980s, for help in some details.

— "progress slowed." Interviews with HAM, 14 July 1970, 1 July 1971, 31 August 1971; HAM to Lewis Mumford, [August] 1938.

— "invasion of France." HAM to Lewis Mumford, 23 December 1941.

— "Harry told himself." Interviews with HAM, 11 and 14 July 1970.

235 "valor-ruined man." *Moby-Dick,* p. 117.

— "shorter critical studies." "In Nomine Diaboli" (1951), "Bartleby and I" (1966), and "Dead to the World: The Passions of Herman Melville" (1967) draw in varying degrees on the biography. So do the Melville "Morsels" which Harry worked on toward the end of his life. These materials will come up for discussion in due course.

— "destroyed in the course of revision." Interview with Eugene Taylor, 2 March 1989.

236 "nothing in the critical literature." A list of the books eligible for comparison would include: Newton Arvin, *Herman Melville* (New York: Sloan, 1950); Leon Howard, *Herman Melville: A Biography* (Berkeley: University of California Press, 1951); Edwin Haviland Miller, *Melville* (New York: G. Braziller, 1975); Lewis Mumford, *Herman Melville* (New York: Harcourt Brace, 1929); and Michael Paul Rogin, *Subversive Genealogy: The Politics and Art of Herman Melville* (Berkeley: University of California Press, 1983).

243 "a screaming altercation." Interview with Conrad Aiken, 28 July 1971.

— "I always do." Conrad Aiken to HAM, 5 February 1940.

246 "reticent about Murr's sexuality." "The Case of Murr," pp. 296–300.

247 "a wicked book." Melville to Hawthorne, 29 June and 17 November 1851, in *The Letters of Herman Melville,* pp. 133 and 142.

249 "other forms of beauty." Gaston Lachaise to HAM, 18 October 1934.

250 "fiery spirit." Interview with HAM, 24 July 1970.

— "described it to Mumford." HAM to Lewis Mumford, [January?] and [March?] 1935.

— "ruled by his sexuality." Interview with Ina May Greer, 4 July 1970.

251 "I'm it." Interview with Ina May Greer, 27 June 1970.

— "the Guidance Pillar." "STED," 1935.

— "Her records." CDM's chronological and topical file; and "HOLA," a hand-printed volume recording key dyadic developments between 1930 and 1945.

252 "The Whip for Slavery." "HOLA," October 1936.

253 "the day would come." CDM's chronological and topical file.

— "Write my words." Ibid.

254 "You shall write *my* book." Ibid.

255 "struggle and tragic dissolution." Ibid.

256 "towered house at Arrowhead." Rogin, *Subversive Genealogy,* p. 230; and Eleanor Melville Metcalf, *Herman Melville: Cycle and Epicycle* (Cambridge, MA: Harvard University Press, 1953), p. 126.

— "the claustrum." Interview with HAM, 6 August 1970.

— "Harry did most of his work." CDM's chronological and topical file.

257 "when your Lord returns." From a folder of dyadic materials entitled "Annuesta: Masc.[uline] Fem.[inine] Authority"; and CDM's chronological and topical file.

— "He made his offerings." Interviews with HAM, 14 and 27 July 1970 and 23 August 1971.

258 "Laughter came." CDM's chronological and topical file.

— "Love-making came last." Interviews with HAM, 27 July and 6 August 1970; and with Lewis Mumford, 15 July 1970.

— "The Tower accelerated everything." Interview with HAM, 27 July 1970.

259 "fruits of her being." "Annuesta: Masc.[uline] Fem.[inine] Authority."

— "timorous, tame penis." Ibid.; and CDM's chronological and topical file.

260 "visions would come to naught." CDM's chronological and topical file.

— "old story all over again." From a folder marked "2" containing fragments from a diary and assorted notes and records by CDM.

262 "This is his message." "Written by Mansol" and "The Way to the Sanctuary" are both stored in the folder marked "2."

264 "his fist and his iron heel." "The Way to the Sanctuary." There is a hint at Christiana's developing problem with alcohol in "Clinicus," Harry's one-act play performed at the Clinic in 1937. One of the male characters challenges Queen Morganatic to a game of squash—"or," he goes on, "shall we make it a drinking bout?" "O, drinking," she replies, "by all means. The harder the better."

265 "beautiful shapes." CDM's chronological and topical file.

10. Chronometricals and Horologicals

266 "At the age of 51." HAM to Josephine Murray, [June] 1945.

— "My office is with the individual." HAM to Lewis Mumford, August 1942.

— "social vacuum." "Preparations for the Scaffold of a Comprehensive System," p. 45.

267 "a new superego." HAM to Lewis Mumford, 20 December 1942.

— "wrote to FDR." Interview with HAM, 30 July 1972. The proposal was properly received by the government, but nothing came of it.

— "great social & moral dilemmas." HAM to Lewis Mumford, June 1943.

— "his word will deliver me." CDM's chronological and topical file.

— "We had given them nothing." CDM to Ned and Elizabeth [Handy], 20 May 1943.

— "retreat for creative writers." HAM to Lewis Mumford, June 1943.

— "into her own depths." HAM to Lewis Mumford, June 1944.

268 "one correction." *Harvard College Class of 1915 35th Anniversary Report* (Cambridge, MA: Cosmos Press, 1950), p. 235.

— "Discussing Eric Fromm's." HAM to Josephine Murray, 10 December 1945.

— "lots of money for research." HAM to Josephine Murray, 30 September and 16 October 1945.

269 "instincts of a true social scientist." Interview with Talcott Parsons, 31 July 1972. "Clyde [Kluckhohn] was more of a social scientist than Harry," Parsons averred. "Harry is a psychologist open to sociological considerations; he's not a sociologist."

270 "self-analytic letters to Josephine." HAM to Josephine Murray, 10 January 1946.

— "another long dive." Ibid.

271 "social relations among young people." Alan Gregg, memo of interview with HAM at the Clinic, 9 October 1940 (Rockefeller Foundation Archives).

— "Harry's notes for the period." "Problems to be Studied, 1941–42" goes on to specify a handful of basic political assumptions: "(1) Democracy is [the] best form of government, its values are worth defending. (2) Fascism must be fought or counteracted until it is dead. (3) Individuals have a common responsibility to the Nation. (4) Government must be improved."

272 "Harry's rousing essay." Interview with Elliott Jaques, 12 December 1972.

— "all this shallowness." "What Should Psychologists Do About Psychoanalysis?" p. 175.

— "Those who continued." Harry first wrote to Alan Gregg about the suspension of the grant during the summer of 1942. Their correspondence on this matter is in the Rockefeller Archives. Harry's "Report of Work at the Harvard Psychological Clinic 1941–1943," along with a bibliography of "Miscellaneous Papers Completed," is available in the same collection.

— "TAT." *Thematic Apperception Test* (Cambridge, MA: Harvard University Press, 1943); and reviews of Carl R. Rogers, *Counseling and Psychotherapy* and of *Studies in Personality,* a collection of essays honoring Lewis M. Terman. The Tomkins volume was published by Harvard University Press in 1943.

— "a brief note on techniques." "Note on the Selection of Combat Officers," *Psychosomatic Medicine*, 5 (1943), 386–391.

— "cutting everything off." HAM to Lewis Mumford, June and August 1942.

273 "monograph." Henry A. Murray and Christiana D. Morgan, *A Clinical Study of Sentiments, Genetic Psychology Monographs*, 32 (1945), 76. The bulk of the writing on the project was completed by the end of the summer of 1943. Harry brought the manuscript to completion on his own at scattered intervals during the following year or so (interviews with HAM, 1 and 3 July 1971, and 18 July 1972).

— "integrity of American society." *Sentiments*, p. 67.

— "fortitude in a foxhole." Ibid., p. 75.

— "existence of evil." Ibid., p. 79.

— "physical timidity. Ibid., p. 84.

— "to live or die for." Ibid., p. 92.

— "fashionable cynicism." Ibid., p. 108.

— "has got the best of him." Ibid., p. 130.

— "victorious armies and navies." Ibid., p. 138.

274 "college intellectuals." Ibid., p. 302.

— "no common enlivening ideology." Ibid., p. 304.

— "Romantic Genius figure." Ibid., p. 79.

— "better fitted for peace." Ibid., p. 149.

— "valuation of individualism." Ibid., p. 304.

— "fairly mediocre." HAM to Lewis Mumford, [November?] 1943.

— "virtues, talents." *Sentiments*, p. 301.

— "amounts to an indictment." HAM to Lewis Mumford, June 1943.

— "*ethos of American culture.*" *Sentiments*, p. 304.

275 "extreme of Christianity." HAM to Josephine Murray, 4 March 1938.

— "endowment of aggressive instinct." HAM to Lewis Mumford, August 1938.

— "selfish country." HAM to Lewis Mumford, n.d. [1939?].

— "made it known to the staff." Interview with Nevitt Sanford, 17 January 1971; and with Robert White, 18 February 1989.

— "solidify the country." HAM to Lewis Mumford, 23 December 1941. Harry was informed and influenced by *Faith for Living* (1940), Mumford's attack on fascism and call to war, as well as by Harold Laski's *Where Do We Go From Here?* (1940) and Max Lerner's *It Is Later Than You Think* (1938), which he urged on Nevitt Sanford (interview with Nevitt Sanford, 17 January 1971).

— "urging the students." From an undated clipping in Harry's records, apparently from the Bryn Mawr student newspaper. Donald MacKinnon wrote to Harry on 5 February 1942, requesting that he come to Bryn Mawr to give a talk on "some psychological aspect of the war."

— "article." *Boston Herald*, 22 February 1942.

276 "strategy and propaganda." Interviews with HAM, 30 July and 31 August 1971 and 11 July 1972.

— "morale in a democracy." Harry wrote to Archibald MacLeish, then at the Office of Facts and Figures, Library of Congress, describing the seminars and offering their services. "These groups are made up of historians, sociologists, cultural anthropologists and psychologists, and they are ready to make short-time or long-time investigations and to mimeograph their condensed reports on any topic that falls within their competence. Among other things, Dr. Allport and myself have been conducting a seminar on the psychology of morale, and we now have collected a number of memoranda on various phases of this problem" (HAM to Archibald MacLeish, 17 January 1942).

— "profile of the Fuhrer." Interviews with HAM, 1 July 1971, 7 July 1972, and 1 March 1986; HAM to Harmon S. Ephron, 31 July 1940. The Vernon essay, "Hitler the Man—Notes for a Case History," appeared in the *Journal of Abnormal and Social Psychology*, 37 (1942), 295–308.

277 "portrait formed itself." "Analysis of the Personality of Adolf Hitler," pp. 1–7, 185, 25–27, 18, and 148–151.

— "questioned two of the women." Ibid., p. 210: "Although the discovery of these sexual patterns is helpful to a psychiatrist in arriving at a complete formulation of Hitler's character and therefore indirectly pertinent to the final diagnosis and the predictions of his behavior, it has no bearing on the political situation."

— "fearing that disgust." Interview with HAM, 1 July 1971.

— "past master." Walter Langer to HAM, 2 September 1943.

278 "without a word." Interview with HAM, 27 July 1984. Harry took the news in stride. He made no public complaint about Langer's use of his ideas and language; nor did he protest for long at the misplaced praise for Langer's achievements in Robert G. L. Waite's Afterword to *The Mind of Adolf Hitler: The Secret Wartime Report* (New York: Basic Books, 1972). A comparison of Harry's original report—a single copy survives at the Franklin D. Roosevelt Library in Washington—with Langer's book reveals that the unacknowledged debts were extensive. Hans W. Gatzke suggests as much in his very damaging review of *The Mind of Adolf Hitler*. He notes that Langer fails to give the names of his associates, adding that "the Murray report . . . proves to be an extensive document, in its conclusions and language not unlike Langer's. . . . Since Dr. Murray wrote his paper at the time Langer did and since Langer states that pressure of time prevented him from showing his report to his collaborators, one cannot help wondering to what extent the Langer report is based on Dr. Murray's version. One wishes this relationship had been clarified" (*American Historical Review*, 78 [1973], 395–396). Walter Langer, along with his brother, William (who was also working for Donovan in the OSS) and Robert G. L. Waite wrote replies to the review but failed to answer the most damaging of its charges. Gatzke observes as much in his response (the entire exchange appears in *American Historical Review*, 78 [1973], 1155–1163).

— "Naval Reserve." Ellsworth Moody to HAM, 25 September 1940.

— "Combat Intelligence Officer." HAM to Lewis Mumford, August 1942.

— "War Office Selection Board." Interview with HAM, 6 August 1971; HAM to Lewis Mumford [November] 1943.

— "Assessment Station S." Interviews with HAM, 3 July 1971; and with Donald MacKinnon, 1972.

279 "Christiana's blood pressure." HAM to Lewis Mumford, [October?] 1945.

— *"pain* can fill the whole world." HAM to Lewis Mumford, November 1943.

— "margin of my fortitude." Ibid.

— "observer at both operations." Interview with HAM, 1 July 1971.

280 "which they read." Denis de Rougement, *Love in the Western World,* trans. Montgomery Belgion (New York: Harcourt, Brace and Company, 1940), pp. 3, 13.

— "twin narcissism." Ibid., p. 46 (de Rougemont's emphasis).

281 "In one mood." Interviews with HAM, 27 July 1970 and 25 August 1971.

— "open up about Harry." Interviews with Robert Holt, 29 July 1970; Elliott Jaques, 12 December 1972; and Ina May Greer, 4 July 1970.

— "terrific fun." Interview with HAM, 3 July 1971.

282 "co-authored account." Henry A. Murray (with members of the OSS Assessment Staff), *Assessment of Men: Selection of Personnel for the Office of Strategic Services* (New York: Rinehart, 1948), pp. 8–20. Those principally involved with Harry in the composition of the book were Donald W. Fiske, Eugenia Hanfmann, Donald W. MacKinnon, and James G. Miller. Much of the writing, along with the overall design and theoretical trajectory of the project, were Harry's. He was characteristically generous in sharing the credit. Harry's "Assessment of OSS Personnel" (with Donald W. MacKinnon), *Journal of Consulting Psychology,* 10 (1946), 76–80, and his paper on "Assessment of the Whole Person," in *New Methods in Applied Psychology* (College Park: University of Maryland Press, 1947), pp. 55–60, are briefer accounts.

— "the Clinic in a nutshell." *Assessment of Men,* p. 3 and passim.

— "He was delighted to find." HAM to Lewis Mumford, 28 April 1944; interview with HAM, 6 August 1971. Interviews with John Bowlby (11 August 1972), Ben Morris (11 September 1972), and John D. Sutherland (28 August 1972)—all closely involved with English officer assessment—were helpful supplements to Harry's account of the visit to England.

283 "Promotion to Major." Interview with Donald MacKinnon, 1972; HAM to Lewis Mumford, 6 June 1944.

— "at college again." HAM to Josephine Murray, 11 April 1945.

— "assessment of Chinese paratroopers." HAM to Josephine Murray, 20 May, [5 June], and 28 June 1945; interviews with HAM, 5 July 1971 and 27 June 1984.

— "enjoyed myself hugely." HAM to Josephine Murray, 2 September 1945.

— "tangible proof." *Assessment of Men,* p. 451.

284 "clinical psychology." Ibid., pp. 462, 492, 462–493.

— "praised the volume." Leonard W. Doob, *Saturday Review,* 31 (May 19, 1948), 10.

— "The picture presented." *Assessment of Men,* p. 393. While it is fair to assume that Harry accepted the judgment advanced here, it may be that the rather labored language of the sentence was the responsibility of one of his co-authors.

— "James Alexander Hamilton." HAM to Mumford, 6 June 1944.

— "had its start." Donald W. MacKinnon, "Pioneers in Assessment" interview with Joseph L. Moses, April 1982.

— "advancing British forces." Interview with HAM, 4 July 1971.

— "China was equally memorable." HAM to Josephine Murray, 2 September 1945.

285 "goodwill and lawfulness." Ibid.

— "*unit affiliation* and brotherhood." HAM to Lewis Mumford, [April] 1945.

— "Jo is also regularly present." HAM to Josephine Murray, 1 March, 11 April, and 20 May 1945.

286 "rumors at Station S." Interviews with Elliott Jaques, 12 December 1972, and James G. Miller, 9 August 1980

— "job prospects." HAM to Josephine Murray, 10 January 1946.

— "I can not predict." HAM to Lewis Mumford, [September] 1945.

— "I'm in transition." HAM to Josephine Murray, 10 January 1946.

287 "tranformation of attitudes." HAM to Josephine Murray, 2 September 1945.

— "more intimately committed." HAM to Lewis Mumford, [September] 1945.

— "several other opportunities." HAM to Lewis Mumford, n.d. [Fall, 1947].

— "the atomic bomb." HAM to Lewis Mumford, [September 1945].

— "One World or No World." HAM to Lewis Mumford, [October?] 1945. Harry made efforts, apparently without much success, to interest the government, and the Rockefeller Foundation, in his project (memorandum, 23 October 1945, Rockefeller Foundation Archives).

— "National Man into World Man." HAM to Theodore Newcomb, 4 April 1946. Newcomb was the Chairman of the Society for the Psychological Study of Social Issues. Harry goes on to propose that the United States stop manufacturing atomic bombs "on the condition that representatives from all other nations" agree to "a plan for the control of atomic energy."

— "creation of a world federation." *New York Times,* 9 June 1948, p. 28; and HAM to Lewis Mumford, 25 May 1948. Harry continued over the years to give time and money to the UWF (interview with HAM, 30 July 1971). Norman Cousins' book on world federalism, *Modern Man Is Obsolete* (1945), had an obvious influence on his thinking.

288 "positive ideal." "Time for a Positive Morality," *Survey Graphic,* 36 (March, 1947), 195, 215.

— "a sequel of sorts." "America's Mission," *Survey Graphic,* 37 (October, 1948), 412, 415. Harry hues to the UWF line in recommending requisite revisions of the United Nations Charter and "an amendment to our own constitution which will permit full participation in a world government" (p. 414). "America's Mission" was subsequently reprinted for distribution by the United World Federalists.

— "commitment to world government." HAM to Lewis Mumford, 17 April 1948.

— "GI culture." HAM to Lewis Mumford, [March] 1948 and 17 April 1948.

289 "negative attitudes." HAM to The Society for the Psychological Study of Social Issues, 12 March 1946. The letter was a response to a request that he chair a

new committee on Psychology in Relation to Maintaining Peace. "I am not invited by the goal of Maintaining Peace," he replied. "Peace is a neutral state, equivalent to Avoidance of War. I should much prefer a positive title, such as 'Advancement of International Relations'. . . . Also, instead of studying the causes of delinquency and neurosis, we should study the stages in the development of the best relationships between individuals, groups and nations."

— "unusually successful relationships." "Proposals for Research in Clinical Psychology," *American Journal of Orthopsychiatry,* 17 (1947), 209–210.

— "the dyad was surely foremost." In an interview on 12 July 1971, Harry acknowledged that his relationship with Christiana formed the "core" and "center" of his research on dyads. By contrast with sociologists, who studied small groups of five and more, Harry "went up to two, and no more than two. The dyad."

290 "the biggest mistake." Interview with HAM, 11 July 1971.

— "a dead duck." Personal communication from Robert White, 22 February 1989.

— "Harry in fact resigned." HAM to Paul Buck, 2 January 1945.

291 "blow off even more steam." HAM to Josephine Murray, 14 November 1945. Buck wrote to Harry on 14 June 1945, to insist on a more detailed explanation for his resignation. The correspondence with Lewis Mumford during this period also suggests that the decision to leave Harvard was an element in a larger strategy.

— "You *are* a statesman." Gordon Allport to HAM, 14 November 1945. Allport wrote again the next day to add that Harry's intervention with Buck would lead to a faculty motion to establish Social Relations.

— "Levellers." Clyde Kluckhohn to HAM, 9 April 1940.

292 "establishment of the Department." Interviews with HAM, 11 and 12 July 1971; Paul Buck, 14 July 1972; and Talcott Parsons, 31 July 1972. Parsons' report on the *Department and Laboratory of Social Relations: The First Decade 1946–1956* (1956) is very thorough on the local background and founding. Ernest R. Hilgard, *Psychology in America,* provides a briefer summary (pp. 599–602) but includes a useful reconstruction of the larger context. George Homans' *Coming to My Senses* (New Brunswick, NJ: Transaction Books, 1984) includes a lively first-person account of leading persons and events (pp. 293ff).

— "successful experiment." Hilgard, *Psychology in America,* pp. 593–602. The experiment was not without its critics. President Conant had in 1945 appointed a commission under the leadership of Alan Gregg to advise him on the future of psychology at Harvard. The so-called "Gregg Report"—"The Place of Psychology in an Ideal University"—though opposed in key respects to interdisciplinary reorganization, was not issued until 1947, too late to influence the formation of Social Relations.

— "epoch-making book." Richard M. Elliott to Oxford University Press, 4 October 1945. *Explorations* was reprinted in 1948 and sold nearly 6,000 copies in the next two years. It had achieved total sales of 10,587 copies by the summer

431

of 1961, when a paperback reprint was arranged. Variously translated, the volume is now regarded as a "classic" in the field.

— "tour of Station S." Edwin G. Boring to Dean Paul H. Buck, 11 and 17 September 1945 (Edwin G. Boring Papers).

— "A much longer piece." "The Test at Station S," *Time,* 47 (21 January 1946), 28; "A Good Man Is Hard to Find," *Fortune,* 33 (March 1936), 93. The *Fortune* essay was written by Osgood Nichols, a veteran of the testing program at Station S and a good friend to Harry in the years after the war (interview with Osgood Nichols, 22 June 1972).

293 "a very legitimate desire." Talcott Parsons to HAM. In his angry letter of 2 January 1945, Harry impresses on Dean Buck that returning to Harvard would disrupt his "little plan . . . for a three-year period of writing."

— "He would be just as marginal." Interview with HAM, 16 July 1971.

— "were never again warm." Interviews with HAM, 25 July 1972; Robert White, 16 and 22 April 1970 and 18 February 1989; and Silvan Tomkins, 28 June 1971. In a personal communication of 22 February 1989, Robert White recalls declining Harry's suggestion that he resign from his new position in order that Donald MacKinnon might take his place.

— "conspicuous personal advantages." Interview with HAM, 15 June 1985.

294 "fussy 'old woman.'" George Homans (*Coming to My Senses,* p. 296) admits to having "enjoyed writing skits" for Harvard social occasions. In one such production he portrayed Gordon Allport "as a bit of an old woman." Allport, he adds, "did not take this sort of thing in good part and put an end to our skits."

— "joust of Olympians." M. Brewster Smith, "Allport, Murray, and Lewin on Personality Theory: Notes on a Confrontation," *Journal of the History of the Behavioral Sciences,* 7 (1971), 353–362. Interviews with Gardner Lindzey (23 January 1972) and Henry Riecken (30 January 1972) yielded similar perspectives on the encounter.

— "Harry's only close friend." Interviews with HAM, 18 August 1970 and 16 July 1971.

— "trusted confidant." "I had a sense that Murray trusted Clyde with certain things in his life more than he did most people" (interview with Ted Kroeber, 17 December 1971).

— "no barriers." Clyde Kluckhohn to HAM, 18 July 1944.

— "the whole man." Ibid.

295 "like no other man." *Personality in Nature, Society, and Culture* (New York: Alfred A. Knopf, 1948), pp. xi–xii, 12–15, 17–18, 27, 35, and passim. Though the introductory chapters appear as co-authored, they were in fact separately composed and then jointly edited and revised (interview with HAM, 16 July 1971). The book is dedicated to Gordon Allport, O. Hobart Mowrer, and Talcott Parsons, "with whom it was our privilege to collaborate in planning the Department of Social Relations at Harvard which is concerned both with personalities and with the socio-cultural matrix in which they develop." The collection met a genuine educational need and enjoyed large sales. A second edition, with minor additions by David M. Schneider, appeared in 1953.

— "awful things." Interview with HAM, 15 August 1970.

— "yet Harry stayed away." Interviews with HAM, 11 and 17 July 1971 and 18 July 1972.

— "summit of experience." HAM to Josephine Murray, 8 April 1946.

— "dyadic letters of the period." I am grateful to Edwin Shneidman for permission to use the wartime letters.

297 "staggering from chair to chair." CDM to Lewis Mumford, 1 January 1944.

— "Christiana's loneliness and deepening self-absorption." Interview with Ina May Greer, 15 June 1970.

— "what is right and what is wrong." From "Pilgrimage of Creation," CDM's typewritten account of the dyad during the war years.

— "before we die." HAM to Lewis Mumford, 6 June 1944.

— "Lead me, my Superior." "Pilgrimage of Creation."

300 "No medieval monk." CDM to Lewis Mumford, 24 September 1944.

— "Ananda K. Coomaraswamy." He was a writer and lecturer on Indian art and metaphysics and the Keeper of Indian and Mohammedan Art at the Museum of Fine Arts in Boston. His wife shared many of his interests.

304 "fueled Christiana's determination." Lewis Mumford to CDM, 25 May 1944, in Mumford, *My Works and Days: A Personal Chronicle* (New York: Harcourt Brace Jovanovich, 1979), p. 181.

— "I have always told Harry." CDM to Lewis Mumford, 18 August 1944.

— "curb on his autonomy." "Pilgrimage of Creation"; and HAM to Lewis Mumford, 6 June 1944.

— "desperation of loneliness." CDM to Lewis Mumford, 21 April and 19 July 1945.

— "autocratic, Mt. Sinai." HAM to Lewis Mumford, 17 October and 25 November 1946, and [February] 1948. Donald L. Miller, Mumford's biographer, draws similar conclusions about the decline in their friendship (*Lewis Mumford: A Life* [New York: Weidenfeld & Nicolson, 1989], pp. 442–443). In a personal communication of 28 July 1970, Mumford traced the break to Christiana's insistence in 1944 that he be drawn into dyadic discussions. "Harry thereafter turned to Jo, Kluckhohn, and science, and became alienated from C. and me!"

11. I Will Gospelize the World Anew

307 "cultural-sociological system." "Preparations for the Scaffold of a Comprehensive System," p. 45.

— "global neurosis." From a talk delivered on Edwin R. Murrow's radio program, "This I Believe," in 1953.

— "World Concord." A summary of the paper appears in the *Proceedings of the International Congress on Psychology* (Stockholm, 1951), pp. 185–186.

— "the constant vision of the Ideal." From a typescript of "World Concord" preserved among Harry's papers. He makes the same case in "Science in Two Societies," a lecture delivered at the Metropolitan Museum of Art in 1952 and reproduced in *The Contemporary Scene: A Symposium* (New York: The Metropolitan Museum of Art, 1954), pp. 31–40. See also *Assessment of Men,* pp. 463–464.

— "an insurgent Id." "In Nomine Diaboli," *New England Quarterly,* 24 (1951), 446, 447, 449. See also "Science in Two Societies," p. 37, and "Individuality: The Meaning and Content of Individuality in Contemporary America," *Daedalus,* 87 (1958), 29–30, and passim.

308 "Youth Culture of mediocracy." HAM to Lewis Mumford, [1952].

— "rid myself of Melville." HAM to Josephine Murray, 10 January 1946.

— "*become* the incarnation of it." HAM to Lewis Mumford, 19 August 1947.

— "General systems theory." "Preparations for the Scaffold of a Comprehensive System," p. 50. Harry discourses at some length on general systems theory in "Preparations" (pp. 50–52), and in the seminal "Vicissitudes of Creativity," in *Creativity and Its Cultivation,* ed. H. H. Anderson (New York: Harper & Brothers, 1959), pp. 100–102. In *Living Systems* (New York: McGraw-Hill, 1978), a copious overview of general systems theory, James G. Miller, Harry's quondam protégé and long-time friend, acknowledges his mentor's "significant influence" (p. xiv) on his work in the field.

310 "Mysterious Woman." A Speech Delivered at the Signet Society, 10 December 1955.

— "participations of two lovers." "Preparations for the Scaffold of a Comprehensive System," p. 23.

311 "self-developing relationship." "The Possible Nature of a 'Mythology' to Come," in *Myth and Mythmaking,* ed. Henry A. Murray (New York: George Braziller, 1960), pp. 351–352.

— "'woman' in his life." "What Should Psychologists Do About Psychoanalysis?" p. 153.

— "Jungian visionary." "The Case of Murr," p. 291.

312 "not a pacifist." Interview with HAM, 14 July 1970.

— "There has been a breach." "Personality and Creative Imagination," in *English Institute Annual* (New York: Columbia University Press, 1943), p. 156.

313 "With his ideal drowned." "In Nomine Diaboli," pp. 449, 451–452.

314 "the role of the creator." HAM to Josephine Murray, 8 April and 13 May 1946.

— "Melville Memorial Room." Interview with HAM, 25 July 1972; and with Robert G. Newman, 20 August 1971. Mr. Newman, Librarian Emeritus at the Berkshire Athenaeum, added many helpful details in a personal communication of 25 April 1989. The Herman Melville Memorial Room finally opened in April 1953. Harry donated the room and much of the collection. Melville's granddaughter, Eleanor Metcalf, and the Morewood sisters, his great-nieces, were also principal donors of books and memorabilia.

— "Melville Society." Tyrus Hillway to HAM, 14 April 1945; personal communication from Donald Yannella, 12 May 1989; and Yannella's tribute in the *Melville Society Extracts,* 78 (1989), 1–3. Harry gave generously of his time and money to the Melville Society. His latest contribution was an endowment of $20,000, established in 1985.

— "interests me immensely." Howard P. Vincent to HAM, 28 November 1945; HAM to Howard P. Vincent, 4 December 1945. Harry reviewed Vincent's *The Trying-Out of Moby-Dick* in *New England Quarterly,* 23 (1950), 527–530.

— "he wrote to Christiana." HAM to CDM, 20 February 1946. "I have Melville in 2 vols ⅘ths finished," he wrote to Josephine on 30 September 1945.

315 "stone pier into the Atlantic." HAM to Howard P. Vincent, [January?] 1948.

— "didn't want to end up there." Interviews with HAM, 9 August 1979 and 20 June 1983.

— "professing psychologist." *Pierre,* pp. vi–vii.

— "superb piece of work." Howard P. Vincent to HAM, 29 September 1947.

— "compactly colossal." Lewis Mumford to HAM, 29 June 1949.

— "Charles Olson." Merton M. Sealts, Jr., *Pursuing Melville 1940–1980* (Madison: University of Wisconsin Press, 1982), p. 101; Aiken to HAM, [1949].

— "Jung professed to like it." C. G. Jung to HAM, 14 September 1949. "The only thing I can say," Jung declared, after complaining of slow progress with the book, "is that I appreciate highly your clear and well-balanced presentation of Melville's case."

316 "spiritual autobiography." *Pierre,* p. xxiv.

— "dedicated love." Ibid., p. xxix.

— "racing tide." Ibid., p. xxvi.

— "eruption." Ibid., p. xxxi.

— "the most personal thing." Interview with HAM, 1 July 1971.

— "fantastic version of reality." HAM to CDM, [5] January 1946.

— "tragic anima." Pierre, p. lii–liv.

— "directing influence." Ibid., p. liii–liv.

317 "immoral, impious, or insane." Ibid., p. lxxx.

— "to the threshold." Ibid., p. lv.

— "treacheries of the heart." Ibid., p. lv.

— "elevating substitute." Ibid., p. lxxii.

— "no satisfactory solution." Ibid., p. xcix.

— "creative religionist." Ibid., p. xcvi.

— "heroic substance." Ibid., p. cii.

— "forces of the unconscious." Ibid., p. xcvii.

— "What is her nature." HAM to CDM, 20 February 1946.

318 "Harry promptly relented." HAM to CDM, 27 February 1946; CDM to HAM, 1 March 1946; HAM to CDM, 5 March 1946.

— "death wish." Pierre, pp. lxxxix–xc.

— "repudiation of the world." Ibid., p. xcvi.

— "wholly unequipped." Ibid., p. xc.

320 "the main things." Interview with HAM, 14 July 1970.

— "Jay Leyda." Interview with Leon Howard, 23 June 1971. Leyda made his research available to Howard, who used much of it in his *Herman Melville, A Biography* (Berkeley: University of California Press, 1951). The volume is dedicated to Leyda, who "possessed," according to Howard, "a hardheaded inquisitiveness which was rare even among scholars" (p. vii).

— "heated meeting." Interviews with HAM, 7 July 1970 and 29 July 1972; and with Harrison Hayford and Howard Vincent, 24 August 1971; Agnes Morewood to HAM, 29 April 1947; and personal communication from Jay Leyda, 14 November 1971.

321 "delays in progress." HAM to Jay Leyda, n.d. [Summer 1947] (UCLA Department of Special Collections); Jay Leyda to HAM, 14 August [1947], and 4 February [1948].

— "waste of time." HAM to Jay Leyda, 15 June 1948 (UCLA Department of Special Collections).

— "cruel announcement." Jay Leyda to HAM, 13 July [1948].

— "shark-pack of rivals." Jay Leyda to HAM, n.d. [March 1949].

322 "cut-throat." Interview with HAM, 3 August 1971.

— "killed his greatest work." Personal communication from Jay Leyda, 14 November 1971.

— "twenty years of research." CDM to HAM, 2 May 1947.

— "cruises to Europe." Interviews with HAM, 16 August 1970, 7 August 1971; and with Arthur Couch, 18 August 1972; Gertrude Macy (Katharine Cornell's secretary) to Josephine Murray, 16 May 1960.

323 "Harry loomed large." Interview with HAM, 17 July 1971. Harry wrote to Christiana in 1945 that Councilman had made a good choice in a bride—"next to Josephine," he added, "the best possible choice" (HAM to CDM, 20 February 1945). Harry's correspondence with Josephine is everywhere indicative of his powerful influence in her life.

— "her own enduring objections." Interview with Ina May Greer, 15 June 1970.

— "Leyda had ruined all that." Interview with HAM, 27 July 1971.

— "They both drank heavily." Interviews with HAM, 18 and 24 July 1972; and with Kenneth Keniston, 27 July 1970; Robert Wilson, 19 August 1970; Gardner Lindzey, 23 January 1972; and Robert White, 18 February 1989.

— "answer of joy and power." CDM's diary, 7 July 1950.

324 "It was understood." Interview with HAM, 31 July 1970. There is evidence—in a folder labeled "Proposition"—that Harry commenced his work during the summer of 1949. No sooner had he taken up his pen, however, than he began to temporize. "Strictly speaking," he wrote, "I shall not start with the proposition but with the scaffolding, or better still with the blueprint, or more precisely, the notes for the blueprint of the Proposition." Little wonder that he never finished!

— "when we love, we live." CDM's diary, 9 and 22 July, 2 and 5 August, and 11 September, 1950.

— "whispering of the 'mysterium.'" CDM's diary, 29 February 1952.

325 "passivity." CDM's diary, 24 and 27 May 1953.

— "faster than I could type." CDM to Lewis Mumford, 2 September 1955.

— "junkets to the West Indies." Interviews with HAM, 16 August 1970 and 27 July 1971.

— "brutally frank." Interview with Ina May Greer, 27 June 1970.

326 "If we didn't write a single word." Interview with HAM, 23 August 1971.

— "The chief feature." *What Joy!* Prologue.

— "possibility of spiritual growth." *What Joy!* ch. 19.

— "Dyle." Ibid., ch. 24.

327 "Hola." Ibid., ch. 4.

— "love's creative evolution." Ibid., chs. 12 and 23.

— "when she turned to natural subjects." Ibid., chs. 10–11.

328 "stations of the cross." Interview with HAM, 15 August 1970; see *What Joy!* ch. 18.

— "greater order of things." Ibid., chs. 4 and 24.

— "It must go on." Christiana numbered Whitehead—with Jung, Henderson, and a few others—among her spiritual "fathers." The two were very close during the years just before the philosopher's death in 1947. One of the paths near the Tower was "named the *Philosophenweg*, because it was here that Altie [Whitehead] used to take his daily contemplative walk" (*What Joy!* ch. 14).

329 "out of me has come this grace." Ibid., ch. 16.

— "a god was being made." Ibid., ch. 4.

330 "success in the dyadic discipline." Ibid., ch. 24.

— "He was confident." Harry's views appear in his Introduction to *Case Histories in Clinical and Abnormal Psychology*, ed. Arthur Burton and Robert E. Harris (New York: Harper, 1947), pp. 1–20. A substantial portion of Harry's original Introduction, prefaced by his brief acknowledgment of gratifying developments in the field, was published in a second volume of case histories, *Clinical Studies of Personality*, ed. Arthur Burton and Robert E. Harris (New York: Harper, 1955), pp. 1–17.

— "His reviews." Review of Gardner Murphy, *Personality: A Biosocial Approach to Origins and Structure* (New York: Harper, 1947), in *Survey Graphic,* 37 (1948), 167–168. See also Harry's review of *Dynamic Psychiatry,* ed. Franz Alexander and Helen Ross (Chicago: University of Chicago Press, 1952), in *Psychological Bulletin,* 50 (1953), 304–306.

— "TAT." Harry gave continuing support to the *TAT Newsletter,* under the editorship of Robert Holt and later of Edwin Shneidman. He wrote a Foreword to *An Introduction to Projective Techniques,* ed. H. H. Anderson and Gladys Anderson (New York: Prentice-Hall, 1951), another for Shneidman's *Thematic Test Analysis* (New York: Grune and Stratton, 1951), and adapted the TAT to the uses of the armed forces—"Thematic Apperception Test," *Military Clinical Psychology* (Washington: U. S. Government Printing Office, 1951), pp. 54–71. His paper describing the TAT, delivered at a meeting of the American Psychiatric Association in May 1950, was published as "Uses of the Thematic Apperception Test," *American Journal of Psychiatry,* 107 (1951), 577–581. He published two other essays in the area: with Anthony Davids, "Preliminary Appraisal of an Auditory Projective Technique for Studying Personality and Cognition," *American Journal of Orthopsychiatry,* 25 (1955), 543–554; and "Theoretical Basis for Projective Tests," summarized in *Proceedings of the Fifteenth International Congress of Psychology* (Amsterdam: North-Holland, 1959), pp. 481–482.

331   "In the same essay." "Research Planning: A Few Proposals," in *Culture and Personality,* ed. S. S. Sargent and M. W. Smith (New York: The Viking Fund, 1949), pp. 208–209, 204. "Toward a Classification of Interactions," Harry's contribution to the Department of Social Relations manifesto, *Toward a General Theory of Action* (Cambridge: Harvard University Press, 1951), displays a similar bent. (The essay was reissued, in slightly shortened form, as "Some Basic Psychological Assumptions and Conceptions," *Dialectica,* 5 [1951], 266–292.)

—   "chronic headaches." Interview with HAM, 17 July 1971.

—   "psychodrama theatre." The fact that the theatre was little used provoked speculation, only half in jest, that Harry had it built to block the path that connected the Baleen to the old Clinic on Plympton Street. It was also observed that Harry rarely, if ever, visited Bob White's establishment. Harry took a warm but rather mixed view of J. L. Moreno, whom he first met in New York in 1947. Moreno "has contributed a lot," he wrote to Mumford. "His methods do not lend themselves to scientific experimentation & verification, and so he is on the periphery—the pioneering periphery—of science, & overlaps, to some extent, the domains of art & religion. . . . Moreno says whatever comes into his fertile head—much of which is Grain, the rest Chaff" (HAM to Lewis Mumford, n.d. [October 1950]). Moreno describes Harry, and the opening of the Harvard psychodrama theatre, in his *Who Shall Survive?* (Beacon, NY: Beacon House, 1953), p. lxxxix–xc.

—   "Harry's grant." "Request for Grant from the Rockefeller Foundation" (Rockefeller Foundation Archives). First approved for 1948–1951, the grant was extended for one year because of the delay in completing work on the Baleen (HAM to Alan Gregg, 26 April 1948 [Rockefeller Foundation Archives]).

332   "Gardner Lindzey." HAM to Robert S. Morison (of the Rockefeller Foundation), 1 September 1949 (Rockefeller Foundation Archives). Interviews with HAM, 16 July 1971; Bert Kaplan, 26 May 1972; Gardner Lindzey, 23 January 1972; Henry Riecken, 17 January 1972; and Robert Wilson, 17 August 1970. Wilson later published a sociological study of American poets, *Man Made Plain* (Cleveland: Howard Allen, 1958), for which Harry wrote a long Foreword.

—   "He observed that competition." Rockefeller Foundation memorandum on the "Psychological Clinic, Harvard University," 18 March 1952; and HAM to Robert S. Morison, 27 March 1952 (both at the Rockefeller Foundation Archives).

333   "dull and desultory level." HAM to Josephine Murray, 16 April 1952.

—   "Morale at the Baleen." Interviews with Ina May Greer, 27 June 1970; Neil Smelser, 13 March 1972; Herbert Goldings, 26 July 1972; Bert Kaplan, 26 May 1972; Henry Riecken, 17 January 1972; and Robert Wilson, 17 August 1970.

—   "I prefer to stay away." HAM to Josephine Murray, 16 April 1952.

—   "It was a great 'mistake.'" Interview with HAM, 27 July 1970.

—   "Getting away with Jo." Interview with HAM, 21 July 1971.

334 "A great moment." Interview with Howard Vincent and Harrison Hayford, 24 August 1971.

— "the very best thing." Lewis Mumford to HAM, 25 February 1952.

— "Aiken was of like mind." Conrad Aiken to HAM, 18 February 1952.

— "Even Charles Olson." Charles Olson to HAM, 16 February 1952.

— "trial of Alger Hiss." Interview with HAM, 19 July 1971.

— "He had asked the students." Interview with David McClelland, 18 June 1970.

— "far more adept." Allen Weinstein, *Perjury: The Hiss-Chambers Case* (New York: Knopf, 1978), p. 492.

— "clean, honest, brilliant job." Lewis Mumford to HAM, 17 January 1950.

— "Nationwide attention." Interviews with HAM, 21 July 1970, 19 July 1971, and 20 June 1983. Harry's dramatic role in the final days of testimony was featured widely in the national press. Most notably perhaps, *Time* and *Newsweek* both carried the story in their editions for 16 January 1950. For a summary of Harry's testimony, see Weinstein's *Perjury*, pp. 492–495. Chambers responded to the damaging portrait in *Witness* (New York: Random House, 1952), pp. 691–692.

335 "started the new year with a bang." HAM to Josephine Murray, 6 October 1952.

— "*Glory in the Highest.*" HAM to Ina May Greer, 25 June 1954.

— "two published papers." "American Icarus," in *Clinical Studies of Personality,* ed. Burton and Harris, pp. 615–641; and "Notes on the Icarus Syndrome," *Folia Psychiatrica, Neurologica et Neurochirurgica Neelandica,* 61 (1958), 204–208.

— "Icarus figure lost definition." Interview with HAM, 16 July 1972.

— "Harry admired Gardner Lindzey." HAM to Josephine Murray, 6 October 1952: "Gardner Lindzey is turning out papers faster than I can read them."

336 "comparative literature seminar." The catalog indicates that Harry co-taught Social Science 4 with Kluckhohn in 1955–1957 and Comparative Literature 270 ("Thematics") with Levin in 1958–1959, 1960–1962. The *Confidential Guide* reports favored Harry's teaching over Kluckhohn's, giving special praise to his preparation and wit. Harry certainly made the effort. In one large class he took the time to memorize the names of all 150 students! (interview with Gardner Lindzey, 23 January 1972). Levin was also pleased with their joint efforts (interview with Harry Levin, 12 August 1970).

— "So did editing." Harry was guest-editor of *Daedalus,* 88 (1959) on "Myth and Mythmaking," and editor of *Myth and Mythmaking* (New York: George Braziller, 1960), which includes his essay, "The Possible Nature of a 'Mythology' to Come." He wrote introductions to both volumes.

— "copy to President Kennedy." Interview with HAM, 17 August 1971. A copy of Hoagland's letter to Kennedy, dated 26 September 1961, and drawing special attention to the section entitled "Toward a Re-Orientation of our Foreign Policy," is among Harry's papers at the Harvard Archives. "Unprecedented Evolutions" appeared in *Daedalus,* 90 (1961), 547–569, and again in *Evolution and Man's Progress,* ed. H. Hoagland and R. W. Burhoe (New York: Columbia University Press, 1962), pp. 137–159.

— "journey on acid." Interviews with HAM, 18 August 1970; Frank Barron, 12 November 1971; Ted Kroeber, 17 December 1971; and Alan Watts, 7 February 1972.

— "brief brush with Huxley." Interviews with HAM, 18 August 1970; and with Evelyn Hooker, 20 December 1971. Huxley made his feelings known at a dinner just after Harry's lecture.

— "with obvious delight." HAM to Lewis Mumford, [August] 1961.

337 "he betrayed no signs." Interview with Frank Barron, 12 November 1971.

— "The winter has been good." CDM to Lewis Mumford, 18 February 1957.

— "accepting their fate." Interview with HAM, 22 July 1971.

— "We have a *very* fine group." CDM to Lewis Mumford, 6 November 1960 and 9 December 1961.

— "Harry made ample provision." "Research plan" for Grant M-1287 (C3S1), September 1, 1959–August 31, 1960.

— "stressful dyadic situation." "Studies of Stressful Interpersonal Disputations," *American Psychologist,* 18 (1963), 28–36. The entire operation is also well described in Harry's "Brief Summary of Baleen Researches," a mimeographed report covering the period 1959–1961.

338 "In his published reflections." "The Case of Murr," p. 306.

339 "holding the bag." Interview with HAM, 24 July 1972. *Aspects of Personality* is mentioned briefly in "The Case of Murr," p. 306.

— "thinking of the Baleen." From Harry's Foreword to *Methods in Personality Assessment,* ed. G. G. Stern, M. I. Stein, and B. S. Bloom (Glencoe, IL: Free Press, 1956), p. 15.

— "The Three Musketeers." Interview with HAM, 21 July 1971.

— "terribly difficult." Interview with Edwin Shneidman, 22 July 1971.

— "Social-class tensions." Interview with Arthur Couch, 18 August 1971.

340 "the most deeply ambivalent." Personal communication from David Ricks, 20 July 1970.

— "what it was that Harry wanted." Interview with Leo McNamara, 18 July 1972.

— "betrayed and abandoned." Interview with Kenneth Keniston, 27 July 1970.

— "once-vibrant being." Kluckhohn died in a Santa Fe hospital on July 29, 1960, of a heart attack suffered the day before while he was fishing in the New Mexico countryside. Harry's words are taken from his tribute to Kluckhohn, read at the memorial service which he organized the following October. Harry was also responsible for the "minute" on his friend's life, read at the meeting of the Harvard faculty on April 11, 1961. It appears in the *Harvard University Gazette* for April 29, 1961, pp. 195–196.

— "as hard on himself." Interview with Ted Kroeber, 17 December 1971.

341 "Hallelujah!" HAM to Edwin Shneidman, 11 May 1961.

— "Respecting you as I do." Edwin Shneidman to HAM, 24 May 1961.

— "that his brain was deteriorating." CDM to Lewis Mumford, 6 November 1960. Earlier that year she reported that "Harry was tired and distressed because he couldn't collect his thoughts clearly for his next effort—and, as usual, began to think that his mind was failing. Well, we all . . . know about that!" (CDM to Lewis Mumford, 28 July 1960).

— "unequal to the set standard." "Preparations for the Scaffold of a Comprehensive System," p. 9.

342 "exclusively experimental specialists." Ibid., p. 8.

— "I sweated gumdrops." Interview with HAM, 6 June 1970.

— "You wade in so fast." Conrad Aiken to HAM, 28 November 1956.

— "I was led on." "Preparations for the Scaffold of a Comprehensive System," p. 53.

— "the temporary Scaffold." *Pierre*, pp. 246–247.

— "dyadic system." "Preparations for the Scaffold of a Comprehensive System," p. 52.

343 "analysis of a homosexual." "Commentary on the Case of El," *Journal of Projective Techniques*, 25 (1961), 406.

— "I wasn't talented enough." Interview with HAM, 2 September 1971.

344 "the child in Harry." Interview with Frederick Wyatt, 27 August 1970. Edwin Shneidman observes in Harry's prose "a constant movement toward ascending synthesis in a series of approximations, serial approximation. That's the beauty of Harry's system," he adds, "and its greatest defect. That is, it has no end . . . there's never a last word; there's only the latest word" (interview with Edwin Shneidman, 15 May 1971).

345 "one of its misfortunes." "Vicissitudes of Creativity," p. 97.

346 "go on happily from here." Ibid., pp. 101, 104–108, 112–118.

— "allegiance to a selected aim." Ibid., p. 108.

— "Harry was surprised." Interview with HAM, 31 July 1970.

— "essay on Conrad Aiken." "Poet of Creative Dissolution," *Wake*, 11 (1952), 99.

347 "interdependence and creation." "Beyond Yesterday's Idealisms," in *Views from the Circle: Seventy-five Years of Groton School* (Groton, MA: Trustees of Groton School, 1960), pp. 375, 377–378. The oration was reprinted in *The Fate of Man*, ed. Crane Brinton (New York: George Braziller, 1961); and in *Man Thinking: Representative Phi Beta Kappa Orations, 1915–1959*, ed. William T. Hastings (Ithaca, NY: Cornell University Press, 1962). An abridged version appeared as " A Mythology for Grownups" in *Saturday Review*, 43 (23 January 1960), 10–12.

— "European races." "Two Versions of Man," in *Science Ponders Religion*, ed. Harlow Shapley (New York: Appleton-Century-Crofts, 1960), pp. 171–173, 178–181. This essay appeared in two earlier, shorter forms: "Versions of Man," in *Man's Right to Knowledge*, 2nd ser. (New York: Columbia University Press, 1955), pp. 34–42; and "Creative Evolution, or A Deity Imprisoned in the Past?" *Christian Register*, 135 (1956), 10–11, 29–31.

348 "Bitchcraft in New England." Interview with HAM, 16 August 1970. "It was a terrible thing to say," Harry admitted.

— "that was a party." Ibid.

— "special TAT issue." *Journal of Projective Techniques,* 22 (June, 1958). Leopold Bellak's warm "Appreciation" (pp. 143–144) must have been especially gratifying to Harry.

— "old friend A. R. Luria." Interviews with HAM, 16 August 1970, 27 July 1971, and 17 August 1971. Harry first met Luria, the eminent Soviet psychologist, at the New Haven International Congress of Psychology in 1929. He nominated his Russian friend for an honorary degree at Harvard in 1974. For a fuller, published report on the trip to the USSR, see Henry A. Murray, Mark A. May, and Hadley Cantril, "Some Glimpses of Soviet Psychology," *American Psychologist,* 14 (1959), 303–307.

— "warm exchanges." "I am disarmed by my admiration for your productivity, felicity and wisdom," wrote Allport on 26 February 1960, and "also by my affection for you." "What a bountiful friend you are!" Frankfurter exclaimed in a letter of 20 July 1961. "I only wish that geography did not separate us so much."

— "gesture of respect." Interview with Silvan Tomkins, 28 June 1971.

— "review of Philip Rieff's *Freud.*" *American Sociological Review,* 25 (1960), 300.

— "over-reaching aspiration." "Preparations for the Scaffold of a Comprehensive System," p. 53.

— "Deepening discouragement." In his "Drive, Time, Strategy, Measurement, and Our Way of Life," in *Assessment of Human Motives,* ed. Gardner Lindzey (New York: Rinehart, 1958), Harry characterizes the American way of life as a godless "marriage of greed and speed" (p. 194).

— "he was increasingly fretful." Interview with HAM, 27 July 1971.

349 "all the newspapers observed." "Mrs. Henry A. Murray Jr., 67, Active in Social, Civic Circles," read the headline in the *Boston Herald* for January 16. The *Globe* and the *Traveler* featured similar messages.

— "burden of remorse." Interview with Carl Binger, 18 April 1970.

350 "out of the abyss." HAM to Lewis Mumford, 22 January 1962.

— "enough flowers." CDM to Lewis Mumford, 20 January 1962.

— "the horrors of life." Interviews with Edwin Shneidman, 15 May 1971 and 22 June 1971; with Jeanne and Robert Shneidman, 24 June 1971; and with Arthur Couch, 18 August 1972. The Shneidmans were especially helpful in providing details on the funeral. "I thought he would be off in a corner absolutely bereft with grief," recalls Edwin Shneidman, "and he was as a matter of fact manipulating—it's a word I don't use often—the whole thing. Then when it came time, and people began to arrive, he then played a very different role."

12. The Oozy Weeds about Me Twist

351 "as her sixties wore on." Interviews with Jeanne and Robert Shneidman, 24 June 1971; Edwin Shneidman, 22 June 1971; and Evelyn Hooker, 20 December 1971. Their views on Christiana's decline were widely shared.

— "green memories." "Josephine Lee Murray 1894–1962," *Radcliffe Quarterly,* 9 (1965), p. 10.

352   "not tried to snatch it." Lewis Mumford to CDM, 8 February 1962. "When Jo died, everyone thought marriage was in sight," recalled Christiana's sister, Mrs. Frank Wigglesworth, in an interview on 1 May 1970.

—   "no inclination at all." Interview with Lewis Mumford, 15 July 1970.

—   "Christiana held on." Interview with Ina May Greer, 15 June 1970.

—   "Harry relented." Interview with HAM, 24 July 1972.

—   "insiders to the truth." It was a "secret from nobody," insists David Mc-Clelland. "Every graduate student knew" (interview with David McClelland, 18 June 1970). Councilman Morgan, Christiana's son, took the same view (interview with Councilman Morgan, 5 March 1989).

—   "duly noted." *Time* (July 13, 1962), p. 42. A much longer notice appeared in the *Harvard Alumni Bulletin* for June 9, 1962.

—   "No more experiments." HAM to Alvan Barach, 9 June 1962.

—   "he met regularly." Marjorie Ingalls (Harry's secretary) to Leo McNamara, 8 March 1962.

—   "Keeping busy." Interviews with HAM, 17 August 1971 and 2 August 1972; and HAM to Lewis Mumford, 12 September 1962.

—   "unfinished projects." HAM to Lewis Mumford, 23 February 1963. The catalogue of unfinished books appears in an undated pamphlet—most likely from the early 1960s—among Harry's papers at the Harvard University Archives.

353   "prodding of interested publishers." In 1963, Arthur Rosenthal of Basic Books proposed the publication of three volumes, one of them to be a sequel to *Explorations* (interview with HAM, 30 July 1972). That same year, Atheneum offered a contract for a collection of essays (Hiram Hadyn to HAM, 17 October 1963). In 1966 Harry signed publication agreements for four volumes of essays with Jossey-Bass.

—   "less ambitious projects." Review of Clyde Kluckhohn, *Anthropology and the Classics* (Providence, RI: Brown University Press, 1961), *American Anthropologist,* 65 (1963), 139–140; of Avis M. Dry, *The Psychology of Jung: A Critical Interpretation* (New York: Wiley, 1961), *Contemporary Psychology,* 8 (1963), 468–469. Harry's Foreword to *The Inner World of Choice* (New York: Harper & Row, 1963) includes a stirring reassertion of his faith in creative evolution.

—   "spills over in a letter." HAM to Lewis Mumford, 7 September 1963. "Dead to the World" was published in *Essays in Self-Destruction,* ed. Edwin S. Shneidman (New York: Science House, 1967), pp. 7–29.

—   "project would have to be scuttled." HAM to Edwin Shneidman, 2 January 1964 and 18 June 1965.

—   "wasted the greater part." HAM to Alvan Barach, 22 July 1967.

354   "this is indeed a *must*." Edwin G. Boring to HAM, 20 January 1964.

—   "'distinguished' critical performance." Howard Vincent to HAM, 23 January 1965. Vincent was the editor of *Bartleby the Scrivener* (Kent, OH: Kent State University Press, 1966), the volume in which "Bartleby and I" was published. The essay was first presented as a paper at the meeting of the Melville Society at Oberlin in November 1964.

—   "That is criticism!" Jacques Barzun to HAM, 14 April 1967. Harry's review of *The Sins of the Fathers* (New York: Oxford University Press, 1966), first published in *American Scholar*, 36 (1967), 308–312, was reprinted in *Psychiatry and Social Science Review*, 1 (1967), 11–13.

— "third force." Interview with HAM, 2 August 1972. Harry's philosophical differences with the "mainstream" of humanistic psychology are clearly set forth in M. Brewster Smith's "Humanistic Psychology," pp. 10–11, 15–16. Rollo May recalled that Harry's retreat from the movement was prompted in part by what he viewed as the personal excesses of some of its members (interview with Rollo May, 20 December 1980).

— "William James Hall." HAM to Leo McNamara, 25 February 1965.

— "I was beginning to have trouble." Interview with HAM, 30 July 1972.

— "Emphysema was detected." Interview with Alvan Barach, 2 July 1970.

355 "viral pneumonia." HAM to Edwin Shneidman, 12 May 1966 and 21 September 1967.

— "gentle plea of beauty." HAM to Jack and Rosemary ("Molly") Pritchard, 29 July 1966.

— "Jung's autobiography." CDM to Lewis Mumford, 8 August 1963.

— "last great creative effort." CDM to Lewis Mumford, 1 October [1966?].

— "The most critical experiences." "A Symposium on Morality," *American Scholar*, 34 (1965), 366. The conference, convened by Hiram Hadyn in New York on January 14, 1965, featured an informal discussion—by Daniel Bell, René Dubos, Harry, and others—on modern values.

— "*Our* book remains." CDM to Lewis Mumford, 31 March 1965.

— "Garden of Eden." Ibid.

356 "disposition of the Tower." Interviews with Councilman Morgan, 5 March 1989, Nina Murray, 20 May 1991, and Ina May Greer, 27 June 1970; personal communication from Edwin Shneidman, 21 November 1990; and Councilman Morgan to CDM, 10 January 1967, and to HAM, 19 April, 20 April, 28 April, and 28 November 1967.

357 "Christiana was gone." Interview with HAM, 24 July 1972; and with Nina Murray, 20 May 1991.

— "before regaining consciousness." HAM to Alvan Barach, 1 April 1967.

— "Christiana's intoxication." Interview with Councilman Morgan, 5 March 1989.

— "last-minute adjustments." Toward the very end of his life, in about 1986, Harry remorsefully reviewed the "clues" of Christiana's suicide for his friend Edwin Shneidman. "I could not clearly judge," Shneidman recalls, "whether H[arry]'s statements were fact or delusion fueled by guilt" (personal communication, 21 November 1990). The suggestion of suicide is also perfectly clear in Harry's account of Christiana's death in his Postscript to the *Vision Seminars*. "Finally," he concludes, "with the lethal mounting of ventricular fibrillations, Christiana Morgan chose her best-loved Caribbean beach, St. John's Island, as locus of her demise" (vol. 2, p. 521).

— "Christiana's last days." HAM to Edward and Elizabeth Handy, 18 March 1967.

358 "circulate the story." There is some suggestion that Harry wrote more often, and in more intimate terms, than was necessary or appropriate. Gardner Lindzey, for example, was surprised to receive the letter describing Christiana's death and puzzled by the announcement of plans for a wedding (interview with Gardner Lindzey, 23 January 1972).

— "happy mother." Councilman Morgan to HAM, 19 and 28 April 1967.

359 "In beauty it is finished." The details of the ceremony, held on May 21, 1967, are preserved in an "Order of Memorial Rite" that Harry made available to the assembled guests.

— "Better to be done with it." Councilman Morgan to HAM, 28 November 1967; and interview with Hallee Morgan, 25 May 1991.

— "surviving my own death." HAM to Ann McDonald, Josephine's childhood nurse, 19 December 1967.

360 "dormant libido." Interviews with Nina Murray, 18 July 1988 and 31 May 1991.

— "Precious Nina." HAM to Nina Chandler Fish, 21 April 1967.

— "keen to live." HAM to Alvan Barach, 20 November 1968.

— "animated 1968 interview." Mary Harrington Hall, "A Conversation with Henry A. Murray," *Psychology Today*, 2 (September 1968), 63.

— "I'm in love." Interview with Maurice Firuski, 19 April 1971.

— "married at Francis Avenue." HAM to Alvan Barach, 9 March 1969; and to Edward and Elizabeth Handy [November 1969].

— "*the* successful relationship." Interview with Isabelle Kendig, 23 July 1970.

361 "references to Piaget." Interview with Nina Murray, 2 August 1971.

— "surest avenue to grief." Personal communication from Nina Murray, 3 December 1988.

— "personological scheme." "Components of an Evolving Personological System," in *International Encyclopedia of the Social Sciences,* vol. 12 (New York: Macmillan and Free Press, 1968), pp. 5–6.

362 "Need." In *Lexikon der Psychologie,* vol. 3 (Basel: Herder Freiburg, 1971–1972), pp. 237–238.

— "breathlessly condensed outline." *Annals of the New York Academy of Sciences,* vol. 291 (New York: New York Academy of Sciences, 1977), pp. 323–331. The title of the piece suggests a much more comprehensive theoretical overview than Harry was actually able—in four packed pages—to provide.

— "obstacles to his ambition." Interview with Barbara Du Bois, 1 August 1972; and personal communication, 16 November 1988. The work on Merrill Moore, and on the Icarus complex, pursued with the assistance of Ina May Greer and others until well into the 1970s, was also left unfinished (HAM to Ina May Greer, 6 July 1976, 27 March 1977, and 30 April 1977; interview with Dan Ogilvie, 2 August 1980).

— "the World's Problem." HAM to Josephine Murray, 16 April 1952.

— "The narrative unfolds." The manuscript of *Dialogues in Search of a Path* is stored with the rest of Harry's papers in the Harvard University Archives.

364 "writing just took care of itself." Interview with HAM, 22 July 1971.

366 "they settled their accounts." HAM to John Parke, 14 January, 14 July, and 28 August, 1974; John Parke to HAM, 12 September 1974.

— "freedom *ad absurdum.*" HAM to Lewis Mumford, 22 April 1967.

— "breeding ground of killers." "A Conversation with Henry A. Murray," pp. 56–57, 61.

— "stupid and unjustified." Interview with HAM, 27 June 1987.

— "another Dark Age." Review of Lewis S. Feuer, *The Conflict of Generations: The Character and Significance of Student Movements* (New York: Basic Books, 1969), in *American Scholar,* 38 (1969), 712, 714.

367 "I am too happy with Nina." HAM to Alvan Barach, 6 December 1969.

— "the apotheosis of silver-screen reality." The tag is taken from Harry's unpublished remarks on Reagan, drafted at the time of the President's awarding the Medal of Freedom to Whittaker Chambers. Both men, in Harry's view, perceived themselves, "Walter Mitty-like," as central figures in "a cosmic melodrama" where Communism and Freedom struggled for the upper hand. "It would not surprise us," he wrote, "that President Reagan should have a soft spot in his heart for cowboy valor, for the good, clean fun of a purifying showdown between the six-gun kid and the desperado gang." Nixon and Reagan, Daniel Aaron recalls, were among the subjects that Harry was sure "to explode on" (interview with Daniel Aaron, 19 February 1989).

— "properly venerated." Donald Yannella, "Henry A. Murray," p. 1.

— "once without his false teeth." Interview with Nina Murray, 3 July 1991.

— "unable to improve significantly." HAM to Alvan Barach, 19 August 1973.

— "wrote to his old nemesis." HAM to Jay Leyda, 16 September 1980.

368 "Allan Melvill's By-Blow." *Melville Society Extracts,* 61 (1985), 1–6. Harry's late writings, not previously mentioned, include a Prelude to *Melville and Hawthorne in the Berkshires,* ed. Howard P. Vincent (Kent, OH: Kent State University Press, 1966), pp. 1–3; a Foreword to the English translation of Franz From's *Perception of Other People* (New York: Columbia University Press, 1971), pp. xi–xxiv; a review (in *American Scholar,* 37 [1968], 536), of Henri Troyat's *Tolstoy* (New York: Doubleday, 1968); and several sketches and obituaries, published and unpublished, of departed friends. Finally, Harry produced four additional "Morsels," all of them very brief, for the *Melville Society Extracts:* "Henry Holt on Melville," 57 (1984), 8; "Another Triumph for Maria's First-born," 58 (1984), 1–3; (with Eugene Taylor), "From Mocha to Moby," 64 (1985), 6–7; and (with Eugene Taylor), "The Lancaster System of Instruction," 69 (1987), 5–6.

— "He had a wonderful time." Interview with HAM, 24 July 1972. *The Study of Lives: Essays on Personality in Honor of Henry A. Murray,* ed. Robert W. White (New York: Atherton Press, 1963), commences with a warm dedication: "To Henry A. Murray this book is presented on his seventieth birthday May 13, 1963, by students and colleagues past and present who will always remember with excitement and gratitude their sojourn in the high invigorating climate created by his infectious zest, wide-ranging awareness, bountiful powers of creation, and staunch fidelity to the increase of human understanding." *Leaves of Green Memories* was privately printed.

— "Henry A. Murray Lectures." The lectures have produced a series of publications, the first of which, *Further Explorations in Personality* (New York: John Wiley & Sons, 1981) is inscribed: "This book celebrates the work of Henry A. Murray and commemorates the 40th anniversary of the publication of his seminal *Explorations in Personality.*" Three additional volumes have appeared: *Personality and the Prediction of Behavior* (New York: Academic Press, 1984); *The Emergence of Personality* (New York: Springer, 1987); and *Studying Persons and Lives* (New York: Springer, 1990).

— "honorary degrees." Interviews with HAM, 15 July 1972 and 9 August 1979.

369 "Henry A. Murray Research Center." It is also the repository for the data on Harvard undergraduates gathered at the Clinic during the 1930s and 1950s. Interview with Nina Murray, 26 February 1989; Radcliffe *Centennial News,* 1 (January 1980), 1, 5. Harry repaid Radcliffe's generosity with a very large bequest to the Murray Center. His intentions in the matter of the gift were held in strict confidence until after his death.

— "his most important writing." *Endeavors in Psychology,* ed. Edwin S. Shneidman (New York: Harper & Row, 1981).

— "Murray's Personology." *Theories of Personality,* ed. Calvin S. Hall and Gardner Lindzey (New York: John Wiley & Sons, 1957), pp. 157–205. A second (1970) and third (1978) edition of the textbook have since appeared. For a further sampling of the scholarship, see James William Anderson, "Henry A. Murray's Early Career: A Psychobiographical Exploration," *Journal of Personality,* 56 (1988), 139–171, and "The Life of Henry A. Murray: 1893–1988," in *Studying Persons and Lives,* pp. 304–334; Alan C. Elms, "The Personalities of Henry A. Murray," *Perspectives in Personality,* vol. 2 (Greenwich, CN: JAI Press, 1987), pp. 1–14; Seymour Epstein, "*Explorations in Personality* Today and Tomorrow," *American Psychologist,* 34 (1979), 649–653; Hiram Hadyn, "Henry A. Murray," *American Scholar,* 39 (1969), 123–136; Mary Harrington Hall, "A Conversation with Henry A. Murray"; Ernest R. Hilgard, *Psychology in America* (New York: Harcourt Brace Jovanovich, 1987), pp. 364–367; Salvatore R. Maddi and Paul T. Costa, *Humanism in Personology: Allport, Maslow, and Murray* (Chicago: Aldine, 1972); Saul Rosenzweig, "Converging Approaches to Personality: Murray, Allport, Lewin," *Psychological Review,* 51 (1944), 248–256; Nevitt Sanford, "Murray's Clinic as a Place to Learn," in *Learning After College;* M. Brewster Smith, "Allport, Murray, and Lewin on Personality Theory: Notes on a Confrontation," *Journal of the History of the Behavioral Sciences,* 7 (1971), 353–362; Smith, "Humanistic Psychology," *Journal of Humanistic Psychology,* 30 (1990), 6–21; and Smith's retrospective review of *Explorations,* "Personology Launched" *Contemporary Psychology,* 35 (1990), 537–539; Rodney G. Triplet, "Henry A. Murray and the Harvard Psychological Clinic, 1926–1938"; and Robert W. White, "Exploring Personality the Long Way: The Study of Lives" (in *Further Explorations in Personality*), and *Seeking the Shape of Personality.*

See also the lively, very positive evocation of Harry in Edwin Shneidman's "A Life in Death: Notes of a Committed Suicidologist," in *The History of Clinical Psychology in Autobiography,* ed. C. Eugene Walker (Pacific Grove, CA: Brooks/Cole, 1991).

— "wonder, gratitude, and homage." Harry's remarks appear in a memorial booklet, *Carl Gustav Jung 1875–1961* (New York: Analytical Psychology Club of New York, 1962), pp. 17–21.

— "For him, the magnetism." "The Humanity of this Man," in *Felix Frankfurter: A Tribute,* ed. Wallace Mendelson (New York: Reynal, 1964), p. 17.

— "Delphic Women." In *Frances G. Wickes* (New York: Analytical Psychology Club of New York, 1968), n.p.

— "Handy in 1980." Harry wrote an unpublished biographical sketch of Handy, and a tribute—also unpublished—to Harvard philosopher Ernest Hocking, both in 1967.

370 "His mind wandered." Personal communication from Nina Murray, 3 January 1979.

— "get around on a cane." Personal communication from Edwin Shneidman, 30 April 1979.

— "a warm friend in later years." Robert Penn Warren to HAM, 10 March 1988.

— "More than any other psychologist." Brewster Smith to HAM, 4 April 1988.

— "Yet he *does* go on." Personal communication from Nina Murray, 1 May 1988.

— "I'm the doctor." Personal communication from Nina Murray, 18 June 1991.

13. The Case of Murr

371 "outstanding psychologists." *New York Times,* 24 June 1988.

— "obituary." *Boston Globe,* 25 June 1988.

— "Praise of a more personal cast." "A Service to Celebrate the Life of Henry Alexander Murray," Memorial Church, Harvard University, 3 October 1988. The service was conducted by Harry's nephew, the Reverend Michael H. Murray. In addition to Gardner, the speakers were Edwin Shneidman, Matina Horner, and Daniel Aaron. A family ceremony for the interment of Harry's ashes was held at Mount Auburn Cemetery on 8 August 1988.

— "romantic charm." Interview with David McClelland, 18 June 1970.

— "When Harry Murray enters a room." "Henry A. Murray," pp. 123, 125.

372 "born into royalty." Interview with Rollo May, 20 December 1980.

— "a master manipulator." Interview with Councilman Morgan, 5 March 1989.

— "fastidious reserve." Daniel Aaron, "A Service to Celebrate the Life of Henry Alexander Murray," n.p.

— "the most imaginative." Interview with Kenneth Keniston, 27 July 1970.

— "the most creative." Personal communication from David Ricks, 20 July 1970.

— "impish man." *Boston Globe,* 17 July 1983.

373 "a Renaissance man." "Against Scientism" (a review of *Endeavors in Psychology*), *New York Times Book Review,* 9 August 1981, p. 10.

— "The most striking thing." Leo McNamara, "Henry A. Murray," an unpublished portrait.

374 "Harry's *Moby-Dick.*" Personal communication from Edwin Shneidman, 23 April 1991.

— "William James and Henry Murray." Howard Gardner, "A Service to Celebrate the Life of Henry Alexander Murray," n.p. "Not since William James," argues Joseph Adelson, "has there been an American psychologist so versatile, nor has anyone else written with equal verve and boldness" ("Against Scientism," p. 10).

375 "Individuality is founded in feeling." "The Case of Murr," p. 293. Harry returns to this familiar passage—from *The Varieties of Religious Experience* (New York: Longmans, Green & Co., 1902), p. 501—in "Dead to the World: The Passions of Herman Melville," p. 11.

— "one long confession of failure." From the copy of "Preparations" in the possession of Ada Allport, the psychologist's widow.

376 "an open system." Edwin Shneidman, "A Service to Celebrate the Life of Henry Alexander Murray," n.p.

— "modern psychology of personality." "Personology Launched," p. 539.

— "centers within the business world." On the influence of OSS assessment in the private sector, see Douglas W. Bray and Donald L. Grant, "The Assessment Center in the Measurement of Potential for Business Management," *Psychological Monographs,* 80 (1966), whole no. 625; and Douglas W. Bray, Richard J. Campbell, and Donald L. Grant, *Formative Years in Business: A Long-Term AT & T Study of Managerial Lives* (New York: John Wiley & Sons, 1974).

— "exploring personality the long way." This overview of Harry's professional contributions is substantially informed by M. Brewster Smith, "Personology Launched," pp. 538–539, and by Robert A. Zucker, "Henry Murray's Legacy," in *Studying Persons and Lives,* pp. 335–340. White's formulation serves as the title for his essay on the Clinic in *Further Explorations in Personality.*

377 "the personal side." Interview with Kenneth Keniston, 27 July 1970.

378 "we must transform or fall apart." "Beyond Yesterday's Idealisms," pp. 371–373.

— "re-examine the classic assumptions." Norman O. Brown, *Life Against Death* (Middletown, CN: Wesleyan University Press, 1959), pp. xi–xii.

— "all metaphors are sexual." *Love's Body,* pp. 236, 244, 249–250.

379 "excessive in its pessimism." See Harry's review of *Civilization and Its Discontents, Atlantic Monthly,* 146 (1930), 14.

— "illness-oriented Freudian system." "Components of an Evolving Personological System," p. 6.

— "continuity through change." "Two Versions of Man," p. 158.

— "cycles of creation." "Beyond Yesterday's Idealisms," p. 379.

— "the boundary between sanity and insanity." *Love's Body,* p. 160.

— "alternative to dualism." Ibid., p. 154.

— "the problem of identity." Ibid., pp. 84, 86, 161. Brown's most recent book, *Apocalypse and/or Metamorphosis* (Berkeley: University of California Press, 1991), the final volume in his trilogy on the human condition, advances a Nietzschean perspective clearly akin to the one adopted in the earlier works. "What does it mean," he asks, "to take one's stand under the Dionysian, rather than the Freudian (or the Marxist) flag? It means to discard the pseudo-scientific posture of clinical detachment or political rationality, and recognize madness as the universal human condition, not the distinctive stigma of a separate class distinguished as insane. It means that madness is not an individual but a social phenomenon in which we all participate collectively: we are all in one and the same boat or body" (p. 180).

379   "embrace the opposite." "Two Versions of Man," p. 180.

380   "synthesism." "Unprecedented Evolutions," p. 556.

—   *"dyadic system."* Ibid.

—   "cross-cultural understanding." Interview with Harvey Meyerson, 11 December 1989. Harry met Meyerson, a veteran Vietnam journalist and Melville enthusiast, in 1973. Their discussions often centered on the perils of dualistic political moralizing and on the urgent need for a more flexible, empathic, and dialectical approach to the world's differences. Harry's ideas on such matters—as represented, for example, in "Unprecedented Evolutions"—were already well formed at the beginning of the 1960s.

381   "Mutual erotic love." "Two Versions of Man," p. 178.

—   "exemplary scientific objectivity." "Preparations for the Scaffold of a Comprehensive System," p. 29.

—   "analysis of what went wrong." "The Case of Murr," pp. 297–300.

382   "personal." *Vision Seminars,* vol. 2, p. 517.

—   "consigned the dyadic narrative." James Hillman to HAM, 9 June 1967. Nina Murray discreetly rescued the manuscript of *What Joy!*

—   "really astonishing." "The Case of Murr," pp. 299.

—   "When he was 9." Ibid., p. 298.

383   "veteran of the amorous wars." I am indebted to Brewster Smith for this insight.

384   "a new family culture." "Vicissitudes of Creativity," p. 117.

—   "Narcism Re-exhibited." Hiram Haydn, "Henry A. Murray," p. 125.

385   "rolled into the basket with a thud." "The Case of Murr," pp. 285, 308.

386   "Decapitated Surveyor." Nathaniel Hawthorne, *The Scarlet Letter* (New York: Norton, 1988), pp. 32–33.

—   "Be true!" Ibid., p. 175.

—   "might ruin your life." Interview with HAM, 1 March 1986.

388   "plunged into it and was drowned." *Moby-Dick,* p. 14.

389   "healthy vision." "The Case of Murr," p. 308.

Index

Herrick, Robert F., 41, 43, 47–48
Hinkel, Beatrice M., 103, 105, 164
Hiss, Alger, 334–335
Hitler, Adolf, 229–230, 266, 275–278
Hoagland, Hudson, 336
Hocking, William Ernest, 141
Hodges, John, 19–20, 30
Holt, Robert, 271, 371
Homans, George, 179
Homans, Peter, 106, 180
Homburger, Erik, *see* Erikson, Erik
Hopkins, F. Gowland, 85
Horn, Daniel, 271
Horner, Matina, 369
Howard, Sidney, 89
Howells, William Dean, 10
Hoyt, Alfred, 30
Hudson, William Henry, 203
Hughes, H. Stuart, 180
Hunter, John, 2
Huxley, Aldous, 336

Icarus complex, 335, 338, 348, 352
Ingalls, Marjorie, 286

Jacques, Elliott, 271–272
James, Henry, 13, 107, 116, 372
James, Henry, Sr., 116
James, William, 35, 73, 89, 107, 219,
    222, 225, 374–375, 377
Janet, Pierre, 146, 218
Jeffers, Robinson, 256
Jones, Eleanor Clement, 197, 199–202,
    204, 232, 330
Jones, Robert Edmond, 90–91, 101, 158
Jung, C. G., 97, 99, 102–105, 107,
    114, 119, 126–128, 131, 133, 145–
    147, 149, 152, 155–163, 170–173,
    178–179, 181–182, 185, 192, 196–
    200, 203, 218, 220, 224–225, 244,
    252, 255, 262, 325, 327, 361, 369,
    373, 383; and antisemitism, 230, 401;
    and Antonia Wolff, 122–123, 127;
    autobiography of, 355; and Christiana
    Morgan, 98–101, 411; and individua-
    tion, 168, 206–208, 231; on Melville,

315; and religion, 104–106; sessions
    with Murray, 120–122; *Psychological
    Types,* 83–84, 92–93; *Psychology of the
    Unconscious,* 99, 101, 105
Jung, Emma, 122–123, 129

Kant, Immanuel, 95, 101
Kaplan, Bert, 332
Kendig, Isabelle, 151, 174, 360
Keniston, Kenneth, 338–340, 372, 377
Kipling, Rudyard, 12
Kluckhohn, Clyde, 218, 230, 271, 291,
    295, 301, 331, 336, 340, 348,
    353, 423
Kluckhohn, Florence, 218, 348
Knight, Kenneth, 256–258
Koch, Sigmund, 341
Kraepelin, Emil, 84
Kroeber, Ted, 338, 340
Kubie, Lawrence, 32, 79–80

Lachaise, Gaston, 249–250, 264, 327
Laing, R. D., 365
Lang, Andrew, 19
Langer, Walter, 174, 227, 276–279, 428
Lashley, Karl S., 149, 184, 188–189,
    212–213, 217–218, 224–227,
    374–375
Lawrence, D. H., 3
Leary, Timothy, 334, 365
Leighton, Clare, 355
Levin, Harry, 336, 439
Lewin, Kurt, 218, 221, 224
Leyda, Jay, 320–323, 367, 435
Lichtenberg, Philip, 332
Lincoln, Abraham, 31–32
Lindzey, Gardner, 332, 335, 338, 369
Lippmann, Walter, 101
Livingston, Goodhue, 332
Loeb, Jacques, 93
Longfellow, Henry Wadsworth, 32
Lothrop, Sam, 25, 29–30
Lowell, Abbott Lawrence, 27, 140–141,
    145, 148, 184
Lunt, Alfred, 89
Luria, A. R., 348

454